The Sociology of Housing

HOW HOMES SHAPE OUR SOCIAL LIVES

Edited by Brian J. McCabe
and Eva Rosen

D1604193

The University of Chicago Press   CHICAGO AND LONDON

The University of Chicago Press, Chicago 60637
The University of Chicago Press, Ltd., London
© 2023 by The University of Chicago
All rights reserved. No part of this book may be used or
reproduced in any manner whatsoever without written
permission, except in the case of brief quotations in critical
articles and reviews. For more information, contact the
University of Chicago Press, 1427 E. 60th St., Chicago, IL 60637.
Published 2023
Printed and bound by CPI Group (UK) Ltd, Croydon, CR0 4YY

32 31 30 29 28 27 26 25 24 23   1 2 3 4 5

ISBN-13: 978-0-226-82851-0 (cloth)
ISBN-13: 978-0-226-82853-4 (paper)
ISBN-13: 978-0-226-82852-7 (e-book)
DOI: https://doi.org/10.7208/chicago/9780226828527.001.0001

Library of Congress Cataloging-in-Publication Data

Names: McCabe, Brian J., editor. | Rosen, Eva, 1983–, editor.
Title: The sociology of housing : how homes shape our social
    lives / edited by Brian J. McCabe and Eva Rosen.
Description: Chicago ; London : The University of Chicago
Press, 2023. | Includes bibliographical references and index.
Identifiers: LCCN 2023004294 | ISBN 9780226828510 (cloth) |
ISBN 9780226828534 (paperback) | ISBN 9780226828527 (ebook)
Subjects: LCSH: Housing—United States. | Discrimination
in housing—United States. | Equality—United States. |
Housing policy—United States.
Classification: LCC HD7293 .S615 2023 |
    DDC 363.50973—dc23/eng/20230309
LC record available at https://lccn.loc.gov/2023004294

♾ This paper meets the requirements of ANSI/NISO Z39.48-1992
(Permanence of Paper).

Contents

How Homes Shape Our Social Lives

Brian J. McCabe and Eva Rosen

Housing structures our health and shapes our social relationships. It is the single largest expenditure in our monthly budgets. For certain households it is a tool for building wealth, while more broadly, it acts as an engine for inequality. Our housing determines where our kids go to school, the types of institutions we can access, and the people we interact with in our daily routines. Depending on our housing situations, our homes either expose us to environmental hazards or shelter us from them. The type of structure we live in and its location shape social relationships and pattern inequality throughout our lives.

Historically, sociologists have considered the role of housing in society only sporadically, often letting it linger on the margins of the discipline (Foley 1980). Even so, housing has deep roots among key sociological voices. Early in the discipline's history, writers from Jacob Riis to W. E. B. Du Bois wrote about the importance of understanding basic living conditions as well as the economic, political, and spatial aspects of housing arrangements for all kinds of social outcomes (Du Bois 1899, 1903; Riis 1890). In 1947, Louis Wirth penned an essay in the *American Journal of Sociology* making a case for the importance of housing as a field of sociological research, arguing that "housing is a social activity." As such, he wrote, "sociology has something to learn from [housing], and it constitutes a subject matter for sociological study" (Wirth 1947). Wirth proposed that sociologists center their scholarship on housing as a social value. He emphasized the role that housing plays in shaping communities and the important relationship between housing and social policy. Sociological research on housing in any of these realms, however, was slow to evolve.

In the 1960s, the study of housing gained momentum within certain corners of sociological analysis. As cities wrestled with problems of poverty and inequality, sociologists focused on the housing conditions of the nation's poorest renters and their consequences for their inhabitants'

health and well-being. The conditions of public housing and the emergence of so-called slum neighborhoods garnered more public consideration as social problems. Sociologists turned their attention to studying
how housing organized social life in these neighborhoods and communities—a tradition that would continue to shape scholars' treatment of
housing within the subfields of community studies and neighborhood
effects (Gans 1962; Rainwater 1970).

More recently, the study of housing has lurked in the background of
specific subfields in sociology (Desmond 2018; Pattillo 2013). Housing
plays a key role within the sociological canon of neighborhood effects,
where it is conceived of as an important community-level attribute that
shapes how neighborhood residents form social connections and build
social capital and collective efficacy (Pattillo 2008; Sampson 2012; Sampson and Sharkey 2008; Sharkey and Faber 2014; Small 2004; Wilson 1987).
Sociologists within this subfield study how housing patterns are related to
neighborhood-level racial segregation (Faber 2020a; Massey and Denton
1993). Urban ethnographers often consider housing in their understanding
of community dynamics (Anderson 1990; Pattillo 2008; Venkatesh 2002).
Sociologists studying political behavior, family formation, economic interactions, and the conditions of poverty have also considered the role of
housing. But by and large, this work treats housing as merely a component
of *other* social processes, dispersing the study of housing among various
subfields. Unlike sociological traditions outside the US, where housing
has been more central to understanding the intertwined social, cultural,
and economic orders (Bourdieu 1984, 1999; Desmond 2018), American
sociology has largely failed to recognize the importance of housing *itself*
as an organizing topic of study.

Other disciplines grant housing a more central place in their research
traditions (Baradaran 2019; Connolly 2014; Hirsch 1983; Rothstein 2017;
Satter 2009; Sugrue 2014; Taylor 2019), but they often do so without the
range of methodological tools and theoretical approaches available to sociologists. Economists primarily understand housing as a market good or
financial transaction. Urban planners and architects emphasize the role
of housing as a place of physical shelter. Geographers consider housing
as a locational attribute within neighborhoods. Political scientists analyze
the ways that housing shapes political behavior and policy preferences.
But as we note throughout this volume, housing is more than a market
good shaped by economic forces; it is more than a physical structure to
be designed and renovated; and it does more than simply position people
within a neighborhood or shape their material interests. Building from
this work across disciplines, sociologists must apply our own theoretical

insights and methodological tools to demonstrate how housing shapes everyday lives and structures social relations.

With this collection of essays, we seek to show the power of the sociological imagination in understanding how housing shapes our social world (Mills 1959). To do so, we draw on a distinct *sociological* toolkit to define a subfield centered on housing. Sociologists are uniquely positioned to understand how housing shapes social relationships, social networks, and family life. We can help to understand how the economic relationships engendered by housing in turn structure power relations and social inequality. We are well equipped to consider how everyday aspects of housing—from the physical structures in which people live to the relationships that their housing situations create—shape social lives in unexpected ways. Put simply, sociologists have an important set of methodological and theoretical tools to help us better understand the place of housing in society.

This volume builds on a resurgent interest in housing to push beyond the boundaries of recent research on the topic. This research has emerged from handful of public issues, including the challenges of public housing (Chaskin and Joseph 2015; Goetz 2013; Popkin et al. 2000; Vale 2013), the crisis of eviction (Desmond 2016), and the impacts of gentrification (Brown-Saracino 2017; Hwang and Sampson 2014). Together, as these public issues reinvigorated the conversation about housing and society, they provided the impetus for a renewed agenda on the sociology of housing. In their own way, the redevelopment of the public housing stock and the ongoing crisis of housing affordability have raised important questions about the changing role of the government in tackling housing insecurity. Gentrification has centered concerns about residential displacement, including the loss of housing and community, as the central problematic of changing neighborhoods. And the devastating impact of evictions has generated an important body of scholarship on the causes and consequences of the housing insecurity in America (DeLuca and Rosen 2022; Desmond 2016; Harvey 2020b; Leung, Hepburn, and Desmond 2021; Purser 2016; Sullivan 2018).

While these public issues point to the prominent role of housing in structuring social life, they are only the tip of the iceberg when it comes to understanding how housing shapes our social world. We are wrestling with the continued aftermath of the foreclosure crisis, including the place of homeownership in American life (McCabe 2016). The deepening problem of housing affordability has created new challenges—especially for the poorest Americans—as they seek residential stability. Renewed concerns about housing quality, including issues of crowding and lead paint exposure, point to the impact of housing on the health of young children (Muller, Sampson, and Winter 2018). The role of housing in patterning racial inequality continues to garner growing attention in the public eye (Dantzler 2021; Dantzler, Korver-Glenn, and Howell 2022). As we bring these (and other) topics to the forefront of public conversations, this volume capitalizes on a resurgent interest in housing within sociology to more formally define a subfield around the topic.

Our volume offers unique opportunities to apply a sociological approach to the relationship between housing and policy. Housing is an important outcome for sociological research. For example, we might measure the quality of housing and research the complicated role of government actors in addressing housing quality issues (Bartram 2022). Sociologists may measure the degree of racial segregation in housing and identify how these patterns change over time or across cities (Logan and Stults 2021). In these examples, housing is an outcome. But at the same time, this volume demonstrates the ways that housing itself shapes social relations and social interaction. This sociological approach to studying housing on both sides of the equation necessitates direct engagement with public policy. While scholars often consider public policy primarily as a tool to remedy major social problems—a mere addendum to the "real" sociological analysis— many of the chapters in this book emphasize that policy itself is intrinsically sociological. They consider housing policy as a causal mechanism worthy of study, rather than merely as an outcome or remedy. This sociological study of policy goes well beyond examining the "unintended consequences" of public policy to understand how it fundamentally shapes social outcomes. In this model, policy is a central component of social structure (DeLuca and Rosen 2022).

By centering sociological research in the study of housing, these chapters bring a diverse methodological toolkit to this core social problem. By showcasing quantitative analysis, in-depth interviewing, ethnographic approaches, and comparative historical research, the contributors point to the methodological depth available to sociologists as they seek to understand housing in society. Although the volume draws primarily on research from the United States, we include some understudied American cases—cities like Boise and Buffalo, for example—to broaden the gaze of sociological research and challenge inherited understandings from a handful of paradigmatic cases. While our emphasis on the American context reflects a recent resurgence of interest in housing and urban issues in the US, we also note the adjacent research on housing in a global context. For example, studies of informality in the Global South (Weinstein 2014), the organizing capacity of emerging right-to-housing movements (Weinstein and Ren 2009), and the promises of social housing (Scanlon, Whitehead, and Arrigoitia 2014) are robust areas of inquiry outside the American context. Although this volume offers only a limited international comparative angle, we acknowledge the contributions beyond the United States with the hope that this volume can foster conversations across national contexts.

To lay the groundwork for a subfield centered on housing, we organize this volume into four thematic sections. In part I, we bring together chapters that consider both current and historic mechanisms shaping inequality in housing. The section integrates research on homeownership, public housing, and local housing policies to examine practices that reinforce racial hierarchies and exclude marginalized groups. While these approaches lean on different policy levers, they each continue to shape inequality, homeownership attainment, and the racial wealth gap (McCabe 2016; Oliver and Shapiro 1997). Throughout the chapters, housing policy emerges not only as a remedy to inequalities, but as a central mechanism in shaping those inequalities.

The opening chapter by Zawadi Rucks-Ahidiana considers the role of federal housing policy in creating the racial wealth gap. While the racial differences in Black-white homeownership opportunities are well documented, the chapter reminds readers of the consequences of this unequal access to homeownership. The federal government, private banks, and real estate agents created practices that systematically excluded Black households from homeownership. As an opening salvo for understanding the multigenerational consequences of historic housing practices, the chapter reinforces the importance of housing for wealth-building and inheritance and documents the enduring consequences of policies that created unequal housing opportunities.

In the next chapter, Allen Hyde and Mary Fischer bring readers into a conversation about trends in Latino homeownership. Latinos are one of the fastest-growing demographic groups in the United States—a fact that underscores the importance of centering their experiences in a sociology of housing. The chapter considers how (and why) Latino homeownership has expanded, but also addresses the enduring structural challenges to creating parity in the homeownership experiences of white and Latino households. As the chapter pushes beyond the inherited framework of the Black-white homeownership gap, it also reminds readers that broad demographic categories like "Latino" mask divergent experiences for subpopulations. This chapter sets the foundation for the subsequent chapter by María Rendón, Deyanira Nevárez Martínez, and Maya Parvati Kulkarni on the historic roots of Latino residential segregation. Drawing on historic residential data on Latinos, in particular those of Mexican origin in Los Angeles in 1930 and 1940, the authors ask scholars to consider local race relations in understudied parts of the country as they work to understand housing patterns. They document the unique history of the Mexican-origin group in Southern California by reviewing accounts of this group's racialization, including their incorporation as expendable labor, which shaped their residential patterns.

The next chapter, by Peter Rosenblatt, recasts research on public housing redevelopment in Baltimore by showing how these redevelopments were used to explicitly preserve the racist status quo in Baltimore. The chapter contributes to a sociology of housing by pointing to the role of housing policy in reinforcing, rather than challenging, the racial order. In the subsequent chapter, Jennifer Darrah-Okike, Lorinda Riley, Philip Garboden, and Nathalie Rita examine how housing policies and academic epistemologies exclude particular social groups. The authors examine issues of access and equity for Native people by bringing an Indigenous Studies perspective to the sociology of housing. To do so, they engage the lens of settler colonialism as a contemporary structure to explain current housing experiences and inequalities. They consider both local and federal housing programs, arguing that the racialization of Native peoples proceeds in distinctive ways with consequences for access to housing.

In the next chapter, Matthew McLeskey explores how landlords can both mitigate and perpetuate neighborhood inequalities in their role managing an older housing stock that exposes residents to toxic hazards such as lead paint. By asking sociologists to consider lead exposure as a form of housing inequality, the chapter urges readers to consider a new set of topics within the sociology of housing as drivers of inequality. In the final chapter of the opening section, Michael Gaddis and Nicholas DiRago provide an overview of audit studies measuring housing discrimination. Discrimination in the housing market is often difficult to detect, but the audit study offers a unique methodological tool to understand where and when discrimination occurs. Gaddis and DiRago review emerging research on new arenas in which renters may encounter discrimination, including rental assistance, short-term rentals, and roommate searches, before offering guidance on how to extend understandings of this type of discrimination to other areas of the housing market.

The chapters in part II offer new perspectives on a growing body of sociological research about housing instability, insecurity, and precariousness. Although much of this research has focused on the process of eviction—including the impact of evictions on households and neighborhoods—recent sociological research has begun to identify other forms of housing insecurity that reshape how people live. Part II offers novel approaches to understanding how housing instability impacts social networks, communities, and social life. These chapters identify forms of housing instability emerging alongside the affordable housing crisis and explain how households respond to this precariousness. In conversation with the chapters in part I, these chapters show how sociological research informs ongoing discussions of housing policy.

The section begins with a chapter by Kyle Nelson and Michael Lens exploring how eviction varies by social context and is shaped by legal statutes and political organizations. While acknowledging the expansiveness of eviction research, the chapter calls for a renewed commitment to understanding the institutional life of evictions, especially as they vary from place to place. Up next, Esther Sullivan takes readers to manufactured homes—an important site of naturally occurring affordable housing in the United States. The chapter draws attention to the unique place of manufactured housing in the landscape of affordable housing, including the financialization of this housing form and its contribution to housing insecurity. Given the prevalence of this type of housing, Sullivan points to manufactured homes as an important place of additional scholarship for the emergent sociology of housing.

Drawing on their extensive research on shared households, Hope Harvey and Kristin Perkins bring insights from the field of family sociology into the realm of housing. Rather than focusing on physical structures or neighborhood location, Harvey and Perkins emphasize the importance of household composition and social relations *within* shared housing arrangements. They argue that shared-housing arrangements can be both a cause and consequence of the physical circumstances of housing insecurity. In the next chapter, Claire Herbert draws on ethnographic and interview data from Detroit to examine squatting as a strategy for survival. Much of the research on squatting positions the practice within the social movements literature, but Herbert positions squatting as a mode of informal housing in a changing city. She acknowledges a variety of reasons for squatting, including as a practice for homeowners to reclaim homes lost to foreclosure. As readers learn about squatting and housing informality in Detroit, the chapter creates an opportunity to reflect on how concepts developed and theorized in the context of the Global South can also help to understand the experiences of households in the Global North.

Finally, part II concludes with a chapter by Christopher Herring that centers the experiences of homelessness in the sociology of housing. While research acknowledges that the experience of homelessness is common for renters at the bottom of the housing ladder, Herring brings attention to the varied pathways through homelessness and the range of ways in which unhoused people exit homelessness into housing. The chapter brings renewed attention to the role of the state in shaping this experience and challenges readers to consider the invisibility of homelessness in the public gaze.

In part III, we introduce questions about housing markets and the supply-side intermediary actors, including landlords and real estate professionals, who facilitate access to these markets. A recent expansion of research on these market intermediaries has led to exciting opportunities to study all sorts of professionals in the housing market and their role in shaping social relations (Balzarini and Boyd 2021; Bartram 2022; Besbris 2020; Desmond 2016; Garboden and Rosen 2019; Gormory 2021; Greif 2022; Hepburn, Louis, and Desmond 2020; Korver-Glenn 2018, 2021; Leung, Hepburn, and Desmond 2021; Rosen 2020; Rosen, Garboden, and Cossyleon 2021; Shiffer-Sebba 2020). The chapters in this section offer a sociological perspective on the construction of local housing markets and their impact on broader patterns of social inequality. In doing so, they highlight a range of supply-side actors, the factors involved in creating housing markets, and the shifting ways in which both public and private development structure inequality.

In the opening chapter, Joe LaBriola interrogates questions of housing supply. He asks where and what kind of housing gets built, and who can occupy that housing. While the domain of markets and supply has long been ruled by economists, LaBriola's sociological approach engages with social movement theories and analyses of the growth machine while reminding readers how the social and political conflicts over housing development, as well as the regulatory environment in which housing is constructed, shape patterns of inequality and segregation. Next, Elizabeth Korver-Glenn, Robin Bartram, and Max Besbris introduce the importance of housing market intermediaries, including developers, building inspectors, public housing authorities, and real estate agents, to the sociological study of housing. Notably, the authors identify a broad set of intermediaries involved in the housing market from both the private and public sectors. Drawing on their own research on real estate agents and building inspectors, Korver-Glenn, Bartram, and Besbris acknowledge the active role of intermediaries in structuring patterns of inequality— although not always in ways that are anticipated. Their chapter invites a broader research agenda into the role of intermediaries in both creating new types of inequality and ameliorating the patterns of unevenness within existing housing markets.

The next chapter redirects sociologists away from the familiar study of housing in gentrifying neighborhoods to consider the housing challenges of urban neighborhoods in decline. Sharon Cornelissen and Christine Jang-Trettien acknowledge that studies of gentrification have captured the sociological imagination, especially as they raise issues of residential displacement. However, the authors stage a critical intervention by reminding readers that low-income neighborhoods experiencing disinvestment are more common than neighborhoods experiencing gentrification. Utilizing two field sites, Baltimore and Detroit, they argue that depopulation, the decline in urban services, and the rise of property abandonment shape the housing experience within these neighborhoods. Their chapter calls for a renewed research agenda to identify the unique set of actors, institutions, and conflicts that exist in these declining housing markets. Krista Paulsen then brings readers back to a fast-growing housing market by introducing them to the city of Boise, Idaho, where the arrival of sharing-economy platforms like Airbnb have transformed the rental housing landscape. Given their novelty, these types of short-term rentals have received limited scholarly attention, but Paulsen explores their complex relationship to the housing market. They raise important questions for sociologists about housing, community, and the financial foundations of the rental economy.

Acknowledging the role of landlords as one of the animating themes of this section, Philip Garboden uses the next chapter to explore the concept of exploitation in housing. Garboden focuses on landlords' relationships with their low-income tenants to develop a theory of rentier exploitation that moves beyond the critique of individual predatory actions and actors to understand how exploitation is structurally embedded in the urban rental housing market. The section concludes with a chapter by Isaac Martin that brings a sociological perspective to issues of housing finance, underscoring how housing is embedded in fiscal relationships. To understand the social experience of housing, Martin argues that we must also pay attention to the financing of housing and the tax policies that shape our housing choices. The analysis in Martin's chapter is particularly significant for understanding homeowners, who uniquely benefit from a handful of behind-the-scenes fiscal relationships that enable the construction and financing of owner-occupied housing.

In part IV, we bring together six chapters to highlight how sociologists can draw important links between racial segregation, social inequality, and housing. We use this opportunity in the volume to look forward and tie sociological studies of housing to a number of important social and policy issues, including racial segregation, criminal justice, and social networks. To begin, Jacob Faber highlights the centrality of racial segregation in understanding how housing shapes our social world. He reminds readers that racial segregation in housing is intentionally produced by people and institutions, emphasizing the inherently social nature of these processes for a sociology of housing.

Continuing an analysis of residential segregation, Erin Carll, Hannah Lee, Chris Hess, and Kyle Crowder investigate how subsidized households make residential decisions in segregated markets. Describing how members of racial and ethnic groups draw on knowledge from their racialized networks to make residential decisions, the authors consider the consequences of racially segregated social networks for housing trajectories. While their chapter draws on qualitative interviews with housing voucher recipients, it has broader implications for understanding the housing search process for low-income households. The next chapter, by Maximilian Cuddy, Amy Spring, Maria Krysan, and Kyle Crowder, continues on the topic of housing search processes by emphasizing the role of family in the search process. The authors point to multiple ways that family networks and resources impact the housing search process, ultimately linking the study of housing and residential mobility back to sociological research related to kinship, family, and social networks.

The chapter by Rahim Kurwa begins to connect the voluminous scholarship on policing and the carceral state with housing scholarship on patterned racial segregation. Kurwa proposes that the social position afforded by homeownership allows those in possession of property to police others, positing a theory of "policing as property," much as Harris (1993) theorized whiteness as property. Kurwa shows how nuisance and crime-free housing ordinances, gang injunctions, and laws barring leases for renters with criminal backgrounds perpetuate racial segregation in housing. The penultimate chapter, by Brielle Bryan and Temi Alao, builds on this relationship between housing and the carceral state by asking how contact with the criminal justice system impacts housing outcomes for those who were formerly incarcerated. The chapter explores the mechanisms, including financial opportunities and social relations, that mediate this relationship. But the chapter also flips this question on its head, asking how housing situations in turn shape criminal justice outcomes—an incisive reminder that the causal arrow points both ways when it comes to housing. Given the significant expansion of the carceral state, as well as the racially discriminatory nature of this expansion, the chapter leaves little doubt that the intersection of housing and criminal justice is a critical avenue for the continued development of a sociology of housing.

Part IV concludes with a chapter by Marco Garrido that explores the divide between formal and informal housing in urban space within the developing world. Garrido argues that this divide between formal and informal is itself a social structure in the Global South, dividing residents into differently valued groups, in much the way that race does in the Global North. While the chapter offers the only explicitly international comparison in the volume, it provides a fitting conclusion by opening lines of inquiry for a more global investigation of housing instability and informality in shaping social structure across different contexts.

Taken together, the collection of chapters assembled in these four sections sets an ambitious and urgent agenda for sociologists. Although the topics covered in the volume are not exhaustive of the research on housing within the discipline, each chapter offers researchers and scholars an opportunity to consider how housing shapes the social world. Taking advantage of the expansive sociological toolkit, the volume reimagines the place of housing studies in sociology. In doing so, we hope it demarcates the boundaries of a new subfield within the discipline.

PART I

Mechanisms of Housing Inequality

1

Housing as Capital

US POLICY, HOMEOWNERSHIP, AND THE RACIAL WEALTH GAP

Zawadi Rucks-Ahidiana

Urban scholars often associate housing with access to resources like schools, playgrounds, grocery stores, and banks. But housing is also a resource and a source of capital (Conley 1999; Taylor 2019). While it is impossible to use a house as a direct payment, owning a home translates to economic capital as collateral for loans that Americans use to pay for their children to go to college, start a business, buy a car, or buy their own home through the gift of a down payment (Squires 1994; Oliver and Shapiro 1997; Shapiro 2004). In fact, for most Americans, the house they own makes up the bulk of their wealth holdings (McCabe 2016; Conley 1999). Yet national policies on homeownership historically had racial restrictions that gave white Americans access to this financial asset and excluded Black Americans, thus excluding Blacks from the foundations of middle-class wealth (Rothstein 2017; Taylor 2019; Satter 2009; Pattillo 2008).

This chapter builds on the work of racial wealth gap scholars to document how racist federal policies created the foundations of today's racial disparities in wealth and to demonstrate how housing contributes to racial disparities in economic stability and intergenerational wealth. I argue that the effects of policies that made homeownership accessible to the white working and middle classes in the 1940s are still present today in three contemporary racial wealth disparities that persist across income categories: (1) Black-white differences in inheritance, (2) Black-white differences in homeownership rates, and (3) Black-white differences in home values. I document these three disparities using survey data, thus demonstrating how housing is a foundation of racial inequality in the United States, not just by providing access to a neighborhood but by providing capital across generations.

Homeownership and the Racial Wealth Gap

For most of the post–civil rights era, Black-white disparities in wealth have persisted at a steady level. The Black-white wealth gap in 2016 was about the same as it was in 1962 when whites held almost seven times the wealth of Blacks (Aliprantis and Carroll 2019). As Oliver and Shapiro describe, today "African-American families thus possess a dime for every dollar of white families' wealth" (2019, 18). Even though Black wealth has increased from an average of $4,000 in 1984 to $17,000 in 2015, white wealth has outpaced this growth, starting at $88,000 and ending at $275,000 (Oliver and Shapiro 2019). While homeownership is a central and important part of wealth holdings for most Americans (McCabe 2016), home values are particularly important for Blacks' wealth holdings. In fact, 75 percent of Black wealth is in home values (Oliver and Shapiro 2019). Thus, patterns of homeownership and home values are central for understanding the racial wealth gap.

Black homeownership has been consistently lower than white home-ownership over time. Figure 1.1 shows census figures of homeownership by race from 1970 to 2010. White homeownership began at 62 percent in 1970 and increased steadily to a height of 75 percent in 2000. While there was a slight decline in white homeownership in 2010, homeowners remained the majority of white households at 71 percent. White homeownership increased between 1970 and 1990, but Black homeownership declined from 51 to 43 percent. The rate recovered slightly in 2000 for Black homeowners, increasing to 49 percent, but declined to 44 percent in 2010.

Hidden between census years in the data shown in figure 1.1 is the most significant decrease of Black-white homeownership disparities post-Emancipation, which occurred before the Great Recession of 2008–2009. Taking advantage of the increased availability of mortgage loans, Blacks purchased homes, increasing the Black homeownership rate. While this trend provided an initial decrease in the Black-white wealth gap, Black wealth suffered tremendously due to the targeting of the Black community with subprime loans and the high rates of foreclosure in the Black community (Wolff 2017b; Rugh and Massey 2010; Faber 2013; Thomas et al. 2018). Furthermore, declines in home prices between 2007 and 2010 disproportionately affected Black homeowners, decreasing their home values by 26 percent (Wolff 2017b; Thomas et al. 2018). White wealth recovered from the recession by 2010, but the impact of the Great Recession extended through 2013 for Blacks (Thompson and Suarez 2015). By the end of 2013, any gains that had been achieved through increased Black

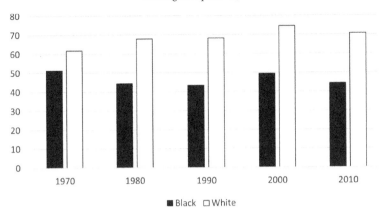

FIGURE 1.1. Homeownership rate by race over time

homeownership were erased as the Black homeownership rate fell to 1992 levels (Wolff 2017b).

Homeownership is thus a central tool in wealth-building in the United States, contributing significantly to both Americans' wealth holdings and racial disparities in wealth. Access to homeownership and mortgage loans has consequences for overall wealth, which in turn has implications for outcomes in health, education, and economic stability (Conley 1999; Boen and Yang 2016; Boen, Keister, and Aronson 2020; Oliver and Shapiro 1997).

Extending Homeownership to the Middle Class

While homeownership today is common among working- and middle-class Americans, owning a home was relatively inaccessible prior to the 1940s. Only affluent households could afford the conditions of mortgage lending at that time, which required 50 percent of the home's value as a down payment, high interest rates, and a period of only five to seven years to pay back the loan (Abramovitz and Smith 2020; Rothstein 2017; Gordon 2005; McCabe 2016). These limited conditions were how banks protected their investments in housing due to the large sums of money involved and thus the high possibility of lenders defaulting on the loan. The conditions of mortgage lending that we know today came as a result of government intervention in the early and mid-1930s. Prior to then, the federal government was uninvolved in the housing market with the exception of the 1916 Federal Land Bank system (Gotham 2002). The shift from a free market to a regulated market came in response to the housing crisis of the Great Depression of 1929 to 1933.

The economic collapse the US faced during the Great Depression had two implications for homeownership. First, the increase in unemployment increased foreclosures among home buyers (Faber 2020a; Jackson 1985; Rothstein 2017; McCabe 2016; Gotham 2002). Second, housing development ground to a halt (Gotham 2002; Jackson 1985; Rothstein 2017; McCabe 2016). As part of an effort to stimulate the economy and address the nation's broader economic decline, New Deal legislation included policies to address the need for new housing development and to promote homeownership.

The first change came in 1932 with the Federal Home Loan Bank Act (FHLB), which extended financial support to local banks, allowing them to make more mortgage loans (McCabe 2016; Freund 2006; Gotham 2002). This legislation was quickly followed by the Home Owners Loan Act in 1933, which established the Home Owners Loan Corporation (HOLC) and allowed the federal government to refinance one million foreclosed mortgage loans (Abramovitz and Smith 2020; Gordon 2005; Gotham 2002; Faber 2020a; Jackson 1985; Rothstein 2017; McCabe 2016). These two efforts focused on alleviating the housing crisis. Subsequent legislative changes focused on expanding homeownership opportunities to working- and middle-class Americans.

The most important piece of legislation was the 1934 National Housing Act, which established the Federal Housing Administration (FHA) and the Federal Savings and Loan Insurance Corporation (FSLIC). Where the HOLC provided temporary relief for banks and foreclosed mortgage holders, the 1934 National Housing Act produced a permanent solution to the concerns that banks had with mortgage lending: a federally insured mortgage loan. Instead of a 50 percent down payment, high interest rates, and repayment periods of five to seven years, federal insurance opened opportunities for home buyers to benefit from terms that were riskier for banks. These terms included down payments of 20 percent or less, low interest rates, and twenty- to thirty-year lending periods (Gordon 2005; Gotham 2002; Rothstein 2017; McCabe 2016). The subsidies and assurances continued in subsequent years, including the 1935 Banking Act, the 1938 Federal National Mortgage Association (Fannie Mae), and the 1944 Veterans Administration Mortgage Guarantee (the VA bill) (Freund 2006; Abramovitz and Smith 2020; McCabe 2016; Rothstein 2017; Squires 1994; Gordon 2005). The latter was particularly important in providing opportunities for veterans to buy a home with no down payment.

With these federal subsidies, banks were willing to take on the risk of mortgage loans to prospective buyers beyond the affluent. This willingness opened opportunities for working- and middle-class Americans and increased home building. However, these opportunities were not widely available to all working- and middle-class Americans, as federally backed mortgage loans were limited to "low risk" investments, thereby producing an institutionalized system of racial discrimination.

How Racism Produced "Risk"

Through the FHA and the VA bill, many working- and middle-class Americans gained access to homeownership, but the vast majority of these Americans were white. Black Americans across all income levels were systematically excluded from homeownership through definitions of what kind of home investments were considered "risky" (Taylor 2019; McCabe 2016). The HOLC defined "risk" by the characteristics of the surrounding neighborhood, relying heavily on the racial demographics of the people living in the area (Taylor 2019; Jackson 1985; Gordon 2005; Faber 2020a; Gotham 2002). While the HOLC only operated from 1933 to 1935 (Gotham 2002), this system of risk assessment—called "redlining"—informed the mortgage lending practices of the FHA and VA through the 1960s (Taylor 2019; Gordon 2005).

Based on the research of University of Chicago economist Homer Hoyt, HOLC developed a grading system to assess for risk using assumptions about neighborhood stability based on racial composition. Neighborhoods that were all-white and predominantly composed of native-born white Americans got an "A" grade and were "green lined" for mortgage loans (Jackson 1985; Gordon 2005; Faber 2020a). Any racial mixing, or the presence of lower-status racial groups including Blacks, Mexicans, and ethnic whites, contributed to a lower grade. While Jewish neighborhoods were generally graded a "B" and racially mixed neighborhoods a "C," majority-Black neighborhoods were systematically graded "D" and "redlined" as unacceptable for mortgage loans (Jackson 1985; Gordon 2005; Faber 2020a; Abramovitz and Smith 2020; Gotham 2002).

While HOLC refinance loans were distributed as needed to address foreclosures regardless of grade (Gordon 2005), eligibility for FHA and VA loans strictly followed the restrictions provided by HOLC risk maps (Gotham 2002; Faber 2020a; Rothstein 2017; Gordon 2005; McCabe 2016; Taylor 2019). Black home buyers struggled to find banks willing to provide mortgage loans, because they did not qualify for FHA and VA loans if they were attempting to purchase a home in a white neighborhood (as doing so would produce racial mixing) or in a predominantly Black one (excluded as grade D) (Taylor 2019).

Even when federal agencies removed explicit racial restrictions for mortgage loans in the late 1940s, the FHA replicated lending patterns to target white neighborhoods with colorblind policies. These regulations included rules that favored large lot sizes for new development, single-family homes, and suburban developments. They also excluded eligibility for multifamily homes, neighborhoods with mixed land use zoning such as industrial and residential, and urban neighborhoods (Abramovitz and Smith 2020; Gotham 2002; Rothstein 2017; Gordon 2005). Thus, while the rules documented in the FHA *Underwriting Manual* no longer referenced a preference for mortgage lending in all-white neighborhoods, the manual still noted a preference for "homogenous" neighborhoods and described neighborhoods with "dissimilar" residents as "unstable" (Gotham 2002).

These policies had two implications for racial patterns of homeownership. First, FHA backed loans predominantly supported white homeowners living in suburban areas. By the end of the 1950s, 98 percent of FHA-insured loans were issued to white households (Abramovitz and Smith 2020). This practice both established the white middle class and created white areas that reaped the benefits of concentrated investment including increasing property values. Second, excluding Black home buyers from federally insured loans limited their options to predatory lending markets. These markets included contract leasing and rent-to-own schemes, which inflated costs, included balloon payments at the end of the contract period, and only resulted in legal ownership if and when the full amount was paid down (Taylor 2019; George et al. 2019; Satter 2009). Thus, when Black people were able to buy homes, they were predominantly overpaying and were highly likely to lose their homes before they ever became the legal owners.

Between 1940 and 1960, homeownership in the US increased from 44 percent to 62 percent due to policy changes and the implementation work of the FHA (Abramovitz and Smith 2020; Taylor 2019). But access to federally insured mortgages was limited to white home buyers in predominantly white neighborhoods (Abramovitz and Smith 2020; Gotham 2002; Hirsch 2006; Rothstein 2017; Gordon 2005; McCabe 2016). The racist policies around "risk" that made Black home buyers and home buyers in Black neighborhoods ineligible for federally insured mortgages meant that the white middle class had access to homeownership for almost fifty-five years before the majority of the Black middle class. Legislative attempts to address redlining as a form of housing discrimination were unsuccessful until the Federal Housing Amendments Act of 1988, which had long-term, damaging effects for racial disparities in wealth (Galster and Godfrey 2005; Quillian, Lee, and Honoré 2020).

Implications for the Racial Wealth Gap

The exclusion of Black Americans and inclusion of white Americans from fifty-five years of homeownership opportunities has had three main implications for the racial wealth gap across Black and white Americans at all incomes. First, it has produced Black-white inequities in inheritance both in the receipt of inheritance and the amount of inheritance received. Second, it has contributed to persistent Black-white inequities in homeownership. Finally, it has created Black-white inequities in housing values. Below, I use data from the 2016 Survey of Consumer Finances (SCF) to demonstrate and explain each of these inequities that contribute to the persistence of the racial wealth gap today.[1]

INHERITANCE

White Americans are both more likely to receive inheritance and more likely to receive a larger inheritance than Black Americans across all income levels. This difference is driven by white middle-class Americans' early access to homeownership, which launched their generational wealth-building. The development and investment in white suburbs meant that the white middle-class people who bought homes in the 1950s have been able to pass on their investment to their children and grandchildren. These investments have provided inheritance and gifts to younger generations of white Americans that allowed them to invest in homes and college education while avoiding taking on debt (Conley 1999; Menchik and Jianakoplos 1997; Avery and Rendall 2002; McKernan et al. 2014). Because early government-backed mortgages were only available for white neighborhoods and predominantly led to investment in white suburbs, property values increased in white suburbs (Flippen 2004). The lack of access to government-backed mortgages in Black neighborhoods contributed to a decline in value through two pathways. First, the lack of financial investment contributed to a decline in property values. Second, the lack of loans produced physical deterioration as white property owners who rented in the neighborhoods opted not to invest in maintaining their properties, and the predominantly Black homeowners who lived in the

---

[1] The SCF is a nationally representative survey conducted triannually by the Federal Reserve Board. In 2016, the survey included 757 Black respondents and 4,467 white respondents across all income levels. For additional information, see Rucks-Ahidiana (2017).

neighborhoods were unable to get loans to pay for needed repairs. Thus, even when Black homeowners were able to pass on their homes to their children, those homes were worth less money and thus contributed to lower amounts of inheritance among Blacks compared to whites.

The 2016 SCF data clearly reflects this disparity in inheritance. Among white respondents, 26 percent had received inheritance, which averaged $66,706. In contrast, only 8 percent of Black respondents had received inheritance, which averaged $10,902. One plausible explanation for these differences is that racial differences in inheritance could be due to racial differences in class background origins. Because the SCF does not include information about respondents' parents' class background, I use respondents' class position as a proxy given evidence that class position is largely stable across generations (Chetty et al. 2014b). Among the survey sample, Black respondents were more likely to be low-income and white respondents were more likely to be middle-income.[2]

However, white respondents were more likely to have received an inheritance across all income levels. As shown in figure 1.2, white respondents were between 14 and 19 percentage points more likely to receive inheritance than Black respondents at all income levels. This finding includes 25 percent of low-income white respondents who had received inheritance compared with 10 percent of low-income Black respondents. While white respondents generally saw a slightly higher rate of receiving inheritance with an increase in income, Black respondents had much more variation. Upper-middle-income Blacks had the highest likelihood of receiving inheritance at 11 percent, but upper-income, lower-middle-income, and middle-income Blacks were less likely to receive inheritance than low-income Blacks. In fact, upper-income Black respondents had almost the same rate of inheritance as low-income Black respondents. This unexpected pattern is likely due to the prevalence of downward economic mobility among Blacks, such that even lower-income Black people would have been likely to receive inheritance from their middle- or upper-income parents (Pattillo 1999).

---

[2] The income categories are based on income quintiles for the full sample using the following distributions: $0–25,000 (low-income), $25,001–48,000 (lower-middle-income), $48,001–80,000 (middle-income), $80,001–150,000 (upper-middle-income), and $150,001 or more (upper-income). Sixty-one percent of Black respondents were either low-income (33 percent) or lower-middle-income (28 percent) compared with only 42 percent of White respondents (21 percent low-income and 21 percent lower-middle-income).

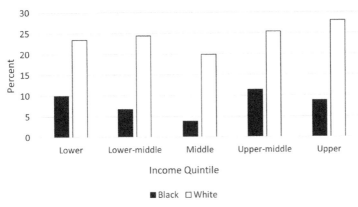

FIGURE 1.2. Received inheritance by race and income

These variations in inheritance receipt among Blacks by income mean that Black-white disparities in inheritance also fluctuate by income level. The largest gap was between upper-income Blacks and whites at 19 percentage points. Black respondents were less likely to receive inheritance and likely to receive significantly less in inheritance than their white counterparts across all income levels.

HOMEOWNERSHIP

These racial disparities in inheritance contribute to racial differences in homeownership. Even when down-payment requirements are low, home buyers still need cash in hand to pursue homeownership. White Americans have a higher homeownership rate than Blacks in part because whites are more likely to have inheritance and more likely to have family members with wealth who can provide a down payment for a home (Conley 2001; Menchik and Jianakoplos 1997).

Overall, 68 percent of white respondents and 42 percent of Black respondents owned their homes. Homeownership rates increased with income across both racial groups. However, racial differences in rates of homeownership were stable even with increased income. As shown in figure 1.3, white respondents were more likely to own their home across all income groups. Among low-income respondents, 45 percent of white respondents were homeowners compared with 27 percent of Black respondents.

While homeownership increased with income for both Black and white respondents, the Black-white disparity in homeownership also increased between lower-middle-income and middle-income respondents.

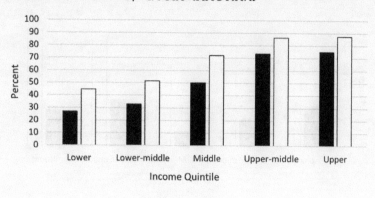

FIGURE 1.3. Homeownership by race and income

For lower-middle-income respondents, white respondents were 18 percentage points more likely to own their homes than Black respondents, compared with 22 percentage points more likely for white middle-income homeowners. Racial disparities in homeownership decreased slightly for higher-income respondents, but Black respondents were still less likely to own their homes. For upper-middle-income respondents, 86 percent of white respondents owned their homes compared with 73 percent of Blacks. This difference was similar for upper-income respondents, as white respondents were 12 percentage points more likely to own their homes than upper-income Black respondents.

Even though upper-middle-income and upper-income Black respondents have higher homeownership rates than lower-income Blacks, their homeownership rates are most similar to that of middle-income whites. Middle-income whites had a homeownership rate of 72 percent compared with 73 percent of upper-middle-income Blacks and 75 percent of upper-income Blacks. Similarly, middle-income Blacks had a homeownership rate comparable to lower-middle-income and lower-income whites of about 50 percent.

HOME VALUES

Finally, even after the federal government, banks, and insurance companies opened opportunities to Blacks for government-backed mortgages, Blacks' options for residential housing continued to be racially segregated due to real estate practices of "steering" customers toward neighborhoods that matched their racial background (Galster and Godfrey 2005; Oh and

Yinger 2015). Because of the disinvestment in predominantly Black neighborhoods, Black Americans are more likely to own homes with lower values than their white counterparts (Flippen 2004). While it is possible that higher-income Blacks are more likely to live in predominantly white neighborhoods than lower-income Blacks and thus could have comparable home values to their white counterparts, the SCF data demonstrates that white homeowners have higher home values than Black homeowners across all income levels.

White homeowners had an average home value of $336,997 compared with $181,595 for Black homeowners, a difference of $155,402. Black-white disparities in home values existed across all income levels. But disparities were greatest among low-income and upper-income homeowners. Low-income Blacks had home values that were 45 percent of the value of low-income whites' homes, while upper-income Blacks had housing values that were 54 percent of upper-income whites' home values. In dollars, that was $130,815 more for low-income white homeowners and $386,791 more for upper-income white homeowners. Differences in home values between the middle-income quintiles ranged from 83 percent of whites' home values for lower-middle-income and middle-income Blacks to 71 percent of whites' home values for upper-middle-income Blacks, as shown in Figure 1.4.

Racial segregation thus contributes to persistent racial differences in home values today across all income levels (Markley et al. 2020; Flippen 2004; Perry, Rothwell, and Harshbarger 2018). These differences are also related to Black-white disparities in inheritance, which may limit Black homeowners' options for purchasing to lower-valued homes across all income levels.

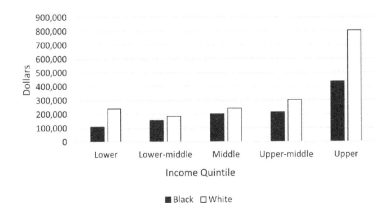

FIGURE 1.4. Home values by race and income

In sum, racial differences in inheritance and homeownership contribute to Black-white disparities in overall wealth holdings. On average, Black respondents held $97,440 in total assets, compared with $485,499 among white respondents, almost five times as much in assets.[3] Among homeowners, the gap was even larger. White homeowners held $692,495 in total assets on average compared with $223,957 among Black homeowners. Given the accrual of home values over time, these disparities replicate themselves over generations, reproducing the racial wealth gap.

Conclusions

The historical legacy of racist policies in mortgage lending continues to contribute to Black-white wealth disparities today. While opportunities and access have opened for Black Americans, the racial wealth gap persists due to the advance access white Americans had to wealth accumulation and the contemporary contributions of racial segregation and steering to differences in home values. Federal homeownership policies established the wealth of the white middle class and significantly contributed to the more limited wealth holdings of Black Americans today. In fact, among the homeowning respondents of the SCF, home values made up 76 percent of white homeowners' assets and 89 percent of Black homeowners' assets.

With home values making up such a significant proportion of asset holdings among homeowners in the US, understanding historic and contemporary patterns and inequities in homeownership is a top priority for scholars of housing. Recent research has begun to document the contemporary racial inequities produced by the historic legacies of redlining (Faber 2020a). Other work is expanding our understanding of how racial inequalities in home values are produced through real estate actors including appraisers, real estate agents, and developers (Howell and Korver-Glenn 2018; Korver-Glenn 2021; Besbris and Faber 2017). Ongoing research continues to document racial discrimination in the mortgage lending process (Steil et al. 2018). Finally, recent studies also look to understand how wealth and debt contribute to housing patterns such as multigenerational households (Houle and Warner 2017).

Although this chapter focuses on inequities between Blacks and whites, a sociology of housing should work to understand historic and contemporary trends in access to homeownership for Asian and Latinx communities

---

[3] Total assets included the amount held in checking accounts, IRA/Keogh, savings accounts, bonds, certificates of deposits, mutual funds, stocks, brokerage accounts, and annuities.

(Hyde and Fischer, this volume). Doing so would help illuminate broader patterns of racial inequities. We know that Latinx and Black communities were targeted for subprime lending through racial segregation and lower homeownership rates (Hwang, Hankinson, and Brown 2015; Rugh and Massey 2010), which could contribute to trends in Latinx homeownership and wealth holdings. Sociologists concerned about housing issues should work to understand how historic patterns of exclusion from homeownership affected Asian and Latinx Americans' residential choices. They should evaluate how social differences within these communities, including class and immigration status, shape homeownership patterns and other housing outcomes.

Finally, a sociology of housing must keep in mind that decisions about where to live or whether to buy a home are about more than neighborhood access. The study of housing is in fact the study of economic stability and intergenerational wealth. Homeownership provides an economic resource that owners can leverage for loans for their present needs, but also provides for future generations through inheritance. By defining housing not just as a place where one lays one's head, but also as a form of capital, the sociology of housing can contribute to our understanding of inequality. This inclusive approach to conceptualizing housing has implications for how we think about neighborhood change and stability, spatial patterns of (dis)investment, and the impact of housing segregation on every aspect of inequality in the United States (Gutierrez, Demby, and Frame 2018).

2

Latino Homeownership

OPPORTUNITIES AND CHALLENGES IN
THE TWENTY-FIRST CENTURY

Allen Hyde and Mary J. Fischer

In the United States, homeownership is commonly viewed as a center-piece of the American Dream (Pais and Ray 2015), conferring both economic and social benefits. Home equity is the dominant component of wealth for much of the income spectrum (Lin and Neely 2020). Home-ownership is also an important form of forced savings. It provides tax benefits, inflation protection, and asset appreciation (Flippen 2010; Martin, this volume). Policymakers and the real estate industry tout the positive impact of homeownership on families and communities, manifested in ways such as increased political participation, community engagement, and pro-civic attitudes. Thus, homeownership expansion has been a public policy cornerstone, despite evidence raising doubts about the wholesale veracity of these claims (McCabe 2016).

The growth of homeownership over the past few decades has brought this "American Dream" to life for many underserved groups, fueling investments in communities as well as anchoring families to the middle class. Latino homeownership has increased dramatically over this time period, although their rates of homeownership still fall well below the rates for white residents. In the mid-1990s, around 41 percent of Latinos were homeowners compared to around 70 percent of non-Hispanic whites; by 2007, these numbers peaked at 50 percent and 76 percent respectively. While homeownership rates dropped during the Great Recession, they rebounded by the mid-2020s (Rucks-Ahidiana, this volume). Latinos have also grown as a share of all homeowners. The Joint Center for Housing Study reports that, from 2000 to 2019, the Latino share of homeowners grew from 7.7 percent to 10 percent. Black, non-Latino residents, by contrast, have lagged behind Latinos in their rates of homeownership and thus far have not experienced the same rebound in homeownership post-recession (Fernald 2020).

This chapter provides an overview of Latino homeowners and

homeownership, a population that often gets less attention as past research tends to focus on the persistent Black/white gap in homeownership (Alba and Logan 1992; Coulson 1999; DeSilva and Elmelech 2012; Kuebler 2013; Kuebler and Rugh 2013; Taylor 2019). While insights from research on Black/white homeownership is important given the history of structural racism in the United States, it does not capture the unique experiences of Latinos in the United States. The treatment of Latinos as a monolith can mask within-group differences by race (e.g., between those who identify as white Latinos and Afro-Latinos), country of origin or ethnicity (e.g., Puerto Ricans vs. Mexicans vs. Cubans) and immigration status (Painter II and Qian 2016a, 2016b; Tesfai 2016). Despite being understudied, Latinos are the fastest-growing ethnic group in the United States, particularly among youth (Frey 2020). We first examine the factors that contributed to Latino homeownership growth during the early 2000s. Second, we discuss constraints that continue to shape access to homeownership for Latinos and that impact housing appreciation, including the relationship between contemporary racial and ethnic segregation and homeownership. We conclude with a discussion of the factors that will likely shape Latino homeownership in the coming years and highlight promising directions for future research.

Latino Homeownership Expansion

Several converging factors help explain why Latinos benefited from homeownership expansion starting in the mid- to late 1990s: regulatory changes that allowed Latinos and other underserved populations to gain greater access to credit and mortgages; the improved socioeconomic position of Latinos in terms of education and income; and the movement of Latinos to new, more affordable destinations in the US.

First, changes in the regulatory environment in the 1990s allowed commercial lenders to loosen credit and down-payment requirements. These lenders responded by expanding subprime loan products that made mortgages more attainable. Of course, the availability of looser credit created considerable risk, which disproportionately impacted aspiring Latino homeowners (Rugh 2015). Government programs, including Federal Housing Administration (FHA) and Veterans Administration (VA)–backed loans, also targeted underserved groups, facilitating the overall expansion of homeownership (Shlay 2006). Compared to white residents, Latinos are more highly represented among FHA/VA loan recipients and are more likely to hold subprime loans (Hyde and Fischer 2021).

Second, the socioeconomic status of Latinos in the United States has been steadily improving over the past few decades (Fry and Taylor

2013). Average educational levels have been on the rise for Latinos, with particularly strong growth among recent immigrants. From 1990 to 2018, the percentage of recent immigrants obtaining at least a BA rose from 10 percent to 26 percent (Noe-Bustamante 2020). Those with more than ten years in the US also saw gains in education (Noe-Bustamante 2020). Latinos' median incomes have correspondingly increased over this period, bolstering the credentials of Latino loan applicants. By 2018, 56 percent of Latinos held FICO scores above the 620 minimum to qualify for a conventional loan and 37 percent above the 700 threshold, which is commonly considered to be "good" credit. These scores help explain Latinos' relative gains in homeownership (Clark 2013; Kochhar, Gonzalez-Barrera, and Dockterman 2009; Rosenbaum 2012) even as access to credit has become more restrictive.

Third, changes in the demographic profile of homeowners mirror Latino population expansion and their movement to new destinations (Kandel and Cromartie 2004; Massey 2008). Latinos comprised over 55 percent of overall growth in the US population from 2000 to 2011 (Motel and Patten 2013) through both migration and natural increase. This population growth coincided with a shift in the locations where Latinos reside. Prior to the 1990s, Latinos primarily clustered in a set of areas often referred to as established destinations because of their long history of attracting new immigrants. These established destinations are concentrated in California, Texas, Arizona, New Mexico, and Florida, as well as in major cities like New York City and Chicago (Zúñiga and Hernández-León 2005; Kandel and Cromartie 2004). While these places continue to be important locations for Latinos, population growth has increasingly been concentrated in new destinations in the Southeast, Great Plains, and Midwest (Marrow 2011; Ribas 2015; Massey 2008; Zúñiga and Hernández-León 2005). These places have lower average housing costs, making homeownership more accessible.

While these factors have helped position Latinos favorably to take advantage of expanded lending opportunities, making inroads into homeownership, there continue to be countervailing forces that constrain access and dampen some of the advantages typically incurred by homeownership. These forces include structural factors impacting *where* homes are purchased and their subsequent appreciation.

The Contemporary Limits to Homeownership for Latinos

Latino homeowners continue to experience conditions limiting both access to and benefits from homeownership. Some of these reasons are tied to historical discrimination that served to undermine Latinos (and other racial/ethnic groups) by largely excluding them from homeownership, as well as geographically constraining housing options for many who have been able to obtain homes. This history is discussed in greater detail by Rucks-Ahidiana (this volume). The broader context of racial segregation and history of access to homeownership forms the backdrop for understanding housing trends for Latinos and other minorities today.

One of the frameworks sociologists have used to understand residential housing patterns is the spatial assimilation model. This perspective views the ability to pay as the main constraint on housing choices. As individuals and groups experience improved socioeconomic status, their housing outcomes should similarly improve, inclusive of both access to homeownership—which is widely believed to be an essential step in status attainment—and neighborhood characteristics. The racial composition of the neighborhood continues to be a key factor in neighborhood attainment. Racial residential segregation in housing has been associated with worse outcomes for minorities and continues to be a limiting factor in home appreciation (Howell and Korver-Glenn 2021). Thus, the spatial assimilation model predicts that as minorities improve their socioeconomic status, they will also become more racially integrated. Overall, this perspective views segregation between white and Latino groups as merely a reflection of differences in the socioeconomic status (SES) or status attainment of these groups. Previous work has indeed found evidence that higher SES Latino families tend to be less segregated from white families than their racial/ethnic counterparts who have lower SES (Clark and Blue 2004; Massey and Fischer 1999). Thus, recent SES gains by Latinos and the corresponding growth in homeownership rates would be predicted to result in lower levels of segregation for Latino homeowners.

However, empirical evidence suggests that Blacks and Latinos do not always get the same returns on improved socioeconomic status as those experienced by their white counterparts. The place stratification perspective helps us to understand these disparate outcomes, asserting that structural racism, like zoning practices and the placement of public housing, limits residential choices and opportunities for racial and ethnic groups regardless of SES (Charles 2003; Pais, South, and Crowder 2012). Indeed, there is substantial evidence that as Black, and to some extent Latino, residents move up the economic ladder, their levels of segregation from white residents and neighborhoods remain relatively high (Massey and Denton 1988; Logan et al. 1996; Fischer 2008; Friedman and Rosenbaum 2007). From this perspective, aspects of the housing system constrain the opportunities of Latinos to gain access to homeownership, especially in higher-resourced white neighborhoods. The racial neighborhood preferences of white homeowners may lead them to move into or out of neighborhoods in response to racial composition or opportunities for equity growth in gentrifying neighborhoods. Still others assert the "buffer hypothesis" that Latinos and other racialized groups of color act as buffers that blur the color line between the strong white-and-Black binary in neighborhoods while promoting multiculturalism, mutual acceptance, and understanding (Alba 2009; Parisi, Lichter, and Taquino 2015).

These perspectives can also help inform our understanding of the experiences of Latino homeowners. In the spatial assimilation model, homeownership can be seen as part of the status attainment process and a key factor signaling upward mobility (Pais and Ray 2015), particularly for Black and Latino families (McCabe 2018). Thus, we would expect that the growth in Latino incomes and SES mentioned earlier in the chapter would result in reduced levels of segregation. However, evidence suggests that the benefits of homeownership for segregation may not be shared universally, a finding that tends to support the place stratification model. Using data from the 2000 census, Friedman, Tsao, and Chen (2013) found that Latino and Asian homeowners tend to be less segregated than renters, although the opposite pattern was found for Blacks. Research also suggests that Black and Latino homeownership tends to be higher in areas with larger co-ethnic bases and areas where there is less residential segregation (Flippen 2010). Segregation can also undermine homeownership for Black and Latino families in different ways (Flippen 2004). For Latinos, clustering and the formation of enclaves likely facilitates homeownership through greater access to Spanish-speaking lenders and real estate institutions, as well as stronger social capital through denser ethnic neighborhood networks. However, clustering often has the opposite effect for Black families due to the legacy of forced housing segregation and disinvestment in those communities. Thus there is growing evidence that patterns of segregation and homeownership operate differently for Blacks than for Latinos, suggesting that scholars need to reconsider theories of segregation based largely on the white-Black binary.

The average neighborhood racial composition among homeowners can also vary by geography, including immigrant destination type. Latinos in established destinations typically have more Latino neighbors due to the larger size of their population, their history of settlement in these areas, and the more expensive housing stock in these communities (Hyde and Fischer 2021). In addition, linguistic and cultural similarities, as well as familial ties, may encourage Latino homeowners to settle in similar neighborhoods (Almeida et al. 2009; Bécares 2014; Hong, Zhang, and Walton 2014). While Latinos on average fare somewhat better than Black residents in terms of converting increased socioeconomic status into more integrated neighborhoods, there is growing evidence that residential outcomes for Latinos are generally more constrained in new destinations compared to established destinations (Fischer and Tienda 2006; Hall 2013; Lichter et al. 2010), as well as in suburban locations shaped by immigration (Jones 2008). This suggests that the overall racial composition and structure of communities is particularly important in shaping outcomes for Latino homeowners.

There is mixed evidence on segregation of Latinos, especially homeowners, in new destinations. Many new Latino destinations have grown due to employment in low-wage sectors, such as agriculture and food processing (Crowley, Lichter, and Qian 2006; Kandel and Parrado 2005). As Latino households move into new destinations, they may become racialized over time and face similar limits to spatial assimilation and residential integration as Black households (Lichter et al. 2010). According to group-threat theory (Blalock 1967; Brown and Fuguitt 1972), abrupt increases of the Latino population in new destinations may lead to increased competition with US-born whites, which may cause greater anti-Latino prejudice as whites see Latinos as a threat to their culture and job prospects. Several studies show that the rapid influx of Latinos can create ethnic conflict, especially in small towns and suburbs with large Black communities or a history of racial oppression (Fennelly 2008; Griffith 2005). Hyde and Fischer (2021) show that both white and Latino homeowners tend to have more Latino neighbors in new destinations or areas with rapid Latino population growth. Overall, segregation continues to be an issue for Latino homeowners; however, it may be more of an issue for immigrants or Afro-Latinos than for white Latinos.

Another constraint on access and location of housing for Latinos is discrimination in housing and lending. In another chapter in this volume on audit studies of housing discrimination in the United States, Gaddis and DiRago summarize recent research using a unique and powerful field-experimental method to make causal claims about discrimination. While evidence of discrimination against Black home buyers is often the strongest, these audit studies show that Latino home buyers and renters often face discrimination and provide insight into how discrimination occurs. While more overt forms of housing discrimination have decreased over the last few decades, less overt forms of discrimination (like steering) are becoming more common.

Contemporary mechanisms of discrimination in lending affect Latinos in several ways. First, fewer commercial bank branches exist in communities of color (Westrich et al. 2007). Second, Black and Latino potential home buyers face higher rejection rates and less favorable terms in securing mortgages than whites even when they have similar credit histories (Ross and Yinger 1999; Oliver and Shapiro 1997). In 2015, 27.4 percent of Black applicants and 19.2 percent of Latino applicants were denied mortgages, compared with about 11 percent of white and Asian applicants (Desilver and Bialik 2017). Third, with fewer mainstream lending entities in their communities, borrowers of color are often targeted for unsustainable, higher cost, subprime mortgages (Rice and Swesnik 2013). In 2015, Black and Latino families were overrepresented among those paying more than 6 percent on a thirty-year fixed mortgage and were far more likely than whites to receive subprime loans (Rice and Swesnik 2013; see also Hyde and Fischer 2021).

A more recent discriminatory mechanism is the seemingly neutral use of algorithms to determine credit worthiness. Although algorithmic lending can reduce discrimination by approximately 40 percent compared to face-to-face lenders overall in terms of pricing (Bartlett et al. 2017), there continues to be bias in this decision-making. Some scholars have suggested that this discrimination is a form of monopoly rent, as people of color are less likely to shop for a mortgage than white home buyers (Woodward 2008; Woodward and Hall 2012). Others point out that algorithms and machine learning themselves reproduce bias on the basis of social categories like race/ethnicity or gender, even when they are omitted from data collection, because algorithms learn from correlations present in existing data (Williams, Brooks, and Shmargad 2018). Thus, machine learning embeds social identifiers into big data sets, which can introduce bias and discrimination into seemingly neutral algorithms. Despite these limitations, there are many reasons to believe that Latino homeownership will remain strong in the years to come.

Prospects for Latino Homeownership Going Forward

The first part of the COVID-19 pandemic saw an uptick in home buying (Demsas 2021b). Home sales from May to September 2020 were significantly higher than in the same months in 2019, in part because families sought more space to accommodate extended working and schooling from home (Fernald 2020). Although housing costs have gone up in nearly every market, continued low interest rates until mid-2022 helped make homeownership relatively affordable for those who managed to maintain their income during the pandemic; these rates also enabled some existing homeowners to lower their mortgage payments through refinancing.[1] While the recent home buyers were overwhelmingly white, Latinos comprised 9 percent of the home purchasers from April to July of 2020 (National Association of Realtors 2021). Over half of the Latino home buyers reported being first-time buyers, compared to only 28 percent of whites (National Association of Realtors 2021). This figure suggests increased upward mobility for at least that portion of the Latino population possessing the requisite assets and income to qualify for these home purchases. The general upswing in home prices has helped homeowners across the board to build equity and grow their financial resources.

In the longer term, Latino homeownership merits attention from sociologists of housing for several reasons. First, Latinos will continue to represent a growing proportion of the population through both natural increase and immigration. Latinos have a relatively youthful age distribution. They are more likely to be entering childbearing years and establishing their households. Immigration and immigration policy will also continue to play a role in understanding the prospects for Latino homeownership. According to the Migration Policy Institute (2019), about a third of the undocumented population in the United States in 2014 owned their own homes. This population of homeowners is particularly vulnerable because of their liminal legal status, which leaves them not only at risk of potential deportation but also excluded from some safety net programs intended to assist homeowners experiencing financial hardship. Lacking papers and fear of deportation can strongly discourage undocumented immigrants from interacting with banks, which can severely restrict their ability to obtain mortgages and interact with lenders, insurers, and other institutional actors (Hall and Greenman 2013; Amuedo-Dorantes and Bansak 2006). Restricted access to lenders combined with potentially reduced economic security can lead to poorer neighborhood and/or home conditions for undocumented immigrants (Hall 2013).

The issues of housing affordability that face many communities will also continue to disproportionately impact Latino households. While it was anticipated that the high percentage of owners behind on mortgages in the pandemic would negatively impact homeownership, it appears now that the government's proactive policy response to the pandemic successfully averted a massive wave of foreclosures (Gerardi, Lambie-Hanson, and Willen 2022). Renters well positioned to purchase homes prior to

---

[1] A recent study found that black and Latino borrowers were less likely to refinance than their white counterparts even after controlling for a range of factors (Gerardi, Lambie-Hanson, and Willen 2022).

the pandemic may no longer qualify, due to the economic toll of the pandemic. Additionally, housing cost–burdened households often skimp on other necessities, such as food, healthcare, and transportation, to make housing payments. These cutbacks on necessary household expenditures can be especially detrimental to children, who are more likely to suffer academic setbacks and have lower overall mental and physical health that may ultimately undermine their prospects for upward mobility moving into adulthood.

Sociologists concerned about housing should also bear in mind the variation and inequality within the Latino community (Martinez and Aja 2021). Theories of race and racism provide insight into the racialization of Latinos in US society within loosely organized racial strata (Bonilla-Silva 2003). While Afro-Latinos may be racialized into the larger "collective Black" category alongside other populations with African or South Asian descent, white Latinos like Cubans and light-skinned segments of the Mexican and Puerto Rican communities may be racialized as whites or "honorary whites" (Bonilla-Silva 2003). Thus, anti-Blackness plays an important role in understanding the experiences of Afro-Latinos relative to other Latino groups. Martinez and Aja (2021) confirm that white Latinos are more likely to own homes than other Latino groups. Broken down by race and ethnicity, white Cubans and other Latinos had the highest homeownership rates; however, Black Dominicans and Puerto Ricans tended to have some of the lowest homeownership rates (possibly due to the long history of racialization of these groups in the United States). Thus, a sociology of housing must acknowledge how race, racism, and ethnicity play an important role in shaping inequality in homeownership among Latinos.

Future Directions for Research

There are several promising directions for future research on Latino homeowners. First, adding to a growing body of literature on housing discrimination for Latino homeowners, sociologists of housing should examine other outcomes, including the opportunities to build wealth and generate equity for Latinos. This type of research will help policymakers evaluate the specific benefits of pro-homeownership policies for the Latino community. In doing so, sociologists should work to understand how these outcomes vary by racial identity, immigration status, and country of origin within the broader Latino community.

Second, we must evaluate the impact of the pandemic on homeowners and future home buying decisions. While it remains too early to draw definitive conclusions, homeownership remains a central component of wealth-building strategies for the Latino community. It will be important to understand how housing affordability programs impact Latino home-ownership and whether programs designed to ensure fair lending practices will further bolster Latino homeownership. Assessing both the short- and long-term effects of these programs will be critical to understanding the Latino homeownership experience.

Third, while there is a substantial body of research on racial discrimi-nation in homeownership and lending, there is more work to be done specifically on Latinos. There is growing recognition of the diversity of experiences among Latinos by race, country of origin, and immigration status that needs to be better captured in research on discrimination. It will also be important to understand how machine learning and algorithms—which form the backbone of the online banking infrastructure that repre-sents a growing share of the mortgage market—impact Latinos' access to homeownership and the terms of the loans offered to them.

Fourth, the sociology of housing can better integrate literature about Latino immigration and housing outcomes. For example, sociologists are well equipped to ask how citizenship (or undocumented) status affects the probability of owning a home and building equity. Some research on nativity, citizenship, legal status, and Latino homeownership in Los An-geles finds that being born in the USA does not predict homeownership; however, undocumented Latino immigrants are the least likely Latino group to own a home (McConnell 2015). Overall, this type of research into different geographic settings and scales can reveal more information about the relationship between citizenship, immigration status, and home-ownership for Latinos.

3

Latinos' Housing Inequality

LOCAL HISTORICAL CONTEXT AND THE RELATIONAL FORMATION OF SEGREGATION

María G. Rendón, Deyanira Nevárez Martínez, and Maya Parvati Kulkarni

Latinos' concentration in low-quality housing in the United States is often depicted as a function of *recent* immigration of unskilled workers. Yet unaffordable, inadequate housing and persistent patterns of segregation are deeply interwoven with Latinos' history of displacement and racial exclusion, particularly in the Southwest. As early as 1908, Jacob Riis would comment on the "filth and squalor" of the Los Angeles "Cholo (Mexican) Courts," noting that "he had seen larger slums, but never any worse" (Housing Commission of the City of Los Angeles, 1909). These housing observations were made *before* the first large wave of Mexican immigrants arrived in the city in the 1920s. By then, local race relations were well established, shaping housing and segregation patterns in the city as well as the future integration of Latinos in the region.

We call for housing and segregation scholars to consider the local historical context of race relations, expanding beyond a Black-white dichotomy to account for the racial exclusion and segregation of other nonwhites. Housing and segregation scholars have focused heavily on the industrial cities of the Northeast and Midwest, shaping our understanding of how race has influenced housing inequality. We know that slums in the industrial cities became stepping stones for white ethnics and that racist local practices and policies segregated Blacks in northern ghettos. How race factored into housing and segregation patterns in other parts of the country is less understood as this subject has been grossly understudied. We contend that to study Latinos' experience with housing inequality, it is important to account for the local history of race relations. In the Southwest, this history includes colonization and the various ways nonwhite groups were historically displaced, expelled, and/or relegated to the worst housing in the region as quickly as whites settled there.

While a deep body of scholarship documents how housing and segregation structured racial inequality for African Americans, similar research on

Latinos is scant and complex, and it reveals contradictions. On one hand, historical studies in the Southwest have long documented high levels of segregation and isolation for the Mexican-origin group (Bogardus 1930; Gamio 1930; McWilliams 1948; Camarillo 1979; Griswold del Castillo 1979; Romo 1983; Fogelson 1967). Today, studies find that racial steering and discriminatory lending practices (Rugh 2015; Rugh and Massey 2010) as well as anti-Latino attitudes and sentiments shape Latinos' housing and residential patterns (Lewis, Emerson, and Klineberg 2011). Yet studies drawing on national-level data find moderate levels of segregation and evidence of spatial assimilation that challenge arguments of a racialized experience (Alba, Logan, and Stults 2000; Massey and Mullan 1984; Logan 2002). These studies examine Latinos' residential patterns through an immigration or ethnicity lens, overlooking the local context of race relations and historical patterns of racial exclusion.

When it comes to the Mexican-origin group, there is tension in the sociological literature, with some scholars suggesting that Mexicans have been incorporated as a racialized group (Telles and Ortiz 2008), while others suggest "delayed assimilation" (Brown 2007). Newly digitized historical census data now allow researchers to compare racial and ethnic groups nationally in new ways, informing our understanding of historical patterns. One such study finds that Mexicans experienced "unique structural barriers" (i.e., racial discrimination) compared to European immigrants between 1850 and 1940 that limited their social mobility across generations (Kosack and Ward 2018). Another finds that Mexican immigrants were just as likely as southern and eastern European immigrants to live next door to native-born Americans during this same period—though the race or ethnicity of these native-born Americans is unclear (Eriksson and Ward 2019).

National-level analyses are important, but to understand the historical roots of Latinos' housing inequality requires accounting for the local context of race relations, including the relational nature of racial formation (Molina 2014). Sociological research shows that social processes underlying housing inequality and segregation, including individual actors' perceptions, decisions, and acts of prejudice, emerge locally (Krysan and Crowder 2017). As Omi and Winant (2014) note, race is "always and necessarily a social and historical process." In Los Angeles and other cities in the Southwest, race relations were shaped by the backdrop of the US-Mexican War, as well as by the earlier colonization of the Spanish empire which stripped native people from their land, relegating them to the bottom of the racial hierarchy in the region. In California, immigration was also a distinct factor, as the state's location along the Pacific Rim made it a draw for Asian immigrants, whose large presence in the 1800s sparked the first immigration-restriction laws in the US (Ngai 2014), including policies of deportation (Lytle Hernández 2017). At the turn of the twentieth century, white settlers imposed anti-Black sentiments on the developing region (Perry and Harshbarger 2019), extending their understanding of race to other nonwhites (Molina 2014).

We account for the unique history of the Mexican-origin group in Southern California by reviewing historical and Chicano/Latino scholarship that accounts for their racialization, including their incorporation as expendable labor, which shaped their housing and residential patterns. We also examine Mexicans' housing and residential patterns in Los Angeles in 1930 and 1940, a critical time for understanding Latinos' racialization, including the roots of their housing inequality. The first large wave of Mexican immigration peaked in the mid-1920s, and the largest Mexican *barrio* emerged in East Los Angeles (Romo 1983). It was then that national rhetoric around the "Mexican problem"—the idea that Mexicans were backward, racially inferior, and unassimilable—emerged, giving way to anti-Mexican sentiment. In 1930, the US census formally categorized Mexicans as nonwhite, and as the Great Depression set in, racial scripts (Molina 2014) associating Mexicans to criminality (Lytle Hernández 2017), disease (Molina 2006), and dependency (Fox 2012) prompted the first large-scale repatriation—or expulsion—of the group. Scholars estimate about five hundred thousand Mexicans and Mexican Americans returned to Mexico by force or "choice" in the early 1930s (Balderrama and Rodríguez 2006; Hoffman 1974; Fox 2012).

Yet examining Mexicans' residential patterns in Los Angeles in 1930 and 1940 reveals that studying this group in isolation is of limited utility. At this time, most Mexicans in the city lived in neighborhoods with other nonwhites. Racially restrictive covenants against Mexicans, Asians, Blacks, and Jews confined these groups spatially. Increasingly, scholars call attention to these groups' shared racialized spaces in the city (Kurashige 2010; Sánchez 2021; Liévanos 2019), or what Liévanos (2019) refers to as the "relational racialization of space." In both decades, Mexicans experienced high levels of segregation from whites, yet few lived in homogenous Mexican communities. Instead, Mexicans, like Blacks and Asians, were more likely to live in racially mixed neighborhoods than in predominantly white *or* predominantly ethnic neighborhoods. While some foreign-born whites lived in these diverse communities, most lived with native-born whites. As scholars note, Los Angeles's diverse communities were racially distinct (Kurashige 2010, Sánchez 2021).

We call for housing and segregation scholars to account for the historical local context of race relations as they incorporate Latinos and other ethnic and racial groups in their analysis. Such an accounting requires understanding how Latinos' racialization intersects with that of other racialized groups—Natives, Asians, and Blacks—whose histories are distinct, yet overlap in significant ways. It also requires understanding how the racialization of one Latino group can extend to other Latinos with distinct migrant histories. Accounting for the relational nature of racial formation—specifically, how racial scripts and racialization processes of one group inform the treatment of others—will be increasingly important to understanding the housing barriers Latinos face not only in regions where they have historical roots, but also in new destinations with distinct histories of race relations. The housing experience and segregation of Latinos is distinct from that of others, yet nonetheless it is "a node in a network of racial projects" (Molina 2010).

Mexicans' Racial Formation at the Intersection of Two Colonial Projects

Darrah-Okike et al. (in this volume) highlight how few housing scholars account for the history of the United States as a settler society. This elision has implications not only for Native people, but also for understanding entrenched patterns of housing inequality and residential segregation of the Mexican-origin group. A well-developed body of literature documents the violence and the racist practices and policies that emerged in American cities to exclude and segregate Blacks (Massey and Denton 1993, Rothstein 2017). The same system of white supremacy that kept Blacks in the Jim Crow South and confined them to ghettos informed the genocide of Native peoples, removing them from their land and denying their citizenship. It informed the racial ideology of manifest destiny (Horsman 1981; Gómez 2018) and the belief that Native Americans "were not fit for self-governance," claims extended to Mexicans whose "indigenous heritage and largely feudal political economy marked them as racially backward," justifying their conquest and land acquisition (Molina 2014, 25).

Mexicans sit at the intersection of this American colonial project and that of the Spanish empire. Though distinct in significant ways, both colonial projects privileged whiteness, denying land ownership to the lower castes, namely indigenous peoples, *mestizos* and *afromestizos*. Rapid development at the turn of the twentieth century in the Southwest accelerated the erasure of this history, its Native people, and the marginalization of "copper-toned" Mexicans, who had long labored and lived in the region. In California, as soon as whites settled in the region, they began to voice concern over the presence of Mexicans, at times referred to as *cholos* ("Cholo

Invasion and Its Bad Results" 1902)—a racialized term originating under the Spanish racial caste system linking Mexicans to their indigeneity (Oliver 1908). It was with the influx of white Americans that the isolation of "lower class" Mexicans in "*cholo* colonies" solidified in the region (Camarillo 1979), as Mexicans were relegated to the "less desirable sections of the city, beyond the railroad tracks" and "where average Americans did not live" (Bogardus 1930).

As historians and Chicano/Latino scholars note, the race prejudice against Mexicans is rooted in "the time when white Americans first came into contact with Indians, Spaniards and Indo-Spaniards" (Gamio 1930, 53). The Treaty of Guadalupe Hidalgo declared Mexicans white by law, but their whiteness was repeatedly challenged in court in the nineteenth and twentieth centuries (Lopez 1997; Almaguer 2016; Gómez 2018; Menchaca 2001; Molina 2014). Californian legislators, drawing from their practice of Black and Native exclusion, clarified Mexicans' "blood quantum." In 1849, a person with "one-half or more Indian blood was considered non-White," and two years later this designation became more restrictive "as people of one-fourth Indian descent were considered non-White" (Menchaca 2001, 221). As land disputes mounted, these racial classifications stripped Mexicans from their land. Those categorized as Indian and nonwhite were denied citizenship rights and land property, while the few elites considered white were allowed to keep their land with proper land documentation on the condition they deny or sever ties to their indigeneity (Cotera and Saldaña-Portillo 2015). As numerous scholars note, Mexicans may have been white by law, but were not so in practice (Lopez 1997; Fox and Guglielmo 2012; Menchaca 2001; Gómez 2018).[1]

Mexicans' history of housing dislocation and residential patterns intertwine intimately with the elimination, racial subjugation, and exclusion of indigenous peoples (Wolfe 2006; Veracini 2010). Race prejudice against "lower class" Mexicans is deeply rooted in this history of America as a settler society and the violent system of white supremacy that denied nonwhites land rights. Imposing a Black-white lens to understand race relations in the Southwest erases this history and the roots of racial exclusion for the Mexican-origin group—as well as for Natives and Asians who have deep roots in the region.

---

[1] The Treaty of Guadalupe Hidalgo declared that Mexicans would be "incorporated into the Union of the United States" with the "enjoyment of all the rights of citizens." Yet only a year later, "the US violated the treaty with respect to the citizenship articles and refused to extend Mexicans full political rights on the basis that the majority population was not White" (Menchaca 1995).

By the time the first large wave of Mexican immigrants arrived in the United States in the 1920s, their racialization and nonwhite status were well established (McWilliams 1948). This racialization shaped Mexican immigrants' incorporation in the labor market, where a dual wage structure meant they were paid less than white immigrants for similar work (Camarillo 1979). Race prejudice also informed Mexicans' segregation in other ways, as they were often prohibited from using local public amenities, like pools or movie theaters, and children were segregated in Mexican schools (Powers 2008; Donato and Hanson 2012; Ruiz 2001).[2] Emory Bogardus, an influential sociologist tied to the Chicago School, noted Mexicans' unique social position in Southern California: "The economic status of the Mexican is lowest on the whole of any race in the city. The Mexican lives, as a rule, in the worst of the house-court" (1916, 398). While some foreign-born whites also lived in these housing courts (Bogardus 1916; Sánchez 1993; Wild 2005; Spalding 1992), most immigrants in the city "were distinguished by race rather than nationality" (and) native-born whites "subjugated and excluded them even more rigorously" (Fogelson 1967, 204). This racial animus extended beyond the foreign born. Gamio (1930) noted that "the second or third generations . . . remained or were kept apart socially, and were almost always called 'Mexicans' . . . Racially they are not wholly or partially American" (53–54). As whites sprawled across Los Angeles, Mexicans and other nonwhites were "barred from subdivisions in greater Los Angeles by restrictive covenants" (Fogelson 1967). "Exploited economically, separated residentially, isolated socially, and ignored politically, these people remained entirely outside the Los Angeles community between 1885 and 1930" (Fogelson 1967, 200–01).

Mexicans' Repeated Expulsion: A History of Housing Displacement

The conquest of the Southwest and legal challenges against Mexicans' whiteness resulted in their loss of land, establishing their precarious housing situation. Mexicans' racialization was further reinforced by working poor, Mexican immigrants' incorporation as expendable labor subject to deportation. Mexican immigration is embedded in a history of expulsion

---

[2] The 1947 *Mendez v. Westminster* case ended school segregation for Mexicans after the judge stipulated that "not only were all Mexicans not Indian" but that "the fourteenth amendment guaranteed them equal rights as citizens."

and housing displacement, which associates the group not only with "foreignness" but with illegality.

Mexicans' mode of incorporation as presumed temporary workers, or "birds of passage," shaped their unique residential patterns and segregation. Mexicans were scattered throughout the southwest region in Mexican colonies, typically labor camps or company towns clustered in or near railroad and farmlands (Camarillo 1979; Gonzalez 1994; Grebler, Moore, and Guzman 1970). These Mexican labor camps varied in size. Some were "small and isolated," like "permanent temporary quarters," while others had "a considerable percent of Mexicans" in small cities or towns where "sometimes 50 or 100 families live in a segregated section of a city or small town" (Bogardus 1934, 21). In these colonies, Mexicans often lived in shack-like housing, among the worst in the region (Gonzalez 1994). Even today, America's deepest pockets of poverty remain in agricultural towns, and some of the worst housing conditions are in Mexican *colonias* along the US-Mexico border where residents lack basic infrastructure like electricity, running water, and paved roads (Nevárez-Martínez, Rendón, and Arroyo 2019; Ward 1999). Many of these communities were ultimately engulfed by rapid urbanization but were originally "invariably 'on the other side' of something: a railroad track, a bridge, a river or a highway" (McWilliams 1948, 217).

Early on, Mexican *colonias* and *barrios* that emerged in Southern California were described as having "little social control" and as places where "personal and social disorganization ranks high" (Bogardus 1934, 21). Other racial scripts unfolded over this time, linking Mexicans to dependency, crime, and disease, justifying racially restrictive covenants and redlining of their communities. As Mexican communities grew and bordered on expanding white neighborhoods, they were subject to local conflict as Anglos resisted their integration—sometimes with acts of violence ("Trouble for Mexicans Brewing" 1909).

Yet another tool used to exclude Mexicans from permanent residential settlement was deportation, a practice that originated first out of efforts to exclude Chinese immigrants in the region (Lytle Hernández 2017). Rhetoric over "the Mexican problem" during the Great Depression galvanized support for the first massive repatriation of Mexican immigrants and Mexican Americans. Other efforts came later, like the national deportation campaign "Operation Wetback" in the 1950s, which existed alongside the binational Bracero Program (1942–1962), which institutionalized Mexicans as temporary migrants (Massey 2007). Deportation campaigns continued into the twenty-first century, uprooting and displacing Mexicans (and other Latinos).

Housing Inequality and the Relational
Formation of Racial Segregation

Racialization processes entrenched Latinos' patterns of housing inequality. Mexicans' racial formation was linked to their indigeneity and racial mixture, as well as to their incorporation as expendable labor. This racial formation informed their segregation, as well as episodes of deportation and housing displacement. Yet the process of racial formation does not emerge in isolation, but rather in a specific context of race relations. We extend the work of Molina (2014), who examines how racial scripts of other nonwhites—Natives, Blacks, and Asians—were drawn on to reinforce Mexicans' racialization in the early 1900s. Housing and residential patterns of the Mexican-origin group in Los Angeles reveals that their racial exclusion was intertwined with that of other nonwhites in the city as well.

We draw on the 1930 and 1940 census microdata (Ruggles et al. 2010) to examine Mexican residential patterns in Los Angeles, comparing these with corresponding patterns for whites (foreign-born and native-born), Blacks, and Asians. Until recently, examining historical residential patterns of the Mexican-origin group was difficult to do. Most historical census data identify Mexicans as white, masking their racialization and complicating our understanding of their segregation. We capitalize on the 1930 census data, the only year when the US categorized Mexicans as a nonwhite racial group, providing a valuable window into their racialization. We then aggregate individual-level data to enumeration districts (similar to census tracts) and map residential patterns across racial and ethnic groups in Los Angeles using a new historical city map available through the Urban Transition Historical GIS Project. We also examine Mexicans' residential patterns in 1940 by extracting the Mexican-origin group from a newly constructed Hispanic variable. We do so to compare Mexicans' residential patterns before and after their repatriation during the Great Depression.

In 1930 and 1940, Los Angeles was a rapidly growing city. It was also about 87 percent white, as most migrants settling in the city were native-born whites from other parts of the country. Most enumeration districts were predominantly white as well—89 percent in 1930 and 84 percent in 1940—but this racial breakdown was not just a function of demographics (see figure 3.1). In 1930 and 1940, nonwhites in Los Angeles—Mexicans, Asians, and Blacks—were highly segregated from whites, and most of them resided in racially mixed communities. Mexicans' concentration in racially mixed neighborhoods contrasts with their hypersegregation in Los Angeles today (Wilkes and Iceland 2004). In 1930, Mexicans made up about

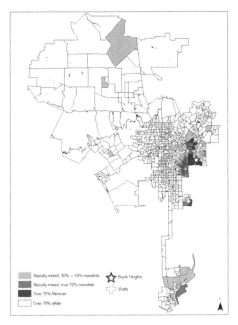

FIGURE 3.1. 1930 racial segregation by enumeration district, City of Los Angeles

8 percent of the city population (a larger community existed outside city limits). This percentage was similar in 1940, though Mexicans were less immigrant in character, partly as a function of repatriations and rise of the US-born second generation. In 1930, over half the Mexican-origin group was foreign born (56 percent) but only a third (32 percent) were so in 1940. Regardless of the immigrant composition of the Mexican community, only 1 percent of enumeration districts in the city were predominantly Mexican (>70 percent) in 1930, with 13 percent of Mexicans living in such communities. This population distribution remained the same in 1940.

Instead, in 1930 and 1940, Los Angeles had several distinct, racially mixed enumeration districts where *most* Mexicans, Blacks, and Asians lived. In line with existing research, our maps illustrate that downtown and the Boyle Heights community of East Los Angeles were racially diverse (Sánchez 2021; Wild 2005). Sánchez finds that Boyle Heights was a "multiracial community made up of Mexicans, Jews, Japanese, African Americans, Armenians, Italians, and scattered native whites for most of its history, well into the 1950s" (2021, 7). By 1940, Little Tokyo—also known then as Bronzeville—was an Asian and Black community (Kurashige 2010). Other racially diverse neighborhoods were near the port of Los Angeles and present-day Watts, areas that were not racially restricted, and

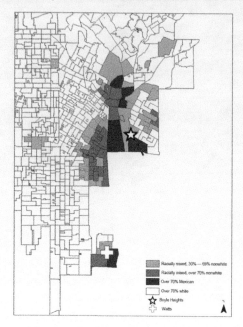

FIGURE 3.2. 1930 racial segregation by enumeration district, inner-city Los Angeles

that were zoned as industrial and developed alongside the transport corridor. A close look at present-day Watts (see figure 3.2), a predominantly Black community in the 1960s but now predominantly Latino, was one of these racially mixed communities. In 1930, a pocket of the city was predominantly Mexican, another Mexican and Black (70 percent racially mixed), and another pocket of Watts was even more diverse, with a mix of Mexicans, Blacks, Asians, and whites (30–69 percent nonwhite).

The extent to which these nonwhite groups lived side by side as neighbors is unclear. Emerging scholarship suggests segregation likely existed at a fine scale in these neighborhoods. In his research on Boyle Heights, Sánchez (2021) found that in the late 1930s, "most residents lived on blocks in which over 80 percent of the residents were of the same racial group" and that there were "significant disparities in rents, housing conditions, and home ownership rates that were largely based on race" (p. 32). Logan and Martinez (2018) find similar patterns of segregation between Blacks and whites at the turn of the twentieth century in neighborhoods once described as racially integrated, encouraging scholars to examine segregation at a fine spatial scale (i.e., in street segments, alleys, face blocks, and buildings.)

In 1930 and 1940, about 55 percent of Mexicans lived in these racially mixed districts in the city, regardless of whether they were foreign or native born. This pattern was similar for Asians. Only Blacks experienced a notable shift in their residential patterns between the two decades. In 1930, 62 percent of Blacks lived in racially mixed neighborhoods, while 21 percent lived in predominantly Black districts (>70 percent). By 1940, the number of Blacks living in racially diverse districts dropped to 46 percent as more Blacks (45 percent) resided in predominantly Black communities. This shift is in line with well-documented growing patterns of racial segregation for the group at this time. Some scholars note the presence of "racially disparaged" whites—Jews and Italians—in these neighborhoods (Sánchez 2021; Wild 2005). Yet we point out that while some foreign-born whites lived in racially mixed districts (~9 percent), the majority (~91 percent) lived in predominantly white districts in both decades, a stark contrast to the experience of nonwhites in the city.

Dissimilarity index measures confirm significant racial segregation across enumeration districts. Blacks experienced the highest levels of segregation from whites in 1930 (.87) and 1940 (.90). In 1930, Mexicans had the second-highest level of segregation from whites (.72) followed by Asians (.68), but these numbers flipped in 1940 as Mexicans experienced a modest decline (.68) and Asians (.73) a slight increase in their segregation. These persistently high levels of segregation in Los Angeles support historical scholarship documenting Mexicans' racialization and segregation across generations. It is striking that Mexicans' segregation remained similar between 1930 and 1940, despite the repatriation of Mexicans after 1930 and lower rates of immigration by 1940. The high levels of segregation for Asians are also notable and in line with existing research. The Chinese community experienced some of the highest levels of racial segregation in the United States (.90 dissimilarity index in San Francisco, California, in the late 1800s) (Eriksson and Ward 2019) and Japanese, forced into internment camps in the 1940s, lived in communities with Blacks prior to urban renewal (Kurashige 2010; Lai 2012). The high levels of segregation of these racialized groups sharply contrast with the low levels of segregation for foreign-born whites in Los Angeles in 1930 (.14) and 1940 (.15).

Los Angeles would remain predominantly white into the 1950s. Racial restrictions against Asian immigration remained, and the Bracero Program allowed Mexican immigrants to work but not reside permanently in the US. It would take civil rights efforts to dismantle racial exclusion in immigration law and abolish the exploitative migrant program. By then, housing and segregation patterns in Los Angeles were firmly in place to welcome the new wave of immigrants, whose integration would inevitably be shaped by the local history of race relations in the city.

Future Directions for Housing and Segregation Research

We offer a starting point for housing and segregation scholars interested in deepening and expanding research that includes the Latinx community and other racialized groups in the United States. We center on the Mexican case to highlight how the local context of race relations shapes housing and segregation patterns in the United States. The Mexican case also illustrates the relational nature of racial formation, important for housing and segregation scholars to consider in their work.

Our snapshot of Mexicans' residential patterns in Los Angeles in 1930 and 1940 confirm historical Chicano/Latino scholarship documenting the racialization and segregation of the group in Southern California. Housing scholars examining the Mexican experience should account for this history, expanding beyond the Black-white binary understanding of race in the United States. Efforts to characterize the housing experience and segregation of the Mexican-origin group as akin to those of white immigrants or African Americans is ahistorical, decontextualized, and theoretically unproductive. To fully understand the role housing plays in reflecting or shaping Mexicans' integration in the United States, it is necessary to account for their unique racialization in the Southwest and for the historical flow of Mexican immigrants for over a century, subject to repatriation and deportation campaigns. Mexicans' indigeneity and racial mixture marked them as distinct from white immigrants. Their immigrant mode of incorporation has reinforced this racialization and resulted in a nonlinear, disrupted integration process. Mexican housing patterns reflect this dual form of racial incorporation as nonwhite and expendable labor.

We also call for housing scholars to account for the relational nature of racial formation (Molina 2014). Our maps of Los Angeles not only capture the racialization of Mexicans, but also that of Asians and Blacks. Scholarship has documented how the housing experience and growing racial segregation of Africans Americans across the twentieth century, including in Los Angeles, significantly reinforced racial inequalities. The residential racial exclusion of Asians and Mexicans took a different form during this period. Notably, immigration law racially excluded Asians (Ngai 2014), and Mexicans' racialization became more tightly linked to their incorporation as expendable laborers, as reflected in repeat deportation campaigns. African Americans were not subject to such practices of expulsion, leaving residential racial segregation—and other forms of violence—as the main linchpin of their racial exclusion (Massey and Denton 1993).

Important empirical and theoretical work remains to be done to better understand the historical roots of housing inequality for Latinos. In the Los Angeles context, there is still much to learn about restrictive covenants— and the social dynamics—that contained nonwhites in racially mixed communities there. We know these neighborhoods were subject to redlining and became sites of large public housing development in later years, but knowledge gaps remain. Some scholars are unpacking the implications of these racially mixed communities and how they differ from the experience of living in racially homogenous neighborhoods. These studies find evidence that this close contact facilitated cross-racial relations and allowed for cross-racial coalitions (Kurashige 2010; Sánchez 2021).

Sociology of housing scholars should examine housing patterns and segregation at a fine scale. While most Mexicans (and Asians) in 1930 and 1940 Los Angeles lived in racially mixed communities, a third lived in predominantly white enumeration districts. What this means is unclear. On the one hand, scholars have long noted that fair-skinned Mexicans (Gamio 1930) experience less discrimination and more easily integrate than those who are darker skinned. Mexicans living in predominantly white districts may have passed as white or been better off financially. On the other hand, segregation occurs at various scales, and a closer analysis of residential patterns within the enumeration district—such as at the street-level—can provide a better understanding of racial integration. Mexicans in predominantly white districts could have still been highly segregated, clustering at the periphery of a community or socially isolated. Scholars have long noted Mexicans' efforts to move out of communities with "disreputable housing conditions" being "usually doomed to disappointment," as they had to "contend with prejudices of (white) Americans" (Bogardus 1934, 19).

As the United States continues to diversify, sociologists of housing will have to expand beyond dominant scholarship to account for changing demographics. It would be a mistake to do so primarily through an immigration lens, as racial and ethnic groups are incorporated in local communities with distinct historical contexts of race relations. To better understand housing disparities, including how housing sustains segregation and other racial disparities, we encourage sociology of housing scholars not only to engage well-established research on segregation, but to account for the relational formation of racial segregation. Doing so will allow for a more expansive understanding of how housing and racial segregation has shaped American society.

4

The Renaissance Comes to the Projects

PUBLIC HOUSING POLICY, RACE, AND URBAN
REDEVELOPMENT IN BALTIMORE

Peter Rosenblatt

Public housing sits at a key nexus for understanding how the politics of urban redevelopment perpetuate racial inequality. Critical urban theorists have crafted compelling arguments for urban growth and redevelopment as inseparable from capitalism and detrimental to the stability of poor and working-class communities. The city is an outlet for accumulated capital (Harvey 1982; Gotham 2006) and its development benefits the interests of place entrepreneurs (Logan and Molotch 1987). This development is carried out through neoliberal strategies of governance aimed at "rolling back" the Keynesian welfare state and "rolling out" policies that expand the reach of the market and intensify competition between places (Peck and Tickell 2002; Hackworth 2007; Brenner 2017). At the same time, sociologists have produced a wealth of studies showing that racial segregation is fundamental to the perpetuation of white socioeconomic advantage (Massey and Denton 1993). Segregation is entrenched in housing markets and reinforced by discrimination (Turner et al. 2013; Rosen, Garboden, and Cossyleon 2021), racialized preferences for neighborhoods (Charles 2006), and the structure of the housing search process (Krysan and Crowder 2017). It is relatively straightforward to treat segregation as a demographic fact and acknowledge that its prevalence in American cities means that the processes of urban redevelopment unpacked by critical urban theorists do not have race-neutral impacts. A sociology of housing, however, allows us to go further and closely examine the ways in which urban redevelopment is inherently racialized.

Using Baltimore as a case study, I focus on public housing and compare housing policy in two time periods: the era of public housing construction, 1933–1950, and the era of public housing demolition and redevelopment that took place under the Housing Opportunities for People Everywhere (HOPE VI) program between 1992 and 2006. Across both eras, public housing was used as a redevelopment tool to clear away blight and strengthen the housing market, alternatively protecting and expanding the central business district. But this process was also explicitly racialized. Black communities were targeted for spatial reconfiguration and displacement in both eras, as public housing policy was used in ways that preserved the racially segregated status quo of the city, particularly in racially homogenous white areas.

In making this argument, and in connecting it to other studies of US public housing policy across places and time periods, I hope to show that a sociological approach is particularly well situated to allow us to understand the complex interrelationship between policy, race, and urban redevelopment. In this way, the sociological study of housing is vital for interpreting social inequality and advancing social justice.

The Era of Public Housing Construction

Concern for the poor, ill-housed, and unhoused may have inspired public housing, but it has long been in tension with downtown preservation strategies and the maintenance of racial segregation. Housing advocates raised issues of poor housing conditions, overcrowding, crime, and disease in cities as far back as the Progressive Era, but it wasn't until the New Deal that federal housing legislation provided widespread funding and established local housing authorities to construct public housing for those at or near the bottom of the housing market (Bauman 1987, Vale 2013). The housing problem was often framed in terms of slums (deteriorated housing and social problems) and blight (falling property values). Differences in framing the problem often related to proposed solutions, with those concerned about slums advocating for more and better housing. Those concerned with blight pushed for ways to protect property values by eliminating unsightly buildings near the central business district (Thomas 2013, Bauman 1987).

The first foray into public housing construction in Baltimore followed the blight line of thinking. In 1933, before federal funding was even available, Baltimore mayor Howard Jackson commissioned a group of architects, planners, and academics to investigate potential sites for public housing. This Joint Commission on Housing in Baltimore released its report the following year, targeting "a ring of blighted residential tracts of the most serious importance and size" surrounding the center of the city. The commission argued that these blighted properties had a deleterious effect on surrounding neighborhoods, which "unless rehabilitated will remain an increasingly serious menace to all properties inside and outside of this ring" (Maryland State Advisory Board 1934).

This "menace" had clear racial overtones. By the 1930s the city's segregation ordinance—and, later, its use of restrictive covenants—had largely confined African Americans to increasingly overcrowded neighborhoods on the east and west sides of downtown. The neighborhoods that made up the "ring of blight" were home primarily to Black residents, and the commission, drawing on the practice of legal, government-supported (de jure) housing segregation, carefully adjudicated between which areas would be served by new public housing for Black families, and which would be better suited for public housing for whites. These decisions were based on the degree of physical decay, but also on the proximity of each site to better-off majority-white neighborhoods. Without fail the committee recommended putting new public housing for whites in neighborhoods that had the best chance of becoming profitable. Thus, an area "close to clerical and other white-collar employees" should "be reused for white low rental [housing]," while an overcrowded portion of downtown that had long been abandoned by whites was described as having "no other value except for Negro residence" (Maryland State Advisory Board 1934).

Using public housing construction to entrench segregation was common in other cities at this time. Historian Arnold Hirsch (1983) showed that white elites in Chicago used eminent domain to clear downtown land for private redevelopment, removing Black residents to new housing projects constructed in majority-Black neighborhoods. While the Chicago Housing Authority attempted to place projects in white neighborhoods as well, their reliance on the city council for site approval meant that these plans were blocked (Hunt 2009), leading to the overwhelming placement of public housing projects in Black neighborhoods and creating what Hirsch called the "second ghetto," an enlargement and institutional transformation of the South Side Black Belt (Hirsch 1983). The story of using public housing construction to bolster segregation has been told in other cities from Philadelphia (Bauman 1987) to Atlanta (Lands 2009, Vale 2013) to Detroit (Thomas 2013). A nationwide study found that African American families were segregated in public housing developments across the country and were more likely than white tenants to be in centralized, high-density projects (Bickford and Massey 1991).

The fate of the central business district became a greater concern in the postwar era, as suburbanization increasingly drew away middle-class, white families from cities. Local governments, buttressed by a growing profession of urban planners, responded with further slum clearance and "renewal" of downtown neighborhoods, displacing residents, a disproportionate number of whom were Black, in service of the reimagined city (Fullilove 2016, Thomas 2013). Across the country, public housing played a significant role in this wave of urban renewal. It often was used for families removed from slum housing; sometimes this process involved incorporating public housing into the design of new developments in the same location as the demolished slums, while other times it meant using housing projects in separate locations for displaced families (Hirsch 1983, Bauman 1987, Hunt 2009). In either case, replacement housing projects, while providing clean, attractive dwellings, often acted to remove the poorest households from the original slum areas (Vale 2013).

In Baltimore, the wartime and postwar process of relocating slums and building replacement housing was overtly racialized. Dating back to the early 1940s, the building of housing for wartime workers drawn to the city's booming steel, ship, and fighter-plane industries took place firmly within the limits of a de jure segregated housing market. Four wartime housing projects were built for "whites only" with little public debate. A fifth, for Black workers, was decided upon only after large protests by white residents blocked construction at the two initial sites (Hirsch 2003). This imbalance fed a postwar housing shortage that was particularly acute for African Americans, who were still largely concentrated in neighborhoods surrounding downtown.

In 1945 the mayor commissioned a new task force on city planning to study these areas, the boundaries of which were very similar to those that the 1934 Joint Commission on Housing had delineated. The 1945 commission weighed the need for housing and the threat of blight spreading and undermining the housing market. This time the racialized justifications for redevelopment were a bit more softly worded. The housing commission sought to target areas for "rebuilding" that were "capable of more or less homogeneous development of some kind" (Baltimore, Maryland, Commission on City Plan 1945). In practice, this guideline meant that the sites targeted were either majority Black or had pockets of African Americans living in a predominantly white area (Rosenblatt 2012).

In the postwar era, the Housing Authority of Baltimore City (HABC) also had to contend with the political difficulty of placing public housing near white neighborhoods. This difficulty was compounded by a 1950 ordinance which required the Baltimore City Council to approve any site for public housing construction. The ordinance gave council members a direct influence in shaping the public housing landscape of the city and allowed individual council members to halt new public housing construction in their districts by appealing to their colleagues. Plans to build housing projects on vacant land in the outlying majority-white neighborhoods of Belair-Edison and Violetville were opposed by local councilmen and neighborhood associations, with 1,500 residents turning out to oppose the plan at a meeting of the Belair-Edison Improvement Association (Henderson 1993). In the face of this opposition, HABC retreated from building on the Violetville and Belair-Edison sites, instead turning to Black neighborhoods close to downtown and building high-rise projects. Over the next forty years these location decisions would be influential in shaping the racial composition of individual public housing projects, as public housing in Baltimore transitioned from a segregated program with both Black and white tenants in separate developments to a segregated program housing almost exclusively African Americans in African American neighborhoods.

In an era of de jure housing segregation, the connections between public housing policy, urban redevelopment, and race are clear. The recommendations of Baltimore's housing commissions in 1934 and 1945 show that a narrative of threats to the housing market was used to drive a racialized process of demolition and selective rebuilding. Resistance from outlying white neighborhoods and their representatives on the city council further stymied attempts to build in a way that challenged the segregated status quo.

The HOPE VI Era

The connections between public housing, race, and redevelopment can also be seen in the contemporary HOPE VI era. By the early 1980s Baltimore faced threats to its economic viability due to the decline of manufacturing jobs, the reduction of federal aid to cities, and the departure of more than one hundred thousand residents over the previous decade. A group of civic and business entrepreneurs, with the support of Mayor William Donald Schaefer, developed a plan to rebuild the city's former port into a retail and tourist destination. The resulting "renaissance" of the inner harbor won widespread acclaim, and was followed in subsequent years by an aquarium, new hotels, and eventually new baseball and football stadiums. In the mid-1990s, public housing redevelopment provided a way to continue this downtown expansion. The administration of Mayor Martin O'Malley worked to more explicitly connect the policies and practices of the housing authority to citywide goals of economic redevelopment and selective neighborhood revitalization. Strikingly, these concerns were couched in the same language of blight as those of the New Deal era. A 2003 report entitled *Revitalizing and Rebuilding the City of Baltimore* quotes, verbatim, William W. Emmart, chair of the Joint Commission that had planned the city's first public housing projects: "To protect the core property and allow the city to survive, a surrounding ring of blight must be razed and the city's 'human resources' must be renewed" (30).

To accomplish these goals, the city adopted a strategy of attacking the worst source of physical deterioration in order to remove excess housing supply and encourage the housing market to operate on its own. This strategy involved a mix of demolishing vacant housing in some areas and acquiring titles and reselling them in others. Beginning early in the first decade of the 2000s, the city and the housing authority acquired five thousand vacant properties and worked with lawyers to clear titles for resale. These vacant houses were seen by planners and city officials as inhibiting the development of the real estate market and were a significant focus of redevelopment efforts in the city.

These plans dovetailed with federal reform of public housing introduced in the 1990s. In a 1992 report, the National Commission on Severely Distressed Public Housing documented the conditions in numerous public housing projects across the nation and called on Congress to address the needs of residents and revitalize the physical condition of several high-rise housing projects across the country. This report, combined with a growing social-scientific consensus about the harm done to children who grow up in neighborhoods of concentrated poverty (Wilson 1987; Brooks-Gunn, Duncan, and Aber 1997) helped spur the creation of the HOPE VI program, which would depart from the National Commission's recommendation for rehabbing housing projects and instead (in most cases) encourage demolition and the rebuilding of mixed-income housing. Mixed-income housing was proposed as an antidote to concentrated poverty, and featured a combination of fully subsidized public housing, "affordable" units partially subsidized for low-income households but not as deeply as the public housing units, and market-rate units with no subsidy. As Vale has extensively documented (Vale 2019; Vale and Shamsuddin 2017), the program took different forms in different locations, with a wide variation in how much of each type of housing was built in the 260 HOPE VI projects across the country, including developments with all-public housing and those with no public housing. Mixed-income housing also meant the permanent displacement of residents of the original housing projects. This was the most controversial aspect of the program, drawing criticism from some activists and scholars (Goetz 2003, 2013; Bennett and Reed 1999), defense from others (Cisneros and Engdahl 2009), and unease, anger, and resistance from residents (Bezalel 2014; Williams 2018).

HOPE VI was also a significant step toward reducing government assistance and encouraging greater reliance on the housing market. Starting in 1996, Public Housing Authorities (PHAs) were encouraged to partner with local development corporations to rebuild housing projects under HOPE VI guidelines. Part of this partnership involved instructing PHAs to see housing developments as a source of revenue. Policies included the use of "income targeting" to allow higher-income families to move into developments, privatization of site planning and management, and the repeal of a long-standing requirement that all demolished public housing units be replaced one-for-one (Smith 2006). Encouraging income mixing on project sites not only deconcentrated poverty; it also lessened PHA reliance on federal subsidies and turned neighborhoods once dominated by publicly funded housing projects into potential sites of private investment.

On the ground in Baltimore, the effect of this shift toward market-oriented housing can be seen in the way mortgage lenders responded to HOPE VI. In a prior analysis (Rosenblatt 2012) I used data from the Home Mortgage Disclosure Act (HMDA) to compare the proportion of mortgage loans approved in the neighborhoods surrounding Baltimore's HOPE VI sites to a group of comparison neighborhoods surrounding family-housing projects that were not demolished. This loan approval rate reflects how willing banks were to invest in a neighborhood. The neighborhood boundaries I use include not only the housing project "footprint" but also the surrounding privately owned housing. In 1994, both sets of neighborhoods contained large housing projects, and both sets of neighborhoods were similarly unattractive to lenders, with loan approval rates below the citywide mean. Yet by 2006 lending approval rates had improved dramatically in the neighborhood around Baltimore's five HOPE VI sites—on average, banks approved 16 percent more home loans in those neighborhoods after the redevelopment of the projects than they had beforehand. This finding contrasts sharply with those in family-project neighborhoods *not* developed through HOPE VI, where loan approval rates declined by an average of 10 percent. By 2006, after the high-rises were torn down and mixed-income communities rebuilt on the HOPE VI sites, loan approval rates were 25 percent higher in the surrounding neighborhoods than in the family-project neighborhoods. This finding holds even when controlling for features of the neighborhood and applicant pool, suggesting that not just the individual HOPE VI projects but the surrounding neighborhoods saw a greater willingness of banks to invest than they might have had the program not taken place.

The positive response of lending institutions to HOPE VI also shows that the program fit with the wider city-planning goals of expanding the housing market in low-income neighborhoods. The city's policy of using governmental authority to demolish or package and resell vacant and abandoned housing to private speculators in order to jumpstart the housing market aligned with the practice of HOPE VI, which also used government policy to demolish buildings and encourage privatization. The HMDA analysis shows that, by increasing the rate of mortgage approvals in the neighborhoods surrounding the "footprint" of the housing projects, HOPE VI helped expand the housing market in low-income neighborhoods.

Other scholarship has drawn connections between HOPE VI and urban redevelopment. One notable way is through research on the connections between the demolition of housing projects and the gentrification of nearby neighborhoods. An early study found that HOPE VI shifted from a focus on highly distressed housing projects to those that were more favorable for private investment (United States General Accounting Office 1998). In a nationwide study, Goetz found that in the early 1990s, cities with higher "gentrification pressure" (expressed as the ratio of median public housing rent to median citywide rent) demolished more public housing, suggesting that in its early days HOPE VI responded to opportunities for economic investment in cities more than conditions in housing projects (Goetz 2013). An examination of HOPE VI in Chicago suggests that the housing authority reduced the allocation of subsidized units in those neighborhoods most amenable to gentrification (Wyly and Hammel 2000). Others have noted connections between specific HOPE VI demolitions and nearby real estate development, from ABLA and Cabrini Green in Chicago to Memorial Homes in New Brunswick NJ, with the implication that cities have used HOPE VI as a way to clear public housing from valuable land and open new sectors to development (Bennett and Reed 1999; Hackworth 2007).

As in the era of public housing construction, public housing policy in the HOPE VI era was carried out in a racialized manner. Nationwide and in Baltimore individual projects chosen for demolition through HOPE VI tended to have a higher percentage of African American residents than the cities in which they were located, suggesting that Black families were disproportionately impacted by HOPE VI (Goetz 2013). While this finding is perhaps unsurprising given the segregating practices that built these housing projects, the Baltimore case also shows that a racialized debate over the placement of public housing occurred in the HOPE VI era as it had in the era of public housing construction.

In 1995, a lawsuit was filed by the American Civil Liberties Union (ACLU) on behalf of fourteen thousand African American residents of public housing in Baltimore. The suit (*Thompson v. HUD*) alleged that Baltimore City, under the aegis of HUD, had not done enough to combat the ongoing segregation of the city's public housing. An initial agreement between both parties, referred to as a partial consent decree, established a housing voucher mobility program and a plan for new, permanent scattered-site public housing units to be built in majority-white neighborhoods. However, just as in previous decades when attempts had been made to expand public housing into majority-white areas, the city faced a rapid backlash to the scattered-site proposal, notably a plan to build ten units in the majority-white northeast Baltimore neighborhood of Hamilton.

City officials were bombarded with complaints from residents when the scattered-site plan was announced, and more than eight hundred angry people showed up to a public meeting at Hamilton Middle School. The complaints[1] revealed the fears of Hamilton residents about the encroachment of Black families and the dwindling number of working-class white neighborhoods in the city. Residents lashed out at the housing authority for planning to turn Hamilton into a "dumping ground" for families displaced from public housing. Many of the complaints made a distinction between Hamilton residents who paid taxes and public housing families who are "given things [and] neither appreciate them nor take care of them." A couple of residents lamented the "deterioration" of Hamilton and wrote of their plan to move out of the city. Yet claims that Hamilton was becoming a "dumping ground" for housing voucher families are not supported by the data. During the years between the demolition of the HOPE VI sites in 1996 and the announcement in 2000 of the ten public housing units to be built, the Hamilton area (home to more than thirty-two thousand people) saw a total of thirteen additional voucher families move in. A more significant change during the 1990s was the racial composition of the neighborhood: 88 percent white in 1990, by 2000 the area as a whole had become only 63 percent white.[2] The language of "decay" and the notion that northeast Baltimore was being "destroyed" by "the mass placement of such people" is more likely a reference to this racial transition.

---

[1] The following quotes come from mailed and emailed exchanges between residents of Hamilton and the office of Sheila Dixon, city council president, between September 2000 and August 2002. Source: Robert L. Bogomolny Library at the University of Baltimore, Special Collections Department, Archive of ACLU of Maryland Records, Thompson v. HUD.

[2] These numbers refer to nine northeast Baltimore census tracts surrounding the proposed HUD sites. Source: HUD Picture of Subsidized Households, 1996 and 2000; and the 1990 and 2000 censuses.

The reaction of Hamilton residents to the scattered-site plan also shows how the previous era of public housing construction that built housing projects disproportionately in Black neighborhoods worked to reinforce a racial stigma linking public housing and Black families. This kind of connection can also be seen in the Housing Choice Voucher Program. Voucher holders often face stigma that can exclude them from socially integrating into a neighborhood (Rosen 2020), while landlords use vouchers to steer tenants to some neighborhoods while excluding them from others (Rosen 2014, 2020). Receipt of a housing voucher, and the associated stigma it bears, interact with race and other marginalized social categories (Rosen, Garboden, and Cossyleon 2021) to shape how tenants are or are not able to use the voucher, resulting in a program that is highly segregated despite removing the financial barrier to accessing housing in most neighborhoods (DeLuca, Garboden, and Rosenblatt 2013; Metzger 2014).

In Baltimore, the Hamilton backlash led to a rapid reversal from the city. At an October 3 public meeting in Hamilton, Mayor O'Malley won the support of the hostile crowd by vowing to halt building the ten units and appeal the initial agreement from the lawsuit. Reversing his earlier written support for the plan, O'Malley told the crowd: "We've been struggling with how to get out from under this [consent] decree," and said that the plan "never should have gotten this far" (Thompson and Shields 2000). O'Malley was not the only politician to avoid upsetting the segregated status quo, even in the face of a court order. City council president (and future mayor) Sheila Dixon wrote in an op-ed to the *Baltimore Sun* that while "no one deserves to live in centers of poverty, crime and despair," she took issue with the racial composition requirements of the consent decree. In 2001 the housing authority backed down from developing the ten units of scattered-site housing in Hamilton; the plan to build permanent public housing in a white neighborhood had been defeated without a single tenant moving in.

Public Housing Redevelopment and the Sociology of Housing

In both eras profiled here, public housing policy was used to respond to redevelopment pressures and was shaped by white resistance to upsetting the segregated status quo. In the era of public housing construction, local commissions comprised of academics and professionals drafted public housing plans to "protect" the city by preserving functioning housing markets inhabited by whites in the areas near downtown. In the HOPE VI era the mayor, the city's Department of Housing and Community Development, and the Housing Authority embraced a triage approach of selectively demolishing or reselling vacant houses that was focused on jumpstarting the housing market in areas where it might be expanded rather than preserving the downtown specifically. This approach dovetailed with the HOPE VI program and helped spark a renaissance of lending in formerly neglected neighborhoods surrounding housing projects. In fact, the tools that had proved successful in redeveloping places like Baltimore's Inner Harbor—public-private partnerships, incentivizing the middle class to return to the city, seeking to incorporate revenue streams from real estate—were harnessed by local and national administrations as a way to change public housing as well. Yet this story also reveals a racialized hierarchy when it comes to delineating the extent of housing policy qua redevelopment. In both eras, plans to place public housing in outlying parts of the city were retracted after white residents protested. The result was that homes were demolished and the geography of Black neighborhoods reshaped in both eras, while the racial hierarchies applied to urban spaces were legitimized and reinforced.

This case study points to a number of other ways a sociology of housing helps us deepen our understanding of how housing policies can produce or reinforce social inequalities. Examples can be seen in studies of how public housing policy has contributed to the well-established subfield of neighborhood effects. Historically public housing policy helped create the kinds of neighborhoods of concentrated poverty, particularly in Black communities, that scores of scholars have shown shape the life chances of adults and children (Wilson 1987; Sharkey 2013; Chetty, Hendren, and Katz 2016). In the HOPE VI era, a recent study by Tach and Emory (2017) used a series of counterfactual comparison groups to show that HOPE VI reduced neighborhood poverty rates and increased the share of white residents in and around the redeveloped housing project neighborhoods, although this change was driven more by the displacement of poor and nonwhite residents of these neighborhoods than by race and class integration.

The Baltimore case also emphasizes the connections between public housing policy and the politics of capital-driven expansion. The concerns about blight, raised in both eras to successfully spur the strategic use of public housing to preserve or expand the housing market, point to the influence of place entrepreneurs (Logan and Molotch 1987) in crafting policy. The efforts of the O'Malley administration to selectively jumpstart the housing market, as well as the way HOPE VI successfully turned public housing projects and the neighborhoods surrounding them into sites of increased investment, point to the "roll back/roll out" dynamic of neoliberal strategies of governance in smoothing the way for privatization

(Peck and Tickell 2002; see also Khare 2018). The Baltimore case also stresses the importance of what Brenner and Theodore (2002) term "actually existing neoliberalism"; local and contested variation in the way historic uses of space, political dynamics, and institutions shape the direction of government programs. In the case of HOPE VI, Vale reminds us that this variation means "paying close attention to the overarching political history of urban development in each city while remaining alert to signs of productive pushback and unexpected victories" (Vale 2019, 18). Emphasizing the links between specific policies and larger dynamics of urbanization pushes us to not only assess the *outcomes* of public housing policy, but also acknowledge the *process* of public housing policy, and with it the potential for doing things differently and even for building a more just city (Bennett and Reed 1999; Brenner 2017).

A sociological approach also points to ways that racial ideologies shape urban redevelopment. In the Baltimore case, this shaping is seen by looking at the places where public housing is *not* built and exploring the rationale for these decisions. Operating under a racial regime (Holt 2000) characterized by de jure segregated public housing, the planning commissions in 1934 and 1945 blatantly used racially identified housing projects to create a racialized spatial hierarchy by regularly placing housing for whites in areas that had the best chance of becoming profitable. In the HOPE VI era, racialized siting decisions continued as politicians conceded to the racist pushback from whites that drew on the language of colorblind racism (Bonilla-Silva 2003). The distinctions made by white protesters in Hamilton between hard working taxpayers and "HUD people" who are "given things" have also been seen in studies of how whites use the language of "taxpayer" to make a claim on privileged status when defending educational segregation (Walsh 2017), and echo the "euphemized racism" found by Michele Lamont (2000) in her study of working-class white attitudes toward Blacks. Paying attention to racial ideologies and their impact on how urban space is organized expands our focus on segregation from a demographic and policy-driven phenomenon to one that more explicitly operates in the realm of *racialization* and *racial projects*, terms that get at the time-specific meaning of race and the way it structures everyday experiences (Omi and Winant 2014; see also Rosen, Garboden, and Cossyleon 2021; Tuttle, forthcoming).

Public housing policy has undergone some significant changes in the past decade. A sociology of housing can help us assess the outcomes of these policies by understanding the impacts of urban redevelopment pressures and the role of racial ideologies. The HOPE VI program officially ended in 2010; its immediate successor, Choice Neighborhoods, seeks to foster public and private investment to make more comprehensive changes to the neighborhoods surrounding "severely distressed" housing projects (USHUD 2021). As Choice Neighborhoods is more explicit than HOPE VI in its aims to redevelop the neighborhoods *around* public housing into mixed-income communities, the connections between public housing policy and local priorities concerning the housing market should be manifest. The question of how these policies disrupt or reify racialized spaces could be further explored to test the conclusions drawn from the Baltimore case.

Another significant change to US public housing policy since HOPE VI is HUD's Rental Assistance Demonstration (RAD). Launched in 2013, RAD offers PHAs a way to change the way they fund public housing from relying on congressional funding to incorporating private-sector funds like mortgage loans. For a sociology of housing focused on the intersections between policy, redevelopment, race, and urban spaces, studies of RAD could test and extend recent work on how mortgage lending transforms cities in highly racialized ways. In the years before and after the housing crisis of the end of the first decade of the 2000s, several studies pointed to the way the legacy of redlining combined with the restructuring of real estate financing to create a racialized market for subprime loans (Wyly, Atia, and Hammel 2004; Rugh and Massey 2010; Rosenblatt and Sacco 2018). This work showed that the policies and practices that facilitated a massive flow of capital into urban areas also followed the contours of a segregated housing market, leading ultimately to a foreclosure crisis borne disproportionately in Black and brown neighborhoods (as well as an eviction crisis among renters of apartments that were foreclosed—see Swartz and Blake 2010). Taking a wider historical lens, Keeanga-Yamahtta Taylor (2019) details how federal partnership with the mortgage finance industry and the reluctance to push for open housing in the late 1960s enabled lenders to exploit a captive market through poorly regulated and exploitative home loans. This "predatory inclusion" (Taylor 2019) of Black home buyers (see also Satter 2009; George et al. 2019) highlights the inseparability of race, housing policy, and capital-driven urbanization. In all these ways, a sociology of housing is well suited to unpack and interpret the complex ways that housing policy contributes to social inequality.

5

Unsettling Native Land

INDIGENOUS PERSPECTIVES ON HOUSING

Jennifer Darrah-Okike, Lorinda Riley,
Philip M. E. Garboden, and Nathalie Rita

Given their origins within industrial America (Du Bois 1935; Park and Burgess 1925; Wirth 1947), it is hardly surprising that urban sociology and the sociology of housing have tended toward a Black/white view of the city. While recent work has brought Latinx and Asian communities into sharper focus (Diaz and Torres 2012; Lin 2008; Oh and Chung 2014; Rugh 2015; Small 2004; Rendón, this volume), these additions have done little to address the erasure of Indigenous peoples and Indigenous epistemologies from our discipline's foundational theories. The absence of Indigenous perspectives on housing and cities is limiting not only because it ignores Indigenous peoples' experiences. It also has implications for sociology's understanding of humans' relations to land, limiting the sociological imaginary to a distinctly Western tradition. Rather than seeing market logics of land, housing, and race as a fait accompli, Indigenous perspectives center historical and contemporary alternatives to such logics.

This chapter draws from Indigenous Studies with a focus on Native Hawaiian scholars and the Hawai'i case. As a distinctive field, Indigenous Studies centers Indigenous people, land, and conflicts over the control and cultural meaning of places. Settler colonial theory—as one strand of this work—highlights how colonization, especially in settler societies like the United States, Hawai'i, New Zealand, and Australia, is an ongoing but never complete process, rather than a past historical event (Kauanui 2016; Veracini 2010; Wolfe 2006).

The growing attention to Indigenous communities within sociology has contributed to the study of race and ethnicity, inequality, the environment, and other subfields, while also linking scholarship to activism, and generating theories better equipped to make sense of Indigenous people's experiences (Fenelon 2014; Garroutte 2003; Glenn 2015; McKay 2019; Norgaard 2019; Rodriguez-Lonebear 2021; Steinman 2016). However, sustained attention to Indigenous people has rarely been brought into urban sociology or the sociology of housing (for reasons including a lack of diversity within the discipline, a long-standing association of Indigenous people with rural places, and the Western/white roots of the field) (Brunsma and Padilla Wyse 2019; Morris 2015).

We suggest three ways in which work that centers Indigenous people and perspectives can inform a sociology of housing. First, the literature on settler colonial theory foregrounds land and the contested colonial dispossession of land, which we argue is a crucial focus in an analysis of housing. This literature discusses "settlement," an expansive term that includes patterns of human habitation, social relations to place, claims to land, and the material and cultural dimensions of shelter (Glenn 2015; Wolfe 2006). Such scholarship pushes us to interrogate the political and cultural dynamics *behind* the construction of land and housing markets, thus expanding the critical and historical purview of sociological analyses of real estate. We trace a direct line from American colonialism, land dispossession, and threats to Indigenous political self-determination to current inequities in housing. The work we discuss below expands notions of "home" beyond material features of shelter toward cultural meanings of place, land, and belonging. This approach stands to reframe social problems like homelessness and housing inequality by situating them in longer time horizons and wider contexts of colonialism.

Second, Indigenous perspectives also identify how the racialization of Native people, along with varied anti-Native racisms, have advanced private-property regimes. Such dynamics are visible in housing policy, which, as we discuss below, continue to define and redefine categories of indigeneity and race via the legal system (Kauanui 2008). In conversation with a sociology of race, this perspective advances a robust integration of the various articulations between racialization, housing policy, and inequality.

Finally, the fields of Indigenous studies and settler colonial theory identify fissures in Western-style real estate markets and, thus, shift attention to the *failures* of colonialism. To put it directly, Indigenous people and Indigenous relations to land persist, though our field has too often ignored these realities (Fenelon 2014; McGregor 2007). Indigenous scholarship pushes us to focus on seizures of land and iterative processes of dispossession, oppression, and attempted assimilation (e.g., Estes 2019). It also foregrounds the ways that Native communities have continually resisted such seizures (Fenelon 2014; Goodyear-Kaʻōpua 2013). In all, Indigenous genealogical connections to land reveal normative alternatives to capitalist inequality in housing and land markets.

Before proceeding, we begin with a brief overview of terms. We use the term "Indigenous" to refer to those who claim ancestral or genealogical ties to a place (prior to colonial contact), or who identify as Indigenous, Native American/American Indian, Aboriginal, or members of First Nations (United Nations 2007). Recognition by settler nation-states is bestowed on certain Indigenous communities through historic documents, such as treaties or modern legal mechanisms (Riley 2016), culminating in purported racial and political identities (Fletcher 2012; Cramer 2006). Even outside official federal recognition, Indigenous nations persist, such as the Lumbee—who are state-recognized—or the lāhui Hawai'i.

The standard categories of race and ethnicity used in sociology often fall short for understanding Indigenous lives. Indigenous peoples maintain political identities that are often at odds with their ascribed categorization as "racial" and "ethnic" minorities (Garroutte 2003; Trask 1999). For example, the terms "Indigenous" or "Native American" often reflect a political or national identity (such as citizenship in one of the 574 federally recognized nations) (Steinman 2016). However, Native American and Native Hawaiian individuals often hold varying racial identities (Kana'iaupuni and Liebler 2005). In the 2010 census, roughly 44 percent of individuals who selected "American Indian" also selected other racial categories (Pettit et al. 2014), and 70 percent of individuals who identified as Native Hawaiian also identified as some other racial categories. These official numbers have been contested for decades, both in terms of accuracy and because they self-identify race rather than political citizenship (Nagel 1997).

Despite the diversity of Indigenous groups, US federal law implies a shared legal—and thus sociological framework—encompassing American Indians and, with key differences, Alaska Natives and Native Hawaiians.[1] Native Hawaiians—also referred to as Kanaka Maoli or Kanaka 'Ōiwi—are the Indigenous people of the Hawaiian Archipelago. As authors, our identities—a white non-Indigenous woman (Jennifer), an Indigenous woman (Lorinda), a white non-Indigenous man (Phil), and a Latina non-Indigenous woman (Nathalie)—influence our understanding of the perspectives discussed here.

Genealogies of Land

We begin with *mo'okū'auhau* (genealogy and continuity), a Native Hawaiian cultural concept as well as methodological/epistemic orientation to research (Wilson-Hokowhitu 2019). Kame'eleihiwa (1992) examines

---

[1] The US does not maintain a formal "government-to-government relationship" with Native Hawaiians, but it has acknowledged a "special political and trust relationship" with Hawai'i's Indigenous population (Corey et al. 2017).

moʻokūʻauhau as a Hawaiian concept of time, which provides an ordering of the universe through an unbroken chain tracing from the gods to human ancestors. We deliberately share a few details of one Indigenous origin story to suggest how sociology may expand its imagination to account for alternative epistemologies and human relations to land.

The *moʻokūʻauhau* traces human lineage from Wakea (Father Sky) and Papa's (Mother Earth) daughter, Hoʻohōkūkalani, who gave birth to a still-born boy, Hāloa Naka. From Hāloa Naka's buried body grew kalo, a staple Hawaiian food. Hoʻohōkūkalani then gave birth to another son, Hāloa, named in honor of his older brother, who was the first Hawaiian person. In this *moʻokūʻauhau*, Hāloa represents to the connection between Hawaiians and the gods and is sustained by his older brother, kalo (Kurashima et al. 2018). From a Hawaiian epistemological perspective, the *ʻāina* (land) is inextricably intertwined with Hawaiian existence, as life itself is grounded within the *ʻāina*. When viewed through an Indigenous economic lens, *wai* (water)— together with *ʻāina*—becomes a representation of *waiwai* (abundance or wealth) (Baker 2018; Kanahele 1986).

This origin story is more than a distant or abstract myth. Native Hawaiians continue to steward ancestral lands and maintain a "sacred connection to the land requiring dutiful, nurturing care" (Goodyear-Kaʻōpua, Hussey, and Wright 2014, 7). Indigenous origin stories beget land-management practices in Hawaiʻi that have nurtured abundance, reciprocity, and sustainability (Goodyear-Kaʻōpua, Hussey, and Wright 2014; Hasager and Kelly 2001; McGregor 2007).

Many Indigenous communities share a similar respect for land, reflected in terms such as "Mother" or "Grandmother Earth" (Smith 2012). Such terms denote sacred reverence for land rather than dominion or ownership (Kameʻeleihiwa 1992). Approaching lands or waters as revered living ancestors differs radically from framing land as a commodity to be owned (as in, e.g., New Zealand's 2017 Te Awa Tupua Act, cited in McAllister et al. 2019). Recognizing the distinctiveness of Indigenous views of land pulls into relief alternatives to capitalist or Western approaches.

While sociologists are used to being critical about the treatment of land as a commodity (or as a "fictitious commodity"), many may be less aware of practical alternatives. In one origin story of modern capitalism from the sociological canon, Marx describes the "bloody" clearing of people from land as a historic moment that birthed modernist property regimes (Marx [1887] 2000, 520–33). Contemporary sociological research extends this tradition by describing the social embeddedness of markets (Granovetter 1985, Somers and Block 2005). And recent research on the sociology of housing advances these insights by showing how regulation and politics allocate risk and reward in housing markets, propel displacement and residential segregation, and structure real estate markets (McCabe 2016, Robinson III 2020b, Sullivan 2018, Taylor 2019).

Indigenous perspectives go beyond this work by showing how American land and housing markets are historically founded in colonial domination, which was supported by legal and racial fictions. For example, a legal fiction called "the doctrine of discovery"—tied closely to the fiction of white racial superiority—was utilized by early settlers to take title to Indigenous lands. This centuries-old principle, described by Moon-Kie Jung as "profoundly white supremacist" (2015, 64), justified US claims of sovereignty over Indian territories on the American continent (Fenelon 2016; Williams 1991a). In the 1800s, the US Supreme Court embedded the doctrine of discovery into US law in ways that justified later settler claims to land titles (Williams 1991a).

Historical accounts of "homesteading" and "settlement" on Native American lands further reveal the foundations of housing markets that extend the purview of sociological accounts (Glenn 2015). On the US continent and in Hawai'i, white Americans and the US government seized land and territory through treaties, violence, legal fictions, and other forms of coerced removal (often justified by racist ideas) (Chang 2010). Land dispossession that unfolded across the American continent and into Oceania has been inextricable from settlement, which is as much about claiming (or conquering) territory as creating homes.

Land dispossession in Hawai'i has a distinct history, but nonetheless reflects American colonial ambitions. In response to anticipated intrusions of foreign imperial powers, leaders of the independent Hawaiian Kingdom initiated the conversion of the traditional land-management system to a Western-style private-property regime beginning in the mid-1800s. This shift also benefited white businessmen who had established lucrative sugar plantations (Kame'eleihiwa 1992). Scholars continue to debate the consequences of this transformation (Beamer and Tong 2016), but what is clear is that the majority of Native Hawaiians did *not* gain fee-simple title during the land conversion (Kame'eleihiwa 1992). As the nineteenth century proceeded, new laws allowing foreigners to buy land further propelled the removal of land from Hawaiian hands (Van Dyke 2008). Private land tenure failed to protect over two million acres of public or "Hawaiian National" lands, which were seized at the time of the illegal overthrow (and eventually transferred to the US government and later the state of Hawai'i) (Van Dyke 2008). Today, Native Hawaiian agencies and advocates continue to fight for a fair share of revenue and authority over these lands (Andrade 2016).

These complex land-tenure changes sit at the roots of contemporary housing inequality facing Native Hawaiians today. In Hawai'i, as early as the 1900s, observers and political leaders began to realize the damage that land alienation was causing commoner Native Hawaiians, many of whom had become "squatters" in their own homeland on the margins of a new capitalist system (Hasager and Kelly 2001).

Urban sociologists have a rich tradition of theorizing the conflict between communities and real estate interests (Logan and Molotch 1987). Literature on gentrification both describes and critiques residential displacement resulting from capitalist processes (Brown-Saracino 2010; Hyra 2017; Smith 1996; Taylor 2002). Some of this scholarship construes the power of capitalist property interests as so overwhelming that it "cleanses" (Wacquant 2008) or "annihilates" (Mitchell 1997) the urban poor from public spaces and neighborhoods. These literatures can be broadened by attention to the contested colonial takings of land—often facilitated by the state—which unleash such conflicts. Moreover, work by and about Indigenous communities refuses to naturalize (or reify) property markets in an even more fundamental way than critical sociological traditions—by describing *and* perpetuating non-capitalist relationships with land.

Reframing Housing Inequities and Homelessness

These perspectives suggest ways to reframe housing disparities faced by Native Americans, which we see as the outcome of land alienation, attempted assimilation, and threats to the political self-determination of American Indians and Native Hawaiians. Native Americans, within and outside tribal (or reservation) settings, face significant economic and housing hardships. The poverty rate of Native Americans in the US in 2010 was 28 percent, compared to 15 percent for other groups. In urban areas, Native Americans are more likely than other groups to be overburdened by housing costs, live in substandard or unsafe housing, and live in overcrowded conditions (Levy et al. 2015). Native Americans are also less likely to own their own homes and more likely to be denied home loans, all else equal (Pettit et al. 2014; Scarborough et al. 2019). Meanwhile, those on tribal lands have been shown to experience more severe physical housing problems than the average US household, including plumbing and heating deficiencies (Corey et al. 2017). Native Hawaiians showed similar patterns, facing higher rates of poverty, overcrowding, and housing-cost burdens than other groups (Corey et al. 2017).

US federal-tribal political arrangements have consistently failed to meet the housing needs of Native Americans (Eagan-Smith 2008; Keeler

2016), while also cutting off the wealth-building opportunities of home-ownership. For the roughly 22 percent of Native Americans who live in tribal areas or reservations (Pettit et al. 2014), regulatory hurdles and other barriers pose obstacles for building affordable housing or securing traditional mortgages (Hillabrant et al. 2004). Similar issues exist on Hawaiian homestead lands—trust lands designated for housing leases for Native Hawaiians, though only a minority of Native Hawaiians live in such areas (Cooke 2012). However, existing research suggests that, when tribal nations have led housing production, with sufficient federal funding, the results have been relatively strong (Eagan-Smith 2008; Corey et al. 2017).

Given their histories of land dispossession, it is not a coincidence that Native Americans and Native Hawaiians disproportionately experience homelessness. Across the United States, 67 out of every ten thousand Native Americans were homeless, second only to Pacific Islanders (including Native Hawaiians) at 160 per ten thousand (National Alliance to End Homelessness 2020). When the multiethnic category of "Pacific Islander" is broken up, Native Hawaiians are disproportionally represented among unsheltered homeless populations in Honolulu (Pruitt and Barile 2020). Despite these statistics, studies on homelessness often overlook Indigenous peoples (Levy et al. 2015).

These issues are visible in the context of Honolulu, Hawai'i's largest city, which has become notorious for its high rates of homelessness, as well as for its punitive approach to unsheltered people (Darrah-Okike et al. 2018). Honolulu was the first place in the US to enact a countywide ban on sitting or lying in public spaces. Even before this ban, the city of Honolulu's sidewalk "nuisance" and public-park closure ordinances forced the removal of houseless communities and sparked criticism and litigation from civil-liberties groups. Viewed through an Indigenous lens, the displaced communities are neither haphazard nor informal, yet exist as places of refuge in defiance of decades of iterative displacement.

Indigenous perspectives also complicate standard policy meanings of "homelessness" by expanding notions of home to include belonging to places that sustain. This view blurs categories of tenure prevalent in a sociology of housing (e.g., renter vs. owner or homeless vs. sheltered) by drawing the distinction between "home" as a place to which one belongs and the material conditions of shelter. For example, community advocates often prefer to use the term "houseless" to homeless, insisting that no Native Hawaiian can truly be homeless in Hawai'i. This language affirms that Hawai'i remains an enduring homeland, and that 'āina (as "land which feeds") provides, even in the absence of permanent material shelter. This argument is manifest in the experiences of houseless communities in *pu'uhonua* (refuges or places of sanctuary). Even when excluded from formal housing markets, they can sustain themselves from *'āina* and *kai* (ocean), and through other strategies for economic survival (Goodyear-Ka'ōpua, Hussey, and Wright 2014; Kelly 2014).

Homelessness should be seen as more than something that disproportionately burdens Indigenous people and, instead, as a symptom of systemic alienation from land. This view stands to reorient the literature on homelessness, which is often studied separately from other housing issues such as urban development, housing and land use policy, and even affordable housing (but see Rita et al. 2021; Herring, this volume).

Racialization and Housing

An engagement with Indigenous scholarship can help advance sociological understanding of the link between housing inequality and race. Housing and land policies have imposed distinctive racial categories on Indigenous communities, often racializing them as neither Black nor white but, yet, as *assimilable into whiteness* (Arvin 2019; Rodriguez-Lonebear 2021). Such policies have been both racial projects and projects of land dispossession, and they reveal the range of racial schema complicit in housing inequality.

Traditionally, American housing policy is seen as reflecting and calcifying the nation's hostility toward Black and, more recently, Latinx communities (Gotham 2002; Korver-Glenn 2018; Massey and Denton 1993; Taylor 2019). Based on this literature, the sociology of housing has persuasively argued that American housing policy was designed as a mechanism of segregation and oppression, one that has both reflected and constituted dominant racial attitudes and hierarchies. For Native Americans and Native Hawaiians, the relevant racial categories and hierarchies differ qualitatively, yet reveal parallel ways that racial technologies have advanced both land dispossession and assimilation.

For Native Americans of the US continent, the federal Dawes Act, or General Allotment Act of 1887, provides an example of how the racialization of Native people went hand in hand with the colonial dispossession of land (Chang 2010). Under the Dawes Act, the dual goal of assimilating Indians and opening land for western expansion was accomplished by creating official tribal-citizen rolls that attempted to document blood quantum for the purposes of determining legal competency and official citizenship (Keeler 2016; Schmidt 2011). The Act undermined collective American Indian claims to property, communal ownership patterns, and cultural relationships to land by allocating "homesteads" to individual heads of house and their dependents. Allotment amounts varied based on family status and blood quantum (Chang 2010). Remaining lands were then sold to white settlers in a "checkerboard" fashion, as land allocation was used to further assimilate Indians. As shown by Rodriguez-Lonebear (2021), the racial project of blood quantum has uniquely involved American Indian people. In the case of Dawes, it caused long-lasting damage to extended kinship systems and promoted heteropatriarchal nuclear family forms by separating families across distant allotments (Glenn 2015).

This history directly influences contemporary Native American housing disadvantage. Scholars estimate that the Dawes Act directly and indirectly propelled the loss of up to one hundred million acres of tribal lands (due to foreclosures, forced sales resulting from nonpayment of taxes, and other market pressures, accelerated in part by the urging of white settlers) (Carlson 1983). Households living in tribal reservations where allotment occurred saw greater losses in homeownership along with increases in household overcrowding than other reservations, all else equal (Akee 2017).

Native Hawaiian housing policy has also institutionalized blood quantum requirements, as seen in the Hawaiian Homes Commission Act of 1921 (HHCA). The Act set aside nearly two hundred thousand acres of lands for Native Hawaiians of qualifying blood quantum to lease "homesteads." Native Hawaiian leaders (Prince Kuhio and territorial senator John Wise, especially) advocated for homesteads as a means to improve the health and well-being of Native Hawaiians. However, because of the influence of white elite landowners, the resulting HHCA not only failed to establish a sufficient land and resource base to "rehabilitate" Hawaiians through housing, it also limited housing benefits to Hawaiians as defined by a 50 percent blood quantum (Kauanui 2008).

Classifying social relations by putative blood "purity" (associated with debunked notions of race as biologically meaningful) is not only at odds with expansive Indigenous practices of kinship, heredity, and genealogy, it also imposes notions of blood dilution toward vanishing identity, consistent with assimilation goals (Kauanui 2008). Sociologists and Indigenous scholars have documented the damaging effects of blood quantum racial schema. For example, racializing Native Hawaiians *through* housing policy has fractured the Hawaiian political community and undermined Hawaiian pursuit of resources (Arvin 2019; Ledward 2007). Pinning rights to land and housing on blood quantum, and allocating housing access through state discourses of welfare deservingness, has occluded Native Hawaiian claims to land based on political status as a sovereign people (Kauanui 2008).

These histories provide context for understanding contemporary housing inequalities as rooted in racial and racist fictions. The Dawes Act and

HHCA are examples of policies that imposed racial schema on Indigenous people, advanced white settler claims to land, and propelled land and housing dispossession of Native people (Chang 2010).

Expanding the Housing Imaginary: Generative Resistance in Housing

Indigenous perspectives have shown that the incursions of colonization are never complete (Estes 2019; Fenelon 2014). This framework offers a valuable corrective to political-economic approaches in sociology that stress the power of capitalism. Indigenous social movements—as well as everyday acts of "sustainable cultural self-determination" (Corntassel 2008) have pushed back against political domination and assimilation (Steinman 2016). For Native Hawaiians, enduring relationships to place, as well as access to housing or shelter, are fundamental to *ea* (cultural and political self-determination) (Goodyear-Kaʻōpua, Hussey, and Wright 2014). Here, we discuss just a few examples of what might be conceptualized as movements to "decolonize housing," which can broaden both our theoretical and normative lenses.

Indigenous communities have generated unique housing solutions, partaken in litigation and lobbying efforts to shape state and federal land and housing policy, formed autonomous communities, and resisted paternalistic social assistance, all while continuing to live in or steward ancestral places. In Hawaiʻi, as elsewhere, non-Indigenous allies have also sought to perpetuate Indigenous models of sustainability and supported varying forms of Indigenous self-determination (Fujikane and Okamura 2008).

For example, cultural advocates have worked to affirm Native land rights protected in the Hawaiʻi state constitution, based on principles inherited from the independent Hawaiian Kingdom (MacKenzie 1991). State laws also protect historic and cultural sites and can be leveraged to stop or significantly alter development (Darrah-Okike 2019a and 2019b). Debates about housing in Hawaiʻi are often closely connected to struggles to protect the cultural meaning of land against its commodification (Cooper and Daws 1990).

Just as Indigenous cultures are neither static nor confined to the putatively "authentic" forms of a distant past, Indigenous relationships to land adapt to and reorient even highly disruptive capitalist incursions. As relevant to the field of housing, Mehana Blaich Vaughan narrates how families from the North shore of Kauai, *noho papa* (continue to dwell), *kupaʻai au* (eat from land), *ēwe ʻōiwi* (maintain genealogical ties), and perpetuate knowledge of place, even after losing their generations-old family homes and lands due to foreclosure, forced sales, property taxes, and legal manipulations amid the in-migration of the global rich (2018). Community actions "honor their homes, whether those homes remain physical places or memories" (Vaughan 2018, 124). Community voices "express *aloha ʻāina* (love of the land) and *kuleana* (right, privilege, responsibility), which transcend ownership and unlike property, cannot be taken away, gated, or sold" (Vaughan 2018, 124).

Historical analyses show other ways that Kanaka Maoli land-management systems have persisted alongside the institutionalization of Western-style property markets. Aikau (2012) describes, for example, the case of Lāʻie, where Native Hawaiians and other Polynesian people continue to cultivate *loʻi* (traditional wetland taro fields), even as they have been employees and lessees of plantation companies and the Mormon church. Groups of Native Hawaiians also found ways to work *within* the privatized system when faced with risk of land loss. In several areas (for example, Hāʻena on the north shore of Kauai or Kahana on Oʻahu), collectives known as *huis* pooled financial resources to purchase large land areas (Stauffer 2004; Vaughan 2018), ensuring access for future generations. Today, these communities do not adhere to "standard" modern tenure or leasing patterns—for example, the residents of Kahana maintain the rights to live on long-term leases in a state park, which they fought to designate as a "living cultural park."

Indigenous communities in Hawaiʻi have also established relatively autonomous (including subsistence-based) villages, some of which have called themselves *puʻuhonua* (places of refuge and sanctuary) (e.g., those in Waimanalo, Mākua, Keaukaha, and Waianae). While a sociological literature might term these "squatter," "informal settlements" or "homeless encampments," such terms are limiting and potentially stigmatizing (Herbert, this volume). These villages have emerged as offshoots of larger movements for Hawaiian political self-determination or have explicitly identified themselves as places of refuge for those without permanent shelters. Unfortunately, throughout modern history, many such *puʻuhonua* have been forcibly cleared by state agencies. In other cases, these communities have made unique compromises with state agencies, thus continuing to reside in homes and shelters that are "off the grid" in more ways than one.

Other communities and tribal nations have advanced their own Indigenous housing paradigms, such as Australian Aboriginals and Torres Straits Islanders, who in the early 1970s created housing models designed to promote community relationships, health, and environmental stewardship (Saha et al. 2019). The Place of Hidden Waters near Tacoma, Washington re-operationalizes traditional designs in order to provide tribal citizens with functional and sustainable housing to support collective wellness (Blosser et al. 2014). Using the methodology of *mo'okū'auhau* we see how these communities draw from their own housing genealogies in order to provide their citizens with services that align with their cultural values and point toward a sustainable future.

Conclusion

Sociologists have long appealed to a "sociological imagination" upon which we base our understanding of lived experiences as reflective of larger social processes (Mills 1959). However, scholars from traditionally marginalized communities have highlighted how limited the imagination of mainstream sociology can be when it refuses to engage with alternative epistemologies. Both theoretically and professionally, this chapter represents a beginning rather than a summary. Few of the citations in this document were of sociologists, even fewer of urban sociologists, and none of those who might be described as undertaking the sociology of housing. Such references largely do not exist. This is a problem that must be rectified if the sociology of housing is to embrace a more inclusive and generative imaginary.

The discipline's failure to engage with this imaginary afflicts us with a double blindness. First, it limits our awareness of social problems that disproportionately affect Indigenous peoples. But it also limits our potential to understand and address those problems. There is little doubt that Indigenous people experience some of the highest rates of housing inadequacy and insecurity in ways that are not fully explained by standard economic variables. We see the roots of such disadvantages in iterative histories of land dispossession, American imperial domination, and related technologies of racial classification—all of which have radically recast human ways of relating to land and nature. At the same time, Indigenous views and practices unsettle the taken-for-granted quality of these foundations of contemporary housing markets; they present alternative origin stories and invite more sustainable (and perhaps more equitable) social relations to place.

6

Affordable Housing Is Public Health

HOW LANDLORDS STRUGGLE TO CONTAIN AMERICA'S LEAD POISONING CRISIS

Matthew H. McLeskey

In 2016, President Barack Obama declared a federal emergency in Flint, Michigan. The city's largely low-income, African American population suffered widespread lead exposure after the city switched its water supply to the Flint River. The water was not treated properly for Flint's aging infrastructure, and lead spread through corroded plumbing (Clark 2018). Flint's crisis made national headlines, but a more mundane route to lead poisoning afflicts millions of US residents who live in homes built before 1978, when leaded paint was banned. Since lead hazards are more prevalent in the older housing stock found in disinvested neighborhoods across the US, low-income, often minority children disproportionately suffer from lead poisoning. According to the National Center for Healthy Housing (2021), lead poisoning forms a "concrete expression of the affordable housing crisis." For sociologists concerned about housing inequality, it is crucial to understand housing as a site where exposure to lead and other toxins contribute to the reproduction of social inequalities.

America's affordable housing crisis is also a public health crisis: the toll of poverty and its health consequences fall disproportionately on communities of color. Muller, Sampson, and Winter (2018, 265) define inequality from lead exposure as "literally embodied," given the relationship between its geographic concentration and its impact on social outcomes. Low-income tenants and homeowners also face uneven exposure to mold, radon, and carbon monoxide; suffer higher rates of stress, asthma, and cancer; and often live in areas considered food deserts, where fresh food access can be lacking (Barr 2019). Racial segregation and neighborhood divestment have resulted in neighborhoods literally toxic to live in for already vulnerable families (Sampson and Winter 2016). Public health scholars have emphasized the need to revitalize housing and neighborhoods to improve health outcomes and economic opportunity (Needleman and

Landrigan 1981; Shaw 2004), but sociologists, too, should consider lead poisoning and other health crises of poverty as a sociological lens into broader social processes. Separate groups of scholars have a good understanding of why low-income, often minority residents find themselves in neighborhoods likely to pose threats to their health—systemic racism, urban abandonment, economic decline—and the lasting effects of these exposures—potentially permanent cognitive and behavioral issues—but sociologists of housing have yet to incorporate a public health perspective into their understanding of the affordable housing crisis.

While anyone who lives in a house or apartment built before 1978 is at risk of lead poisoning, the problem is particularly acute for renters, who have limited control over their physical environment and often fear repercussions from complaints. In the US, the responsibility for making rental properties "lead-safe" is left largely in the hands of landlords. Landlords often fail to meet the challenge. Recently, sociologists of housing have turned their attention to landlords as central players in mitigating and perpetuating neighborhood inequalities, with important consequences for tenants (Greif 2018). Landlords are "a critical intermediary force" in tenants' lives (Rosen 2014, 311). They sort and select tenants during a housing search, determine their well-being during housing tenure, and have considerable power to end their housing stay. For sociologists of housing, a study of landlords' role in addressing—or ignoring—lead paint in housing illustrates the policy decisions and regulatory gaps that allow underresourced cities and landlords to fail their already vulnerable residents.

This chapter provides evidence to understand lead exposure as a distinct form of housing inequality, and one which opens new terrain for researchers. The threat of lead exposure shapes the lives of tenants and landlords, influencing housing choice, neighborhood characteristics, and property values. Landlords bear responsibility for tenants' well-being but are the most recent mediators between the often dilapidated state of a housing supply shaped by a history of repressive policymaking. Present-day landlords rent units in disinvested neighborhoods that originated from the racial and economic "redlining" practices of midcentury (Rucks-Ahidiana, this volume; Rothstein 2017; Desmond and Bell 2015). Landlords did not create the lead crisis, but they must mediate it so as to reduce its impact on tenants, all while trying to generate profits. If we are to understand how racial and economic inequalities are maintained, it is critical that we understand how renters do or do not encounter lead in their residences.

The Lead Landscape in US Rental Housing:
Concerns for Tenants and Landlords

The prevalence of lead hazards has made housing a public health risk in most American cities. While industrial sites can deposit lead in the soil of nearby neighborhoods, and plumbing inside and outside housing can expose families to leaded water, this environmental harm can also be caused by a more visible feature of dilapidated housing: paint. According to the Centers for Disease Control (2022), lead-based paint and dust are some of the most widespread sources of lead exposure for young children. Approximately twenty-nine million housing units have lead-based paint and dust hazards; about 2.6 million of these are home to young children. Lead poisoning rates are higher in inner-city, low-income, and minority neighborhoods compared to white, affluent, and suburban neighborhoods, and thus form a crucial yet understudied public health dimension of urban poverty.

Most lead poisoning occurs in smaller, often one- or two-unit, properties owned by small-scale landlords with limited resources in historically underprivileged neighborhoods (Rosenberg, Gardner, and Rickard 2018, 51). Demographically, Yeter, Banks, and Aschner (2020) found African American children living below the poverty line are twice as likely to have elevated blood lead levels compared to white or Latino children living below the poverty line. Researchers have found similar racial disparities in lead exposure across neighborhoods, including how lead exposure remains concentrated in isolated neighborhoods in deindustrialized cities such as Chicago and Detroit (Moody, Darden, and Pigozzi 2016; Sampson and Winter 2016). In an analysis of over one million blood tests in Chicago from 1995 to 2013, Sampson and Winter (2016) found that the city's African American and Latino neighborhoods contain the highest levels of exposure.

Continued lead exposure provides a pathway through which inequalities are reproduced, yet scholars do not fully know how tenants perceive lead risks, how they experience lead exposure, or the nature of their interactions with their landlords about lead threats. For example, what roles do lead threats and landlord behaviors play in tenants' housing choices, or in housing instability resulting in relocation?

Landlords hold significant power over tenants' lives. Most obviously, they are intermediaries both into and out of housing, via decisions about who can rent where and when the tenant must leave. Landlords also make important decisions about maintenance that impact tenant well-being as well as their own financial stability—decisions that include lead abatement. Landlords have the responsibility to maintain or renovate properties to keep tenants safe, even if the costs threaten their profits.

Landlords occupy a complicated place in urban housing markets, controlling the supply and influencing rent prices amid economic and infrastructural decline. Sociologists have studied landlords' influence over rental markets and housing supply, particularly profit-making strategies in low-income neighborhoods (Garboden, this volume; Balzarini and Boyd 2021); tenant screening (Reosti 2020); how landlords mold renters into ideal tenants (Rosen and Garboden 2022); and why landlords threaten eviction even when they don't intend to evict (Garboden and Rosen 2019). Scholars have also noted how policies intended to protect low-income renters, such as nuisance laws, can inadvertently make them vulnerable to landlord retaliation (Greif 2018, 2022).

Landlords' decisions about how they address the presence of lead in their properties enacts all of these dynamics, in large part because their properties are often worth little. As a result, the consequences of lead paint exposure contribute to enduring patterns of segregation, discrimination, and inequality, but scholars know little about landlords' role in managing lead exposure in homes (Muller, Sampson, and Winter 2018, 268). The inspections associated with the Housing Choice Voucher (HCV) program provide renters with some protections. Rosen (2020, 146) has shown how landlords in the program will sometimes go to great lengths to assure a "lead safe" status, including installing drywalling over existing walls, but few protections exist in the private rental market.

The housing policies aimed at keeping tenants safe from lead poisoning and landlords responsible for keeping properties habitable can, paradoxically, burden tenants and incentivize questionable landlord behavior. While landlords exert significant influence in housing markets, they do so within various federal, state, and local housing policies governing the tenant-landlord relationship (Hatch 2017). Weak policies regulating lead risks in rental properties are more attuned to development than to public health, while landlords remain profit-seeking. How landlords choose to abate lead threats remains an unexamined dimension of this profit strategy. In low-income neighborhoods, the investment needed to mitigate lead risks to tenants often proves costly, and local regulations may not require landlords to do so.

Consequently, how landlords manage lead risks on their properties influences rental market dynamics, particularly landlord-tenant conflict and turnover. Landlords' management of lead poisoning risks has broader impact on the availability—and sustainability—of affordable housing in rental markets that are already cost-prohibitive to tenants.

The Regulatory Framework of Lead Abatement

Federal law banned the use of leaded paint in 1978. Since then, federal law has required landlords to provide tenants information about known lead paint risks in housing. The 2010 Environmental Protection Agency Renovation, Repair, and Painting Rule (RRP) set additional standards for renovations that may disturb paint in pre-1978 buildings. Aside from these rules, federal and state laws do little to protect children from lead paint hazards in non-government-subsidized rental housing. Instead, local jurisdictions address lead paint exposure through housing code enforcement and public health laws (Korfmacher and Hanley 2013). The regulatory framework assuring lead-safe housing varies widely across cities, specifically the extent to which property registration pairs with the timing and frequency of a housing code inspection, or whether a city requires landlords to register their properties at all. Some cities require that rental properties pass inspection for housing code compliance, but the timing of these inspections varies. Some cities require housing code inspections when landlords register their units with a rental registry rather than when tenants move in, and then only for buildings of three units or more.

Indianapolis, for example, does not require landlords to undergo pre-rental inspections (Indiana Advisory Committee 2020). In Detroit, landlords must register properties and pass an inspection, including lead-safe status, annually, but the city struggles with consistent enforcement (MacDonald 2019). Cleveland added lead safety requirements to its rental registration program in 2019, requiring landlords to acquire a lead-safe certificate for each occupied rental (Human Impact Partners 2020), while the lead prevention policy in Buffalo did not until recently provide regular interior inspections for lead in one- or two-unit rentals (Magavern 2018).

This survey of cities shows how lead abatement laws vary widely, yet empirical evidence suggests that more-proactive regulatory frameworks can have dramatic effects. More-proactive rental inspections have been associated with decreasing lead poisoning rates. A study examining Cleveland, Greensboro, Philadelphia, Rochester, and Toledo found that proactive rental inspection programs led to decreased blood lead levels among children and a reduction in hospital bills (Fedorowicz, Schilling, and Bramhall 2020). Landlords have a role to play in both mitigating and ameliorating social inequalities in American cities. Stronger regulatory frameworks can allow them to be better providers of affordable housing to low-income tenants in search of safe housing.

Lead in Declining Cities: The Case of Buffalo

This chapter uses Buffalo as a case for understanding landlords' and renters' experiences with lead exposure. It draws on semi-structured interviews with landlords, tenants, legal professionals, and housing advocates that explored how landlords experience lead abatement policies while coping with maintenance burdens and how their actions impact tenants' well-being. Buffalo provides a case of urban decline: its poverty levels, segregation measures, and lead poisoning rates resemble those in other declining cities (Abdi and Andrews 2018; Blatto 2018). With a housing stock that is one of the nation's oldest, Buffalo has over 120,000 housing units built before 1980 (Rosenberg, Gardner, and Rickard 2018, 7), and 46 percent of its renters pay over 35 percent of their income in rent (Rosenberg, Gardner, and Rickard 2018, 68).

Buffalo proves a useful case for understanding the link between lead threats and landlords' ability to provide safe housing. Shortly after the fieldwork for this study (2017–2019), city officials adopted more-proactive inspection measures in the rental housing market. In late 2020, city lawmakers passed an ordinance expanding municipal inspection requirements to include previously exempted one- and two-unit rental buildings every three years. Landlords must also submit documentation of instances when the county health department has cited the property for a lead violation. Why did the city introduce new rental regulations? In 2020, the Department of Housing and Urban Development's (HUD) Lead-Based Paint Hazard Reduction Program began providing grants for cities to address the problem of lead in rental housing (Williams 2020). Buffalo's receipt of a $2.3 million grant from this program assisted lead paint removal programs run by the county health department, relieving landlords of some of their cost and maintenance burdens.

Two themes emerged from this fieldwork: landlords' struggle to balance investment and maintenance in the midst of a declining local economy and landlords' desire to minimize conflicts with tenants to prevent turnover and vacancy. From a landlord's perspective, the threat of lead exposure creates maintenance burdens and legal liabilities. These challenges can be so great that some threaten to opt out of the rental market altogether when presented with potential enforcement. Landlords must also weigh whether to disclose risks to tenants beyond what is required in their lease, as doing so risks losing tenants.

In many cities, renter families concerned about lead risks can contact the health department for an inspection. Many tenants decline to do so, however, whether because they seek to avoid potential conflict with their landlord or because they are concerned that reporting might force them to move. Aside from inspections and tenant requests, cities learn of lead-laced properties when children's blood tests reveal high lead levels. New York requires doctors to test children with a blood lead test in their first year and again at age two. For children up to age six, pediatricians ask at each visit about ways a child may have had contact with lead (NYSDH 2019). Regardless of how awareness of a lead risk emerges, confirmed evidence of lead exposure can trigger contact with institutional forces such as the public health department and housing court, which affect both tenants and landlords—albeit in dramatically different ways.

Lead: A Persistent Burden and Threat

Landlords undertake a calculus of what their budget allows them to fix that weighs the cost of immediate maintenance needs against long-term improvements, including lead abatement. When a basic feature of housing habitability breaks, like a sink or radiator, the landlord must fix it immediately if they hope to pass an inspection or lease the unit to a new tenant. Mason, an African American male in his thirties, owns seven rentals in Buffalo. Five are single units and two are double units, which means that none of his properties met the pre-2020 standard for a housing inspection. Mason does most of the maintenance himself, only hiring additional workers when needed to assure "things are done right." While Mason has a long wish list of renovations he would like to make, realistically, he focuses on the ones he *can* make.

To fully update a dilapidated but rentable unit into something lead-free, a landlord would need to essentially build a new unit—the goal with older housing is to make it "lead safe," but the extent of the repairs determines when repairs might need to be done again. However, landlords who operate in low-income neighborhoods are reluctant to make repairs without a guarantee on their investment. Mason described how the most lead-safe practices were not necessarily the most financially smart. A landlord would need to make an investment that might not guarantee a financial return, even in the long term, due to being in a low-income neighborhood unlikely to attract renters who could afford its increased rent. A cheaper approach, as Rosen's (2020) research in Baltimore shows, is to simply drywall over the existing walls, but this leaves the problem to be fully remedied later, possibly by a new owner. New property owners are never quite sure what hazards may exist behind their walls or how long more recent renovations might protect tenants from them, and tenants are unsure about their actual level of safety.

Ollie, an African American landlord living on the East Side who owns three properties, described his difficulties in keeping units safe to rent. He painted one of his rentals three years prior, touched it up a year later, but noticed how recently "probably less than 3 percent of the house, if that, has some peeling spots . . . it's just something you have to budget for, and it's not cheap." Each spot requires scraping, priming, and touching up, and the costs add up. "It could be upwards of a thousand dollars or more," Ollie explained with frustration, "and it's tedious and costly." This process requires plastic sheeting as well, in addition to paint. To truly do the job right, Ollie should be a certified lead remediation specialist. Without that training, he or his workers might accidentally release more lead into the air and soil, as dust, than he removes.

Muller, Sampson, and Winter (2018, 268) argue that landlords likely justify the presence of lead paint on their properties through the language of cost. When landlords in Buffalo enroll in the city rental registry, they must attest that they will use lead-safe renovation practices as advised by HUD and the EPA. The EPA RRP rule, in turn, requires contractors working on pre-1978 housing to undergo EPA-authorized lead renovation training. In practice, many small-scale landlords, as Mason and Ollie's cases show, cite steep costs and do the minimum to follow regulations, and the city does not press the issue due to lack of adequate enforcement mechanisms. Just as landlords use tactics in tenant screening and selection that have socially unequal outcomes while staying within the bounds of discrimination law (Reosti 2020; Rosen 2014), landlords use similar tactics to frugally keep units habitable and lead-safe so as to still generate profit, but similarly socially unjust outcomes can occur for tenants if such tactics go awry and lead exposure occurs.

While he takes pride in ensuring the safety of his units, Mason prioritizes his time. He considers lead risk to be an important issue, but it does not garner more attention than other kinds of routine maintenance. Abating potential, or even known, lead risk gets wrapped into a larger list of maintenance requests. "Unless I've got an hour to kill, I don't like to go there for that," he commented, explaining that he only attends to peeling paint if it was a specific request from a tenant or the health department. And yet, the potential for lead exposure occurs with even a few paint flecks or unsettled dust from a floorboard. Feeling overburdened by the abundance of flaking paint spots, Mason does not seek them out. Instead, he abates possible lead issues by repainting or resealing when at a unit that has "three or four or five things you have to get done, and they're usually small things but still longer trips that can be four hours for eight different things."

Small-scale landlords trying to stay financially afloat in disinvested neighborhoods more often than not operate within a logic of "deferred maintenance." This strategy keeps small-scale landlords afloat, but it has long-term, potentially irreversible effects on children's lives. When informed by a court or a city agency that they *must* address a lead issue, landlords may attempt to deflect responsibility, pointing to the condition of schools or other areas, including relatives' homes, where the child spends time. The city's fine structure incentivizes landlords who do acknowledge responsibility to act swiftly, if perhaps superficially. Chipping paint from moved furniture, for example, might be more easily painted over than sanded, repainted, and vacuumed, because the deeper renovation could disturb tenants' day-to-day lives. In effect, these landlords "are betting on today" (Desmond and Wilmers 2019, 1113) by exploiting their tenants' limited options.

Many tenants, like Angela, defer to their landlord about what constitutes a lead risk and the best way to abate it, whether because of a lack of knowledge or fear of risking their housing security. A white, single mother of three in her forties, Angela described how her front porch repeatedly flakes in an area where her kids play. "All the landlord does is repaint after winter breaks," she says, describing how he patches the eyesore spots with what she felt was inadequate paint because it made her porch slippery and difficult to walk on during winters. When her youngest child tested positive for lead, she assumed it came from there, but she could not confirm where his exposure originated. In Angela's case, a positive blood lead test done during a routine pediatric visit triggered a home inspection from the health department.

Working in and around the Regulatory Context

Landlords can have mixed responses to new regulations, but their response tends to be dictated by the impact on their profits. In Detroit, landlords sued when the city adopted a more proactive rental inspection policy (MacDonald 2019). Other landlords, as shown by Desmond and Wilmers (2019), advocate for a stronger regulatory environment on the premise that clear expectations create predictability for landlords and tenants alike. Ultimately, this approach also focuses on profit-making, as landlords do not want to experience gaps in their rental incomes or unexpected costs.

When Nikki, an African American landlord of six properties in her fifties, discussed her experiences overseeing rentals with potential lead risks, she declared she was interested in renting to Housing Choice Voucher (HCV) holders because their "up-front inspection [required by HCV] takes care of whatever problems I don't know about and I can get rid of them" before the tenants move in. She preferred this approach to the uncertainties associated with the private market, for instance, in a property that she doesn't realize needs lead abatement. Nikki's approach to updating her units between tenants typically includes covering any flaking paint and deep-cleaning to remove leaded dust so that it can pass an HCV inspection before tenants move in. Due to the city approving the property up front, she feels relieved of both the burden and initial liability.

In general, landlords prefer abatement strategies that keep tenants in their properties, as vacant units represent lost income. In some cases, however, landlords respond to a report of lead exposure by requesting or requiring that their tenant leave. Noelle and Bobby, a white couple in their midthirties, rented out a single one-family unit a few blocks from where they live. They were alarmed when the health department alerted them that two of the children living in the rental had high blood levels of lead. The notice caught them by surprise, as the couple were confident that they had abided by all the appropriate lead safety requirements. Bobby, having worked in construction, felt personally devastated by the possible health consequences facing their tenants.

An additional inspection by the health department, triggered by their tenants' pediatrician appointment, revealed that multiple layers of older paint hid under the layers Bobby had put down during the renovation. The health department deemed the unit uninhabitable without an overhaul that included replacing the windows and removing the carpet. At this point, the unit was neither rentable nor sellable. Fearing that either their tenants or the health department might take them to housing court, Bobby and Noelle informally "evicted" their tenants and helped them find a new place to live. Balzarini and Boyd (2021) note how informal, "off-the-books" evictions are increasingly common among small-scale landlords. While it is a social good that their tenants can find lead-safe housing, the process of moving, especially abruptly, is burdensome on tenants and thus a social harm. How regulations regarding lead exposure influence this process remains an untapped area of research.

Noelle and Bobby's single unit had not been subject to inspection. Instead, the couple took what Benfer (2017, 495) calls the "wait and see" approach. As both they and their tenants soon learned, this approach can produce multiple burdens, including physiological consequences and the burden of finding new housing. Noelle remarked how larger property owners use lead-certified contract workers because they can afford them— "it saves them hassle," she exclaimed, "but not everyone can afford that." Bobby attended a lead-safe certification training to make sure they got it right this time.

For landlords like Noelle and Bobby, the fallout of a lead exposure means stress and a financial setback. The situation is more dire for tenants. For example, Jada, a single Latina woman in her late twenties, was dealt the dual blow of learning that her daughter had been exposed to lead and having to find a new place to live. Her daughter's positive blood test triggered an inspection during which the health department deemed her apartment uninhabitable. Jada soon secured safer housing with a reputable landlord through a friend, but she was left to grieve the possibility of her daughter suffering permanent learning deficits because of prolonged lead exposure. She recounted how this experience would "haunt me the rest of my life."

Landlords with larger property portfolios are typically more proactive, in part because they can take advantage of economies of scale to reduce their overall risk and have more resources to tackle such challenges. Miles, a property manager in his early forties with an MBA and eighteen properties, divulged how he overcomes "the challenges and risks" of lead threats in his rental housing. He sees the challenge and risk as affecting not just the tenants, whom he claims to be concerned about, but also his reputation as a landlord. He therefore actively manages lead exposure by testing for lead at every possible opportunity, with or without his tenants' knowledge. Any time a tenant needs a hole fixed, for example, he tests for lead. These routine tests give him confidence about the lead status of any given wall. When he notices other spots, like window trim, that "may be a lead hazard with time," he plans to deal with it later. This plan usually entails one of his maintenance workers going into the unit and pretending to fix something else. This strategy allows Miles to prevent conflicts over lead safety and prevent lead exposure and shows how landlords with the means will abate lead in their rental units without notifying tenants about the true nature of their visits. While not common in the data analyzed for this chapter, future research would benefit from interrogating the maintenance and rehabilitation strategies landlords employ in the private rental market.

Not all landlords have Miles's ability to engage in questionable tactics to keep tenants safe. Landlords use different strategies depending on their means; yet none of these strategies amount to proper protection from lead hazards. Tenants suffer when landlords make ad hoc decisions on limited budgets. At minimum, a more proactive regulatory framework requiring that vacant units be inspected before new tenants move in can assure that tenants are living in a lead-free, or at least lead-safe, living space. Such requirements would provide a frame of reference for understanding what deterioration has occurred to the unit. They would also help assuage or address concerns if a tenant fears a lead risk exists or when a child's lead diagnosis occurs.

Policy Implications and Future Research

Flint has become synonymous with lead poisoning, but lead poisoning associated with older housing stock is endemic in the US. This fact should alarm researchers interested in the relationship between housing and health, as inequality in housing access shapes the lives of low-income families. During the height of the Flint crisis, at least three thousand areas had recorded lead poisoning rates at least double those in Flint. While concentrated in cities, they also occur in rural areas. Any place with older plumbing, dilapidated housing, and industrial waste could pose lead risks to residents. In a sense, the US *is* Flint (Pell, Schneyer, and Sullivan 2017).

To make housing healthier, cities must devote resources toward more substantial lead paint remediation, transforming "lead-safe" housing into "lead-free" housing. The cost of such investment seems pale alongside what the American Academy of Pediatrics estimates as the economic and social damage caused by the lead epidemic: $50 billion in annual health-care costs, $17 to $221 saved for every $1 invested to reduce lead hazards in housing, twenty-three million total lost IQ points, and one in five attention deficit hyperactivity disorder cases (Healthy Children 2019). If more cities updated their housing policies to focus on prevention rather than exposure, threats of exposure would decrease. Cities practicing "secondary prevention"—abatement after exposure occurs—but concerned with residents' long-term health could target resources toward proactive policies to limit lead exposure in marginalized neighborhoods: expanding inspections to include all landlord-owned rental properties, not just three-unit and larger buildings; including interior "dust-wipe" tests, even if external visual inspection does not identify lead hazards; and requiring periodic lead-specific inspections to ensure proper occupancy status (Magavern 2018; Benfer 2017). Stronger regulatory frameworks provide models for guaranteeing healthy housing rather than just accountability for it being unsafe.

Sociologists understand that where people live affects their overall well-being. For urban sociologists occupied with cities or neighborhoods as their frame, shifting to housing, particularly its physical features, allows for a fuller grasp of the struggles of urban life, and also what is needed to make cities flourish. Unsafe housing is not just a symptom of poverty—it can be a cause. Two different rental units sitting side by side on the street, owned by the same landlord, could pose different lead risks depending on multiple factors: the choices of previous occupants and owners, renovation history, and proximity to other hazards. Proactive, rather than reactive, attention to housing makes vulnerable families safer and enriches struggling communities. As the case of lead and landlords shows, reactive approaches to housing policy put the lives of families at risk.

A sociological approach to housing shows how housing forms a key determinant of health. Scholars have much to learn about how environmental risks shape housing outcomes, because so much of the housing available to low-income families could be toxic. Health disparities across race and socioeconomic class exist within a milieu of health risks stemming from an unjust housing system, as public health risks are embedded within the relationship between housing and inequality.

Housing policy should address the needs of America's most vulnerable. A sociology of housing understands that a public health crisis such as lead exposure is also an affordable housing crisis. It acknowledges that we cannot expect landlords to act as de facto public health managers, responsible as the frontline defenders against lead exposure when they operate in markets incentivizing profit-seeking. While their practices impact the safety of renters, landlords are also subject to historic patterns of inequality, particularly racial discrimination, that may make the lives of many landlords only slightly less precarious than those of their tenants. In the long term, the complicated cases of landlord decision-making and landlord-tenant interaction illustrate the need for real transformation of affordable housing. We need significant public investment in housing to increase the well-being of communities in the long term.

7

Audit Studies of Housing Discrimination

ESTABLISHED, EMERGING, AND FUTURE RESEARCH

S. Michael Gaddis and Nicholas V. DiRago

Before civil rights legislation in the 1960s prohibited numerous forms of housing discrimination, various actors in the housing sector (e.g., real estate agents, landlords, and mortgage brokers) could engage in discrimination with impunity (Massey and Denton 1993; Squires 2017). In the years that followed the introduction of anti-discrimination laws, many of these actors changed their behavior to engage in more subtle forms of discrimination while avoiding legal and social penalties (Gaddis 2019b; Massey 2005). Discrimination became more private and difficult to detect. This shift rendered two of the primary tools of social scientists—surveys and interviews—less effective in documenting discrimination. Facing potential legal repercussions and social stigma by admitting to engaging in discrimination, respondents likely began lying to researchers. This type of behavior—what researchers call "social desirability bias"—reduced the accuracy and validity of survey and interview research examining discrimination (Pager and Quillian 2005).

And yet, over the past few decades, social scientists have increased their scholarly output examining discrimination (Crabtree et al. 2021). Arguably, the development and expansion of the audit method have played an outsized role in the increased attention devoted to discrimination (Gaddis 2018a; 2018b). Audits are a specific type of field experiment researchers use to examine discrimination (e.g., gender, racial/ethnic) across contexts (e.g., employment, housing) and geographies (Pager 2003; Quillian et al. 2017). Researchers use these covert experiments to make strong causal claims about discrimination since it is otherwise difficult to document using surveys and interviews (Gaddis 2019b).

Fair-housing committees and activists began conducting small-scale housing audits in the 1940s (Cherry and Bendick 2018). The UK Parliament authorized the first significant housing audit to examine discrimination based on race and immigration in England in the late 1960s (Daniel

1968). Since then, the US Department of Housing and Urban Development (HUD) has conducted four (1977, 1989, 2000, 2012) large-scale in-person audits of purchase and rental markets across the US (Oh and Yinger 2015; Turner et al. 2013; Yinger 1995). Before the 2000s, researchers primarily conducted in-person audits that were subject to high costs and complex implementation. Resource constraints often limited the conversation to documenting the existence of discrimination, and scholars conducted few small-scale in-person housing audits (see Galster 1990a, 1990b; Yinger 1986).

In the twenty-first century, audits have become more common due to the rise of online applications for housing and employment and easy access to decision-makers across many contexts via email. These correspondence audits present advantages over in-person audits because they require fewer resources and are easier to design, implement, and scale up. They also, however, present two distinct disadvantages compared to in-person audits. First, researchers can examine a more limited range of outcomes, typically electronic interactions and often only those at the very early stages of the decision-making process. Second, researchers face more constraints in signaling pertinent characteristics (e.g., race/ethnicity via names rather than visually) and may accidentally capture multiple forms of discrimination by violating the excludability assumption (Crabtree et al. 2022). Overall, these trade-offs mean that social scientists can more easily examine interactions between characteristics, geographic differences, and contextual nuance in discrimination, but with limitations on outcomes and questions about construct validity (Gaddis 2018a).

Although housing audits initially focused on examining differences by race as a means of investigating the effectiveness of the Civil Rights Act of 1968, researchers have expanded housing audits to examine discrimination based on gender (Hogan and Berry 2011), sexual orientation (Ahmed and Hammarstedt 2008), parenthood (Galster and Constantine 1991), disability (Ameri et al. 2019), criminal record (Evans, Blount-Hill, and Cubellis 2019), and immigrant generation (Gaddis and Ghoshal 2020). Research has examined a variety of outcomes, including whether inquiries received any response, what type of information was provided in the response, and whether inquirers were steered to other properties (Auspurg, Schneck, and Hinz 2019; Gaddis 2018a; Quillian, Lee, and Honoré 2020).

Sociologists are particularly well suited to examine housing discrimination as it intersects with numerous core areas of study: communities, families, gender, inequality, neighborhoods, organizations, poverty, race and ethnicity, and sexual orientation, to name a few. The study of housing discrimination captures interactions between individuals with different levels of power and status (e.g., prospective homeowner and realtor), individuals and racialized organizations (e.g., borrower and mortgage lender), and between individuals with a government intermediary (e.g., housing voucher holder and landlord). Beyond individual interactions, sociologists are also concerned with the broader social structure and the embeddedness of explicit and implicit racial decision-making, policies, and organizations (Bonilla-Silva 2003; Ray 2019). These concerns have led sociologists to make critical contributions to the study of contextual effects, durable inequality, neighborhood selection, and mechanisms of neighborhood inequality (Korver-Glenn 2018; Krysan and Crowder 2017; Sampson, Morenoff, and Gannon-Rowley 2002). Thus, it is clear that sociologists have a lot to offer to the study of housing discrimination through the use of audits.

We build on previous reviews of housing audits and focus attention on emerging areas of inquiry, suggest new avenues of research pursuits, and highlight areas where the contributions of sociologists are critically important. First, we briefly review the long history of housing audits, beginning with in-person HUD audits. Next, we discuss three emerging areas of housing audit research—housing choice vouchers, short-term rentals, and roommate searches—and highlight important findings, innovations, and areas of weakness. Finally, we conclude with a discussion about future directions of housing audits, including using experiments to test for ways to reduce discrimination, using additional data to examine the mechanisms of housing discrimination, and designing modified audits to explore discrimination in other stages of housing exchange.

Previous Research on Housing Audits

The first HUD housing audit used white and Black testers to examine discrimination in the purchase and rental housing markets (Wienk et al. 1979). Researchers found discrimination against Black testers in reported housing availability, treatment by real estate agents, reported terms and conditions, and the types and levels of information requested by real estate agents. Subsequent HUD-sponsored audits added tests for Hispanic housing-seekers and examined racial steering (Turner, Struyk, and Yinger 1991), added tests for Asians and Native Americans (Turner and Ross 2003; Turner et al. 2003, 2013), and examined housing discrimination based on disability (Turner et al. 2005; Levy et al. 2015). These Housing and Discrimination Studies (HDS) found that some forms of discrimination, such as racial/ethnic discrimination in showing units, have decreased over time. Other forms of discrimination, such as racial/ethnic discrimination in steering, have increased over time.

Researchers and fair-housing organizations conducted numerous small-sample in-person housing audits from the 1970s through the early years of the first decade of the 2000s. Most of these studies document racial discrimination against Black, and sometimes Latino, buyers and renters across multiple outcomes (Galster 1990a, 1990b; James, McCummings, and Tynan 1984). To our knowledge, only two published non-HUD audits from this period of over thirty years in the US examined housing discrimination based on a characteristic other than race/ethnicity. Galster and Constantine (1991) examined rental housing discrimination based on gender and parenthood and found that single women with and without children faced significant discrimination compared to men. Additionally, in an analysis of Boston audit data, Yinger (1986) found that couples with young children faced slight discrimination compared to single adults and couples with older children.

Housing audit researchers have included social class signals (Hanson and Hawley 2011; Hanson, Hawley, and Taylor 2011) or credit scores (Ewens, Tomlin, and Wang 2014) to examine variation in racial/ethnic discrimination by SES. Others have included signals for criminal records and health conditions (Henkels 2020). Finally, researchers examine targets of discrimination through a broader range of racial/ethnic (Carpusor and Loges 2006), gender, and sexual orientation (Murchie and Pang 2018; Schwegman 2018) statuses.

While the HUD audits were critically important in providing methodological guideposts and leading the way for future audits (Gaddis 2018a), they were conducted to provide national estimates of discrimination and as enforcement tools in support of anti-discrimination legislation (Fix and Struyk 1993; Oh and Yinger 2015). In contrast to the broad answers provided by the HUD audits, many of the correspondence audits conducted in the twenty-first century have focused on very narrow slices of housing discrimination. In the next section, we highlight some emerging areas of research where scholars have addressed more nuanced sociological research questions.

Emerging Research

HOUSING CHOICE VOUCHERS

Researchers have begun using audits to test for discrimination against tenants who pay for housing with the help of a Housing Choice Voucher (HCV), also known as "Section 8." By subsidizing poor households' rent in privately owned units that meet basic safety standards, the HCV program reduces barriers to decent housing and promotes physical and financial security (Rosen 2020). However, three gaps in the HCV program have led to failure in the stated goal of facilitating social mobility for residents of poor neighborhoods. First, landlords often exclude voucher holders from affluent neighborhoods while seeking them out in low-income areas (Garboden et al. 2018; Rosen 2014). Second, information is scarce on using HCVs to move to more advantaged neighborhoods (DeLuca, Garboden, and Rosenblatt 2013). Third, Congress only funds HCVs for fewer than a quarter of eligible households (Moore 2016). Many analysts argue that reforming and expanding the HCV program would reduce housing insecurity, poverty, and racial inequality (e.g., Collyer et al. 2020; Desmond 2016; Rosen 2021). Critics caution against relying on discrimination-prone landlords in the private market to reduce housing inequality and recommend policy adjustments (e.g., updated legislation, increased enforcement, and expanded use of small area fair market rents) to attenuate discrimination.

Experimental evidence of landlords' discriminatory behavior toward HCV holders contributes to this debate. The most comprehensive audit of HCVs found that landlords discriminate by refusing vouchers altogether or prioritizing applicants without vouchers over voucher holders (Cunningham et al. 2018). HUD-commissioned researchers fielded a multistage experiment in five US cities in 2016 and 2017. A white woman first responded by telephone to apartment advertisements and asked whether the landlord accepted HCVs. Teams of white, Black, and Latina women then attempted to schedule and appear at in-person appointments with purportedly HCV-friendly landlords in three of the five cities. In the first stage (n=3,780), landlords refused vouchers at widely varying rates, from 15 percent in Washington, DC, to over 75 percent in Los Angeles and Fort Worth. Landlords were more likely to refuse HCVs in more affluent neighborhoods; conversely, rejection rates were lower in high-poverty neighborhoods. In the second stage (n=694), testers in the HCV and control groups had comparable success securing appointments by phone. In the third stage (n=509), however, landlords were 12 percent more likely to appear at appointments scheduled with testers in the control group. Landlords also told testers in the HCV group about fewer or different available units.

Beyond contextual differences by neighborhood poverty, the HUD-commissioned study provisionally attributes variation in rates of voucher refusal to the strength of local anti-discrimination laws. Two audits have tested this hypothesis directly, providing preliminary supporting evidence (Faber and Mercier 2022; Moore 2018). In each of these studies, discrimination against HCV holders was at least partially attenuated in cities where anti-voucher discrimination was illegal, controlling for characteristics of the advertisement, housing unit, neighborhood, and local housing market. These results, however, are vulnerable to confounding from local voucher payment levels and other variable aspects of local implementation. Although local laws may attenuate levels of discrimination against HCV holders, it is unclear whether these laws can completely eliminate discrimination against HCV holders.

Correspondence audits also provide evidence on statistical interactions between applicant race and voucher use, a possibility raised but not tested by the HUD-commissioned study. In one experiment in Washington, DC, in 2015, landlords were over twice as likely to respond to applicants in the control group than those indicating HCV status (Phillips 2017). The penalty for voucher use increased with rental cost and was two to four times the penalty for Black applicants. The two penalties were additive and noninteractive. Researchers fielded a second wave in 2017, after local regulations were amended to allow higher HCV subsidies in costlier neighborhoods (Aliprantis, Martin, and Phillips 2022). The voucher penalty's magnitude, positive association with rents, and additive relationship with the penalty for Black applicants were relatively stable. However, new HCV holders were more likely to lease up in costlier neighborhoods after the regulations changed. A third audit across fourteen cities found a comparable voucher penalty and a similarly additive, noninteractive relationship between voucher status and race (Moore 2018). Conversely, the final audit, covering the broadest geographic area (thirty-one cities), found that Black and Hispanic housing-seekers only faced discrimination when *not* indicating HCV status (Faber and Mercier 2022). Additionally, this audit tested parental status and found that this effect was driven by Black housing-seekers signaling that they had a child. Overall, these results suggest that landlords discriminate based on race and voucher status but generally do not use these characteristics as proxies for one another when determining whether to accept HCVs.

These audit studies on housing voucher discrimination do more than simply document levels of discrimination. They test specific mechanisms and highlight why the sociological phenomena of neighborhood context and intersectionality matter. First, these studies show that while landlord discrimination against HCV holders is high in low-poverty neighborhoods, landlords in high-poverty neighborhoods have fewer qualms about HCV holders. Interviews with landlords confirm these results (Garboden et al. 2018; Rosen, Garboden, and Cossyleon 2021). These findings show that HCVs likely will not contribute to mobility without additional policy interventions and enforcement but will instead keep low-income families in high-poverty neighborhoods. Second, these studies show that although race and HCV status do not interact to intensify discrimination, landlords do discriminate more against Black mothers. This finding raises an important question about whether landlords assume Black women HCV holders have children if the subject is not explicitly discussed in their correspondence.

SHORT-TERM RENTALS

Short-term rentals (STRs) are houses, apartments, condos, or accessory dwelling units (ADUs) owned by individuals or organizations that guests or tourists can book online, typically for less than a month (Guttentag 2015; Paulsen, this volume). Several audit studies analyze STRs, most of which focus on Airbnb—the largest platform for STRs. In sociology, researchers usually approach STRs as cases of political and economic restructuring (Vallas and Schor 2020). Sociologists of housing have focused mainly on links among STRs, speculation, rents, neighborhood change, and community disruption (Guttentag 2019; Hoffman and Heisler 2020). As emerging audit research demonstrates, however, STRs also reveal largely unexamined mechanisms of discrimination and the shortcomings of policies designed to reduce it (see Cheng and Foley 2018).

Two correspondence audits have examined racial discrimination on Airbnb. The first examined host responses in five cities in 2015; landlords accepted 42 percent of requests from Black applicants, compared to 50 percent from white applicants (Edelman, Luca, and Svirsky 2017). A relatively distinct subset of serially discriminatory landlords accounted for the bulk of this disparity, which varied little with housing units and landlord characteristics. Along with this audit, public awareness of discrimination on the platform and a series of lawsuits led Airbnb to change their policy requiring guests to include a photograph and their full name before completing a booking (Murphy 2016; Schor and Vallas 2021; "Settlement Reached in Airbnb Discrimination Case" 2019). A second study, conducted from 2016 through 2018, also explored five US cities, though only one city appears in both studies (Cui, Li, and Zhang 2020). A 19 percent disparity emerged between Black and white applicants. When applicants' profiles included positive reviews from past STR hosts, however, new hosts did not discriminate against Black applicants.

There is also experimental evidence of ableism in STRs in the US. In a correspondence audit of Airbnb in 2016, hosts were between 18 and 67 percent less likely to pre-approve requests from applicants indicating they needed accommodations for a disability than from paired control applicants (Ameri et al. 2019). Levels of discrimination varied by the disability indicated and accommodations requested, but they were robust to the onset of nondiscrimination policies and consistent across housing unit characteristics. The authors argue that their findings reveal a gap in the Americans with Disabilities Act, which protects individuals with disabilities from discrimination in hotels but not STRs.

Research on STRs, particularly audit studies of STRs, is a relatively new and burgeoning area. Still, this research uncovers at least three important broad sociological findings. First, racial discrimination may be concentrated among a small set of serial offenders. This finding is echoed in a recent large-scale employment audit as well (Kline, Rose, and Walters 2021; Kline and Walters 2021). Second, certain policies may work to exacerbate or attenuate discrimination. While Airbnb's actions to remove picture requirements likely reduced some forms of racial/ethnic discrimination, other forms may have arisen in the void (e.g., based on names). Similarly, adding federal protection against discrimination based on disability status in STRs would likely attenuate another form of discrimination on these platforms. Finally, this research also shows that small pieces of positive information might change stereotypes or assumptions to reduce levels of discrimination in STRs. As a whole, these audits uncover important mechanisms of and, perhaps, solutions to discrimination in a new housing context.

ROOMMATE SEARCHES

Another new area of housing correspondence audits examines the process of roommate selection. Nearly 6 percent of the US adult population—more than fifteen million people—currently live with unrelated roommates who are not romantic partners (US Census Bureau 2017), and the total number to ever live with a roommate is likely much higher. Roommate selection is an even more integral part of the housing search process for the young and highly educated; 16 percent of individuals with at least a bachelor's degree who are in their twenties live with a roommate (Lauff and Ingels 2013). Thus, roommate correspondence audits capture a very different housing search process for the young, geographically mobile, and highly educated demographic who move to costly urban areas and often cannot rent, much less purchase, housing units on their own (Olsen 2014). This demographic group likely has different economic and social considerations that influence the housing search process compared to older individuals, less educated individuals, or those with families. Still, the decisions these individuals make influence segregation, access to resources,

commute times, and the overall quality of their neighborhoods for themselves and others, and in turn influence future downstream outcomes
as well.

Three studies examine roommate discrimination via correspondence
audits by responding to individuals who post advertisements on Craigslist
looking for roommates (Gaddis and Ghoshal 2015; 2020). Each ad represents an individual who already lives with one or more roommates and
is looking for a new person to fill a recently or soon-to-be vacated room.
Across multiple cities, the authors find evidence of discrimination against
Black, Hispanic, Asian, and Arab Americans. These disparities differ by
geography. In one study, the authors find tentative evidence supporting
the ethnic competition hypothesis; Arab American room-seekers experience higher discrimination in some cities when listings are in areas with
high population concentrations of Arabs and in proximity to mosques
(Gaddis and Ghoshal 2015).

These roommate search studies find significant racial discrimination
against a number of racial/ethnic groups in an increasingly important
area of housing, particularly for young people in urban areas. We believe
these studies present three important sociological points. First, racial/
ethnic discrimination occurs in housing situations that are not exclusively
economically driven. While many theories of discrimination are based
in economic contexts, these audit studies of roommate selection show
that social contexts can lead to similar discriminatory processes. Second,
geographic context, or more specifically the racial/ethnic composition
of local area, is important. Third, beyond race and ethnicity, signaled immigration generation is an important characteristic that may lead to additional discrimination. These studies once again highlight the importance
of intersectionality in housing discrimination.

Future Research

RESEARCH DESIGN AND CONCEPTUALIZATION

Many concerns remain about the difficulties presented by correspondence
audits in signaling certain characteristics, especially race and ethnicity.
Scholars have examined the validity of using names to signal a host of
characteristics, including age, social class, race/ethnicity, and immigrant
generation or citizenship status. Researchers often must use names to
indirectly signal these characteristics when they cannot use more direct
signals (e.g., explicit statement, photos). Recent research shows that racial
perceptions of white and Black names are often linked with social class

(Crabtree et al. 2022; Gaddis 2017, 2019a) and that racial perceptions of Hispanic and Asian names are linked with immigrant generation or citizenship status (Gaddis, Kreisberg, and Crabtree 2021). Beyond methodological concerns, the signaling issue raises important questions about why decision-makers discriminate. In housing contexts, for example, much of the discrimination uncovered by audit studies may in fact be at least partially driven by discrimination based on SES or social class. These issues present new opportunities for sociologists of housing discrimination to disentangle the effects of these signals and examine discrimination based on intersectionality—particularly between race and class.

Correspondence audits represent a specific type of research design. Well-executed audit studies have high internal validity and can capture a very real experience in precise contexts (e.g., for people who use Craigslist to look for a rental unit). However, audits often capture only one type of interaction in a given stage of the housing exchange process (e.g., initial emails with a landlord and no face-to-face contact). Researchers should take sampling bias seriously and distinguish between two aspects of external validity: the realism of the scenario and the generalizability of the scenario. Especially in emerging areas of research, few studies identify exactly who are the populations of interest, address the extent to which their data represent them, and analyze data or interpret results accordingly. Instead, many studies take for granted the populations that use housing listing services, STR platforms, and the representation of other common sources of data for audits. Some authors might argue that their studies are primarily concerned with internal validity: broadly representing real-world processes and populations matters less than causal identification within the sample.

A given study's data may only enable authors to identify, say, a disparity of x percent that surfaces in paired responses to Craigslist advertisements for apartments in the cheapest quartile in five large cities. This causal effect is well-identified but highly circumscribed. In short, without additional data, such an audit answers a very narrow research question. Researchers could bridge this causal effect to the larger questions that will draw many readers to the study by marshaling supplemental data or consulting existing theoretical, quantitative, and qualitative research. For example, scholars might use a representative survey to show what percentage of people in those five cities use Craigslist to search for rental housing and examine potential heterogeneity by household income. This research might also benefit from a discussion about the decision to select cities into the sample and how representative these cities are of all US cities with regard to demographic composition, political and economic arrangements, and pertinent historical dynamics.

Future audit studies of housing in the US should reflect more clearly the ways in which discrimination compounds over the multiple, heterogeneous, and path-dependent stages of housing exchange (Bell 2020b; DeLuca, Wood, and Rosenblatt 2019; Korver-Glenn 2018, 2021; Krysan and Crowder 2017). Audit methods can measure discrimination in some stages but are inappropriate for others. For some auditable stages of housing exchange, in-person testing is the only viable route to experimental data. Regardless of the stages any given study examines, however, audit researchers should aim for more than quantifying the magnitude of discrimination. Guided by theory and empirical research, they should present audits' findings and limitations in view of the wider process of housing exchange.

Some stages of housing exchange are amenable to audit studies in principle but difficult to audit in practice because verisimilitude is difficult to achieve. For example, researchers might wish to audit rental or mortgage applications, which usually collect confidential data to screen applicants' incomes, credit scores, residential histories, or encounters with the legal system. Audit researchers would have to coordinate with a prohibitive number of actors to ensure testers' applications return convincing results. For the foreseeable future, observational studies are better suited to analyzing stages of housing exchange that involve third parties and personal or proprietary data.

Although correspondence studies are increasingly popular approaches to the auditable stages of housing exchange, in-person audits with live testers remain vital to comprehensive experimental data on housing discrimination. Today, researchers can increasingly field correspondence audits cheaply online. They can also achieve considerable external validity because many stages of housing exchange often transpire without in-person interaction. Correspondence audits, however, are not well suited to every stage of housing exchange in the US. Many stages continue to occur primarily in person, especially unit showings. Individuals are susceptible to discrimination in these stages. Relying on correspondence studies overrepresents earlier and more impersonal stages of housing exchange in the literature at the expense of later and more interactive stages. Researchers should prioritize, and funders should increase resources for, auditing face-to-face and in-person interactions in housing markets about which automated or remote data collection is impossible. Following testers through multiple stages of housing exchange by combining correspondence and in-person testing will better capture the contours of discrimination.

NEW DIRECTIONS

The correspondence audit method excels at providing information on the "what," "where," and "who," but comes up short in answering the "how" and "why" questions of discrimination (Gaddis 2019b). Scholars have suggested that the body of knowledge on processes of discrimination would benefit from coupling audit data with additional data sources such as survey or interview data (Gaddis 2018a; Pedulla 2018). Many such examples exist in the literature on discrimination in the labor market (Pedulla 2016; Quadlin 2018), but none among housing discrimination studies. This is a significant oversight in the literature. Do landlords discriminate against Black or Hispanic housing-seekers due to assumptions about their ability to pay rent? Do hosts on STR platforms discriminate against disabled individuals due to perceived accessibility gaps in their dwelling? A well-designed correspondence audit coupled with interview or survey data might provide answers to these and other important questions about the mechanisms of discrimination. Moreover, understanding these mechanisms is crucial to designing potential interventions that may attenuate or eliminate discrimination.

Audits have potential contributions beyond estimating causal effects and may prove especially useful in guiding new policy aimed at reducing discrimination. Multiple divisions and offices within the federal and local levels of government in the US conduct audits for the purpose of anti-discrimination enforcement, and findings from audits in the 1970s and 1980s helped strengthen the fair-housing enforcement system (Cherry and Bendick 2018; Yinger 1998). Researchers often wish to help identify illegal or discriminatory behavior in support of reforms that would curb it or to assess existing anti-discrimination policies. For example, a study's motivation, and many policymakers' concern, might be to identify how much anti-Black discrimination occurs in low-income rental housing markets in US cities and what policies can mitigate it. Scholars should consider building such tests of policy interventions into audit studies to increase the value of such projects.

At least two recent audit studies have tested whether targeted message interventions reduce discrimination. In an in-person audit study of rental housing in New York City, researchers worked with the city government to design and test two types of interventions (Fang, Guess, and Humphreys 2019). In the "monitoring condition," some landlords received a personalized phone message from a city employee reminding the landlord about fair-housing laws. In the "punitive condition," other landlords received a similar message with more details, including information about the monetary damages for engaging in illegal discrimination. Under both conditions, discrimination against Hispanic testers was attenuated, and in the monitoring condition, discrimination against Black testers was attenuated. In a correspondence audit of rental housing across ninety-two US cities, researchers implemented a similar messaging intervention (Murchie, Pang, and Schwegman 2021). The authors found that the intervention attenuated discrimination for Black men and to a lesser degree for Black women, but that there was a quick fade-out effect of the intervention.

Promising new versions of the correspondence audit may present a pathway for researchers to examine discrimination in other stages of housing exchange. For example, to examine discrimination in college admissions, some researchers have emailed admissions counselors with basic questions (Hanson 2017; Thornhill 2019). A normal correspondence audit, however, cannot examine actual admissions outcomes since a researcher would be forced to somehow fake key information like high school transcripts and SAT scores. A recent study found a creative way around this obstacle by recruiting real subjects who were matched on similar characteristics and then applied to colleges using their own accurate information (Stewart and Uggen 2020). This "modified audit" design could be used in housing studies of discrimination to examine the stages of mortgage approval, appraisals, and reference checks, among others. Researchers might recruit a team of real testers to use their own information in other stages of housing exchange.

Conclusion

Social scientists, fair-housing agencies, and the federal government have conducted housing audits, both in-person and correspondence versions, to examine discrimination in the US since the 1960s. These studies have consistently uncovered racial/ethnic discrimination in multiple stages and contexts of the housing exchange process. In recent years, scholars have expanded audits to include additional characteristics and contexts. Beyond traditional housing rental and sale audits, research has started to examine discrimination across three emerging areas of audits: Housing Choice Vouchers, short-term rentals, and roommate searches. These audits have uncovered new discrimination on the basis of race/ethnicity, SES, and disability status.

We suggest that scholars looking to conduct their own audits of housing discrimination should integrate core questions from the sociology of housing into their designs. Specifically, they should engage questions about whether and why discrimination varies by geography and neighborhood context, how housing discrimination changes individual preferences and creates cumulative disadvantage, and what mechanisms lead to housing discrimination. These questions remain relatively underexplored in the audit literature, and scholars might address them either through innovative or modified audits or by combining other methods with audits.

Researchers should carefully consider other design issues, such as the choice of pairing correspondence, the best method for signaling characteristics, and the population to which they can generalize their results. Additionally, while some stages of the housing exchange process lend themselves well to auditing, researchers should consider whether they can implement a modified audit in other stages to expand knowledge of discrimination in housing. Future experiments should also include experimental treatments to test for ways to reduce discrimination and additional data beyond the experimental data to test for mechanisms of discrimination. If researchers follow these and other new paths, the next decade will likely bring significant advances in our understanding of housing discrimination.

PART II
Housing Insecurity and Instability

8

Centering the Institutional Life of Eviction

Kyle Nelson and Michael C. Lens

Eviction has long been a critical problem for tenants facing it, landlords initiating it, social movements fighting it, and lawyers litigating it. Until Desmond's *Evicted: Poverty and Profit in the American City* in 2016, however, eviction existed as a "hidden housing problem" in academic research (Hartman and Robinson 2003). That does not mean that sociologists never studied eviction, nor that eviction is historically a rare phenomenon (cf. Desmond 2016). Sociologists have long studied eviction in adjacent research into residential mobility, slum housing, housing precarity, urban renewal, gentrification, and social movements. What *is* new is sociologists' understanding of eviction as a primary mechanism in reproducing economic, housing, gender, and racial inequalities in urban neighborhoods across the United States (Desmond 2016). In this chapter, we situate eviction research within a broader sociology of housing. Crucially, eviction informs the sociology of housing by illuminating the causes and consequences of losing it.

What is eviction? Following Hartman and Robinson (2003, 462–67), we define eviction as a process whereby a landlord or landowner dispossesses occupants of their homes. We choose this phrasing to avoid conflating the broader social phenomenon of eviction with its legal-bureaucratic realities in the United States (see Weinstein 2021; Nelson et al. 2021b). For example, our definition is inclusive of formal and informal evictions (Desmond and Shollenberger 2015) as well as legal and illegal ones. This definition includes eviction occurring via processes like mortgage foreclosure (Stout 2019), eminent domain (Gans 1962), third-party policing (Kurwa 2015), and disciplinary housing policies (King 2010). While not all are eviction in a legal sense, these cases highlight myriad ways that the threat of housing loss shapes peoples' experiences of place, home, and identity, bridging the phenomenology of dispossession with macrostructural analyses of land ownership, power, and urban political economy (Nelson 2022).

These examples are connected by the legal-bureaucratic institutions that play essential roles in legitimating a fundamental power imbalance whereby owners' property claims supersede occupants'. In the United States, property has long afforded owners privileges from formal citizenship to enfranchisement, as well as the power to write the rules of the game while mobilizing institutions (from law to politics) to maintain their interests (e.g., Nedelsky 1990). The historical nature of these entitlements is exemplified by not only the pursuit of and reification of private property, but also by the tremendous imbalance between federal support for homeowners and that for renters (McCabe 2016; Taylor 2019; Rosen 2020). Thus, eviction (and how we analyze it as a sociological object) lays bare fundamental inequalities in ordinary peoples' abilities to formally make claims to place and home in ways that are both culturally taken for granted and institutionally sanctioned.

In the sections below, we first review eviction research in sociology, which has traditionally focused on eviction's *individual* life—particularly its social demography and tenants' outcomes—and eviction's relationship to the political economy of housing. We then discuss the methodological and interpretive benefits of studying eviction's *institutional* life, a new approach that, among other things, complements existing research while eliding ongoing data challenges in this burgeoning field. Specifically, drawing on insights from our research studying eviction case processing, we show how incorporating analyses of eviction's institutional life into future research benefits qualitative and quantitative sociologists alike.

Eviction's Individual Life, Past and Present

Many studies of eviction use the language of "crisis" (e.g., Desmond 2016), but a relatively neglected body of research from the late nineteenth century to the present suggests that housing precarity and eviction, in particular, are normal, rather than dysfunctional, elements of urban housing markets (e.g., Du Bois 1899). Thus, instead of asking why eviction is happening *now*, a sociological lens asks why eviction has persisted across time and place, policy context, and legal regime.

After a flurry of sociological research on housing insecurity at the turn of the twentieth century, however, subsequent eviction research appeared primarily in law reviews and policy-oriented journals, focusing on eviction's prevalence and the inequities endemic to eviction case processing in courts (see reviews in McCarthy 1979, Hartman and Robinson 2003, Engler 2009). By 2012, however, sociologists "rediscovered" eviction and confirmed insights into what we call eviction's "individual life." "Individual life" research primarily focuses on eviction's social demography and how eviction affects peoples' life chances, where researchers analyze eviction as an outcome or as a social mechanism explaining variation in outcomes.

Research on eviction's social demography is remarkably consistent, as analysts continue to confirm a core empirical finding in increasingly expansive data sets: eviction as an outcome is unequally distributed in the population. Black tenants, in particular, face eviction in US housing courts across the United States far more often than other sociodemographic groups (Desmond and Gershenson 2017; McCabe and Rosen 2020; Hepburn, Louis, and Desmond 2020). Increasingly, researchers find that Latinx tenants are also overrepresented in eviction rolls in United States cities, suggesting that groups that are socially marginalized are more likely to face eviction than more socially advantaged groups in a given metropolitan area (Crowell and Nkosi 2020; Kim, Garcia, and Brewer 2021).

The literature makes clear that race matters, but the likelihood of being evicted is also a function of gender identity and family status. Confirming observations first made by Bezdek (1992), newer quantitative research finds that women, particularly Black and Latinx women, are far more likely to be evicted than women in other racial groups and men of any racial group (Desmond 2012; Desmond and Gershenson 2017; Hepburn, Louis, and Desmond 2020). Families with children are also at increased risk of eviction relative to families without children (Desmond et al. 2013; Lundberg and Donnelly 2019). While this research primarily focuses on compositional effects rather than causal claims, it nevertheless illuminates potential relationships between eviction, housing discrimination, and enforcement of anti-discrimination housing laws.

To date, however, few studies have seriously evaluated the extent to which racial and gender discrimination explain discrepancies in eviction filing outcomes. In an ethnographic study of landlords and tenants in Milwaukee, however, Desmond (2012) provides evidence that gender and race-based discrimination, in tandem with broader structural factors, explain landlords' eviction decisions and Black women's overrepresentation on eviction dockets. In a quantitative analysis, Greenberg, Gershenson, and Desmond (2016) show that racial discrimination explains why Latinx tenants in Milwaukee are evicted in higher numbers from predominantly white neighborhood than from less segregated neighborhoods. Others note that unequal enforcement of housing policies such as nuisance ordinances (Desmond and Valdez 2013), regulations against "unauthorized tenants, crime and drugs" (Kurwa 2020b), and discriminatory third-party policing (Kurwa 2015) may explain divergent eviction outcomes among demographic groups.

Another body of research situates eviction as a mechanism in explaining variation in tenants' life chances by showing how eviction shapes tenants' housing, health, and employment-related outcomes (DeLuca and Rosen 2022). Starting from the influential finding that eviction is a mechanism explaining the reproduction of urban poverty (Desmond 2012), research shows that experiencing an eviction puts tenants at risk of negative mental and physical health outcomes (Desmond and Kimbro 2015), employment insecurity (Desmond and Gershenson 2016), family instability (Desmond, Gershenson, and Kiviat 2015), and prolonged housing insecurity (Desmond 2016), among other effects. Many of these effects emerge as tenants work to secure subsequent housing with evictions on their record, a mark affixed to their credit reports that many landlords use to disqualify rental housing applicants (Kleysteuber 2006). Not only is eviction unequally distributed in the population, its effects further reproduce inequalities in tenants' lives long after "eviction events" conclude.

Eviction and the Political Economy of Housing

Eviction also fundamentally exists in relation to broader political economies of housing. While common sense suggests that macroeconomic dynamics drive filing trends (Lens et al. 2020), research into eviction filings must consider the political contexts and economic calculus scaffolding landlords' decision-making processes (Burawoy 2017). At risk is conflating eviction filings, which do not automatically result in lockouts, with eviction's broader economic, political, and social realities (Nelson et al. 2021b). Where formal evictions filed through the legal system may be low, for example, official statistics may not capture the reality of informal evictions that circumvent the legal system (Gromis and Desmond 2021). In Los Angeles, for example, low eviction filing volume likely reflects higher costs of filing rather than a decreased prevalence of housing insecurity and precarity (Lens et al. 2020; Nelson et al. 2021a, 2021b).

Garboden and Rosen (2019) describe a different filing dynamic—serial filing—where landlords use the legal system to coerce tenants into paying rent or discipline them into being "ideal" tenants. In jurisdictions with high court filing fees, however, serial eviction is less prevalent (see also McCabe and Rosen 2020; Leung, Hepburn, and Desmond 2021). The phenomenon of serial eviction is an important rejoinder to overly economistic portrayals of housing markets because it shows how legal systems, landlords' biases, and tenant protection policies differentially shape landlords' eviction filing decision-making processes. Eviction in these cases may have little to do with "removal." Instead, landlords exploit the legal system to collect rent and/or harass tenants (Garboden and Rosen 2019; Rosen and Garboden 2022).

In the tradition of Gans (1972), serial filing illustrates eviction's functional relationship with the political economy of housing, as well as the broader fields of municipal finance and state bureaucracy, where legal fees can generate significant revenue. A related literature, however, describes the workings of the "eviction economy," an economy of services ancillary to the legal eviction process but essential in enacting eviction (Purser 2016). Seymour and Akers (2021), for example, show how the foreclosure crisis presented an investment opportunity for a new generation of landlords who transformed "tax-reverted properties" into profitable, oftentimes low-rent rental housing stock (see also Fields 2018). Foreclosure is not only a form of eviction in and of itself, but it also enables a predatory economy where occupants, either renters or underwater owners, become targets of eviction.

Lax government regulation exacerbated the foreclosure crisis, but public agencies themselves also commonly evict tenants (Harrison et al. 2021) and may also influence the likelihood of eviction through housing and land use policy. Sullivan (2018) powerfully shows how state-driven affordable housing development and changing land use dynamics along peripheral urban areas have resulted in mass trailer park evictions when governments target these parcels for affordable housing and commercial-retail development. Lundberg and colleagues (2020) argue that subsidized housing generally shields low-income populations from eviction, though public housing agencies do evict, and at similar rates as the private rental industry (Gromis, Hendrickson, and Desmond 2022).

Finally, sociologists have analyzed how transformations in the landlording industry have affected eviction dynamics. Whereas most sociological research focuses on "mom and pop" landlords operating in low-income neighborhoods (e.g., Desmond 2016), these landlords are being replaced by a new class—typically referred to as institutional investors, corporate landlords, or large owners—who view rental property as an investment vehicle as much as housing (Lee 2017; Ferrer 2021), are less lenient than mom-and-pops when it comes to serving tenants with eviction lawsuits (Raymond et al. 2018), and are more likely to serially file on tenants (Immergluck et al. 2020; McCabe and Rosen 2020). Thus, changing material conditions in rental properties owned by institutional investors are slowly starting to shift commonsense notions about how and why eviction occurs in the United States.

Eviction's Institutional Life

Building on an extensive body of research in law journals, one promising direction for sociologists studying eviction involves analyzing what we refer to as eviction's "institutional life" (Nelson et al. 2021b). Distinct from aforementioned research on eviction's individual life, research into eviction's institutional life centers analyses on institutional forces shaping eviction case processing, case outcomes, and tenants' experiences of eviction. Our definition of "institutional" is intentionally broad, including state bureaucratic organizations that process evictions and related housing issues like courts, housing authorities, and code-enforcement departments; social movements contesting eviction; the political coalitions comprised of advocacy organizations, law firms, and tenants' unions, on the one hand, and landlords' interest groups, on the other; and state bureaucracies (e.g., law enforcement organizations), institutional investors, and contracted laborers comprising "eviction economies." In exploring eviction's institutional life, researchers might incorporate insights from diverse fields like organizational sociology (e.g., Powell and DiMaggio 1991), law and society (e.g., Sarat 2004), and ethnomethodology (e.g., Garfinkel 1967).

Likewise, researching eviction's institutional life also entails analyses of institutional forms of social action, particularly the strategies tenants, landlords, lawyers, caseworkers, and street-level bureaucrats use to navigate eviction case processing, and how interactional and institutional determinants of eviction outcomes vary by actor, organization, and jurisdiction. For example, eviction outcomes are shaped by institutionally grounded processes that make the civil justice system a site in which existing social inequalities are reproduced and amplified (e.g., Sandefur 2008). One set of explanations as to why suggests that tenants are likely to lose cases by default—or as a result of failing to file an answer or appear at a court date—when cases are complex (Larson 2006), when legal procedure is unintelligible (Steinberg 2015), and when litigants have had frustrating appearances with the legal system in the past (Sandefur 2007). Others, however, show that tenants rarely win in court because while most landlords are represented by lawyers, few tenants go to court with legal counsel (Seron et al. 2001). In this research, enduring "access to justice" gaps explain why so few tenants successfully defend themselves against eviction, though researchers can only speculate about the precise social mechanisms shaping associations (Greiner, Pattanayak, and Hennessy 2013; Sandefur 2015).

While qualitative researchers may struggle to identify broader trends in eviction filings and outcomes, they can illuminate the social mechanisms and institutional contexts that explain how *and* why the broader trends exist that quantitative researchers observe. Nelson (2022) describes how informal dimensions of eviction case processing became institutionalized in Los Angeles, California, and explores how these institutional idiosyncrasies shape both tenants' responses to their landlords' lawsuits and eviction defense lawyers' expertise in settlement negotiations. Two institutional factors are particularly consequential in Los Angeles. First, eviction case processing occurs in the eviction hub, a regional network of courtrooms dispersed throughout Los Angeles County, in a "master calendar court" configuration. Second, eviction case processing occurs on an accelerated timeline, different from other forms of civil litigation, necessitating that tenants respond to their landlords' lawsuits within five court business days.

These factors generate institutional configurations that explain important variation in eviction case outcomes, as well as their underlying sociological meanings. For example, tenants actively troubleshooting eviction lawsuits may nevertheless default, as they do not have time to shift their understanding of "housing trouble" to align with the court's definition of an eviction before the court-mandated five-day response window expires. While some eviction default outcomes may represent tenants' nonparticipation (e.g., Larson 2006), the first author's ethnographic study of eviction's institutional life in tenants'-rights clinics shows how time and space pressures generated from these institutional configurations make default outcomes likely even as tenants actively troubleshoot the cases against them (Nelson 2021).

If tenants avoid default, then courts assign landlords and tenants trial dates. Instead of remaining cases being adjudicated at trial, however, most will settle due to institutionalized informal settlement negotiations. Plaintiffs' lawyers tend to coerce tenants without lawyers into accepting disadvantageous settlements (Summers 2022), but tenants with lawyers may be able to use the legal process to their advantage. They are able to do so because the eviction hub described above processes cases in a master calendar court configuration where cases originate in one courtroom and are tried in another. As a result, a backlog builds as cases must first be approved for advancement in one courtroom before being "sent out" to another. Since landlords' lawyers typically charge their clients hourly or by session (and tenants' lawyers are either free or fixed fee), the legal process can become costly for landlords when tenants have lawyers by their side. Whereas time pressures make default outcomes likely for tenants at T_1, they can help eviction defense lawyers construct leverage in difficult-to-win cases at T_2, incentivizing landlords and their lawyers to settle on terms that can be favorable to tenants (or risk the uncertainty inherent in letting judges and juries determine case outcomes at trial). Though only an estimated 9 to 11 percent of tenants go to court with lawyers, defense lawyers are able to turn a punishing process into a possibility for tenants to keep their homes in an uncompromising housing market (Nelson 2022).

As noted above, landlords in Baltimore, Cleveland, and Dallas—places with vastly different institutional configurations from Los Angeles—use the courts to enact "serial filing." In some jurisdictions that enable serial filing, there is evidence that some landlords use the eviction process disciplinarily, to collect rental arrears or to harass tenants by threatening them with eviction. In Los Angeles, however, formal evictions may be more likely to result in displacement because going to court is far more expensive in LA than in other areas (e.g., Nelson et al. 2021b, 704). Thus, while evictions are processed similarly across jurisdictions, formal and informal elements of institutional configurations vary significantly in ways that shape the social meanings of eviction outcomes, as well as lawyers' and tenants' strategies for navigating case processing in state bureaucracies like civil courts.

The Eviction Data Problem

The lack of comprehensive and consistent data on eviction has long been a major obstacle to incorporating eviction into the sociology of housing. New efforts such as the Eviction Lab at Princeton (Desmond et al. 2018) and the Anti-Eviction Mapping Project have addressed this lack in part by cataloging eviction events across time and place. But these efforts leave important gaps that sociologists must address if they are to quantitatively analyze eviction's forms (e.g., Aiello et al. 2018; Porton, Gromis, and Desmond 2021). Chief concerns are data availability, comparability, and accuracy, all of which are complicated by concerns over privacy.

Every jurisdiction with property taxation authority maintains reliable property ownership records, but there is no analogous administrative data system that collects data on rents, tenants, and landlords. Oddly, the very bureaucracies tasked with processing eviction are rarely able to account for anything beyond the number of eviction filings. Furthermore, while the US Census Bureau estimates the number of rental units and reports median rents by various levels of geography, these rents are self-reported by tenants and subject to measurement error and time lag. When scholars fail to critically engage these data, they all too often reify "official statistics," conflating them with the underlying processes that they putatively represent (Kitsuse and Cicourel 1963).

This lack of comprehensive data on rental units has led some to call for rent registries, which several jurisdictions have adopted thus far (Phillips 2020). A rent registry can provide researchers with the universe of rental agreements, with potential to observe rent prices, lease duration, and importantly for eviction scholars, how each lease term ended. Scholars can then know the share of rental arrangements that ended through some form of involuntary displacement, and potentially the reasons for that displacement. At present, these data do not exist, even for public housing or units under rent control, meaning credible estimates on eviction's prevalence (in its many forms) vary considerably, with much error (Gromis and Desmond 2021). The lack of comprehensive data negatively impacts not only scholars, but also advocates and policymakers, who find it very difficult to estimate the scope of the eviction problem and to progress toward alleviating it.

Inconsistent data collection processes make it difficult to compare eviction outcomes across jurisdictions, which matters because eviction's institutional life varies so much (Nelson et al. 2021b). For example, variation in eviction case processing may be attributable to state and local laws and policy frameworks, such as tenants' rights and housing policies (Hatch 2017). Thus, even data on eviction filings may not be comparable across jurisdictions with different filing incentives arising from variation in legal protections and rent caps (Nelson et al. 2021b). Comparison difficulty is further compounded by variation in housing markets, which is vast (Garboden and Rosen 2019; Leung, Hepburn, and Desmond 2021). This is not to say that comparison is impossible or a worthless endeavor, but rather that it must be empirically grounded in sociological analyses of eviction case processing.

The Eviction Lab has worked to overcome issues of availability, completeness, and comparability in the collection and dissemination of eviction data. Much of this work entails making data from third-party vendors available to scholars, advocates, and the public. In many ways, these data help overcome many of the problems discussed above (Leung, Hepburn, and Desmond 2021). In practice, however, even these data are often inaccurate and incomplete. Porton, Gromis, and Desmond (2021) discuss the inherent inaccuracies in court records and the implications for tenants and scholars. They find that an average of 22 percent of eviction records are either ambiguous or incorrect about case resolution, which, aside from causing problems for researchers, threatens tenants' ability to obtain lease applications years down the line. To what extent has data inaccuracy compromised sociological research on and understandings of eviction? In our experience, combining the expertise of qualitative and

quantitative researchers offers one way to account for eviction's data quality problem by specifying the strengths and weaknesses of data sources
and anticipating how they may bias research findings (e.g., Lens et al. 2020;
Nelson et al. 2021a).

Once more, particularly in states like California that seal records when
tenants successfully fight against an unlawful detainer petition, these records are incomplete. Record sealing laws are essential to protecting tenants from having eviction filings attached to their rental histories, where
they could be (legally) discriminated against by future potential landlords
(Kleysteuber 2006). However, sealing bedevils quantitative researchers,
advocates, and policymakers alike in their attempts to discern whether
eviction filings are increasing in particular jurisdictions and the factors
motivating filing trends. It also makes it difficult to study several eviction
phenomena, including serial filing, relationships between housing conditions and filings, and factors associated with successful tenant outcomes
at court. That said, these data challenges only limit a subset of quantitative
research. Qualitative research, particularly ethnographic, interview-based,
and archival analysis, can uncover important eviction insights despite
these limitations to administrative data access (e.g., Desmond 2016; Nelson 2021; Garboden and Rosen 2019)

Eviction outside the Courts

Landlords use many means—legal or not—to evict tenants and get out of
leases they do not want. This reality presents an additional layer of complexity when trying to assess eviction's prevalence and who is being evicted
when. An example of eviction that operates outside the court system, but is
entirely legal, exists in California through the state's Ellis Act (1985).[1] The
act allows landlords to evict tenants legally if their petitions to do so are
approved by local housing agencies. Typically, landlords file Ellis Act petitions to exit the rental market through condo conversion, redevelopment,
or sale of land or property, while circumventing eviction court. Reporting
requirements make these data available to scholars and advocates, but various agencies, sometimes within the same jurisdiction (e.g., Los Angeles
County), collect these data in different forms that make them difficult to
locate. Only recently have scholars and advocates began accessing these
data and using them to monitor tenant displacement (Nelson et al. 2021a).

---

[1] Ellis Act evictions are part of a larger category of "no-fault evictions" where landlords
may evict tenants without alleging a lease breach (Nelson et al. 2021a).

Other forms of eviction that frequently go undetected are almost entirely out of the reach of researchers. Landlords may induce tenants to leave for several reasons: perhaps the market is hot, or they have some retaliatory and/or predatory scheme to shake down tenants unaware of their rights (which depending on the jurisdiction, may or may not be very extensive) (Garboden and Rosen 2019). Reliable estimates of these forms of displacement are hard to come by. One attempt suggests that informal evictions may indeed be more prevalent than formal ones. Gromis and Desmond (2021), for example, comparing data from the Eviction Lab and the American Housing Survey (AHS), estimate that there are 5.5 informal evictions for every formal eviction filed.[2]

Conclusion

Eviction research has already produced important insights into eviction's individual life—particularly its social demography and effects on tenants' life chances—and its relation to the broader political economies of housing. This literature has refocused scholarly attention in sociology and other disciplines on a social problem that researchers as recently as twenty years ago described as hidden. Studies of eviction are now contributing valuable insights into research on housing markets and residential mobility by illustrating a common mechanism through which tenants are coerced into moving. We argue that centering eviction's institutional life generates a perspective that can address many of the questions left over in extant research while illuminating exciting directions for future research. Engaging with institutional perspectives situates eviction research in both the broader sociology of housing and within empirical and theoretical

---

[2] Desmond and Shollenberger (2015) use Milwaukee Area Renters Survey (MARS) data, a precursor to the Eviction Lab data set, to further elucidate the limitations of the AHS. MARS could be a source for evaluating the commonality of eviction over time, but the questions in this survey have been criticized as not likely to capture evictions in a consistent way (Desmond 2016). The most pertinent question traditionally asks tenants to choose among several "main reason(s) for moving," of which eviction is only one option. The question does not distinguish between formal and informal evictions. Depending on how respondents interpret the question, it could be overcounting formal, court-based evictions or undercounting informal evictions (Desmond and Shollenberger 2015). While the new AHS "eviction module" better approximates the frequency of informal eviction, researchers note that it likely undercounts formal evictions when compared to estimates by the Eviction Lab (Gromis and Desmond 2021; see also Collyer, Friedman, and Wimer 2021).

traditions in other disciplinary subfields from law and society to the sociology of organizations, occupations, and work.

Furthermore, adopting an institutional perspective will enable sociologists to address long-standing methodological challenges inherent to studying social problems using administrative data (Kitsuse and Cicourel 1963). Better and more accessible administrative data alone cannot solve the problems motivating researchers in a given field, but we show how qualitative and quantitative sociologists can collaboratively use disciplinary perspectives and tools to address these limitations in practice. Researchers must comparatively and critically analyze how institutional factors shape eviction case processing dynamics, documentation and measurement practices, and meanings of outcomes produced in administrative data sets. Doing so enables a distinctly sociological analysis of an enduring social problem while contributing to the resurgence of sociological research on housing.

9

Manufactured Housing in the US

A CRITICAL AFFORDABLE HOUSING INFRASTRUCTURE

Esther Sullivan

Sociological scholarship on affordable housing has largely focused on government-subsidized housing and housing assistance programs. However, the last four decades of US housing policy have successively chipped away federal funding for affordable housing, so that today less than 2 percent of the nation lives in public housing and only one in four households that qualifies for federal housing assistance receives it (HUD n.d.). In an era of federal disinvestment in housing production and assistance, unsubsidized modes of affordable housing are more important to low-income residents and should be more central to the sociology of housing.

Manufactured housing (MH) is one of the largest sources of unsubsidized affordable housing in the US (CFED 2010). Its affordability comes from economies of scale in the factory production process, rather than from federal or state subsidies. MH costs less than half as much as traditional site-built housing per square foot (US Commerce Department 2010). The US Census Bureau (2019a) estimates 17.5 million Americans live in manufactured homes, also called mobile homes or trailers. Entities like the Manufactured Housing Institute (MHI) and the Urban Institute cite this figure much higher—at twenty-two million, indicating a lack of basic understanding and systematic data on this housing type (Choi et al. 2019, MHI 2020). Throughout the 1980s, MH was the fastest-growing housing type in the US (Scommegna 2004). In the 1990s, manufactured homes were responsible for 66 percent of new affordable housing produced in the US (Apgar et al. 2002). MH is also a primary vehicle for low-income homeownership. In 2011, 70 percent of all homes sold under $125,000 were manufactured homes (MHI 2012). Yet manufactured homeownership has critical differences from traditional homeownership and all manufactured homes (whether owned or rented) face challenges that are both unique to this type of housing and that offer broader lessons for the sociology of housing.

This chapter explores distinct dimensions of MH including: the social stigma surrounding the housing form; the legal and policy factors that contribute to its marginality; the resulting spatial inequalities that impact its residents; the risk of eviction for residents living in manufactured home parks; and the financialization of MH communities, including the links between financialization and housing insecurity. Beyond being a source of shelter, MH is a cultural artifact, imbued with meaning, status, and stigma. Few other housing forms are as widely vilified as "trailer park" housing. This stigma shapes subjective perceptions of MH and its residents, as well as objective treatments of MH in planning regulations.

In this way MH is also a socio-legal object: a range of codes, ordinances, and zoning regulations structure whether, where, and how MH can be located and positioned relative to "conventional" housing. Over the last century, these planning practices have segregated and marginalized MH. The implications are far-reaching, as this chapter explores: manufactured homes are clustered into informal subdivisions and mobile home parks where they are exposed to environmental hazards as well as, in the latter case, insecure land tenure that predisposes residents to eviction. Despite this unequal cultural, legal, and spatial treatment, MH remains crucial to US households jostling to secure housing they can afford during a continued national affordable housing crisis. This fact has not gone unnoticed by private investors, who are consolidating ownership of manufactured home parks under corporate, institutional, and private-equity investment. This process has important parallels to the financialization of housing more broadly and corporate ownership expanding within other affordable housing stocks. In these ways, manufactured housing is a site where housing studies intersect with the sociology of culture, community, and a range of social, spatial, and economic inequalities.

Stigma and Spatial Marginality

Despite its central role in affordable housing in the US, manufactured housing occupies a marginalized sector of the housing market and an almost completely ignored area of study within the sociology of housing. MH is socially stigmatized in tropes of seedy "trailer trash" residents and seedier "trailer parks" where manufactured homes are often located. MH is also spatially stigmatized by a century of urban land use regulations that have segregated and marginalized MH, clustered MH into manufactured home parks (MHPs), and contributed to patterned spatial inequalities for MH residents.

While the term "mobile home" is commonly used to describe these homes, the term is a misnomer that has led to significant confusion about the *immobility* of MH and its widespread use as *permanent* affordable housing. Technically the term "mobile home" refers to a prefabricated home built before 1976 when the National Manufactured Housing Construction and Safety Standards Act (the "HUD code") went into effect. Homes built after that date should be referred to as "manufactured homes," which are post-1976 housing units built in a factory and then transported on a permanent chassis to be placed on a foundation on site. While these homes are constructed on a chassis that allows them to be transported, modern MH is designed to be permanent housing and is meant to be "mobile" only this once, from the factory to the site of installation. The Manufactured Housing Institute estimates that 90 percent of MH is never moved after it is installed.

The innovative affordability of MH means that it houses a disproportionately low-income population. The median annual household income for MH residents is $28,400 compared to a national median of $52,250; more than 22 percent of MH residents have incomes at or below the federal poverty line (Fannie Mae 2019). Importantly, MH is made even more affordable when located in MHPs, where residents can place manufactured homes on rented lots. Indeed, in MHPs, poverty rates are higher. Durst and Sullivan (2019) estimate 31 percent of MHP households are living in poverty. While these communities offer a deeply affordable housing option, the segregation of MH into MHPs and away from other housing forms contributes to a pervasive stigma surrounding the housing form.

My own work ties MH stigma to the political economy of regional land markets and the regulatory processes that shape them. Through an architectural and legal history of trailers, mobile homes, and manufactured housing, my book *Manufactured Insecurity* (Sullivan 2018) traces how a century of restrictive planning regulations resulted in the spatial containment and social marginalization of MH. This "sociospatial stigma" began not long after the invention of the first travel trailers of the 1920s, which were a luxury item of the very wealthy who could afford an automobile to tow an "auto camper" (Wallis 1991). But the Great Depression–era use of mobile homes as low-cost permanent housing fueled resistance to the homes and their residents. City councils across the nation responded to public objections by enacting restrictive ordinances and exclusionary zoning for MH. These actions followed the late-nineteenth-century precedent of using zoning regulations to exclude socially undesirable ethnic minorities, pushing them into Chinatowns and other ethnic enclaves (Bernhardt

1981). As MH grew in numbers during the 1950s and 1960s, so did ordinances, covenants, and municipal regulations that restricted the placement of MH (Sullivan 2018).

This treatment continues in planning policies today. Jurisdictions restrict the placement of MH and the development and location of MHPs
through a variety of planning and regulatory tools (Dawkins and Koebel 2010). A legal analysis of MH zoning nationwide finds manufactured
homes "face insurmountable zoning barriers in many states," including
total exclusion, exclusion from residential zones, exclusionary use of aesthetic standards, and requirements that MH be restricted to manufactured
housing parks (Mandelker 2016, 278). As a result, the American Planning
Association found that MH is relegated to undesirable nonresidential areas and "mislocated' on inferior lands in commercial and industrial zones
(Sanders 1986).

Much of the existing research on MH revolves around the symbolic dimensions of trailer park life, focusing on the cultural elements of the housing form and the experience of social stigma for residents. Those interested
in the symbolic dimensions of housing have explored the ubiquity of mass
media and popular-culture imagery that depicts MH residents as transient,
destitute, and morally deficient (Kusenbach 2009), the essential elements
of so-called trailer trash. The epithet "trailer trash" can be understood as
a racialized concept, which "marks out certain whites as a breed apart, a
dysgenic race to themselves" (Wray and Newitz 1997, 2). In their comparative ethnography of white, African American, and Latino/a MHPs,
Salamon and MacTavish show that the trailer trash image does not impart
that "particular sting" for African American and Latino/a MH households
as it does for whites (2017, p. 122). Indeed, Latino/a manufactured homeowners experience upward mobility and see MH ownership as "a positive
marker of their personal and collective identities" (Kusenbach 2017, 30).

This research on the symbolic dimensions of MH shows that the experience of housing stigma is complex and is felt differently across racial and
ethnic groups. As noted, manufactured homes make up the vast majority
of very low-cost new homes (70 percent of homes sold under $125,000)
(MHI 2012). Achieving the status of homeownership may counter the
stigma of trailer housing for Latino/a households. While whites remain
the largest share of MH residents (69 percent are non-Hispanic white),
nationally Latino/a households and American Indian or Native Alas-
kan households make up a greater share of MH owners than site-built
homeowners. For instance, while MH accounts for only 5.4 percent of US
homeownership, among Latino/a households MH accounts for close to
10 percent (Reed and Ryan 2021), making it an important component of

growing Latino/a homeownership (see Hyde and Fischer, this volume). The opposite is true for African Americans and Asians, who are under-represented among MH residents compared to site-built residents (CFPB 2014). The low representation of African Americans in MH may be related to the large share of homeowners living in manufactured housing (nationally about 68 percent of MH households are homeowners) coupled with the lower representation of African Americans among homeowners due to the legacy of racially discriminatory housing policy in the US.

In light of the stigmatized place of MH in the pantheon of housing types and the patterned inequalities facing MH discussed below, it is clear that the demographic makeup of MH residents is a site where the sociology of race and ethnicity and the sociology of housing meet. Understanding how access or preference drives certain groups into MH ownership is especially important considering growing rates of MH home purchases among African American and Latino/a households, which have well surpassed rates for whites in recent decades (Apgar et al. 2002). Given the spatial inequalities discussed below, sociologists of race and ethnicity may consider how low-cost manufactured homeownership contributes to the reproduction of historic housing disparities, such as neighborhood access and wealth generation.

Segregation and Spatial Inequality

The cultural stigma that surrounds MH and the exclusionary planning practices that relegate MH to less desirable locations have resulted in spatial patterns where MH is segregated from traditional owned and rented housing: clustered alongside other manufactured housing and located in areas where residents are exposed to significant sociospatial inequalities. These spatial inequalities demonstrate why housing arrangements matter for sociology; in the case of MH they structure access to basic resources such as water and exposure to environmental hazards such as natural disasters.

Durst and Sullivan (2019) demonstrate that nationally manufactured housing is highly segregated from other types of housing. Of the nearly seven million occupied MH units in the country, approximately 69 percent are located within a half block of another manufactured home, while only 4 percent of conventional owner and renter housing units are located within a half block of MH. In other words, the vast majority of MH is grouped together and segregated from other types of housing, both owned and rented.

On top of this high degree of segregation, MH is clustered into two distinct community types: *manufactured home parks* (MHPs) and *informal subdivisions* (ISes). Durst and Sullivan (2019) estimate that 2.7 million MH units, 39 percent of all occupied MH, are located in MHPs, while nearly 2.1 million, 30 percent of all occupied MH, are located in ISes. As described above, MHPs are private businesses owned by private landlords where homeowners *rent* lots to place their homes, even though the vast majority of MHP households are homeowners.[1] ISes are rural residential subdivisions where developers subdivide and sell plots of land to homeowners under minimal regulatory control and with little infrastructure (often lacking paved roads, streetlights, sewer service, and sometimes even piped water and electricity) (Durst 2018; Durst and Ward 2015). IS residents utilize manufactured housing or rely on "self-help"—building the home themselves over years—often using manufactured homes in the interim period or as part of their final housing design (Durst 2018). Durst and Sullivan (2019) highlight that ISes serve as one of the most affordable housing options in the US and an important means of low-income homeownership. Informal subdivisions have been studied as *colonias* along the US-Mexico border, where 19.2 percent of the occupied housing stock is MH (HAC 2012). *Colonias* are defined narrowly by federal and state law as low-income informal neighborhoods built before 1990 and located within 150 miles of the US-Mexico border.[2] The term "informal subdivision" expands this limited policy definition and is used more broadly to include both *colonias* as well as neighborhoods with similar characteristics that were developed after 1990 and outside 150 miles of the US-Mexico border (Durst 2015; Durst and Ward 2015).

More than two-thirds of all occupied MH in the country is clustered in these two community types, which should make them key sites of interest for both sociologists of housing and environmental sociologists. The clustering of MH into MHPs and ISes is important because both communities are associated with distinct spatial inequalities. Below I discuss two examples—access to clean water and sanitation and exposure to environmental hazards—to illustrate the nature of these spatial inequities.

WATER INSECURITY

Safe and reliable water and sanitation are essential for health and well-being. This truth is being underscored by the COVID-19 pandemic at the

---

[1] A smaller subset of MHPs are cooperatively owned by residents, which provides protection against many of the predatory practices found in privately owned parks.

[2] Cranston-Gonzalez National Affordable Housing Act, S. 566, Texas 101st Congress (1989–1990), https://www.govtrack.us/congress/bills/101/s566.

same time as the extent of water insecurity in the US is being exposed by citizens and scholars alike. In the United States, an estimated 471,000 households or 1.1 million individuals experience water insecurity, defined as the absence of a piped water connection (Meehan et al. 2020). The primary household characteristics associated with water insecurity are fourfold: unplumbed households are more likely to be headed by people of color, earn lower incomes, rent their residence, and live in manufactured homes (Meehan et al. 2020). Manufactured homes are 2.5 times more likely to lack complete plumbing than other types of housing (Deitz and Meehan 2019). Living in a manufactured home is significantly, negatively correlated with water service reliability, even after controlling for other explanatory factors such as race and income (Pierce and Jimenez 2015).

The segregation of MH into MHPs and ISes likely plays a key role here. In the case of MHPs, private landlords own the land under residents' homes and have a financial incentive to limit investments and upgrades to MHP infrastructure. Water systems serving MHPs are more likely to be in violation of health standards (US Water Alliance 2019). In their study of Los Angeles County, Pierce, Gabbe, and Gonzales (2018) found that access to water was worse in MHPs than the county average. Nationally, households living in MH are nearly 20 percent more likely to have suffered a service shutoff than those living in other housing units; households in MHPs were over three times more likely than other households to experience at least one water outage a year (Pierce and Jimenez 2015). In 2012, the Environmental Protection Agency cited MHP landlords for more than 4,300 Clean Water Act violations at fifteen MHPs and more than nine hundred Safe Drinking Water Act violations at thirty MHPs in Pennsylvania alone (US EPA 2012).

Likewise, water insecurity has been well documented in *colonias* along the US-Mexico border, where inadequate water and sanitation are pervasive (Jepson and Vandewalle 2016). Water reliability also impacts residents across informal subdivisions, even newer non-*colonia* ISes with water and wastewater infrastructure, because households often cannot afford water connections (24 percent of IS respondents reported that they lived on the lot without water service for a period of time) (Durst and Ward, 2015). Since MHPs are often zoned out of residential zones and ISes develop in exurban and rural areas, both communities are often located in peripheral locations where the prohibitive costs of extending public services mean residents receive substandard services (Shen 2005, 4).

ENVIRONMENTAL HAZARDS

A range of studies has also demonstrated that MH tends to be located in more hazardous areas relative to site-built housing and thus is heavily impacted by environmental disasters. During Hurricane Andrew (1992) manufactured homes were twenty-one times more likely to be destroyed than site-built homes (Morrow 1999). This likelihood is not due to the structural characteristics of MH alone. One study in South Florida calculated that 33 percent of all manufactured homes in the area were in the hundred-year floodplain and 27 percent were in the storm surge zone (Prasad and Stoler 2016).

Policies that determine the location of MH likely play a key role in their vulnerability to environmental hazards. Shen's (2005) geospatial analysis of one North Carolina county finds that MH is not only sited on flood-prone land but is also located further from positive community facilities such as health care facilities, employment centers, and educational institutions as well as public services such as fire stations and police. Flanagan et al. (2011) argue that MH is less resilient to natural hazards because of its frequent location on the outskirts of cities and away from critical mitigating infrastructure. In Colorado, Rumbach, Sullivan, and Makarewicz (2019) demonstrate that MHPs were home to more socially vulnerable households and were exposed to flooding at a higher rate than housing generally; at the same time, MHPs were severely disadvantaged in post-disaster recovery policies.

The clustering of MH into these two community types calls for better data on both MHPs and ISes, as well as better analysis of segregation by housing type. Case study research on MHPs and ISes suggests that these communities are exposed to concentrated forms of economic, social, and environmental vulnerability. However, many of these studies have been done on a statewide or local scale. Currently there is no systematic national data on the locations of either community type, though roughly two-thirds of MH is located in these communities. The US census records data for mobile homes but does not differentiate between MH on privately owned lots, on owned lots in ISes, or on rented lots in MHPs. Machine learning and big data (a national data set of building footprints released by Microsoft) are opening up new avenues of research that may provide first-time systematic national data on MHPs (and ISes) in the US (Durst et al. 2021).

Eviction and Housing Insecurity

The clustering of MH into MHPs also has important implications for the housing security of millions of individuals living in the 2.7 million manufactured homes that are located in these land-lease communities. Eviction scholarship has documented the pervasiveness of eviction for renters in low-income urban communities (Desmond 2016). Evictions drain households' material resources and negatively impact physical and mental health for both adults and children, and these effects can endure for years following an eviction (Desmond and Kimbro 2015).

In MHPs, an estimated 80 percent of households are homeowners (HAC 2011), but as my own research shows, these lower-income home-owners are not protected from the impacts of eviction (Sullivan 2017, 2018). In MHPs, only about 14 percent of households also own the property under their homes; instead, most rent the lots where their homes are placed (HAC 2011). I conducted a comparative ethnography over seventeen consecutive months within closing MHPs in the two states with the largest MH populations (Texas and Florida) to document the unique challenges that individuals, households, and entire communities face during mass evictions from MHPs (Sullivan 2018). This ethnography centers *land tenure* in the analysis of eviction and reveals how the divided homeowner/land-renter tenure of MHP residents creates multiple forms of housing insecurity.

Homeowning households living on rented lots in MHPs lack many of the benefits associated with traditional homeownership, including both financial and residential stability. MHP households (even those that own their homes outright) are subject to frequent lot-rent increases and addi-tional, often arbitrary, park fees that escalate their monthly housing costs (PESP 2019; Consumers Union 2001). Landlords control investments in the property upkeep and infrastructure, an arrangement that impacts home values and likely contributes to the issues with water access and environmental hazards outlined above. Ultimately, because MHP prop-erties are owned by private landlords, they can legally close at any time, with only thirty days' notice to residents in many states. MHP closures are frequent, as urban redevelopment and suburban sprawl pressure landlords to sell or redevelop MHP properties. When MHPs close, residents strug-gle to move both themselves and their homes. Relocations can cost more than the homeowner paid for the home (estimates range from $5,000 to $15,000). According to one study, this cost represents five to seven years' worth of accrued equity for manufactured homeowners (CFED 2010).

Residents who are able to move their manufactured homes face seri-ous challenges relocating them. Current demand for affordable housing means vacancy rates in MHPs are commonly in the single digits. Because residents are evicted en masse when MHPs close, they must compete with each other for available lots in other MHPs. In my study, residents' rents doubled or even tripled in new MHPs, many of which were corporately owned. MHP closures set off a cycle of housing insecurity for many residents; they also seriously impacted residents' health and well-being and ruptured the social networks on which residents had formerly relied (Sullivan 2018).

Households who could not move their manufactured homes fared much worse than households who did relocate their homes. In the MHPs where I lived and was evicted alongside residents, about one-third of homes were deemed structurally unsound for a relocation. These residents lost their homes and all their accrued equity, sometimes selling homes to landlords for a fraction of their purchase price. Because many households owned their homes outright and paid only $200-$300 monthly lot rent, evicted residents searched but simply could not find comparable affordable alternatives. As others have documented in cases of housing insecurity, residents transitioned to doubling up with friends and family (Wright et al. 1998; Harvey and Perkins, this volume), to squatting (Herbert 2021), and to homelessness (Crane and Warnes 2000). For these MHP residents, the most fundamental benefits of homeownership—equity and shelter—were lost.

Private Equity and Manufactured Home Parks

Eviction is just one of the ways that MHP land tenure produces housing insecurity. Even when parks remain open, residents are subject to frequent rent hikes and predatory landlord practices. Salamon and MacTavish (2017) use the concept of the Mobile Home Industrial Complex to describe the interrelated functions of mobile home manufacturers/sellers, lenders, MHP owners, and managers. This web of actors presents MHPs as an affordable alternative but traps residents with high interest loans, depreciating home values, rising lot rents, and hidden fees. The need for affordable housing in MHPs and residents' inability to move homes to avoid predatory landlord practices makes them vulnerable to exploitation. These same features also make MHPs a highly stable source of revenue for investors and a valuable site of entry for global finance.

The twin processes of financialization and economic inequality are arguably defining developments of the twenty-first century. As economic sociologists have shown, the transformation from manufacture-driven to finance-oriented economies in the US and across the globe has restructured income dynamics as well as social relations and can be seen as a key driver of economic inequality (Lin and Tomaskovic-Devey 2013). The same processes are restructuring peoples' relations to their homes. The increasing dominance of the finance sector in the provision of housing, both via the securitization and repackaging of mortgage debt into tradable financial products and via the increased significance of residential real estate as an investment tool, is thus an area where the sociology of housing speaks to economic sociology and related subfields. The growth of the MH sector is a material expression of the ongoing commodification of affordable housing, as global finance reaches ever deeper into low-income housing stocks.

My research on MH is an attempt to reframe analyses of affordable housing away from individual extractive relationships between residents and landlords and to show how an international "mobile home empire" of linked industries both produces and profits from housing insecurity in MHPs (Sullivan 2018, 161). Over the last decades, MHPs have increasingly been consolidated under corporate ownership and become a favored "undervalued asset" for Real Estate Investment Trusts (REITs) (Sullivan 2018). These processes have clear links to the wholesale buying of "toxic assets" in rental housing markets after the real estate collapse of 2008, so that today "global corporate landlords [have] become deeply rooted in local residential markets, controlling hundreds—sometimes thousands—of units in single districts or counties" (Rolnik 2019, 267).

Currently, the emergence of private-equity investment in MHPs marks a new phase in the financialization of low-income housing. The largest owners of MHPs in the US are now billionaire investors Warren Buffet and Sam Zell and global private-equity firms like Blackstone and the Carlyle group. Private-equity firms generally seek to generate 15–25 percent annualized returns by investing in businesses, making changes to those businesses to increase cash flow, and selling those businesses or taking them public through an IPO after four to six years (PESP 2019). Generating this rate of return necessitates raising rents and fees in MHPs. In the last few years, some of the largest private-equity and real estate investment firms in the world have made major investments in MHPs. The Private Equity Stakeholder Project (2019) cataloged $1.77 trillion in MHP investments made by a wide range of global institutional investors. The impacts of institutional and private-equity investment in MHPs have been severe for the residents living there. As just one example, MH Action documented the experiences of residents in MHPs purchased by Havenpark Capital Partners, a private real estate investment firm operating in several states. Residents in these communities reported dramatic increases in lot rent (as much as 50–60 percent), minimal community maintenance, and arbitrary and punitive rules (MH Action 2021).

The private-market provision of affordable housing has been shown to be central in low-income rental markets, where the extractive relationship between landlords and tenants creates chronic insecurities for residents (Desmond 2016). MHPs ask us to think through how the commodification of affordable housing operates well beyond individual landlords and includes multiple forms of extraction that occur at different levels, up to the level of some of the largest global investment firms. The rush of global capital into MHPs may be a bellwether for processes of extraction and capital accumulation that target other stigmatized or "toxic" housing investments.

Conclusions

Manufactured housing represents a critical but understudied source of affordable housing and a growing source of low-income homeownership in the US. The historical and contemporary treatment of MH in planning and law has created sociospatial stigma. Cultural tropes treat MH residency as a proxy for transience and moral deficiency, while MH is highly segregated from other forms of housing, clustered into MHPs and ISes, and relegated to undesirable land in commercial and industrial zones or in the exurban hinterlands outside metro areas altogether.

For housing practitioners, this segregation is a clear call to address the spatial relegation of MH and increase the affordable housing stock by removing historic ordinances and regulations that prohibit or restrict manufactured homes. For sociologists of housing, the sociospatial stigma surrounding MH and the processes whereby unwanted uses (and the low-income people that reside there) are zoned into less desirable urban space challenge us to investigate how physical space both signifies and reproduces social power. In Bourdieu's classic understanding of "site effects," social space organizes itself through hierarchical classification that is naturalized through the inscription of social distinctions into the physical world. Simply put: "spatial distance affirms social distance" (Bourdieu 1999, 126). Wacquant updates Bourdieu by conceptualizing territorial stigmatization as a primary mechanism through which advanced urban marginality is produced and maintained in the "hyperghettos" of the US (2016). For the sociology of housing, this segregation of MH serves as a call to investigate the symbolic dimensions of spatial marginalization by housing type (whether that be rentals, voucher housing, informal housing, or other housing forms). It also serves as an invitation to study the technologies of governance—regulations, ordinances, land use codes, city plans—that sociologists too often see as the purview of urban planners and practitioners.

Territorial relegation has largely segregated MH from other housing. Scholarship on owners and renters has identified segregation by housing tenure as a potential contributor to spatial inequalities and a notable dependent and independent variable in analyses of housing policy (McCabe 2016). The segregation of MH has important implications for spatial inequalities, an area of future study for this housing stock. More broadly, sociologists of housing should interrogate segregation by housing type as a dimension of sociospatial inequality in the US.

The dynamics that underpin the marginalization of MH are especially important given the documented spatial inequalities associated with the segregation and clustering of manufactured housing into MHPs and ISes. While the space of the chapter only covers three such inequalities—water insecurity and exposure to environmental hazards for all MH residents, and eviction for residents of MHPs—more work needs to be done to investigate a wider range of inequalities facing this housing type. More broadly, research needs to examine intersections between segregation by housing type and inequities in the built environment, including the most basic inequalities like access to running water, which in turn reflect structural inequalities of race and class.

Finally, the consolidation of the MH sector under corporate ownership and private-equity investment is a call for sociologists to analyze housing through the lens of financialization. The commodification of housing has spread even to the lowest-income sectors of the market and the dual crises of housing affordability and housing insecurity must be understood within this new global political economy. Through the lens of financialization, the rise of MH exposes the ways that housing exploitation intersects with other inequalities. One of the largest private-equity investors in MHPs, Apollo Global Management, is the owner of the for-profit college chain University of Phoenix and is also the largest subprime installment lender in the US (PESP 2019). The inequalities facing MH are inseparable from larger processes in which insecurity itself (whether housing insecurity, educational insecurity, or financial insecurity) has become a site of capital production.

Manufactured housing is a prototypical example of why the four-decade-long shift to the private provision of affordable housing "works" for private operators and for investors who can claim it "works" for residents, who can thereby access shelter they otherwise wouldn't be able to afford. Yet the outcome is a system in which housing insecurity has become a primary feature of housing affordability for residents of manufactured housing.

10

Shared Housing and Housing Instability

Hope Harvey and Kristin L. Perkins

When we think about housing, we typically focus on the physical structure or its neighborhood location. Yet research clearly shows that household composition (who lives together inside the home) and changes in composition are also consequential for a range of outcomes, including health and economic well-being for adults, as well as behavioral, educational, and psychological outcomes for children (Cavanagh and Fomby 2019; McLanahan, Tach, and Schneider 2013; Musick and Bumpass 2012). Household composition is intricately connected to the physical spaces in which families live, as decisions about with whom to live often shape where one lives and vice versa. Despite the links between housing and household composition, research on household composition remains primarily the domain of family sociologists and demographers, whose focus is predominantly on the nuclear family unit—the presence or absence of parents, their romantic partners, and their minor children—rather than the full composition of the household. We encourage sociologists of housing to bring the physical and spatial component of housing into the study of household relationships and household composition changes by attending to full household composition and its interactions with residential location and mobility.

Attending to all household members who share a home, rather than focusing solely on nuclear family relationships, is increasingly important. A large and growing share of children in the US—especially those in nonwhite, low-income, and unmarried-parent families—share a home with individuals beyond the nuclear family, such as extended family or nonrelatives. Over 15 percent of children live with a parent and an adult extended family member or nonrelative, and the proportion of children who live in such shared, or "doubled-up," households has steadily increased in recent decades (Harvey, Dunifon, and Pilkauskas 2021). These households are typically short-term arrangements; the movement of extended family members and nonrelatives in and out of children's homes contributes substantial instability to children's lives (Perkins 2017a). The social processes that unfold when shared households combine, co-reside, and dissolve are consequential for the individuals involved.

Shared households are inherently both physical and social arrangements, encompassing a range of topics central to the discipline of sociology, including family structure, family instability, housing needs, and residential mobility. Yet this line of research has been and remains diffused across sociological subfields. Family demographers have begun documenting the prevalence of shared households and their instability (Pilkauskas and Cross 2018). Urban sociologists and poverty scholars also recognize that shared households are important, but typically study them as *physical housing*, describing how extended family and friends provide temporary shelter for families in need (Desmond 2016; Edin and Shaefer 2015). Family sociologists, demographers, urban sociologists, and poverty and inequality scholars have all contributed to our knowledge about shared households, but mostly in isolation.

We summarize foundational contributions sociologists across these subfields have made to understanding shared housing and its instability, describe how our work builds on this research, and chart a path for future research on shared households and their instability. We argue that adopting the theoretical and empirical orientations of sociologists of housing, centering the physical and social aspects of housing, would strengthen future research. We encourage sociologists of housing to integrate insights from across sociological subfields, taking a holistic approach to the causes and consequences of household sharing and instability. We also identify a need for new data that capture complex household compositions, housing status and changes, and interactions between these factors. Our orientation toward shared housing and housing instability is intentionally inclusive of all shared-housing arrangements, including those formed with grandparents, other extended family, and nonrelatives. Because our work builds primarily on family sociology research, our essay focuses on families with children, but we conclude by describing the promise that research on household dynamics holds for understanding other demographic groups—from immigrants to the aging population—to highlight the broad importance of this line of research for sociology.

Lessons from Foundational Research on Shared Housing

In this section we highlight the contributions of poverty scholars, family sociologists, and urbanists to our collective knowledge about shared housing and housing instability. These subfields typically approach shared housing in one of two ways: as a physical arrangement or as a social arrangement. In each case we note how a holistic, unified approach would provide a more complete analysis of the phenomenon of shared housing and enable richer theorizing on social processes surrounding shared housing.

SHARED HOUSEHOLDS AS EMERGENCY HOUSING

Poverty and housing scholars highlight the role of shared households as a safety net. Families move in with extended family or nonrelatives in response to emergency housing needs and when they are priced out of the private housing market or unable to access public housing assistance (Clampet-Lundquist 2003; Desmond 2016; Edin and Shaefer 2015; Leopold 2012; Rosen 2020; Seefeldt and Sandstrom 2015; Skobba and Goetz 2013). Shared-household members often have poverty-level incomes; by increasing the number of adults (and potential incomes) in the household, sharing housing can reduce household-level poverty (Mutchler and Baker 2009; Mykyta and Macartney 2012; Rendall, Weden, and Brown 2021; Reyes 2020).

At the same time, shared households can expose families to crowded or otherwise unsafe conditions (Edin and Shaefer 2015; Seefeldt and Sandstrom 2015; Welsh and Burton 2016). Limited space, resource constraints, and incompatible lifestyles often make shared households conflictual and precarious (Bush and Shinn 2017; Clampet-Lundquist 2003; Skobba and Goetz 2013). Because shared households provide vital but often unstable emergency housing, living in someone else's home for economic reasons is considered a "hidden" form of homelessness by many researchers, policymakers, and housing advocates (Lee, Tyler, and Wright 2010; National Alliance to End Homelessness 2020; National Center for Homeless Education n.d.), and shared households are common among families at risk of homelessness (Bush and Shinn 2017; Fitchen 1992).

This research has yielded key insights into the role of shared housing as a housing safety net. However, more research is needed to examine the full range of circumstances that lead families to share housing, beyond housing crises. Likewise, beyond insights about conflict, knowledge of shared-household relationships and functioning is limited. Continued attention to the dynamics of forming and living in shared households and recognition that they involve a social household, as well as physical housing, will be key.

SHARED HOUSING AS (AN UNSTABLE) HOUSEHOLD STRUCTURE

Alongside research on shared households as safety nets, demographers and family sociologists investigate the social aspects of shared housing as a *household structure*, defined by co-residence with any adult beyond the nuclear family, regardless of motivations for living together or who the householder is. Traditionally, family demographers and sociologists studying children's increasingly complex family structures focused exclusively on parents, their romantic partners, and their minor children. Scholars expanding the scope to include other adults in children's households examine the prevalence, correlates, and potential effects of shared households. Many studies focus specifically on multigenerational households (with a child, parent, and grandparent), others consider extended kin co-residence, and some capture all shared households, whether formed with extended kin or nonrelatives (Amorim 2019; Aquilino 1996; Augustine and Raley 2013; Cross 2018; DeLeire and Kalil 2002; Dunifon, Ziol-Guest, and Kopko 2014; Entwisle and Alexander 1996; Hao and Brinton 1997; Kang and Cohen 2017; Mollborn, Fomby, and Dennis 2011; Pilkauskas 2012; Pilkauskas and Cross 2018; Sigle-Rushton and McLanahan 2002).

Sharing a household has become a common experience for children (Harvey, Dunifon, and Pilkauskas 2021); nearly half of mothers in urban areas lived in a shared household by the time their child turned nine (Pilkauskas, Garfinkel, and McLanahan 2014). Rates of household sharing are higher for younger children; economically disadvantaged children; children with younger mothers; African American, Asian, Native American, and Latino children compared to white children; and children with single or cohabiting mothers compared to those with married mothers (Amorim, Dunifon, and Pilkauskas 2017; Cross 2018; Kreider and Ellis 2011; Pilkauskas 2012, 2014; Harvey, Dunifon, and Pilkauskas 2021; Pilkauskas 2012; Pilkauskas and Cross 2018).

Family sociologists and demographers focus primarily on who is in the household—whether a child is living in a multigenerational, extended, or shared household—and typically pay less attention to the shared physical housing. These scholars rarely distinguish between shared-household members who are "guests" in someone else's home and householders who are "hosting" an extended family member or nonrelative (Cohen and Casper 2002 and Whitehead 2018b are exceptions). Yet, the housing and poverty literature described above suggests that these experiences typically differ dramatically: guests are often precariously housed and reliant on others for housing, while hosts have their own housing which they share with others. Overlooking physical housing arrangements has limited our understanding of how the causes, prevalence, and consequences of living in shared housing may differ for guests and hosts.

Shared housing should be understood in a context of instability. Sixty-two percent of shared households experienced some change in composition within one year and 93 percent experienced change within five years (Glick and Van Hook 2011). Family instability, measured via parental divorce and re-partnering, generally has negative effects on children's cognitive outcomes and behavior, and on adolescents' school engagement, emotional well-being, and behavior (Cavanagh and Fomby 2019). Broadening the scope to include extended family members and nonrelatives who join and leave children's households is necessary to give us a full understanding of instability and its consequences. For very young children, household transitions involving extended family members are more common than transitions involving parents, though these two types of changes often co-occur (Mollborn, Fomby, and Dennis 2011). Measuring changes involving only mothers' romantic partners, the traditional family instability approach, means we miss household changes involving extended family members and nonrelatives: on average, children experience 1.2 changes involving parents by age eighteen compared with three changes involving extended family members and nonrelatives (Raley et al. 2019). A higher share of Black and Latino children experience extended family transitions compared with white children; in the short term, these transitions are negatively associated with cognitive scores for white and Black toddlers, but not Latino toddlers (Mollborn, Fomby, and Dennis 2011). Although family sociologists and demographers have begun to consider instability stemming from shared-housing arrangements, questions remain about whether the consequences of this instability are similar to those of nuclear family instability and how the mechanisms driving any effects may be similar or different.

INTERACTIONS BETWEEN HOUSEHOLD COMPOSITION CHANGES AND RESIDENTIAL MOVES

Absent from much research on family instability is an explicit acknowledgment that family instability often also involves a residential move for the child (exceptions are Mollborn 2016; Fomby and Mollborn 2017; and Raley et al. 2019). For example, parental divorce and remarriage are both associated with an increased probability of moving (South, Crowder, and Trent 1998). Residential mobility has negative effects on children's well-being, on average: children who move have lower test scores and educational attainment, worse physical and mental health, and higher rates of delinquency and substance abuse than children who do not move (Jelleyman and Spencer 2008; Perkins 2017b; Vogel, Porter, and McCuddy 2017; Ziol-Guest and McKenna 2014). Moves prompted by household composition changes can propel families into neighborhoods more or less conducive to child well-being (South, Crowder, and Trent 1998).

Residential mobility is a change in physical location that can be both cause and consequence of the composition and social arrangement of one's household. Bringing shared housing into focus for sociologists involves acknowledging this interaction. Household composition changes and residential moves may prompt or correlate with changes in childcare arrangements or household resources such that sharing housing may be a marker for exposure to other forms of instability (Fomby and Mollborn 2017; Mollborn 2016). Likewise, entries into, exits from, and transitions between shared households may be accompanied by a change in environment if the host lives in a different neighborhood than the guests' prior or subsequent housing. Mothers who live in the home of extended family are less likely to live in poor neighborhoods compared with mothers who do not live with extended family (Whitehead 2018b), and school district quality is one reason some grandmothers share their housing with younger generations (Goodman and Silverstein 2002).

Centering Shared Housing

While urban sociologists and poverty scholars recognize the housing function that shared households can serve, the study of shared households and instability—like the study of household composition more broadly—has primarily been the domain of family demographers. We draw on our own research to illustrate the contributions that studying shared housing and instability can make to sociology. First, we demonstrate that qualitative data provide essential insight to understanding roles and relationships in shared households. Next, we turn to long-term consequences of shared housing and instability for children, estimated using longitudinal quantitative data. Finally, we describe how combining the study of housing and household composition provides a more holistic understanding of the instability families face. Throughout this section, we argue that shared housing and its instability are themselves worthwhile topics of inquiry and are not simply cases of housing insecurity or family structure. We also expound on the implications of our findings for future research and explore the unique strengths that sociologists, particularly sociologists of housing, can bring to this subject.

HOUSEHOLD ROLES AND RELATIONSHIPS

Qualitative research shows that parents' housing status—whether they are "guests" living in someone else's home or householders "hosting" additional adults in their own home—dramatically shapes their interpretation of living in shared households (Harvey 2020a). As described, family demographers rarely distinguish between shared-household guests and hosts. The importance of householder status underscores the necessity of approaching shared households as both a social and physical arrangement. Hosts retain authority within the home, even when guests can afford to live independently and even when they contribute economically. Hosts' symbolic position as the householder and housing support provider, and their ability to evict unwanted residents, reinforces this authority. Because guests rely on hosts for housing (even if they have other options) and have less authority within the home, parents interpret being a guest as inconsistent with their identities as adults and good parents. Thus, even parents who would consider hosting a shared household express unwillingness to be long-term guests. Although shared households can be beneficial, they can also exert a psychological toll on guests, who often subscribe to traditional ideals about family life and residential independence despite structural constraints to achieving them (Harvey 2020a).

Most discussion of shared households from a housing perspective focuses on guests rather than hosts. Yet qualitative data show that shared households can benefit both hosts and guests. Hosts typically understand themselves to be support providers, but many have needs that guests can help meet. For example, guests help pay rent and utilities, share resources like food, and provide services like childcare and eldercare (Harvey 2018a). Although guests' needs typically drive household sharing, some guests consider how the arrangement may benefit the host when deciding whether to move in, and hosts' own economic and childcare needs may influence their decision to allow guests to join their household (Harvey 2020c). Although hosts can benefit from sharing housing, adding adults to the household can also strain limited resources for impoverished householders (Harvey 2018a). These findings show the value of studying hosts of shared households as a distinct group and of theorizing the role these households play in their lives, as well as in the lives of guests.

Qualitative data on shared housing are uniquely suited for examining roles, relationships, and processes within shared households and for understanding how parents interpret and navigate life in these arrangements, illuminating families' experiences in doubled-up households in ways that survey data cannot. These insights can strengthen the growing quantitative literature by suggesting mechanisms through which shared households can affect families and showing how current categorizations of shared households might be refined to better match how families experience these arrangements.

Qualitative insights about how household members understand and experience shared housing differently as "hosts" and "guests" reveal critical gaps in academic understandings of the prevalence, characteristics, and consequences of shared households. Survey data show that living in shared households as a host and as a guest are both common for children in the US. As of 2018, nearly 8 percent of children were guests in shared households—i.e., with a parent in the home of an extended family member or nonrelative—and nearly 8 percent were hosts—i.e., in a household headed by a parent or a parent's romantic partner, that also includes an adult extended family member or nonrelative (Harvey, Dunifon, and Pilkauskas 2021). Guests occupy a precarious position relative to hosts in terms of socioeconomic status and length of residence in shared households. Children whose mothers have less education and whose mothers are unmarried are more often guests than hosts, while more advantaged children are more often hosts than guests. Moreover, guests remain in shared households for longer periods than do hosts—potentially suggesting a lack of other housing options—and those who do transition often experience instability (Harvey, Dunifon, and Pilkauskas 2021). These findings reinforce the necessity of understanding the dual role of shared households as social household composition *and* physical housing arrangement and suggest that future research should analyze hosts and guests as distinct groups. More broadly, they highlight how qualitative research can inform the ways we conceptualize and measure shared households, which can in turn improve quantitative analyses.

LONG-TERM CONSEQUENCES OF SHARED HOUSEHOLDS AND INSTABILITY

While qualitative data are well suited to identifying household roles and relationships, prospective survey data allow sociologists to identify complex household relationships, track household membership and residence over time, and estimate the prevalence and consequences of shared households and instability. Available data are unable to capture the full complexity of shared households and instability—a point we return to later in this chapter—but they do demonstrate that shared households are both common and consequential for families.

Childhood years spent in some shared-household types have enduring links to outcomes closely tied to long-term well-being. Time spent living in shared housing with grandparents has little association with health and educational attainment in young adulthood after accounting for selection into these households, but co-residence with other extended family or nonkin is linked to lower educational attainment and higher rates of obesity (Harvey 2020b). Although researchers often group all shared-household types together or focus only on multigenerational households, these findings suggest that different household compositions may create distinct environments for children.

The long-term consequences of household composition changes likewise demonstrate the value of studying shared housing. Observing children for two years, Perkins (2017a) finds that a substantial share experience a household composition change involving extended family or nonrelatives, particularly Black and Hispanic children and children living with one parent. Approximately 40 percent of children experience a household composition change involving extended family or nonrelatives before age eighteen. Half of these children (20 percent of all children) live with the same parent(s) throughout childhood but have extended family or nonrelatives leave or join their households at some point before age eighteen (Perkins 2019). Focusing narrowly on the nuclear family classifies the 20 percent of children who experience no parental change as having stable families, though they experience household composition changes involving others that could disrupt caregiving and material and nonmaterial resources. Measuring changes involving only parents and their romantic partners ignores potentially consequential changes affecting nearly 40 percent of children.

Exposure to household composition changes involving extended family and nonrelatives is both common and consequential, with negative effects on children's educational attainment similar in magnitude to the negative effects of parental divorce and re-partnering (Perkins 2019). Children who experience such changes are less likely to graduate from high school and less likely to enroll in postsecondary education than children who experience no changes in household composition. Among white children, the predicted probability of graduating from high school is 0.83 for children who experienced changes involving extended family or nonrelatives compared with 0.87 for children who experienced no household composition changes. The corresponding predicted probabilities of enrolling in postsecondary education are 0.45 and 0.51.

Together, qualitative and quantitative findings that broaden the scope of research on family structure and instability to consider shared households

144 HARVEY & PERKINS

and their instability show the value of considering all adults (not just the child's parents and their romantic partners) when examining relationships and processes in children's households, tracking changes in children's home environments, and assessing the consequences of these changes.

COMBINING THE STUDY OF HOUSING
AND HOUSEHOLD COMPOSITION

A more holistic view of shared housing and instability bridges research on residential mobility and family instability. Changes in household composition involving extended family members and nonrelatives and changes in residence often co-occur. Over half of renters in Milwaukee, Wisconsin, who recently moved experienced a concurrent change in household composition (including romantic partners, extended family, and nonrelatives) (Desmond and Perkins 2016a). Families with young children are more likely to experience simultaneous changes in residence and household composition, exposing children to multiple types of changes in their developmental environment (Desmond and Perkins 2016a). Children who experience frequent changes in household composition before age eighteen also have the highest rates of residential mobility. Compounded change, a change in household composition combined with a residential move, is associated with lower educational attainment compared with children who move homes but whose household composition remains stable (Perkins 2017c). Studying the independent and joint influence that residential moves and household composition changes could have on child and adult well-being offers a ripe opportunity for sociologists of housing to approach housing as both a physical and social arrangement.

Advancing an Integrated Approach
to the Study of Shared Housing

Research on shared housing and housing instability by family sociologists, demographers, urbanists, and poverty and inequality scholars has expanded rapidly in recent years, reflecting a growing recognition that households are often more complex than previously acknowledged. This complexity challenges scholars approaching housing as a physical arrangement to consider the social and familial processes occurring in shared households; likewise, scholars approaching households as the site of family growth, socialization, and change should acknowledge the physical context in which those processes are unfolding. To date, however, these subfields lack a coherent approach to studying shared households and their instability. Disparate subfields tend to approach the study of shared housing from either a physical, place-based perspective highlighting shelter and material need, or a social and family-process perspective examining relationships and instability within the home, but they rarely conceptualize shared housing as both a physical and social arrangement.

We argue that shared housing and instability should be central to the emerging subfield of the sociology of housing, rather than relegated to the periphery of other subfields. Rather than treating shared housing as simply one form of housing insecurity, sociologists of housing should center shared housing and its instability as worthwhile topics in their own right. This research should build on other subfields. Approaching shared housing and its instability from a sociology of housing perspective, however, would allow scholars to take a holistic view of families' motivations for living in shared households, the composition of and roles within these households, and the consequences of instability inherent in these arrangements in a way that poverty scholars, urbanists, and family demographers may be reluctant to pursue. That is, sociologists of housing may be better equipped to illuminate the full extent of the causes and consequences of these arrangements and their instability than scholars from other subfields, who focus on isolated aspects of these arrangements.

Moreover, because shared households remain understudied, many questions remain. Sociologists are well poised to take advantage of synergies from studying shared housing and its instability with both quantitative and qualitative data. More research is needed on the meaning of living in shared housing. Whether shared households help or harm is difficult to determine because the counterfactual for shared housing is not clear—for example, would families in shared housing otherwise be homeless or would they live independently?—and may vary across different household types. Research on the determinants of entry into and continued residence in shared housing (as both host and guest), how the household formation process unfolds, and how guests understand and weigh their housing alternatives can help answer this question.

Additionally, theorizing the meaning of living in shared households and the effects of these arrangements requires a better understanding of how families experience and navigate daily life in shared households. We encourage researchers studying these questions to take an inclusive view of shared households, paying particular attention to the dimensions along which these arrangements may vary. Many potential dimensions may be worth studying: reasons for sharing a household, household headship, housing characteristics like crowding, and household member characteristics like age. We especially encourage research on different household compositions; prior research focused disproportionately on multigenerational households, and we know much less about how these households are similar or different from those shared with other extended family or nonrelatives. Researchers should also continue to explore variation by race and ethnicity (Reyes 2018, 2020; Whitehead 2018a, 2018b).

Research on family structure and family instability should consider the full composition of individuals living in children's households, including extended family and nonrelatives, and should make explicit the distinction between household composition and householder status. Research on shared housing should acknowledge the changes in both residence (physical) and household composition (social) that occur as shared-housing arrangements form and dissolve. It will be worthwhile to consider the consequences of changes associated with shared housing, measuring independent and interactive effects of changes in household composition and residential mobility.

Our research focuses on families with children, but research on shared housing and instability should not be so limited. Shared housing provides housing for many groups, including adults recently released from prison (Western 2018) and recent immigrants (Bashi 2007; Menjívar 2000). Research on the transition to adulthood examines the shared households, particularly intergenerational households, of young adults who "failed to launch" or "boomeranged" back into their natal home (Newman 2012; Sassler, Ciambrone, and Benway 2008; South and Lei 2015). Given the striking increase in three-generation households, scholars should examine how the growing population of older adults experiences shared households and how their economic and care needs shape decisions to live in shared households.

Finally, a coherent approach to studying shared housing and housing instability requires better quantitative data capturing both complex household compositions and housing status and changes. Despite the prevalence of shared households, most surveys continue, at least implicitly, to assume respondents live in single-family households. Survey questions such as those about food insecurity are often asked at the household level, making it difficult to answer questions about shared-household functioning, such as how expenses and resources are shared. Despite the importance of host/guest status for how families experience shared households, many oft-used surveys (e.g., the Panel Study of Income Dynamics [PSID] and the National Longitudinal Survey of Youth [NLSY]) do not identify the household lease/mortgage holder. Without better data on complex households, the role of these arrangements in shaping sociological outcomes of interest and the ways their effects may vary by host/guest status will remain poorly understood.

Most longitudinal data sets measure household relationships relative to one household member and do not identify the relationships between all household members. In 2017, the PSID introduced a family relationship matrix documenting relationships among members of the same family unit; yet, even this helpful step toward understanding complex family arrangements provides limited insight into shared households, which nearly always contain multiple family units, and the matrix does not identify relationships across units. Sociologists may be reluctant to consider co-residence with extended family and nonrelatives because existing data are limited to a subset of relationships in the household. Inferring household relationships that are not directly documented is a laborious process relying on logic and assumptions rather than stated relationships (see Harvey, Dunifon, and Pilkauskas 2021; Perkins 2019). Surveys that only identify household members' relationships to the household head constrain researchers' abilities to understand the relationships between non-head household members, as well as the full complexity of shared households.

Moreover, relationships that surveys do capture are likely measured imperfectly. Unrelated shared-household members often describe their relationships in fictive kin terms and reveal their lack of blood or marriage relationship only in response to direct questioning (Harvey 2018b). More-precise household relationship measures might help researchers avoid misclassifying households formed by nonkin using fictive kin terms as extended family households. Finally, few surveys gather extensive data on residential moves, making it difficult to study the important connections between residential instability and household composition instability.

We encourage sociologists of housing to embrace topics on shared housing and housing instability as key research questions that they are uniquely qualified to pursue. As eviction, housing instability, and housing unaffordability capture more attention inside and outside the academy (Nelson and Lens, this volume; Herbert, this volume; Herring, this volume; LaBriola, this volume), we argue that shared-housing arrangements can be both cause and consequence of these circumstances and are a topic worthy of explicit consideration in their own right. The coronavirus pandemic has laid bare the necessity of stable housing for public health, and the social and economic disruption caused by the pandemic is only the most recent phenomenon prompting families to use shared housing as a survival strategy. Sociologists of housing should build on and integrate foundational studies by poverty scholars, urbanists, and family demographers to advance future research on shared housing and housing instability using a holistic approach that acknowledges the physical and social implications these arrangements have for individuals and families.

11

Informal Housing in the US

VARIATION AND INEQUALITY AMONG
SQUATTERS IN DETROIT

Claire Herbert

Amid growing economic inequality and rising housing costs in the US, more individuals and households are seeking alternative methods for securing shelter and creating home. No longer considered merely a condition of the developing world, researchers have been documenting various informal housing practices across the US and other regions in the Global North. Homeowners in high-cost cities build unpermitted housing units (Wegmann 2015). Poor rural households self-build housing in informal subdivisions (Ward 1999). Residents priced out of local housing markets create tent encampments (Herring 2014; Sparks 2017) or live in RVs (Wakin 2005). And in disinvested neighborhoods in Rust Belt cities, squatters take over vacant houses (Herbert 2021; Becher 2014).

Existing scholarship tends to frame squatting as either a social movement (in Global North contexts) or a condition of poverty (in Global South contexts). This chapter explores a third framing, squatting as a type of informal housing, that is emerging in the United States. In Detroit, Michigan, individuals and families take over housing with a diverse set of backgrounds and motivations that reflect the changing socioeconomic experiences of US Rust Belt cities. "Survival squatters" seek shelter, "holdover squatters" hope to remain in homes they have lost, and "homesteader squatters" actively choose to occupy housing as an alternative lifestyle. Their markedly different resources and pathways to informal housing shape their experiences: salient inequalities are reflected within different types of informal housing.

As broader social and economic trends in the US continue to constrain affordable housing options for the poor and middle class, individuals and families come to rely more on informal, and often creative, housing solutions. Informal housing reflects and interacts with broader shifts in formal housing and economic markets, urban and rural conditions, family/ household structures, social norms, and inequality. Despite this recent

wave of scholarship, sociologists of housing have been reluctant to recognize the extent of informal housing practices in the US: informality
has largely been viewed as a condition of the Global South. But as the
subject is an emerging area, there is much that scholars still don't know
about informal housing in the US. By their very nature, informal housing
processes are also relatively hidden and difficult to track, meaning social-
scientific understanding of the phenomenon is necessarily incomplete.
The research methods and analytic tools of sociology can help identify
and quantify the prevalence of these often hidden practices and make
sense of informal housing as a social phenomenon that defies existing
typologies and categories. Sociologists must integrate informal housing
practices into their understandings of the causes and consequences of
housing instability. And planners and policymakers should consider informal housing practices as a kind of planning-by-doing that suggests creative, locally responsive alternatives.

Regional Contexts and Conceptual Advancements

In terms of scale alone, informal housing merits attention from sociologists of housing. In the US, scholars estimate over 50 percent of new housing units in four major cities are unpermitted (Brown, Mukhija, and Shoup
2020) and count at least 2.1 million housing units in informal subdivisions
(Durst et al. 2021). While there are no current estimates for the number
of people illegally occupying housing in the US, scholars estimate that
globally over one billion people—that is, one in eight—squat on land or
in housing (Neuwirth 2007). Broadly, most research on squatting coheres
into two relatively distinct literatures that focus on different regions and
largely rely on different interpretive frameworks: squatting as a mode of
survival used by the poor in "developing" countries and squatting as a form
of social protest in high-cost European cities. Until recently, scholars have
paid little attention to informal housing—and squatting in particular—in
the US. Much of the extant sociology of housing is influenced by broader
idealistic understandings of the US as a place where the rule of law is
comprehensive and equally applied (Larson 2002). Existing research has
nevertheless used different language to describe informal practices in the
US. The poor use "underground" strategies for "making ends meet" (e.g.,
Edin and Lein 1997; Venkatesh 2006), and middle-class residents engage
in "do-it-yourself" practices to fulfill desires (Douglas 2018).

In the context of expanding economic inequality and housing conditions that are increasingly unaffordable even for the middle classes, we
can expect that people from varied backgrounds will turn toward informal

means to meet housing wants and needs as well. By failing to recognize the presence of informal housing in the US, scholars miss the opportunity to engage and learn from informality scholarship in other regions and thereby risk reproducing problematic policy responses (like overregulation; see Durst and Wegmann 2017). Sociologists should care about informal practices—both within housing and beyond—because they reflect and exacerbate inequalities but can also be central pathways for innovation, adaptation, and social change (Roy 2005).

SQUATTING FROM SOUTH TO NORTH

Over the past fifty years, scholars have learned a great deal from studying squatting as a mode of informal housing in the Global South, where poor households often self-build housing on land ringing the edges of rapidly growing cities. Over time, these informal settlements have expanded to form what are sometimes referred to as shantytowns or slums. Scholarship in this arena has progressed from treating informality as a problematic condition of poverty to a form of resistance embodied in everyday survival (Bayat 2000). In many instances, squatters form alliances which are central for their success in taking over land, forming communities, and leveraging their numbers and political power to pressure government for regularization (giving occupants title to the property) or to create alternative housing (e.g., Perlman 1976; Bayat 1997; Auyero 2000; Roy 2002; Holston 2008).

The second body of scholarship uses a social-movement lens to study squatters in high-cost European cities (though not exclusively; see Holm and Kuhn 2017 and Esposito and Chiodelli 2021). In cities like London or Amsterdam, squatters often target vacant government-owned buildings, where occupiers leverage the social/political expectation that government take an active role in housing provision to garner favorable public sentiment and gain continued access to these spaces. While this literature overwhelmingly focuses on squatting as a form of social protest aimed at engendering broader social, economic, and cultural shifts, scholars highlight that these movements mobilize squatters with various motivations, ranging from the need for shelter to the attempt to undermine the private-property regime and create mini-utopias (e.g., Kearns 1979; Martínez 2020). A similar lens has been used in very limited US research examining efforts by anti-poverty group ACORN to support squatters (Atlas 2010) or occupations in Lower East Side Manhattan in the 1970s to the early years of the first decade of the 2000s (often in conversation with European scholarship; see Pruijt 2003 and Starecheski 2016).

More broadly, however, squatting in the US has been dismissed as unique, ungeneralizable, and/or ephemeral. Yet historians affirm that squatting, as a strategy used by settlers in the colonization of North America, was influential for US expansion (Jindrich 2017). Other scholarship has observed squatting in the US, but in manifestations that don't fit a social-movement framework, such as in New Orleans (Marina 2017) or Rust Belt cities (Gowan 2002; Venkatesh 2006; Becher 2014) where rising vacancy rates have created opportunity for squatting (Herbert 2021). One study counted 388 squatters in a Chicago Housing Authority building slated for demolition (Popkin, Cunningham, and Woodley 2003). Recent media has documented squatters across US cities, including Buffalo and Long Island, NY; Richmond and Oakland, CA; Portland, OR; Las Vegas; Chicago; Philadelphia; and Miami (see Herbert 2018b).

While a social-movement framework may be useful or appropriate in some contexts, it misses the way that types of informal housing like squatting connect with widespread problems in the sociology of housing, including homelessness, affordability or stability, vacancy rates, subprime lending, eviction, or access to homeownership. Broad national trends like increasingly unaffordable housing markets, financialization of housing, and a shrinking middle class motivate taking a wider lens toward understanding the phenomena of squatting in the US. Rather than studying squatting as a radical social movement or a condition of poverty, this chapter considers squatting as an informal adaptation to the poverty, precarity, and opportunity that persist in the US.

INFORMAL HOUSING

Since Peter Ward's (1999) work on *colonias*, which analyzes poor households' self-built housing on illegally subdivided peri-urban land in Texas, scholarship has been documenting the growth in form and number of informal housing practices in the US. Homeowners in Los Angeles violate local ordinances by subdividing their homes and lots, building units for kin or to rent for income (Wegmann 2015). Residents priced out of California cities live in RVs (Wakin 2005) or encampments (Herring 2014). Home buyers use informal methods like quit-claim deeds when they cannot get a conventional mortgage (Way 2010; Jang-Trettien 2022). And in cities like Detroit, squatters illegally occupy vacant houses (Herbert 2021).

As literature on informal housing expands, so have theoretical works that refine our definitions and concepts. Common definitions draw from scholars originally analyzing informal economies in the Global South. Informal practices are those "unregulated by the institutions of society, in a legal and social environment in which similar activities are regulated" (Castells and Portes 1989, 12), or those that "fail to adhere to the established institutional rules or are denied their protection" (Feige 1990, 990). Castells and Portes (1989) argue that informal practices achieve a level of social legitimacy, even if only among a subgroup or population, which distinguishes them from *illicit* criminal activity. Informal practices may use illegal/noncompliant *means*, like squatting or unlicensed food vending, to pursue socially legitimate *ends*, like sheltering one's family or generating income (see Herbert 2018a; Devlin 2019).

A central insight from the informality literature centers on the state's role in the proliferation of informal practices via the regulations it creates and enforces (and/or fails to enforce). Durst and Wegmann (2017) argue that informality in the US housing market manifests in three different domains. The first, informality as noncompliance, entails housing practices that are noncompliant with existing regulations. When homeowners create unpermitted garage units, they produce housing that is noncompliant with building codes or land use ordinances. The second entails nonenforcement by regulatory agencies/the state (which can co-occur with noncompliance). When city officials fail to hold homeowners accountable for their vacant, blighted properties and squatters move in, nonenforcement has helped engender noncompliant occupation. Cities that don't enforce camping bans on public property contribute to the expansion of tent encampments. The third, informality-as-deregulation, involves the absence of regulations of certain activities, such as property title transfers outside the mortgage market (Jang-Trettien 2022). Sociologists have identified the way housing laws and regulations have been used to mediate the impacts of inequality (Desmond and Bell 2015), but informal housing may reflect, reproduce, or mediate inequalities through different interactions of behavior on the one hand, and through law, regulation, and enforcement on the other.

Other recent work aims to promote cross-region dialogue on informality (Aguilera and Smart 2016; Devlin 2019). Harris conceptualizes informal housing as manifesting along a continuum that varies according to "the extent to which a regulation is violated, the seriousness of consequences, and the number of people or regulations involved" (2018, 9). At one end is "latent" informality, which refers to the possibility of practices being in violation of laws/regulations, as with once-rural self-built housing that *becomes* informal (as noncompliant) through municipal incorporation. As a relatively isolated instance, squatters in a city like Seattle could be considered "diffuse": they are engaging in individualistic, weakly coordinated, geographically dispersed practices that are largely hidden from the regulatory eye. But as practices grow in number and coordination, they be-come "embedded," a term that describes practices common within a par-ticular social group, characterized by cooperation, physical concentration, and popular legitimacy (akin to squatters in European cities). Informal practices then cross another threshold into "overt" when their number and visibility increase such that authorities cannot help but notice. The final threshold is crossed as overt practices continue to grow in number and impact, becoming "dominant," whereupon informality comes to "shape the mode of the state governance itself" (Harris 2018, 12), as Roy (2005) argues is the case in much of the Global South. Harris's continuum helps situate different types, manifestations, and contexts of informal housing within one framework to identify commonalities and differences.

Scholarship on squatting from across the globe demonstrates how local conditions lead to different manifestations of illegal property/land occu-pation. Housing affordability for both renters and owners varies greatly by region, influenced by spatial, economic, and political differences. These same variations shape the kinds of informal housing practices that arise in a given neighborhood, city, or region. In the US, research shows how these practices vary in high-cost growing urban centers (Wegmann 2015), declining cities (Becher 2014; Herbert 2021), or rural areas (Ward 1999). In cities like Detroit, abundant vacancy provides spatial opportunity for squatting, and underfunded local governments cannot reliably enforce property-related laws. Here, broad socioeconomic trends, including tax and mortgage foreclosure, eviction, and lack of affordable housing, create both need and opportunity for squatting, and disaffected young adults see the possibility for an alternate lifestyle.

The squatters in Detroit who are the focus of this research are noncom-pliant with existing property laws, but authorities promote squatting by failing to enforce regulations for both legal owners and illegal occupants.[1] Detroit squatters sit somewhere between Harris's (2018) modes of "dif-fuse" and "embedded" informalities, as their number, level of cooperation, concentration, and visibility fluctuate across Detroit's varying sociospatial conditions of vacancy, abandonment, and deterioration. Adding on to these schematics, this chapter illustrates the importance of recognizing variation within different manifestations of informal housing. As with other domains of housing, like renting and homeownership, residents of

---

[1] Data for this chapter comes from a larger study of property informality in Detroit. I conducted four and a half years of ethnography and sixty-five in-depth interviews with illegal property users, other residents, and city authorities. See Herbert 2021 and 2018b for more detail.

different backgrounds, social classes, and locations experience different obstacles to and impacts from informal housing arrangements.

Typology of Squatters in Detroit

To advance understanding of informal housing in the US, I present a typology of squatters, a useful approach for early analysis of relatively understudied, hidden phenomena. The analytic categories in my data arise from a combination of class, race, and place-based backgrounds common among squatters. "Place-based background" refers to squatters' history in and experience with the city of Detroit, a racially segregated, declining city of concentrated disadvantage (Jang-Trettien and Cornelissen, this volume) with over seventy-eight thousand vacant buildings at the time of this research (Detroit Blight Removal Task Force 2014). For younger newcomers to the city, Detroit's vacancy and lack of regulatory enforcement present enticing opportunities for unique engagement with city property and land. For many longtime Detroiters, the conditions of the city present obstacles they have struggled to navigate for decades.

Three types of squatters emerged in my typology: survival, holdover, and homesteader squatters. For each type, squatting is connected to their experiences with other domains of formal housing. "Survival squatters" are predominantly very poor, longtime residents of the city who take over property to secure urgent needs for housing and avoid doubling up or homeless shelters. In my study, they were overwhelmingly Black, tended to be over the age of forty, and commonly had children. Many had struggled with various personal crises, such as unemployment, drug addiction, custody battles, neighborhood or family violence, or the death of a child (see Herbert 2018b). "Holdover squatters," typically Black, longtime residents of Detroit over forty, are former renters or owners who remain in their homes after tax or mortgage foreclosure. More economically stable than survival squatters but still poor, some aimed to live rent-free as long as possible, while others sought to regain ownership of the property. "Homesteader squatters" are predominantly white, younger newcomers to the city who are dissatisfied with mainstream cultural ideals (such as the increasingly out-of-reach American dream of single-family suburban homeownership) and seek alternative lifestyles. They took over property in Detroit to "homestead" by starting urban farms and often ended up purchasing the properties they squatted—an uncommon pathway into homeownership.

These categories are flexible and could change over time as squatters' orientation toward their housing practices changed, often with an influx of resources that altered the conditions of their occupations (Herbert 2021). These ideal types primarily differ across four dimensions: (1) their motivation, or, alternatively, their entry into squatting; (2) their future goals; (3) the material conditions of their housing; and (4) their own views on their practices. In my book *A Detroit Story: Urban Decline and the Rise of Property Informality* I also detail how the state responds differently to each of these types and to other informal uses of property in ways that further entrench long-standing inequalities (Herbert 2021).

SURVIVAL SQUATTERS

Survival squatters were motivated to squat in order to combat housing instability and homelessness. Those in my study had housing careers littered with shelter stays, doubling up, and evictions. Many single mothers with large families had struggled in severely overcrowded apartments. For these Detroiters, squatting was but one of many tactics for remaining sheltered through hard times. For example, when an apartment subsidy ended, a renter might move into a squatted house until they could secure another affordable place to live. Survival squatters often scouted out potential houses to occupy or learned about recently vacated homes from friends or family. Others stumbled across their house while homeless and decided it was better than their existing situation. Some of the survival squatters in my study had occupied the same house for upward of three years.

The material conditions of survival squatters' houses were very rough and commonly lacked basic utilities, appliances, or complete protection from the elements. Having been previously abandoned, these houses had often been stripped of anything that could be sold, including heating units, appliances, copper pipes, and electrical wires. Many of these houses had been neglected for years and had leaky roofs, cracked foundations, or problems with mold, mildew, or pest infestations.

Homesteader squatters often took over houses in similar condition, but survival squatters lacked the resources to mediate the poor conditions of their housing. Many got by selling food stamps, scrapping, or hustling up odd jobs; others were employed but couldn't make ends meet. This left little to no money for home improvements. Pressing conditions, however, often led to creative solutions. Survival squatters often salvaged supplies from other nearby abandoned properties to improve their homes, such as carpeting for the floors or wood to board up windows. Many also relied on assistance from friends or family, who helped fix the electrics and plumbing or illegally connected the home's utilities. Because survival squatters did not anticipate a lengthy future with the house, many hesitated to make significant investments. Like many other poor people in the United States, survival squatters live in substandard conditions (Krieger and Higgins 2002; Clampet-Lundquist 2003; McCleskey, this volume).

While squatting helped these individuals navigate significant obstacles, survival squatters were not particularly keen on the practice. Mothers, especially, often expressed feelings of failure but also relief at having a place to live with their children. Survival squatters consistently expressed a desire to move past squatting to find comfortable, stable, safe housing. For them, squatting was a last-resort kind of practice rather than a desired arrangement.

By claiming properties to live in, survival squatters asserted their agency to resist the oppressive racial and economic forces that circumscribed their lives. In this way, they made a concerted decision to squat, but they chose squatting from among very few, undesirable options. Like many other poor renters, survival squatters don't lack agency: they lack options (DeLuca, Wood, and Rosenblatt 2019).

HOLDOVER SQUATTERS

While survival and homesteader squatters made a concerted choice to take over properties, holdover squatters entered informal housing through a change in their legal situation: they *became* squatters when the home they owned or rented was foreclosed, reflecting how informal housing is constituted in relation to law and state enforcement. The holdover squatters in my study either didn't know the property was being foreclosed (surprisingly common in Detroit) or decided to roll the dice and remain in their home for a period of time. Many did not self-identify as squatters. It is possible that many holdover squatters, some of whom had been property owners themselves, would not have been comfortable taking over a vacant house, which involves trespassing and sometimes breaking through boarded up doors or windows. At the same time, participants in my study expressed little concern about getting into trouble for their practices.

Holdover squatters had varied goals. Former owners often wanted to try to buy their homes back. Former renters sometimes wanted to purchase the home if it came up for sale at the county property auction. Others hoped to economize by living rent-free as long as they could or until they found another suitable home. Some renters were surprised to find the house was being foreclosed and decided to roll the dice and continue living in the property. Others inherited homes from family members, only to learn of an exorbitant delinquent tax balance and impending foreclosure, so they lived in the house to keep it safe while they tried to regain ownership.

In comparison to the properties typically claimed by survival and homesteader squatters, holdover squatters' homes tended to be more livable since they had not recently been vacant. Housing deteriorates quickly when empty and unattended, and in Detroit scrappers quickly strip salable materials from these properties. Holdover squatters usually had appliances, some form of heating, and functioning utilities. But even so, these houses were often deteriorated and poorly maintained. When landlords stop paying taxes it signals they are milking the property—extracting as much profit as possible while doing little maintenance, perhaps with the intent of walking away (very profitable in Detroit; see Mallach 2014). Homeowners facing tax or mortgage foreclosure had often put off home repairs in hopes of keeping up with other payments.

Holdover squatters were the most varied in terms of how they felt about their now illegal occupation. Nearly all of them, however, viewed the transition as fraught with uncertainties. As noted, the impending foreclosure itself was sometimes a surprise, especially for renters. Many were unclear about the legal implications of living in their homes after the foreclosure was finalized. Occupants were concerned that, once they were technically squatters, they could possibly lose legal utility service, that Child Protective Services could take their children, that they would be violating their parole, or that they would be confronted by new owners if the property was purchased at auction. At the same time, Detroit is home to various housing activist groups who often join forces to help each other answer these questions, as well as to resist or navigate foreclosure and eviction processes.

Holdover squatters, particularly homeowners, also shared the sentiment of grief. Some homeowners had owned their houses for decades, having raised their children and even grandchildren there. They had poured love, sweat, and time into their homes. Devastated by having had their homes taken for tax delinquency, older homeowners often continued their tenure, wrecked with anxiety waiting for—and yet dreading—the day a new owner might show up and demand they move out.

HOMESTEADER SQUATTERS

Homesteader squatters actively desired this mode of informal housing. For these squatters, illegal occupation was a fun, adventurous experience and often a pathway to inexpensive legal homeownership. In contrast to survival squatters, homesteaders were enticed by the opportunities squatting offered rather than pushed by pressing needs, like shelter. Many sought low-cost housing, some wanted to invest their labor to improve a property, and others were drawn to the possibility of also occupying surrounding vacant lots for gardening or farming. Taking over housing freed homesteader squatters from reliance on menial jobs they detested and allowed them to devote time to their passions—art, farming, activism, etc. The homesteader squatters in my study overwhelmingly ended up purchasing their properties (often via the tax auction) and settling in these homes in Detroit.

Homesteader squatters' houses were often in very rough condition initially, because they took over vacant houses slated for foreclosure or already taken by the city for tax delinquency. They were frequently in even worse condition than survival squatters' houses. Their willingness to live in these houses seemed to happen for two reasons. First, homesteader squatters prioritized location over immediate livability. Those in my study tended to congregate near other homesteaders and sought houses with vacant lots adjacent for farming or gardening. Second, they planned to invest time and resources to improve the house and commonly had other places to live while they initially cleared out the house or made it livable. Homesteader squatters commonly used unconventional methods for improving their homes, like making windows with cemented glass bottles, supplying water via catchment systems, or building furnaces out of fifty-five-gallon drums. Because they intended to purchase their homes and live in them for an extended period, they considered these expenses relatively safe investments.

Homesteader squatters viewed their practices very differently from other squatters. For them, squatting was desirable and fun, an enticing opportunity. Many homesteader squatters, having moved from the surrounding suburbs, were able to quit menial, low-wage jobs and cherished their newfound time. For homesteaders like them, Detroit, with its proliferation of vacant properties and limited municipal capacity for enforcement, offered the space to be freed from the confines of nine-to-five jobs and the hindrance of bills to pay, and to instead creatively live off the land and spend their time in ways that were gratifying and meaningful. Many expressed great pleasure in the simple activities of gathering and chopping wood, growing their own food, and scavenging resources for home renovations from nearby vacant buildings.

Inequality and Informality in the Sociology of Housing

Amid declining real wages, increasing economic insecurity, and rising housing costs, individuals and families from varied socioeconomic groups in the US have turned toward informal ways of securing housing and making home. As the dream of homeownership (McCabe 2016) and heavily consumer-oriented lifestyles become further out of reach of more middle-class people, some are embracing alternative ways to realize their dreams and/or even rearticulate their goals. For some young people, doing so means taking over abandoned houses and lots in declining cities to farm, finding happiness and home as urban homesteaders. Families experiencing generations of precarity find themselves scrambling under more dire economic conditions. Without enough affordable, stable housing to meet demand (Skobba, Bruin, and Yust 2013; Rosen 2021) and discriminatory practices by landlords (Hogan and Berry 2011; Rosenblatt and Cossyleon 2018), squatting in vacant houses provides respite from the problems of shelters (Stuart 2016; Herring, this volume) or doubling up and overcrowding for poor residents (Harvey and Perkins, this volume). The subprime mortgage and foreclosure crises (Hernandez 2009) continue to impact poor homeowners and renters who find themselves living in a home they no longer have legal right to, a situation that leaves occupants at great risk of threats of or actual eviction (Desmond 2016; Garboden and Rosen 2019). The squatters in my study are not only the destitute and homeless, but also poor families making the best of rather undesirable options, disaffected young adults in search of an alternate American dream, and former homeowners holding onto their houses post-foreclosure.

Because squatting by definition involves occupying property that one cannot legally claim, scholars may be tempted to understand squatting and other informal housing practices through the lens of deviancy. Deviance is a central concept in sociology, and some theorists argue that deviance is a key mechanism for producing change in societies over time. When an increasing number of people violate norms (like squatting instead of renting an apartment), societies typically either impose sanctions (like criminalizing squatting) or adjust their norms to include these formerly deviant practices. However, a deviance frame fails to capture the structural features of the housing market that motivate or push individuals and families into modes of informal housing. Given the urgency of finding solutions to the crisis of housing, sociologists might foreground the innovative dimensions of informal housing practices and pursue legal and regulatory shifts that can improve the material conditions, safety, and stability for informally housed residents. Put another way, imagining solutions to the housing crisis in the US and globally requires actively reassessing what constitutes a "deviant" housing practice. Scholarship focused on the Global South has increasingly shifted how informal economies and housing are understood: not as forms of deviance, but rather as a kind of planning-by-doing that models alternative practices that could be formalized and supported by the state (Roy 2005), thereby eliminating the stressors and repercussions of living in violation of the law.

Formulating sensitive responses to informal housing also requires that scholars and policymakers give careful attention to the way inequalities are nested within different informal housing practices, reflected in the varied motivations and resources presented in this chapter. Some policies may aid certain informally housed residents but not others. For example, creating more streamlined pathways to homeownership may suit homesteader or holdover squatters, but not survival squatters, who largely aren't interested in owning the houses they occupy. They have a much greater need for expanded access to subsidized housing, especially larger units for families. Relatedly, policies that help some informally housed residents may hurt others. A policy making vacant, disused homes more readily available for purchase may benefit homesteader squatters but could increase the precarity of survival squatters by increasing the demand, particularly from newcomers, for the kinds of houses survival squatters rely on for shelter. Similar dynamics may be at play in other kinds of informal housing. A new regulation limiting the amount of time an RV can be parked on the street in Seattle may be burdensome for a recently evicted family who now find it harder to park near their children's school. Conversely, a single thirty-something programmer who moved into an RV because he was tired of sharing a house with five roommates may not be bothered by the requirement to move his residence because he enjoys seeing new parts of the city.

As the sociology of housing expands to consider informal or "deviant" modes of housing, there are many questions to answer. Future research should deploy unique research methods to uncover the prevalence of different modes of informal housing (such as Durst et al. 2021). Researchers should further compare what types of informal housing arise in urban versus rural contexts, such as the prevalence of illegally subdivided houses in high-cost cities (Wegmann 2015; Patterson and Harris 2017) or *colonias* (Ward 1999; Durst 2015) and manufactured home communities in rural areas (Durst et al. 2021). Research might investigate how local conditions like sprawl, gentrification, and/or segregation influence informal housing patterns. Informal housing is also an arena ripe for cross-national comparisons; scholars can pick up on recent work aiming to synthesize and promote comparison between and across the Global North and South (Aguilera and Smart 2016; Harris 2018; Devlin 2019; Herbert 2021). Finally, just as decades of housing research have uncovered the impacts of various forms of housing for broad sociological problems such as health outcomes, educational attainment, child and family well-being, racial inequality, and wealth accumulation, we need to understand how informal housing impacts these outcomes as well.

12

Housing Deprivation

HOMELESSNESS AND THE
REPRODUCTION OF POVERTY

Chris Herring

In a recent essay, sociologist Mathew Desmond (2018) not only laments the fragmentation of housing research in US sociology, which this volume seeks to remedy. He also notes that the study of homelessness has become "something quite distinct from the study of housing." "As scholars became more interested in describing the subculture and survival techniques of street people," Desmond writes, "the link between homelessness and housing dynamics evaded serious treatment." This disconnect between housing and homelessness is in part historical. The meaning of "homelessness" in the US and much of the Global North prior to the 1980s differs drastically from its usage today. For sociologists of this earlier era, homelessness mostly meant living outside the family unit, not the absolute lack of housing in shelters or on the streets. Encampments of migrant workers or "hobo jungles" existed as stop-off points near railroad depots, but these were temporary waystations between jobs. In cities, homeless men primarily resided in single room occupancy (SROs) residential hotels or flophouses comprised of cubicles (Rice 1918; Anderson 1967; Sutherland and Locke 1936).

In Chicago School sociologist Nels Anderson's classic *The Hobo*, the "housing problem" refers to poor housing conditions, not a lack of housing (1967, 39). Studies in the boom years following World War II never mention housing shortages or affordability as a cause of homelessness (Shlay and Rossi 1992).

By the late 1970s and early 1980s, as the number of people without access to housing exploded across US towns and cities, social analysts were quick to point out the distinctive features of this "new homelessness" (Dear and Wolch 1987). Scholars attributed increased homelessness not only to economic restructuring in the labor market and the deinstitutionalization of asylums, but also to a new lack of affordable housing. A two-million-unit surplus of cheap housing in 1970 turned into a

3.7-million-unit deficit in 1985 (Blau 1993). The flophouse and cubicle hotels had largely been demolished and replaced by office buildings, luxury condominiums, and apartments (Groth 1999). Whereas HUD subsidized 203,046 new public housing units at its peak in 1976, President Reagan halved the budget for assisted housing several years later (Crump 2002). Only in the 1980s did activists promote the term "homelessness," thereby replacing the predominant labels of "vagrant," "beggar," and "bum" that were increasingly covering the pages of newspapers to draw attention to the condition's roots. Soon, shelters rapidly expanded. Between 1984 and 1988, over 3,500 new homeless shelters opened throughout the nation (Jencks 1995). And yet this number was still grossly inadequate. It suddenly became common to see the down-and-out sleeping in doorways, in cardboard boxes, and in tents under freeways.

Yet despite the general recognition that lack of housing affordability is a key contributing factor to homelessness in this new era, it has only been in the past decade that sociologists have more rigorously linked housing precarity to homelessness. A number of studies have shown that homelessness rates tend to go up in a community when housing costs exceed the reach of poor people (Byrne et al. 2013; Hanratty 2017; Lee, Price-Spratlen, and Kanan 2003). Recent research has also shown that in communities where the average renter spends more of their income on rent, the rate of homelessness rises much more quickly; areas with more income inequality are also associated with higher rates of homelessness (Glynn, Byrne, and Culhane 2018). In their recent book *Homelessness is a Housing Problem* (2022) Colburn and Aldern found that housing market conditions, such as the cost and availability of rental housing, offer a more convincing explanation for homelessness than conventional beliefs about drug use, mental illness, poverty, generosity of public assistance, or the weather. The last decade has also seen a boom in eviction research revealing the mechanisms through which the poor become unhoused (Desmond 2016).

While there is a growing stream of sociological research linking the lack of affordable housing (Labriola, this volume) and evictions (Nelson and Lens, this volume) *funneling people into homelessness*, this chapter discusses *pathways through homelessness* and *exits from homelessness into housing*. In particular, it focuses on the state's role in shaping these trajectories. Drawing on recent sociological studies and my own fieldwork in and on the streets, shelters, and homeless housing programs of San Francisco, the chapter pushes sociologists to consider three themes. First, it integrates housing into poverty research by reconceptualizing homelessness as not merely the outcome of poverty, but a catalyst in its reproduction and shaped heavily by the state's policing and provision of shelter. Second, the chapter strengthens the links between studies of homelessness and housing policy by pointing to the limits and pitfalls of rehousing those who have been chronically unhoused through Housing First. Finally, the chapter concludes by considering how state policies across public space, shelters, and homeless housing programs collectively work to neutralize homelessness by depoliticizing and invisibilizing the social problem. I argue that the use of ethnography and community-based research are particularly useful sociological tools in exposing and politicizing state efforts of neutralization.

Pathways through Homelessness

Experiencing poverty without a home amplifies negative outcomes of poverty. Homelessness has devastating biological consequences through increased food insecurity, exhaustion, stress, and reduced access to medical care (Brown et al. 2016). It can trigger and catalyze mental health and substance use disorders (Castellow, Kloos, and Townley 2015) and it erects multiple barriers to maintaining employment (Desmond and Gershenson 2017). However, the deepening of poverty experienced through homelessness cannot be conceptualized as a mere absence of housing and neglect of governmental response. Instead, the poverty of the unhoused is exacerbated in distinct ways by agencies of the welfare and penal state and varies widely depending on their pathway through homelessness.

First is the role of criminalization on the unsheltered. After first being evicted from their homes, the unsheltered regularly experience secondary evictions from public spaces. While housing status has been shown to play a unique role in the criminalization of poverty due to criminal records (Bryan and Alao, this volume) and residential segregation (Faber, this volume), people's lack of housing status also places them in the crosshairs of the penal state. Jim Crow, anti-Okie, "ugly" and vagrancy laws long empowered police to manage the down-and-out. But in 1972, the judicial reversal of anti-vagrancy laws led US cities to restrict a wide variety of behaviors associated with homelessness, including panhandling, sleeping in parks and sitting on sidewalks (Ortiz, Dick, and Rankin 2015). In 2019, the National Law Center on Homelessness and Poverty found that more than half of the 187 counties in its sample banned camping and sitting, lying down in public, or loitering and begging in particular places. More anti-homeless laws have been passed in US counties between 2009 and 2019 than in any previous decade, and most counties have multiple laws on the books. California counties each have an average of more than ten anti-homeless laws, while Los Angeles and San Francisco have seventeen and twenty-four, respectively (Fisher et al. 2018). Each law may target one or two behaviors; collectively, they effectively criminalize homelessness.

In addition to the challenges wrought from day-to-day survival on the streets, the enforcement of anti-homeless laws results in a secondary marginalization. Whereas sociologists have long documented blatant police harassment against the unhoused (Aulette and Aulette 1987; Bittner 1967; Snow and Anderson 1993), recent scholarship has focused on how even the seemingly mundane enforcement of civil infractions can deepen poverty. Beckett and Herbert (2009) describe how enhanced trespassing ordinances and park exclusions in Seattle effectively banish individuals from certain areas of downtown. The impaired mobility banned people from maintaining relationships with those who resided in certain areas of town and restricted access to social services, medical care, and shelter in zones of exclusion. Duneier's (1999) ethnography of homeless street vendors in New York City and Gowan's (2010) of San Francisco recyclers document how intensified policing interfered with the rehabilitative forces of houseless people's work that allowed them to maintain a sense of dignity in avoiding illegal or charitable means of survival. In LA's Skid Row, Stuart found that new tactics of "therapeutic policing," which pushed people into shelter, failed to increase the provision of services or reduce crime (2016).

In collaboration with San Francisco's Coalition on Homelessness, colleagues and I carried out a community-based survey of 351 unhoused individuals and forty-three in-depth interviews in the city about their experiences of criminalization (Herring and Yarbough 2015; Herring et al. 2020). We found that in the previous year, 70 percent of those surveyed had been forced to move by an officer, 69 percent had been cited, and 46 percent had had their tents or other belongings confiscated by city workers. We found that nearly 90 percent of citations given to homeless people each year for sitting, camping, or loitering go unpaid. The unpaid citations resulted in arrest warrants and suspensions of driver's licenses, erecting further barriers to employment, housing, and services.

Even simple move-along orders and sanitation sweeps mean that people lose medicine, protection from the elements and personal property, including identification to access benefits. The policing also catalyzed racial inequality. Not only are African Americans more likely to experience policing since they more often experience homelessness, but among the currently homeless, Black survey participants experienced move-along orders, citations, and police searches at rates nearly 10 percent higher than those of their white counterparts. Even though a single move-along order or citation may seem inconsequential or even a form of "soft-glove policing," these orders and citations produce a "pervasive penalty"—a sequence of criminal justice contact pervasive in both its breadth and its frequency across the unhoused population.

As part of my ethnographic research in San Francisco (Herring 2019a), I spent fifty-seven nights sleeping on the streets in encampments and more than one hundred days following people as they acquired food, shelter, benefits, and money and interacted with the local welfare and justice systems. I also went on ride-alongs with police officers and sanitation crews. I experienced and witnessed interactions between police and homeless people nearly every day. Several times, I saw people refuse to go to the hospital to address serious medical issues because they were afraid that their tents and belongings would be confiscated if they were admitted. The move-along orders and sweeps aimed at keeping people invisible from other residents and business owners put social services, food, and toilets farther from reach. They created conflicts, encouraged theft among those on the streets, and increased the vulnerability to assault. Although the officers I observed saw their dispatches as a pointless shuffle—"a big game of whack-a-mole," as one described it—their actions pushed people further into poverty and ossified their homelessness.

Despite rhetorical overtures of coercive benevolence that view policing as a means to push unhoused people into services and shelters, the empirical evidence suggests otherwise. Our survey in San Francisco found that only 12 percent of participants had been offered services by law enforcement—usually a sandwich or a pamphlet—and that less than 5 percent were offered shelter. Rather than clearing the streets, 91 percent of survey respondents reported shortly returning to residing in public space after their most recent move-along order because they had nowhere else to go. Although urban sociologists and geographers have long documented the use of zero-tolerance policing campaigns to cleanse public space of unwanted populations in areas of gentrification, bourgeois leisure, and downtown business districts (Mitchell 1997; Smith 1996), the San Francisco findings show how the policing of homelessness perpetuates the very "urban disorder" that such enforcement claims to reduce (see also Sparks 2017).

As the criminal justice response to homelessness ratcheted up over the past decade, the welfare system responded with the provision of shelter. In 2019, more than 1.4 million people utilized temporary homeless shelters in the US (HUD 2019). While counties focused almost exclusively on investing in permanent supportive housing after a decade of shelter ambivalence, many are now seeing a resurgence of shelter development. The past decade has also been marked by a proliferation of new institutional models, including massive mega-shelters, smaller-scale dormitory settings and outdoor tiny-home communities Although typically managed by nonprofit providers, these shelters are funded and regulated through local, state, and federal agencies.

As part of my ethnographic fieldwork in San Francisco, I spent ninety-six nights residing in the city's shelters and shadowed a group of social workers who work inside them. Most of the unhoused research companions I came to know there preferred the shelters to the streets (Herring 2019a). This finding aligns with an extensive scholarship that examines shelters as spaces of care—where physical (clothing, feeding, and healing) and emotional (listening, offering advice) forms of support occur that shield those unhoused from predation, stigmatization, and criminalization (Cloke, May, and Johnsen 2011, Lancione 2014). However, like all forms of housing assistance in the US, exclusions and restrictions prevent many unsheltered people from entering in the first place. On any given night in the US there are estimated to be at least two hundred thousand more unhoused people than available shelter beds (United States Department of Housing and Urban Development 2019). In San Francisco, 8,011 people experiencing homelessness were tallied in the city's 2019 single-night count, but the city only has 3,400 available shelter beds (ASR 2019). To gain a guaranteed shelter bed, individuals must be referred by the Department of Public Health for a special medical condition or participate in the city's workfare program. Other scholars have noted similar requirements, such as participation in drug rehab regimes (Gowan 2010, Stuart 2016) or religious services (Herring and Lutz 2015).

However, individuals who hold a job, receive disability or retirement benefits or fail to meet a number of other conditions cannot qualify. They must wait for a ninety-day bed, which typically takes 1–2 months. Once a bed is obtained, the person will have to exit after ninety days, get back on the list, and wait again. Without a guaranteed bed, one can always seek a single-night bed. These beds are never guaranteed and require four- to ten-hour waits in lines outdoors. While waiting, I regularly witnessed solicitations for sex, threats of violence, and conflicts between frustrated clients. Even with these arduous waits, many people end up sleeping in chairs or outside in lines after having waited hours for beds that are all taken.

The conditions within shelters deepen deprivation and poverty for some and fossilize impoverishment for others. Many of my research companions found advantages to residing outside as compared to shelters. For some, doing so was a means to preserve a sense of autonomy (Snow and Anderson 1993) and community (Herring 2014, Sparks 2017) that the rule-ridden shelter erodes. Others could better pursue a self-sufficient living in the informal economy that shelters restrict through limited workfare options and early curfews (Duneier 1999, Gowan 2010). Many avoided shelters due to the stress, violence, and sickness that congregative living exacerbated (Hopper 2003) or simply wished to remain with their partners, pets, and property in privacy that nearly all shelters prohibit. For those who did manage to maintain residency in a temporary shelter, shelters were still experienced as traumatic institutions as compared to their former housed lives.

Rather than a stepping stone out of homelessness, the shelter was more often experienced by my research companions as a temporary rest stop with bridges to nowhere (Herring 2019b). In contrast to HUD–mandated homeless counts that portray a static perception of sheltered and unsheltered homeless individuals, there is a high rate of churn between street and shelter. Of those we surveyed living on the streets or in their vehicles, we found that 15 percent had been sheltered at some point in the last month, nearly 40 percent had utilized a shelter in the past year, and 81 percent of those unsheltered had either used or tried to access shelter in the past (Chang et al. 2020). The two most prominent shortcomings according to the surveys and echoed in my fieldwork were a lack of meaningful resources to (a) exit homelessness through housing assistance and (b) address employment, behavioral, or mental health challenges. Shelter residents typically perceived these institutions as sociologists have long portrayed them—places of discipline, medicalization, and social control (Stark 1994, Lyon-Callo 2008). However, due to the lack of aid on offer to exit homelessness, shelter residents primarily saw these methods of control geared toward warehousing—spaces to monitor and contain those without housing rather than bringing them back into the social fold (Hopper 2003, Desjarlais 1997).

The long-term embedded ethnographic and survey research reviewed here challenges the dichotomous folk myth of the unhoused being either "service-resistant" or "shelter-dependent." These studies instead reveal how chronic scarcity, programmatic restrictions, and squalid conditions of shelter provision largely explain the persistence of street homelessness. At the same time, the portrayals of institutionalized malaise among longtime shelter clients ignore the structural limitations of the welfare state's aid in exiting out of homelessness. As calls for both a "right to shelter" and a "right to housing" grow in progressive political corners, it's essential that sociologists of housing and homelessness continue to scrutinize not only the quantity of shelter and housing provision, but their quality, condition, and ability to meet the needs of their residents to link them back into housing. Otherwise, the provision of both shelter and housing can be used to exclude and isolate marginalized groups while perpetuating their poverty.

Exits from Homelessness

Although a number of my research companions in San Francisco scrambled back into the private housing market on their own or with the aid of family or charity, those who were rehoused through state assistance most often relied on Permanent Supportive Housing (PSH). Since early in the first decade of the 2000s, Housing First and PSH have become the new policy orthodoxy for ending homelessness. Prior to Housing First, there existed a "treatment-first" and transitional housing model. These programs tied the provision of housing to an individual first engaging in drug treatment, job training, or employment and continuing that engagement or being evicted. The philosophy of Housing First is that adequate housing is a precondition for recovery, rather than a means-tested, compliance-based, welfare benefit (Tsemberis, Gulcur, and Nakae 2004). Housing First moves those experiencing homelessness directly into housing, without requirements of treatment, employment, or training. Individuals are moved either into scattered-site units in the private market or into entire buildings, leased by counties, where they are offered social workers and other supportive services.

Like Housing Choice Vouchers, public housing, and other affordable housing programs restricted by limited resources, PSH is far from an entitlement. Although frequently framed as a rights-based housing intervention, in reality eligibility is often treated as a medicine-based intervention, prioritizing only the most elderly, sick, addicted, and disabled. Today, over two hundred US cities have implemented some sort of Housing First approach, and the model has been adopted in other countries including Australia, Japan, and Canada, as well as across the EU.

While there is little sociological research into how and why certain individuals manage to navigate their way out of homelessness and into PSH (exceptions include Osborne 2019; Gong 2019), there exist volumes of medical, policy, and social science research on the positive impacts and benefits to those who receive housing. This research points to improved health outcomes, more stable housing tenure compared to treatment-first housing, and reductions in government costs through savings on services and incarceration (Woodhall-Melnik and Dunn 2016, Culhane 2008). In my ethnography I followed nine individuals from the streets and shelters into PSH and got to know dozens of other PSH residents in the process. I observed firsthand how Housing First stabilized the health, safety, and well-being of nearly everyone who received it. However, I also frequently witnessed threats of eviction and unstable exits from the city's supportive housing back into homelessness.

My observations were substantiated in an independent audit by the city's Budget and Legislative Analyst's Office. Following a cohort of supportive-housing residents who entered housing in 2010–2011, the study found that 47 percent had left four years later (San Francisco Budget and Legislative Analyst Office 2016, 8). Other studies that track housing retention in PSH for 2–5 years find similar rates of exit, with rental tenure hovering between 50 percent and 65 percent (Nelson et al. 2014; Waegemakers and Schiff 2014; Stefancic and Tsemberis 2007). Of the nearly six hundred people currently experiencing homelessness surveyed, nearly one-third (29 percent) reported living in some form of government-subsidized housing directly prior to their current episode of homelessness, including 13 percent in PSH (Herring, Yarbrough, and Alatorre 2020). Nearly one in five (18 percent) participants reported that they had previously been in PSH.

Despite these findings, there has been little research examining why and how people exit supportive housing or the outcome of those exits. While Housing First works to end homelessness and mitigate the symptoms of extreme poverty for those who can maintain their residency, for others it merely pauses homelessness while instantiating new forms of deprivation, exploitation, and social suffering. The challenges some people faced being rehoused varied depending on whether they had spent their years unhoused primarily on the street or in shelters. Those coming from the street struggled more with hoarding, lack of privacy, and increased surveillance and restrictions. While those who had primarily lived in shelters often experienced PSH as less restrictive and more private than shelter, they also found it more isolating and filled with new dangers. For many, the years of living on the streets or in shelters created the very barriers for them to stabilize in new housing.

Compared to the shelters and streets, PSH was experienced as a service-rich environment. Nonetheless, none of my research companions felt the supports offered were adequate to pull them out of poverty. Even with their various income from disability, social security, or general assistance, most were surviving on between $200 and $500 in disposable income after rent. Everyone I came to know in PSH relied on donations from food banks and many ate more than half their meals at local soup kitchens. Some recycled and others continued panhandling. Many did occasional odd jobs under the table, including those who participated in workfare programs. Beyond this shared lack of monetary support, many felt that there were not adequate health, employment, or behavioral resources to keep them stably housed.

Others found the environment unsupportive. It actively contributed to psychological distress, drug use, and a cycle of short-term jobs that frustrated aspirations of attaining a mainstream lifestyle (see also Gong 2019). Although the leases in PSH are less precarious than those in the private market, the rental agreements were nonetheless far more tenuous than I expected (see also Hennigan 2017). Some of my research companions were evicted due to lapses in benefit incomes, while others who managed to get work and move off benefits found themselves short on rent due after losing a job and awaiting the reinstatement of their benefits.

While Housing First alleviates forms of suffering faced on the streets and in shelters, the existing scholarship has nonetheless failed to adequately assess the permanence or supportiveness of this housing for the poor. Longer-term longitudinal studies across a greater diversity of permanent supportive-housing programs and other forms of government-provided housing would address part of this knowledge gap. Just as important is the need for qualitative studies to examine the reasons people exit government-sponsored housing more generally and the well-being of tenants across low-income housing programs.

Challenging the Neutralization of Homelessness: New Directions for Research

In 1988, Marcuse reflected that "homelessness is shocking to those who are not homeless because it exposes misery in the midst of plenty and represents alienation from home in a home-based society" (83). Pressured by the public to act, policymakers were faced with a dilemma. On the one hand, they were unable to incite a public-policy revolution guaranteeing housing for all who needed it that would actually solve homelessness; on the other hand, they faced a legitimation crisis of ignoring the problem altogether. Their solution, as characterized by Marcuse, was to "neutralize homelessness" by concealing and depoliticizing the social problem.

Today, state officials continue to conceal homelessness. They do so both abstractly—through definitions and statistics—and concretely—by pushing them out of sight and out of mind. Starting early in the first decade of the 2000s, HUD began requiring counties across the country to count the numbers of people sleeping outside and in shelters on a single January evening every other year. Government reports, books, newspaper articles, and most scholarly articles nearly always refer to this "point-in-time count." In 2019, there were 567,715 people experiencing homelessness in the US (United States Department of Housing and Urban Development 2019). 356,422 people were counted as "sheltered" and 211,293 as "unsheltered."

First, setting aside the obvious limitations to getting an accurate count of those "sleeping in areas not meant for human habitation"—a metric that includes not only people sleeping in public spaces, but also those sleeping in less visible places like vehicles and squats—these tallies are also confounded by varying definitions of what counts as a "home." Unlike HUD, the Department of Education considers any family doubled up with family or friends or staying in a hotel or motel to be homeless. In San Francisco, families in SROs may be counted as homeless, but in other cities they may not be.

A second difficulty arises in measuring homelessness via data collected on a single night. For instance, in 2019 the US Department of Education found that 1,280,866 students had experienced homelessness in the last year, double the single-night count of adults alone. San Francisco's HUD count found that on a single night 3,357 people were "sheltered"; however, their shelter-system data showed that over ten thousand people had used shelter at some point over the course of the year. The city's Department of Public Health data showed that at least nineteen thousand of their clients had experienced homelessness in the past year compared to the city's point-in-time count of 8,011. While each of these numbers has its role in shedding light on the issue, the default position among politicians, the media, and even many advocates when talking about homelessness is a sole reliance on point-in-time counts—tallies that minimize the issue and simultaneously concentrate on and undercount the most visible forms of homelessness.

Overreliance on the HUD definition contributes to a narrow, static vision of homelessness. This vision fixates homelessness as an individual trait and permanent status, as opposed to recognizing it as the dynamic and diverse social condition that it is: a common, rather than exceptional, experience among the poor in the US today. This chapter has tried to break with this static conception on two fronts—by spotlighting the dynamic links and trajectories between street and shelter, and between houselessness and housed. Doing so helps us reconceptualize homelessness as not merely the outcome of poverty, but a catalyst in its reproduction. It is not a static status, but a critical moment in the oscillations between housed and unhoused—one with lasting impacts.

The second step in challenging the neutralization of homelessness is politicizing homelessness. There is a rich sociological legacy pointing to how the failure of markets to provide enough housing for all who need it and the rollbacks of state aid both contribute to the housing crisis. From a different angle, this chapter has pushed us to consider homelessness not as simply the outcome of state neglect, but instead as a condition highly mediated by the penal and welfare state. The chapter spotlights not only how shelters and policing deprive and dispossess the unhoused, but also how they hide it, either indoors within shelters or by banishing it into the invisible urban margins.

There is an urgent need to scrutinize emerging trends of invisibilization and depoliticization of homelessness. In 2018, a federal appeals court ruled that arresting or citing homeless people when no shelter is available is cruel and unusual punishment. However, rather than facilitating real solutions, cities are instead forging new paths to hide unsheltered people under programs of "therapeutic" and "complaint-oriented" policing highlighted in this chapter. By pushing people into increasingly marginalized spaces or restrictive short-term pop-up shelters, officials increasingly proclaim that they are ending homelessness when they are instead simply moving it around (see Rankin 2020).

With increasing scrutiny over the use of arrests and over-policing, officials have rebranded "zero-tolerance policing" in a number of liberal cities as "clean and healthy streets initiatives." Under the guise of public health and sanitation efforts, officials utilize purportedly nonpunitive practices of move-along orders and encampment clearances—practices that are, in the eyes of many of my research companions, often more punitive than citations, arrests, or even short incarceration. When governments fail to invisibilize the problem, they depoliticize it by shifting the blame to the homeless themselves. With the new boom of shelter development, officials increasingly proclaim that they are now providing a right to shelter (accompanied by an obligation to use it) to a "service resistant population," without acknowledge that service's chronic scarcity and inaccessibility. In the case of PSH, officials are quick to refer the press to the numbers of new entrants into housing units, but do not even track data on evictions, let alone the reasons for such exits.

Sociological methods are especially well equipped to interrogate problems like homelessness and informal housing that are easily concealed and depoliticized. Ethnographic observations of street-level bureaucrats provide a more accurate assessment of state policies *in practice* as opposed to policies and laws as they exist *on paper*. Ethnographic observations made alongside those experiencing houselessness reveal the impacts of policies and state officials on their daily lives and social relations.

The San Francisco survey data featured in this essay was drawn from studies that used community-based research methods, partnering with a local advocacy group to design, implement, and analyze survey data (see Alatorre et al. 2020). We trained and hired a team of houseless peer-researchers who were currently residing in shelters, on the streets, or in transitional housing. Working with a trusted community group and utilizing researchers with intimate knowledge of homelessness increased the survey response rate, helped us reach the most marginal groups, and enriched interviews on sensitive topics like criminal records, illegal activities, and experiences with police. Together these methods can make visible and politicize the state's role in the shadowy corners of the byzantine shelter systems and encampments where the precariously housed and unhoused take refuge.

Finally, there is a need to strengthen the links between a sociology of housing and a sociology of homelessness. This chapter points to two additional paths for future research. First, there is a need to better understand the process of rehousing and pathways out of homelessness. While there is general consensus among social scientists that the primary challenge to bridging people out of homelessness is the lack in *quantity* of deeply affordable housing, less attention has been given to the *quality* of this housing in addressing the needs of the formerly homeless. In addition, the extant research on eviction has focused primarily on evictions from the private market and says less about the processes through which people are evicted from public or subsidized housing. The findings presented here from San Francisco show that for too many, permanent supportive housing is often not an end to homelessness. While sociologists have played their part in pushing affordable housing higher up the political agenda in arguing for an expansion of the Housing Choice Voucher Program, for public housing, and for permanent supportive housing for the most vulnerable, they must continue to critically scrutinize these programs' shortcomings so that they meet their policy goals of bringing people out of homelessness and preventing it to begin with.

PART III

Housing Markets and Housing Supply

13

Housing Supply as a Social Process

Joe LaBriola

The topic of housing supply in the United States has traditionally attracted more scholarly attention from urban planners, economists, and political scientists than from sociologists. Nevertheless, sociologists have much to contribute to knowledge on the social dynamics underlying new housing construction; indeed, what gets built where in cities has historically been a central concern of urban sociologists. The preeminent sociological theory on the determinants of land use—the growth machine theory of Harvey Molotch (1976) and John Logan (see Logan and Molotch 1987)—highlights the power of business interests, landowners, and developers to push through desired residential development. However, residents who live near proposed housing construction are also powerful social actors who often have the motivation and resources to oppose new housing. In many cities, the political process through which new housing is approved gives these residents ample opportunities to push back on new housing. Ultimately, the housing that is—or is not—built in neighborhoods reflects social conflict and debate about not just what neighborhoods should look like but also who should be able to live in them.

Housing supply is also a distinctly sociological topic because it has important consequences for several dimensions of inequality and segregation. It is thus concerning that that housing supply in the United States is failing to keep up with demand. In the wake of the Great Recession, the rate of new housing construction markedly slowed down in the United States. From 1968 to 2007, an average of 6.3 housing units were built per thousand residents; from 2008 to 2020, this number dropped to just under three units per thousand residents (author's calculations from census data). While rates of new housing construction increased during the COVID-19 pandemic, demand for housing has also spiked, as measured both by large increases in national house prices (US FHFA 2022) and large decreases in the amount of time homes are on the market (Realtor.com

2022). Though housing supply is constrained to an extent by the amount of available land, it is generally possible to use land more intensively to build more housing (Been, Ellen, and O'Regan 2019). As such, insufficient housing supply in the United States is ultimately a *social* problem, and solving this problem requires attention to the institutions that govern housing supply as well as the actors who struggle over whether or not housing is built.

In this chapter, I first cover the consequences of insufficient housing supply for various measures of inequality and segregation. I then expand on sociological approaches to understanding battles over land use, including a growing interdisciplinary literature that highlights and grapples with existing residents' opposition to new housing supply. Next, I outline regulations that govern not just the type and amount of housing that can be built, but also the process through which new housing may be approved by cities. Here, I highlight a growing interdisciplinary literature that demonstrates how these regulations contribute to inequality and segregation in the United States. Before concluding, I highlight my own research on the origins of residential growth controls in California, where I find evidence that these controls were used to enforce racial residential segregation in the post–civil rights era. I close by proposing some potentially fruitful directions for sociological research on the causes and consequences of housing supply.

Housing Supply and Inequality

Perhaps the foremost reason that sociologists are concerned about issues of constrained housing supply is its effect on affordability. Over the same time period that new housing supply has slowed down, the United States has experienced a growing crisis of housing affordability. National house prices have risen by about 50 percent since 2012 in real terms (US FHFA 2022). This shift has made the "American dream" of homeownership increasingly unattainable, especially for Black, younger, and lower-income households (Kneebone and Trainer 2019). The affordability crisis is also felt by renters. In 2018, half of renter households spent over 30 percent of their household income on rent, with a quarter of renters spending over half their household income (Salviati 2019). Low-income households, which disproportionately experience severe rent burden (Desmond 2016), have been priced out of rental markets across the nation: a minimum-wage earner cannot afford an average two-bedroom rental in any county in the United States (National Low Income Housing Coalition 2017). These trends may then imply greater income-based inequality in the amount of resources households can use to consume non-housing goods.

While the housing affordability crisis has several causes, there is a growing academic consensus that the slowdown in new housing supply has contributed to higher housing prices within metropolitan areas (Been, Ellen, and O'Regan 2019). New housing supply lowers rents in the neighborhoods where it is built (Asquith, Mast, and Reed 2020; Pennington 2021; Li 2019; though see also Damiano and Frenier 2020) and lowers house prices at the lower end of the housing market by allowing higher-income residents to "filter up" into more expensive, newly constructed housing (e.g., Mast 2019). Importantly, though, increased housing supply is unlikely to completely solve affordability issues for lowest-income households (Pattillo 2013; Zuk and Chapple 2016; Been, Ellen, and O'Regan 2019; Damiano and Frenier 2020; Phillips, Manville, and Lens 2021), pointing toward the need for policies like housing subsidies and rent control that can help with housing affordability for low-income households.

A second reason housing supply should be of interest to sociologists is that it also affects the likelihood of residential displacement and gentrification (e.g., Zuk et al. 2018). Residential displacement is a negative outcome of concern because it disrupts affected residents' social ties and access to social and economic resources. Theory suggests that greater housing supply may forestall price increases that would otherwise drive displacement, either because existing renters can no longer afford to live in their neighborhoods or because landlords would be less likely to evict tenants in order to charge higher rents to new tenants. Recent research finds evidence for this relationship between housing supply and displacement. While subsidized housing appears to be more protective against displacement than market-rate housing, both forms of housing supply effectively combat displacement (Zuk and Chapple 2016; Pennington 2021).

While sociologists debate the extent of gentrification and of the harms gentrification causes (e.g., Brown-Saracino 2017), there is little doubt that gentrification has become more common in urban areas in the United States in the past few decades. Recent sociological research highlights that gentrification-fueled displacement is unequally patterned by race (Hwang and Ding 2020). There are potentially conflicting mechanisms underlying the relationship between housing supply and gentrification. On one hand, because housing is expensive to build, developers will usually price new market-rate housing at the top of the rental market so that their investment will be profitable. This pricing strategy means that, in general, residents of newly built housing are likely to be more affluent than other neighborhood residents (e.g., Pennington 2021). On the other hand, if new housing is not provided in neighborhoods that are highly desirable, high-income households will bid up the price of existing properties, pushing low- and middle-income households out and thus fueling gentrification (e.g., Hwang and Lin 2016; Phillips, Manville, and Lens 2021). While more research remains to be done, it seems plausible that this latter mechanism has more substantially contributed to gentrification recently, given low rates of new residential construction that would directly drive gentrification via the former mechanism.

Finally, housing supply has important implications for sociologists interested in spatial and environmental inequalities. Insufficient housing supply near dense employment centers causes many workers—typically, those who have less ability to pay—to live far from their work. This, in turn, generates socioeconomic and racial inequalities in access to city resources and in time spent commuting to work (e.g., Kneebone and Holmes 2015; McLafferty and Preston 2019), alongside increases in greenhouse-gas emissions associated with greater commuting (e.g., Ewing and Cervero 2017) and suburban or exurban development (e.g., Jacob and Lopez 2009). Additionally, the lack of housing supply in areas with higher wages blocks workers who are living in lower-wage areas from moving to better economic opportunities, in the process slowing income convergence between residents of high- and low-wage areas (e.g., Ganong and Shoag 2017).

Battles over Housing Supply and Land Use

Understanding battles over housing supply and land use in United States cities requires understanding the groups of actors who participate in these battles and what they have at stake. These battles can be usefully framed in terms of Logan and Molotch's growth machine theory, which highlights tensions between the *exchange value* and the *use value* that can be derived from land. On the one hand are those who seek to profit from the development of land for residential use. This group includes private housing developers, who build nearly all new housing in the United States (e.g., Andrews 2020) and who can be thought of as driven to maximize revenues and minimize costs. These goals largely explain why private developers seek to build housing in areas where housing costs are higher, as well as why many new apartment buildings are so aesthetically similar (e.g., Sisson 2018). Additionally, nearby landowners and business owners may be motivated to seek greater residential development because it then leads to greater demand for services, higher land values, and ultimately more profits for owners of capital. The growth machine suggests that this coalition of profit-seekers is usually powerful enough to push through desired development, whether residential or commercial (Logan and Molotch 2007).

On the other hand, existing residents of neighborhoods often have reason to believe that new residential development will negatively affect the use value they derive from their home and their neighborhood. As a result, they often organize to fight residential development. These residents express a variety of different concerns about the potential negative effects of new housing development on neighborhood use values. Despite ample evidence of the environmental benefits of denser housing, environmental objections to proposed new housing remain common. In an analysis of community meetings in Massachusetts, Einstein, Glick, and Palmer (2019) find that concerns about how new developments will affect the local environment are some of the most frequent objections raised. Residents also commonly voice aesthetic objections to proposed residential structures and claim that they do not fit in with neighboring properties. Nearby neighbors may also complain that the new structure may block the views or light they used to enjoy (e.g., Monkkonen 2016; Dougherty 2017). Another common set of concerns refers to the impact that new residents will have on neighborhood parking and traffic, as well as on community services and amenities. Finally, residents may also be concerned that new residents will bring crime or a decline in neighborhood character or quality (Dear 1992). In affluent and whiter neighborhoods, these concerns may be driven by a desire to exclude low-income (e.g., Duke 2010) and/or minority households (e.g., Farley et al. 1994; Bobo and Zubrinsky 1996) from moving in.

In addition to concerns about use values, homeowners may also be concerned about how nearby residential development might affect the exchange value of their homes (e.g., Logan and Molotch 2007; Einstein, Glick, and Palmer 2019). Homeowners are motivated to protect their home values because homes constitute the largest portion of most homeowners' wealth in the United States (e.g., Kuhn, Schularick, and Steins 2020) and these investments are more difficult to hedge against than other investments. For homeowners, threats to use values are often threats to exchange values as well, since home values are tied not just to the quality of the residential structure and property on which it sits, but also to the bundle of amenities provided in the surrounding neighborhood and city (e.g., Fischel 2001). Further, even if nearby residential development will not necessarily affect homeowners' use values, homeowners may still financially benefit from blocking new housing if doing so will prevent housing supply from expanding to meet demand, thus leading to an increase in house prices. However, opposition to new housing does not appear to be completely driven by homeowner concerns about exchange values, given that in some circumstances renters may oppose nearby housing at the same rate as homeowners (e.g., Hankinson 2018).

Finally, residents may oppose nearby residential development for ideological reasons that do not neatly fit into the above categories of use and exchange value. One important reason for objection is that new development will simply result in large profits for housing developers that are not shared with the surrounding community (Monkkonen and Manville 2019). Residents may sense that housing developers are bending the rules, getting special treatment, or benefiting unethically from building housing in a time when prices are so high (Roth 2007). Residents also object because they believe that the needs and desires of residents should be prioritized over those of newcomers or outsiders (Wong 2018). Manville and Monkkonen (2021) call this perspective *localism*, and find it to be more common among residents who are white, affluent, conservative, and/or homeowners. Finally, residents who hold less egalitarian ideologies are more likely to oppose nearby housing construction, though experimental evidence suggests that the negative effects of homeownership on attitudes toward nearby development are stronger than the positive effect of holding a more egalitarian ideology (Marble and Nall 2021).

Regulations and Institutions Governing Housing Supply

Linking attitudes toward proposed new housing and rates of new housing supply are local regulations and institutions that govern the process of approving new housing. While states have the power to regulate land, states have generally given municipal governments leeway to enact land use regulations that control what types of new housing can be built where (e.g., Hirt 2015; Gyourko and Molloy 2015). The local nature of land use regulation sets up a collective-action problem in high-demand metropolitan areas that can result in insufficient housing supply in the aggregate (e.g., Fischel 2008). Namely, while city residents might economically benefit from the employment growth that results from an increase in the size of the metropolitan area (e.g., Hsieh and Moretti 2019), they might also prefer that new housing goes elsewhere in the metropolitan area. As such, studying regulations around residential land use provides a lens to examine both how cities incorporate the feedback of residents in setting policy and how areas with fragmented governments do (or do not) coordinate in dealing with policy externalities.

The most central land use regulation is the ability to "zone" land so that it can only be legally used for specific purposes—typically, residential, commercial, or industrial use. Though there are areas where these codes can overlap, it is common for residential uses to be prohibited in areas zoned for industrial or commercial use (Hirt 2015). Land zoned for residential use often carries additional zoning regulations that further delimit what types of residential structures—from stand-alone single-family homes to tall apartment buildings—can be built on the land. Because these codes affect density on the underlying land, the relative proportion of residential land zoned as single-family versus land zoned as multifamily has a direct effect on housing supply. In particular, it is difficult to add more housing in areas zoned for single-family housing that are already built out, since there is nowhere for new homes to go. In contrast, additional housing is easier to build in areas that allow for multifamily housing, since denser new housing can take the place of less-dense old housing.

Cities also enact other types of regulations for residential buildings that directly affect the amount of housing on land zoned for residential uses. For instance, cities can specify that residential structures can only be built on lots that exceed a minimum size or that they do not exceed a given height. Less directly, cities may set conditions—like contributing fees toward the provision of public infrastructure like roads, schools, and water supplies—that housing developers must fulfill in order to build new housing. These conditions then may limit housing supply by making building new housing less profitable for developers.

Measuring the effect of these land use regulations on national-level housing supply and costs is somewhat complicated by the fact that many state- or national-level surveys that contain city- or county-level data on land use regulations (e.g., Lo et al. 2019; Gyourko, Hartley, and Krimmel 2019) cannot fully capture the important within-jurisdiction heterogeneity in regulation. However, studies using these data, as well as more detailed within-city data on land use regulations and data on correlates of regulation, almost all find evidence that land use regulations increase house prices and reduce residential construction (Gyourko and Molloy 2015). Stringent land use regulations are strongly correlated with rates of homelessness (Raphael 2010) and exacerbate residential segregation by household income (Rothwell and Massey 2010; Lens and Monkkonen 2016) and race (Rothwell and Massey 2009).

Cities also affect housing supply by setting the process through which new housing must get approved before it is built. Specifically, land use regulations prescribe that residential projects above a certain size, or that would require waivers to existing zoning codes, receive approval at public zoning and/or planning board meetings (Einstein, Glick, and Palmer 2019). Even when a proposed residential project meets all existing zoning codes, vocal enough opposition can convince cities that the project needs to gain board approval at public meetings (e.g., Dougherty 2017). These meetings then provide opportunities for nearby residents to voice their support for or opposition to the proposed project. Though this feature of the approval process ostensibly empowers all community members to participate, these meetings are disproportionately dominated by those who oppose new housing—a group Einstein, Glick and Palmer (2019) call *neighborhood defenders*, and who are often colloquially known as NIMBYs (standing for "Not in My Back Yard").

One reason for this group's dominance in the approval process is structural. While there already exists a constituency of nearby residents who might be concerned about the impact of new housing, the beneficiaries of the new housing do not yet exist as a constituency (Einstein, Glick, and Palmer 2019; Dougherty 2020). Participation in these meetings also skews toward more affluent homeowners, who are more likely to have financial and emotional stakes in defending their neighborhood (e.g., McCabe 2013; Einstein, Glick, and Palmer 2019; Hall and Yoder 2022). This finding is consistent with work in political sociology and political science highlighting that better-resourced citizens (in terms of time, money, and civic skills) have greater capacity to participate in local politics (e.g., Brady et al. 1995). It helps to explain the more general sociological paradox that increasing the number of avenues of participation in local decision-making may actually widen inequalities in political influence (e.g., Lee, McQuarrie, and Walker 2015; Levine 2017).

At meetings to discuss the fate of residential projects, neighborhood defenders may bring up a variety of concerns unrelated to the regulatory issues that triggered the meeting in the first place. Board members may then ask the housing developer to conduct further studies to address these concerns. Additionally, neighborhood defenders may also sue the city and the developer to block the proposed project. As Einstein, Glick, and Palmer (2019) explain, these tactics may reduce the supply of new housing in several ways. First, these tactics may delay housing construction, since conducting studies to address neighbors' concerns and fighting lawsuits over proposed developments takes time. Second, these tactics may reduce the size of new housing projects, either because the zoning or planning board will request a smaller project, or because developers will proactively create projects with fewer units in order to stave off potential opposition. Finally, these tactics may block housing development altogether. Strong enough opposition from neighborhood defenders may convince zoning or planning boards to vote against proposed housing. In some cities, the costs (in time and money) associated with fighting neighborhood defenders may be high enough to discourage developers from building housing.

Origins of Residential Growth Controls

My own research on this topic focuses on the origins of residential growth controls in the post–World War II United States. While zoning regulations date back to the early twentieth century, it was only in the 1960s and 1970s that cities began to implement land use regulations that were designed to control residential growth citywide (Molotch 1976). The spread of residential growth controls across the country was rapid. In 1971, Petaluma, California, a small city located about an hour north of San Francisco, passed one of the first limits on new residential construction (Logan and Zhou 1990); four years later, over three hundred jurisdictions had enacted their own growth controls (Burrows 1978). However, this spread did not happen evenly. Understanding which cities adopted residential growth restrictions can help us understand the conditions under which communities construct boundaries to limit outsider access to community resources.

Previous work has offered several hypotheses as to why residential growth controls spread at this particular point in time. One explanation centers on a growing recognition of negative environmental externalities of residential sprawl, like loss of the natural environment and increased pollution (e.g., Brueckner 2000). A second prominent explanation focuses on the increasing suburbanization and metropolitan fragmentation of the United States (Fischel 2001). Because suburban homeowners generally worked in different cities than where they lived, their political interests shifted away from promoting commercial and industrial health in their city and toward protecting their financial and psychic investments in their homes, which could be threatened by an influx of new housing and new residents. A third explanation suggests that affluent communities passed growth restrictions in order to exclude poorer households, who might harm nearby property values and receive more in government transfers than they paid in taxes (e.g., Fischel 2004).

In my research (LaBriola 2023), I put forth an alternative explanation that makes central the role of race in the advent of residential growth controls around this time (see also related work by, e.g., Rothstein 2017; Trounstine 2020; Sahn 2022). By the end of the 1960s, many of the mechanisms that had been used to legally enforce racial residential segregation, like redlining, racial covenants, and blockbusting, had been outlawed by legislative and judicial action (e.g., Rothstein 2017). White households thus faced the threat of racial integration at the same time that they began to lose their monopoly on political power in cities (e.g., Self 2003). I posit that these forces, which drove many white households to racially homogeneous suburban cities (Boustan 2010), also drove the passage of residential growth controls in these cities as a way to enforce de facto racial segregation when de jure segregation was no longer possible. Using data on the passage of residential land use regulations in California cities from 1970 to 1992, I show that cities that were whiter than their surrounding metropolitan areas were significantly more likely to pass explicit controls on residential growth, even after controlling for environmental attitudes, suburban status, and economic factors. To reiterate some of the earlier discussion on the consequences of constrained housing supply, these restrictions have inflated the house values of predominantly white homeowners, monopolized city resources for white residents, and made it more difficult for nonwhite households in the metropolitan area to transition to homeownership.

Directions for Future Research

Sociologists are well positioned to contribute to this burgeoning literature on housing supply, given our discipline's long history in researching the connections between institutions, laws, and power; the social origins of belief formation; the social embeddedness of economic institutions; and the roots of economic, social, and racial inequalities. Below, I suggest a few potentially fruitful research agendas for interested sociologists.

First, social movement scholars may do well to consider the rise in the last decade of pro-housing development movements whose members often self-identify as "YIMBYs" (standing for Yes in My Back Yard). These movements have organized to speak at zoning meetings on behalf of proposed housing developments, to overturn laws that restrict housing production in more affluent neighborhoods, and to mobilize consciousness about insufficient housing supply as a key social and political problem (e.g., Dougherty 2020). While YIMBY movements are young, they appear to have been influential in securing some important political victories, including resolutions to eliminate single-family zoning in Portland, Minneapolis, Sacramento, and Berkeley (Mervosh 2018; Bailey Jr. 2020; Clift 2021; Yelimeli 2021). There appears to be much to learn about what makes YIMBY movements more successful in some cities than in others, whether YIMBY movements can successfully join forces with existing anti-displacement, housing affordability, and tenants' rights movements (e.g., Dougherty 2020), and what types of messages might be most effective in persuading residents to support more inclusionary zoning (for recent work on this topic, see Demsas 2021a).

Second, urban sociologists might wish to reconcile growth machine theory with research that highlights the power of homeowners and residents to block nearby residential development. A new synthesis that combines the strengths of growth machine theory with the strengths of the literature summarized in this chapter may be better able to explain the power of homeowners in determining land use in urban as well as suburban cities (e.g., Been, Madar, and McDonnell 2014), and perhaps better recognize how calls that "the status quo should always be treated as possibly better than the growth alternative" (Logan and Molotch 2007) may bring about undesirable inequalities.

Finally, to that end, much work remains to be done by sociologists interested in stratification and inequality to more fully understand how insufficient housing supply and rising housing costs over the last decade have widened economic and racial inequalities between households and neighborhoods. For example, in my own recent work (LaBriola 2023), I show how rising house prices have accounted for most of the growth in the median white-Black wealth gap between 2013 and 2019. White households have benefited more from rising house prices than Black households, both because white households are more likely to own homes and because white households own more expensive homes. These trends are likely to have been exacerbated during the COVID-19 pandemic, as low mortgage rates and the desire for more space in one's home have driven up demand for housing, while rates of new housing supply remained flat (Demsas 2021b). More optimistically, sociologists might usefully document how the end of exclusionary zoning within cities may reduce income and racial segregation in the years to come.

14

Housing Market Intermediaries

Elizabeth Korver-Glenn, Robin Bartram, and Max Besbris

The housing market is replete with intermediaries—individuals who are positioned between residents and housing resources and who use their positions to construct, maintain, or expand markets.[1] For example, real estate agents, by organizing open houses, negotiating deals, or managing applications, connect buyers with sellers and renters with landlords. Housing authority workers process applications for vouchers to be used in the private rental market and dole them out to poor renters. Appraisers assign value and provide prospective buyers and current owners with prices on which to base market decisions. Housing court lawyers can help renters facing eviction remain in their homes. And mortgage lenders provide the capital with which to buy or renovate a property. Housing market intermediaries can also limit or enable people's access to housing in many ways. Building inspectors can reduce or enhance property owners' chances for refinancing by issuing or ignoring code violations; mortgage lenders can ensnare homeowners in predatory mortgages or provide relatively fair financing; and landlords and property managers can trap renters in exploitative leases or keep rents affordable. A sociology of housing requires analytic attention to these myriad housing market intermediaries since they affect whether and under what conditions individuals and households can access and maintain access to housing as well as help determine the affordability and quality of that housing.

---

[1] We use the term market "intermediary" because of its purchase in other sociological subfields, namely economic sociology (Bessy and Chauvin 2013), but also because "broker" refers to a specific actor in housing transactions. Additionally, "brokerage" is a broader concept referring to various activities connecting two parties to each other—trading on gaps in social structure—that captures a wide range of market and nonmarket activities (Stovel and Shaw 2012). But see Korver-Glenn (2021) for a use of "broker" that intentionally intersects and expands these meanings.

In this chapter we show the utility of intermediaries as a wide category of analysis, particularly for understanding how housing inequality interacts with other forms of social stratification across axes such as gender, class, and race and ethnicity. We summarize recent research and unpack how the work of public- and private-sector intermediaries—such as housing developers, building inspectors, real estate agents, mortgage lenders, appraisers, landlords, housing authority caseworkers, mobile home park operators, and property managers—leads to more or less stratification in the housing market. By and large, intermediaries reify racialized, gendered, and classed housing markets. That is, market intermediaries do their work within the context of various socially oppressive systems that influence their behavior (Connolly 2014; Gurusami and Kurwa 2021; Taylor 2019), and they animate these systems in their everyday work. For instance, intermediaries often use (presumed) individual- and community-level racial identity as a heuristic to determine distinct courses of action, resulting in unequal outcomes for individuals and neighborhoods. And they match people, products, and places, using racial categories for this work: Real estate agents steer white homeseekers away from neighborhoods of color (Besbris 2020; Galster and Godfrey 2005; Korver-Glenn 2021), lenders offer unfavorable mortgages to Black and Latinx borrowers at higher rates than financially comparable white applicants (Faber 2013, 2018b; Rugh 2015), and bureaucrats zone neighborhoods for different uses depending on their population demographics (Rucks-Ahidiana, this volume). However, intermediaries may also act in ways that counter systemic forms of inequality (Bartram 2021; Korver-Glenn 2021). Thus, intermediaries can reinforce *or* resist hierarchies and contribute to *or* mitigate the stratification of residential patterns and market processes.

A sociology of housing should focus on intermediaries not only because their work leads to particular housing market outcomes, but also because doing so provides bridges to other subfields. Economic sociologists, for example, are keen to know how intermediaries affect the structure of markets. Scholars of consumption and decision-making want to understand why consumers choose certain products (e.g., a home or neighborhood) over others and what role third parties play in adjudicating between different goods and services. Sociologists of work seek to understand whether the conditions under which intermediaries labor make for good or exploitable employment and how different on-the-job pressures shape intermediaries' styles or strategies of brokering. Finally, given the key part housing plays in generating inequality, scholars of stratification will be curious to know how intermediaries' work leads to more inequality or yields more equitable outcomes. Indeed, focusing on housing market intermediaries illuminates specific mechanisms that connect housing to inequality.

What Is a Housing Market Intermediary?

Market intermediaries can be "the *distributors* that buy and resell products, the *matchmakers* that put into contact partners of exchange, the *consultants* that produce advice to their clients . . . and the *evaluators* that evaluate products, individuals or organizations" (Bessy and Chauvin 2013, 84; emphasis original). In the housing market, intermediaries include a wide set of actors who can fulfill one of these roles; for example, appraisers are clear evaluators. Or intermediaries can fill multiple roles—real estate agents act as matchmakers, consultants, and evaluators. Moreover, different types of intermediaries have varying levels of professionalization. Some, like mortgage bankers, are members of clearly defined occupations that require professional training and licensure. Others, like landlords, are minimally regulated; performing their intermediation does not require accreditation.

Housing market intermediaries can work in the private or the public sector. And while many intermediaries gain financially from their work, private- and public-sector intermediaries have distinct economic motivations. To be profitable in the private sector, intermediaries usually must find ways to increase or intensify their market interventions—whether by seeking higher amounts of percentage-based commission, expanding the number of clients in their portfolios, or some other means. By contrast, public sector intermediaries do not earn a commission. Instead, public intermediaries work in salaried or waged positions and their earnings are generally unaffected by the number of clients they have or cases they complete. These distinctions blur, however, particularly in the context of contemporary public-private partnerships and urban growth coalitions. Additionally, government regulations and deregulations shape the capacity of private intermediaries—for example, mortgage lending is dependent on state policy (Aalbers 2019; Gotham 2009; Kohl 2020)—and certain private intermediaries are publicly funded (e.g., landlords who accept housing vouchers from low-income renters [Rosen and Garboden 2022]).

In capturing a wide set of housing market actors, our definition of housing market intermediaries draws attention to a range of activities that can be accomplished through a variety of means. This broad definition also allows us to better theorize the housing market as a market. Housing, after all, is a commodity; studying the conditions under which a commodity is produced and consumed is key for sociologists interested in how a given market stratifies individuals and groups within it (Engels 1935; Pattillo 2013).

What We Know about Real Estate Agents and Landlords

The study of housing market intermediaries is not a completely new endeavor. In fact, some intermediaries, namely real estate agents, have preoccupied scholars of housing for decades. Since the 1950s, most residential real estate transactions in the US have been facilitated by real estate agents, and their involvement in sales has only grown (Hornstein 2005). As the civil rights movement drew attention to racial discrimination and unequal outcomes in housing, scholars began to examine the racial attitudes and practices of real estate agents—given their central role in sorting home-seekers (Helper 1969). In the decades since, a great deal of research has consistently shown that real estate agents routinely discriminate against homeseekers of color. They steer white homeseekers to predominantly white areas with access to more amenities and higher-quality housing stock. By contrast, they steer homeseekers of color to neighborhoods with higher proportions of people of color, relatively fewer amenities, and lower-quality housing stock (Besbris and Faber 2017; Galster 1990a; Galster and Godfrey 2005; Korver-Glenn 2021).

The consequences of this discrimination are myriad and pernicious (see Krysan and Crowder 2017 for summary). While the most egregious forms of discrimination (e.g., refusing to meet with homeseekers of color) seem to have attenuated, agents continue to engage other forms of unequal treatment with adverse outcomes for people of color. For example, after government prohibitions of overtly racist practices like redlining, housing covenants, and steering, agents began what Taylor (2019, 5) calls "predatory inclusion": the processes by which "African American homebuyers were granted access to conventional real estate practices and mortgage financing, but on more expensive and comparatively unequal terms" relative to whites (see also Roscigno, Karafin, and Tester 2009). The unequal access to and conditions of homeownership across racial and ethnic groups contribute to wealth, health, education, and employment inequalities, among many others (Conley 1999; Shapiro 2017; Zavisca and Gerber 2016).

More recent work has expanded the scope of research on real estate agents. Research demonstrates how they affect prices, neighborhood reputations, and growth-oriented development decisions (e.g., Besbris 2020; Kimelberg 2011; Korver-Glenn 2021). Overall, this research argues that agents' work generally has perverse effects at an aggregate scale and that it reifies existing inequalities. But a key contribution of this recent research is its focus on agents as market actors who affect housing decision-making and outcomes in numerous spheres, including evaluation and valuation (Besbris 2016; Benites-Gambirazio 2020). Importantly, this focus reveals how agents' financial and professional interests can lead to adverse outcomes for individual consumers as well as for communities. For example, Besbris (2020) found that neighborhoods with higher house prices have more real estate agents, and that neighborhoods with more real estate agents experience increases in house prices at a higher rate than those with fewer. Over time, the benefits of high house value, e.g., better-funded schools, accrue in already advantaged places. Agents, in other words, foster the reproduction of neighborhood inequality and class segregation.

Other recent work has focused on landlords, similarly treating them as intermediaries who actively intervene between supply and demand (Garboden and Rosen 2018, 2019). That is, while landlords are supplying rental housing to renters, rental markets do not naturally find equilibrium; rather, landlords sort prospective renters and treat them differently depending on their race, class, household composition, and other characteristics such as whether they have a housing voucher. For example, Rosen (2014, 2020) found that landlords in Baltimore steered poor, Black renters who used housing vouchers to the lowest-quality housing stock in their property portfolios (see also Besbris et al. 2022). This housing was in some of the city's poorest and most segregated neighborhoods, and since voucher holders regularly faced discrimination in the market, they had few alternative options (Rosen, Garboden, and Cossyleon 2021). Other work demonstrates that landlords discriminate against renters of color (Hanson and Hawley 2011; Ondrich, Stricker, and Yinger 1999), as well as renters with children (Desmond et al. 2013) and same-sex couples (Schwegman 2018). Landlords also disproportionately evict and exploit poor renters (Desmond 2016; Desmond and Perkins 2016b). Moreover, landlords steer prospective renters when they advertise their available housing and when they correspond with prospective tenants (Boeing et al. 2021; Hanson, Hawley, and Taylor 2011), and they do so in ways that reify existing racial-spatial hierarchies (Besbris, Schachter, and Kuk 2021; Kennedy et al. 2021). Their discretion in steering renters to specific housing units and neighborhoods continues even in the face of laws meant to curtail discrimination (Reosti 2020).

While this prior work has illuminated how real estate agents and landlords discriminate against and exploit homeseekers and residents—and are therefore integral to the maintenance of sociospatial inequalities—there are a variety of other intermediaries who affect the structure of the housing market.

What Other Housing Market Intermediaries
Should Sociologists Study?

Landlords and real estate agents are not the only intermediaries home-seekers interact with when they search for or exchange a home, and they are certainly not the only actors whose work determines the distribution and value of housing. A robust sociology of housing needs to examine the other public- and private-sector actors involved in the market.

PUBLIC-SECTOR INTERMEDIARIES

One understudied yet key set of housing market intermediaries works for the state. These intermediaries evaluate property taxes, make decisions about zoning exemptions (Hirt 2015), dole out citations for regulation violations (Bartram 2019; Kurwa 2020b), and decide who is eligible to receive housing vouchers and other forms of government assistance and relief. While they do not work on commission and their work is not oriented around personal profit, their decisions shape housing prices as well as access to housing markets. The concept of the growth machine (Logan and Molotch 2007), which describes political-economic coalitions between city governments and private interests, suggests that city workers work at the behest of elites to intensify land value. In this way, city workers make decisions that protect property values for middle- and upper-class (white) homeowners and investors, incentivize new developments (though only in particular types of neighborhoods), and penalize low-income residents and residents of color as well as the businesses they own (Fairbanks II 2009; Lipsitz 2011; Sutton 2015; Valverde 2012). While most studies of city government workers center on the ways their decisions shape racial and economic inequality, others have pointed to decisions and preferences of planners, policymakers, and law enforcement that reinforce normative ideals of what constitutes a household and what kind of housing should be built to maintain these ideals (Groth 1999; Herbert 1996; Norman 2011). In other words, public-sector housing market intermediaries often work in ways that reify various forms of social and geographic inequality.

Yet state intermediaries and elite capitalists are not always aligned. Gotham (2002), for example, highlights the conflicts between city officials and elites that delimited growth policies in Kansas City, Missouri. Pacewicz (2013) shows how technocratic intermediaries can use novel financial tools in ways that are not always aligned with the interests of elites. Others have illuminated the discretion and cultural and professional logics of state-employed housing market intermediaries. Becher (2014), for example, shows that city officials assign value according to perceptions of effort that owners have put into maintaining the property. In turn, this valuation shapes how property owners are treated and compensated in the case that the city uses eminent domain to take their property.

Accounts of code-enforcement officials—workers employed by local municipalities who inspect properties for safety and nuisance issues—also illuminate intermediaries' contributions to housing market inequality. For example, Bartram (2022) finds that, while code-enforcement inspectors in Chicago make efforts to "go easy" on small-time landlords and low-income property owners, the structures in which their decisions are embedded end up bolstering growth machine priorities (see also Proudfoot and McCann 2008). Public intermediaries also include the myriad actors who investigate the behavior of residents who receive state-subsidized housing and punish them when they break the rules (Kurwa 2020b; Ocen 2012). Existing research on various public-sector housing intermediaries thus points toward both subtle departures and similarities with their profit-oriented counterparts in the private sector.

PRIVATE-SECTOR INTERMEDIARIES

Recent research also centers relatively understudied private-sector intermediaries who construct, maintain, or expand the housing market. Given the breadth and depth of data available due to the Home Mortgage Disclosure Act (HMDA), for example, researchers have highlighted how mortgage lending companies and loan officers control access to mortgage loans and distribute them in unequal ways. Like the real estate agents in the 1960s and 1970s who steered Black women to predatory loans, mortgage lending companies and loan officers have disproportionately steered Black and Latinx mortgage borrowers into subprime, predatory loans in the first two decades of the twenty-first century (Faber 2013, 2018b; Rugh 2015; Rugh, Albright, and Massey 2015). Women—especially women of color—also continue to be exploited through subprime loans and low-quality housing (McCormack and Mazar 2015; Wyly and Ponder 2011). While discrimination has long been a feature of mortgage lending (Hanson et al. 2016; Ross and Yinger 2002), the subprime crisis presented new opportunities for researchers to examine both the processes by which mortgage loan intermediaries use racial status to determine individual creditworthiness and to investigate how financialization itself is a racialized process (Massey et al. 2016; Robinson III 2020b; Steil et al. 2018). There is increasing evidence that lenders discriminate, but how and why this discrimination occurs remains understudied. Future work should interview lenders and mortgage bankers, observe their training and the workplace dynamics that potentially prompt discriminatory behavior, and examine the technologies and algorithms they use to assess risk.

Appraisers are also key intermediaries in valuation processes. Far from merely "reflecting" the market in assessments of home value, appraisers actively shape home value through appraisal methods (e.g., the choice of "comparable" sales data), assessments of home sellers, and interpretations of neighborhoods (Howell and Korver-Glenn 2018; Korver-Glenn 2018, 2021). Given intractable levels of racial housing-wealth inequality, unequal returns on investment across housing in racially distinct neighborhoods (Flippen 2004), and the increasing correlation between neighborhood racial composition and housing value (Howell and Korver-Glenn 2021), more research on appraisers is certainly warranted. How do appraisers draw neighborhood boundaries? How do they decide that one unit is comparable to another? And how might this work change depending on the demographics of the prospective buyer or current resident?

With respect to rental markets, emerging research centers the key role played by property managers—those hired by landlords or property owners to do the day-to-day work of overseeing rental property. Property managers' work ranges from screening prospective renters, hiring leasing and maintenance staff, and making decisions about property maintenance expenditures and rental prices, to evicting renters, among other activities. In fact, new evidence suggests that tenants in units maintained by property managers suffer more negative outcomes than their counterparts in units managed directly by landlords. Property managers are more likely to avoid service requests and use nonresponse tactics (thus inhibiting renters' ability to resolve conflicts or maintenance issues), are more likely to use exploitative rent and fee arrangements, and have higher eviction filing rates (Korver-Glenn 2020; Leung, Hepburn, and Desmond 2021)—though these higher filings rates may be due, in part, to the fact that property managers are more likely to be used by large corporate landlords who are more likely to file than small individual landlords (Garboden and Rosen 2019).

There are, however, some market intermediaries who seem to improve outcomes for housing consumers—though these are generally public- and not-for-profit market actors. For example, nonprofit housing counselors foster residential mobility to less segregated neighborhoods, and renters who use them tend to experience more residential stability over time (Darrah and DeLuca 2014). Renters fare better in housing court when they are represented by attorneys, and locales that mandate legal representation for tenants in housing court may have slightly lower eviction rates (Ellen et al. 2021; Seron et al. 2001). More generally, future research should explore the possibility that intermediaries may reproduce or exacerbate existing inequalities at some times while contesting those inequalities and providing more just outcomes at others (Bartram 2022; Rosen and Garboden 2022).

Intermediaries, Social Ascription, and Market Actions

Intermediaries' discriminating and matchmaking actions can construct, restrict, maintain, or expand housing markets. First, housing market intermediaries of all types discriminate—or treat people and places differently. Put another way, intermediaries use race, gender, class, and other status markers as shorthand heuristic cues when they connect, expand, or simply intervene in the market; because intermediaries often interpret these cues hierarchically, the actions they take lead to unequal outcomes.

For instance, appraisers use neighborhood racial and income characteristics to do the work of valuation (Howell and Korver-Glenn 2018, 2021; Korver-Glenn 2018, 2021). Appraisers perceive neighborhoods of color as places that have low housing demand, low-value and low-quality homes, and high rates of crime. They assume that homes in neighborhoods of color can only be compared to homes in the same or other neighborhoods of color—which they perceive to be similarly low-value—and they choose appraisal data that reflect these assumptions. In doing so, they treat homes, homeowners, and neighborhoods in qualitatively distinct ways, devaluing houses in communities of color relative to houses in white neighborhoods.

Second, intermediaries use socially ascribed identities to match people and homes to places. Following a broader cultural logic—underwritten by historic and contemporary federal, state, municipal, and subdivision or neighborhood policies and codes—intermediaries assume a logic of social and physical homophily when making these matches: e.g., white people do and should live near other white people; homes near each other are and should be physically similar; low-income people do not and should not live near high-income people. They then match people and homes to places with the perceived "same" characteristics—and these characteristics predictably reflect and reify broader social hierarchies *and* reflect and reify spatial distinctions (Besbris and Korver-Glenn 2022; Lipsitz 2011; Taylor 2019). For example, local zoning commissioners and municipal government officials generally refuse to allow mobile home parks—among the most affordable of housing arrangements for low-income people—in most parts of a given locale. As a result, mobile home parks are often far from amenities, sit on environmentally toxic or vulnerable land, and experience a broad sociospatial stigmatization (Sullivan 2018).

Moving forward, we recommend that future research explore how the changing ethnoracial dynamics of US cities and rural places—specifically, their increasing ethnoracial diversity—factor into intermediaries' discriminating and matchmaking behavior. Past work has generally focused on intermediaries operating in poor and highly segregated neighborhoods (especially highly segregated Black neighborhoods) and on intermediaries' interactions with Black and poor housing consumers. Understanding sociospatial inequality requires more attention to those at the top who hoard opportunities and resources and the processes by which they maintain their spatial privilege (Besbris 2020). Moreover, we encourage future research that examines intermediaries' social ascription of people and places. How do intermediaries perceive and act on others' citizenship status, sexuality, language/linguistic cues, employment status, or physical appearance with respect to matchmaking? And how do the identities and social locations of intermediaries themselves shape their work?

Comparison across intermediaries is also warranted. Conceptualizing housing market intermediaries as members of an occupation or profession may illuminate the importance of professional education, the ways in which they are regulated by the state, their professional organizations, the amount of control they have over their own labor, and their occupational closure relative to other, similar market actors (Garboden, this volume). For example, Besbris (2020) links real estate agents' continued racist practices, in part, to their inadequate training. Shiffer-Sebba (2020) attributes some variation in landlord practices to the pathways by which they became landlords, demonstrating that those who actively pursue landlordism as a career are more likely to exploit tenants. And Bartram (2021) suggests that the physical nature of building inspectors' work shapes how they view urban inequality.

More research on the various aspects and conditions of intermediary labor would allow researchers to make claims about how to best mitigate against the inequality-reproducing actions of intermediaries described above. Are intermediaries less likely to discriminate when they are required to have more training or are subject to more stringent regulations? Or do more regulations have unintended consequences—e.g., do intermediaries pass on the costs of regulation to their clients (see Greif 2018)? Have recent widespread eviction moratoriums and housing activism changed landlords' sensibilities? What are the "spillover" effects of city growth and decline on intermediaries' actions? Do racial sorting and discrimination change when intermediaries' racial identities match consumers' racial identities? How does one set of intermediaries shape the work of others? And to what extent are any horizontal relationships among intermediaries a path toward creating equitable housing markets?

Conclusion

As the many examples in this chapter suggest, housing market intermediaries—actors who are positioned between people and resources and who use their position to build, sustain, or expand housing markets—are of theoretical and empirical import to the sociology of housing and urban sociology as well as to other subfields, including economic sociology; work and occupations; sociology of gender, sexualities, and family; and the sociology of race and ethnicity. The "housing market intermediary" construct is broad, bringing together analytically a diverse range of actors across private and public sectors. For now, this broadness is necessary to better understand the myriad ways intermediaries affect the housing market. While a small handful of housing intermediaries have been the subject of sociological inquiry for some time, others have not. Similarly, scholars are only just beginning to understand how the conditions of intermediaries' labor shapes the work that they do.

Within the sociology of housing, a deeper focus on intermediaries has illuminated and can continue to illuminate the reproduction or change of structural inequalities. After all, residential mobility, differences in housing tenure across social groups, and segregation are, in part, the result of the work of intermediaries like real estate agents, landlords, housing counselors, and housing attorneys. The racial wealth gap and housing asset inequality more generally are, in part, the result of the work of intermediaries like mortgage bankers and appraisers. And differences in housing quality across neighborhoods and groups are the result, in part, of the work of housing market intermediaries like building-code inspectors, developers, and local politicians who control zoning. Indeed, it is crucial to better understand intermediaries because their work occurs at the intersections of individuals' housing options and experiences and structural housing dynamics, including financialization, (de)regulation, steering, and more. As a result, intermediaries are the face of housing inequality and merit close attention within the sociology of housing.

15

Housing in the Context of Neighborhood Decline

Sharon Cornelissen and Christine Jang-Trettien

In recent years, gentrification has captured the imagination of sociologists and the public alike, dominating conversations about the transformation of cities from New York City to Detroit. In this chapter, we direct sociologists' attention away from housing in gentrifying neighborhoods to housing amid decline. Neighborhood decline and disinvestment are more common than gentrification in low-income neighborhoods: quantitative studies have found gentrification to be concentrated in the nation's most prosperous cities, while it remains rare in smaller cities and in neighborhoods on the urban periphery (Brown-Saracino 2017). In the one hundred largest metropolitan areas of the United States, 40 percent of poor tracts lost population during both the 1990s and the first decade of the 2000s, while only 20 percent of poor tracts gained population during both these decades (Small, Manduca, and Johnston 2018).[1] Poor, declining urban neighborhoods exist across the postindustrial Midwest and Northeast, as well as slow-growth cities in the South (Small, Manduca, and Johnston 2018).

In addition to depopulation, many poor urban neighborhoods have seen persistent and deepening poverty over time. In the last two decades, a growing number of neighborhoods have seen poverty rates increase. Between 2000 and 2016, the number of high-poverty census tracts in the United States—those with poverty rates over 20 percent—grew more than 50 percent, rising from 13,400 to 20,600 tracts (Joint Center for Housing Studies 2018, 16). Most low-income, Black neighborhoods do not see reinvestment, but remain poor and disinvested even decades later (Hwang and Sampson 2014; Perkins and Sampson 2015).

---

[1] Small, Manduca, and Johnston report distributions based on the median city, while we report averages here.

In this chapter, we outline a research agenda for a contemporary *sociology of housing in the context of neighborhood decline*. We define "neighborhood decline" as a type of neighborhood change characterized by growing neighborhood poverty, decreasing housing values, and the deterioration of neighborhood services through the withdrawal of public and private investment capital (Hackworth 2019; Mallach 2018).[2] This disinvestment encompasses banks marking neighborhoods for limited services (Puchalski 2016), cash-strapped school districts closing public schools (Ewing 2018), cities cutting public services (Kinder 2016), and landlords neglecting maintenance. Neighborhoods experiencing decline have historically lost population and seen a rise in property abandonment (Hackworth 2019). We argue that trajectories of decline, including depopulation, can significantly shape the lived experiences of residents, thereby making their urban experiences distinct from residents in stable or growing neighborhoods (Cornelissen, forthcoming).

This chapter also emphasizes how urban decline has disproportionately affected Black Americans. Decline has been the result of sociopolitical and historical urban changes, but also of the troubled history of racism in the United States. The consequences of these racist legacies reverberate to this day. Hackworth determined that 74 percent of residents living in declining neighborhoods in American Rust Belt cities were Black (2016, 275). Scholars of neighborhood poverty have also shown the intergenerational consequences to growing up in disadvantaged neighborhoods. Sharkey found that two out of three Black children who were raised in the poorest quarter of neighborhoods continued to live in the poorest neighborhoods as adults (2013, 45). Many Black Americans continue to live in cities and communities that have borne the brunt of economic restructuring and political disinvestment (Sharkey 2013, 47). Since individual economic fortune for many Black Americans is tied to Rust Belt cities, urban decline is a mechanism that perpetuates racial inequality.

We argue that housing scholars can benefit from adopting a framework of urban decline. Contemporary housing inequality is often conditioned by neighborhood decline. Eviction, for example, may vary by neighborhood conditions, with landlord practices shaped by poorly maintained housing stock and declining property values (Rosen and Garboden

---

[2] We argue that all neighborhoods can experience decline. Certain studies distinguish between "already declined" and "declining" neighborhoods, with only neighborhoods above the county, Metropolitan Statistical Area, or city median household income qualifying as potentially declining. However, since disinvestment and depopulation can continue to happen in "already declined" neighborhoods, we make no such distinctions.

2022). Decline also provides opportunities to better theorize racial inequalities, as neighborhood trajectories often determine access to housing and homeownership. Moreover, research on decline balances out the disproportionate focus on gentrification, allowing us to identify processes unique to decline that are detrimental to residents and neighborhoods. Finally, an urban decline framework can sharpen our understanding of ongoing sociopolitical transformations shaping housing inequality, such as the fallout of subprime lending and COVID-19.

To push this agenda forward, we identify several promising areas for studying housing decline. These areas include examining how policies and practices of local governments impact housing markets. They also include looking at the role of homeowners and investors in shaping housing conditions, as well as at the emergence of informality in declining neighborhoods (Jang-Trettien 2022). Finally, they include examining residents' experiences of living in declining neighborhoods and the meanings those residents attach to their homes and communities.

Housing amid the Peak of Urban Decline

In the twentieth century, cities in the United States, especially in the Northeast and Midwest, experienced explosive urban growth as they became industrial powerhouses. Between 1900 and 1930, Chicago's population nearly doubled from 1.7 million to 3.4 million residents (US Census Bureau 1999). A 1927 Detroit planning map designated almost one-third of the city as "future downtown" (Thomas 2013, 37). Many newcomers were African Americans fleeing the Jim Crow South and seeking better jobs. Yet opportunities associated with this growth were not evenly distributed. While cities rapidly built new neighborhoods to accommodate the hundreds of thousands of migrants, newer neighborhoods were restricted to white families. Racist laws, mob violence, and intimidation were used to exclude nonwhite residents (Boyle 2007; Sugrue 1996). As a result, Black families were usually relegated to substandard homes in cities' older cores. A study in Baltimore found that half of all Black renters were living in structurally deficient housing (Stegman 1972, 8). Moreover, while Black families were restricted to a small area of the city—even as thousands of newcomers arrived every year during the Great Migration—Black neighborhoods often became extremely overcrowded. Landlords demanded inflated prices for subdivided apartments with shared bathrooms (Wilkerson 2010). Most banks refused to lend to Black families, forcing would-be Black home buyers to depend on intermediaries who used exploitative land contacts and who sometimes profited doubly as both broker and seller (Satter 2009).

After World War II, the seemingly limitless growth of cities came to an end. Industries reduced jobs through automation, moved to new facilities in the suburbs, or moved to the Sun Belt and abroad, where nonunionized labor was cheaper. Suburbanization coupled with deindustrialization led to a mass migration of white residents out of cities—a path that remained blocked for Black families (Rothstein 2017). As deindustrialization and suburbanization starved cities of jobs, people, and tax income, the burden of coping with depopulated urban neighborhoods fell on the mostly Black and impoverished residents who remained. Between 1950 and 2010, Baltimore lost 34.6 percent of its population (Stoker, Stone, and Worgs 2015), while Detroit lost over 60 percent (Dewar, Seymour, and Druță 2015).

Depopulation and deindustrialization depressed the housing market. Disinvestment is often seen as the result of decisions made by rational actors seeking to optimize economic gain while minimizing risk (O'Flaherty 1990). However, disinvestment decisions are not informed by economic considerations alone. Racism was instrumental in shaping urban decline and its housing markets. Sometimes housing segregation was enforced by violent white mobs (Sugrue 1996). Oftentimes racism in housing was *legally* enforced, with the federal government furthering racial segregation nationwide. Through racially exclusive FHA mortgage loan guarantees, the federal government sponsored white families' home buying in the suburbs across the nation, while it denied loans to Black families and in Black neighborhoods (Rothstein 2017). This denial depleted credit from Black communities and furthered housing decline in these areas. While the federal government outlawed housing discrimination by race with the 1968 Fair Housing Act, persistent patterns in mortgage redlining remained well into the 1970s (Taggart and Smith 1981). Redlining also continued in home insurance markets (Squires and Velez 1987), as companies avoided majority-Black neighborhoods or only offered services at inflated premiums.

The calculus of racism also affected disinvestment decisions by local governments and landlords. Sternlieb and colleagues found that in Newark, New Jersey, white landlords were much more likely to abandon properties than landlords of color, especially if their tenants were Puerto Rican or Black (1974, 329–30). And in their seminal book *A Plague on Your Houses* (1998), Wallace and Wallace showed how New York City's decision to selectively cut fire services in poor neighborhoods during the early 1970s devasted neighborhoods like the South Bronx.

During the 1970s and early 1980s, politicians and journalists articulated an increasing sense of an "urban crisis," as they witnessed urban decline across the country. Ethnographers responded by describing what it was like to be housed amid urban decline. We learned about the discomforts, risks, and health hazards of living in the Pruitt-Igoe public housing project in St. Louis (Rainwater 1970) or the wood-framed shacks of a place its researchers called "the Flats" (Stack 2008). Some ethnographies also offered broader analyses of housing decline, stigmatization, and revaluation (Anderson 1990; Rieder 1985; Zukin 1989). Karn et al. (1985) described how home buyers in declining neighborhoods often rely on informal knowledge and hearsay in property transfers, leading prices to wildly fluctuate. Anderson analyzed how white newcomers created value in disinvested Black neighborhoods through their "discovery" of "antique" homes—a process premised on their white privilege (1990, 26). Finally, ethnographers described how those living on the margins are housed, such as street corner men (Anderson 2003), squatters (Kearns 1979), and crack house residents and visitors (Williams 1991b).

Contemporary Housing amid Pockets of Decline

In the contemporary era, cities have followed increasingly divergent trajectories. By the 1990s, cities such as New York, San Francisco, and Boston were thriving. A handful of cities that benefited from economic globalization became the pinnacle of the new urban hierarchy (Sassen 2001). Cities have also benefited from immigration (Vigdor 2014) as well as from young professionals and empty nesters moving back downtown (Zukin 1989). Yet cities such as Baltimore and Detroit continue to struggle with depopulation. If urban decline in the previous era was national in scale, decline is now regional, occurring predominantly in cities that were formerly dependent on manufacturing. Geographically, they tend to be concentrated in the Northeast and Midwest, as well as some cities in the South (Small, Manduca, and Johnston 2018). They include neighborhoods in both small and larger cities, near downtown or on the urban fringes (Hackworth 2019; Mallach 2018).

Urban decline in the contemporary era has also been influenced by broader economic trends, including financialization, the crash of the housing market, and the rise of institutional investors following the economic downturn. From the late 1990s to the middle of the first decade of the 2000s, the subprime lending industry flooded the market with high-cost, high-risk mortgage loans. The easy access to credit contributed to surging housing prices, notably in California, Florida, and many parts of the East Coast (Immergluck 2009). Black and Latino borrowers received a disproportionate share of subprime loans (Been, Ellen, and Madar 2009). Subprime lenders and brokers targeted minority neighborhoods, especially in highly racially segregated metropolitan areas—a process that has been called "reverse redlining" (Hwang, Hankinson, and Brown 2015; Rugh and Massey 2010). Subprime lending and the ensuing wave of foreclosures were highly racialized processes that stripped wealth from minority households and neighborhoods. Problems following foreclosures were often worse for neighborhoods in older cities, where the housing stock is more susceptible to deterioration. In Detroit, property values fell precipitously due to large numbers of mortgage foreclosures and the recession that began in 2008. This decline exacerbated the city's fiscal crisis, and in 2013 Detroit became the largest city to declare bankruptcy in US history.

There is also the growing realization that urban decline is a global process of urban transformation that affects not only cities in the United States, but also, for instance, those in Germany, the UK, Canada, and China (Hartt 2021; Pallagst, Wiechmann, and Martinez-Fernandez 2013). Since the first decade of the 2000s, the notion of "shrinking cities" has become a master framework for understanding urban decline and sustainable policy responses. Within the United States, detailed case studies have emerged of persistent decline in cities such as Cleveland, St. Louis, and Flint (Hackworth 2019; Mallach 2018; Tighe and Ryberg-Webster 2019). Particularly notable is the so-called Detroit School of urban studies, most of it springing from the University of Michigan (Cooper-McCann et al. 2017; Dewar and Thomas 2012; Galster 2019; Thomas and Bekkering 2015). Its authors have addressed questions such as how to rebuild shrinking cities (Ryan 2012) and how residents cope with vacated structures (Herbert 2018a; Kinder 2016).

Neighborhood Decline and an Agenda for Sociologists of Housing

We propose a research agenda for a *sociology of housing in the context of neighborhood decline,* an area that is little recognized within urban sociology but potentially affects all fields of housing research. Most literature in the sociology of housing is organized thematically and focused on broad social problems, including eviction, housing affordability, health hazards of housing, and the racial wealth gap. When scholars compare housing inequalities across neighborhoods, they often use the proxy of poverty rates as a core indicator of urban disadvantage. But poverty rates can hide underlying neighborhood inequalities, notably trajectories of decline, stability, or growth.

We propose a conceptual shift of studying housing through the lens of neighborhood decline. While poor neighborhoods can be growing, stable, or declining, *declining neighborhoods* create unique contexts for housing markets, often invite distinct institutional responses, and sustain local (and informal) housing practices by renters, homeowners, and investors. Specifically, we argue that the framework of urban decline creates four opportunities for housing scholars.

First, it allows scholars to *situate contemporary housing inequalities, as conditioned by historical and ongoing trajectories of urban decline*. For example, Manduca and Sampson demonstrated how exposure to toxic neighborhood hazards—including high incarceration rates, violence, and lead—independently predicted children's long-term well-being in Chicago, beyond traditional measures such as neighborhood poverty (2019). They also showed how exposure to these hazards was highly clustered and segregated, such that there was "almost no overlap in exposure rates for blacks and whites" (2019, 7773). Thinking through decline can help researchers operationalize community disadvantages beyond current characteristics, to include *processes* such as depopulation, pollution, historical violence, and public disinvestment—all more dynamic examples of urban trajectories. We can also think about the added value of considering urban decline for studies that do not currently use this lens. For instance, we may gain new insights about eviction in inner-city Milwaukee (Desmond 2016) if we explicitly consider its context of postindustrial decline, the role of an aging and ill-maintained housing stock, and the ways in which depressed property values shape landlords' practices.

The lens of urban decline also helps housing scholars better *theorize contemporary racial inequalities in housing* by focusing on historical trajectories of urban decline in predominantly African American neighborhoods in the Midwest, Northeast and select cities in the South. This awareness allows us to better understand issues like the persistence of the Black-white homeownership gap, which stood at 30 percent in 2019 (Choi et al. 2019; Rucks-Ahidiana, this volume). Black homeownership rates are among the lowest in highly segregated, postindustrial northern cities, including Albany and Syracuse, New York; Minneapolis, Minnesota; and Milwaukee, Wisconsin (Choi et al. 2019, 12). A focus on urban decline can help historicize contemporary racial inequalities in housing and neighborhoods, and theorize ongoing decline as part and parcel of that inequality.

Additionally, more work on urban decline would *balance out housing scholars' disproportionate focus on gentrification*. The relative attention paid to gentrification suggests that it is the main threat afflicting contemporary cities—even as many more poor neighborhoods are facing decline. Mirroring some of the questions of the gentrification literature, we believe that much can be gained by understanding contemporary processes of housing disinvestment, housing abandonment, and the experiences of living in a home amid decline. What do rates of eviction look like in declining places? What are the mechanisms leading residents to lose their homes? Who are the investors operating in allegedly disinvested neighborhoods, and how they do make money? We also think that gentrification scholars can benefit from a better understanding of housing amid decline because decline is often a precondition of gentrification.

Finally, a focus on urban decline would also attune scholars to *ongoing sociopolitical and structural transformations shaping cities*, such as the fallout of the subprime mortgage crisis, financialization, and the rise of a new investor class. These transformations include risks still on our horizon, such as the spreading evictions resulting from COVID-19's economic fallout. We understand urban decline as shaped by ever-changing historical conditions, rather than as a bygone feature of our cities' past.

Promising Subfields of Housing amid Decline

We believe that our proposed conceptual shift can generate fresh questions and ideas for the sociology of housing. In this final section we will outline promising research areas for studying housing amid decline.

First, policies and practices for how local governments tax, buy, sell, and classify disinvested property can significantly impact local housing markets. How do cities classify and value (Becher 2014) so-called blighted homes and with what consequences? How much property tax do residents of homes rendered worthless have to pay every year, and what penalties do they face when they fall behind? Work by Atuahene and Berry (2019) has shown how Detroit's 2010s tax foreclosure epidemic, when thousands of Detroiters lost their homes, was partly shaped by faulty property tax assessments—because evaluations were inflated due to lagging computer systems, and city assessors were reticent to fix the mistake. More sociologists could analyze the bureaucracies and everyday decisions behind zoning, mapping distressed areas, public property auctions, and code enforcement.

Second, housing researchers should attend to the role of homeowners in declining markets, and to the informal housing markets that may emerge. In many disinvested neighborhoods, staples of formal housing markets—such as mortgages, sales through realtors, home inspections, and warranty deeds—are rare. Lenders have minimum loan amounts for mortgages that exclude depressed markets. Real estate agents also do not operate in these markets because they typically work on commission and have higher profitability in other markets. Consequently, homeowners in declining neighborhoods tend to depend on informal housing market activities, including informal home repair and alternative financing arrangements such as contract-for-deed purchases (Herbert 2021; Immergluck 2018; Jang-Trettien 2022; Kinder 2016). A recent Pew Study showed that approximately one in five home borrowers used alternative financing at least once in their adult lives, making alternative financing a highly understudied topic (Pew Charitable Trusts 2022).

There are still a lot of questions to be answered, including: what practical and financial barriers home buyers in highly disinvested neighborhoods face, and how longtime homeowners in declining neighborhoods cope with diminishing equity and uncertain prospects. Future research can also address how properties are valued and financed in informal markets, how informal markets intersect with (racial) inequalities, and to what extent informal market activity can help mitigate or propel neighborhood decline.

Third, real estate investors are instrumental in sorting renters across neighborhoods, impacting housing conditions and use, and shaping the outcome of policy programs (Rosen 2014; Travis 2019). In his book *Evicted*, Desmond described how landlords profit in disinvested neighborhoods. One Milwaukee landlord used a local social services agency to fill units (2016, 19). Other studies show that landlords rely on housing vouchers to fill their units in disinvested neighborhoods—places where the vouchers are the most profitable (Rosen 2014). However, as Mallach (2014) argues, investors are more than just landlords. They also flip properties and purchase them for speculative purposes. Scholars should look at the role of investors more broadly, examining who they are and how their profit strategies influence, and are influenced by, neighborhood decline.

Finally, a promising research area examines residents' lived experiences of homes and property in declining neighborhoods. Such examination means looking at people's housing options, the meanings people attach to their homes and neighborhoods, and the ways they cope with and devise solutions for problems associated with decline. Residential arrangements may look different in declining neighborhoods. In her study of Park Heights, Baltimore, Rosen (2020) showed the proliferation of "rooms-for-rent" (p. 62), where landlords furnish apartments and rent out each room to a different tenant (Freeman 2017). In addition, drug and alcohol rehabilitation centers and halfway homes are common in declining neighborhoods (Rosen 2020). Housing-insecure residents may also double up with adults outside their nuclear family (Harvey 2020a) or stay in rent-by-week motel rooms (Dum 2016). These living arrangements indelibly shape residents' conceptions of home and neighborhood. They are also likely to shape romantic relationships, parenting practices, employment options, and residential preferences.

As neighborhoods decline, the question of what meanings residents attach to their homes and neighborhoods becomes particularly urgent. Narratives of neighborhood violence may shape residential relocation decisions (Rosen 2017), and historical experiences with violence often haunt present vigilance and profoundly impact home and street life (Cornelissen 2022). A popular urban-planning solution for urban decline has been "right-sizing" cities (Hackworth 2019). Right-sizing proposes gradually erasing the most disinvested neighborhoods from the map through ad hoc housing demolitions, through active neglect, and by envisioning post-urban futures (Clement and Kanai 2015). Considering these policies, it is even more important to know what residents hope and fear for their declining neighborhoods and homes. In her ethnography of the extremely depopulated Brightmoor neighborhood in Detroit, Cornelissen (forthcoming) found that most longtime residents expected that homes would be rebuilt and saw themselves as residents of an urban neighborhood rather than of a ruralized post-urban space. Living through urban decline shaped how these residents imagined the neighborhood's urban future. More research needs to be done on how residents make sense of urban decline, including experiences of loss and staying in place amid decline.

To cope with the problems associated with urban decline, residents often devised their own solutions. Kinder (2016) called this phenomenon "self-provisioned urbanism," which she traced to the rise of neoliberal market logics and the retrenchment of city services—especially in revenue-strapped cities such as Detroit. For example, she described how Detroiters acted as informal realtors to recruit new neighbors or took on the role of city workers to maintain vacant property on their blocks. Herbert's (2021) work on Detroit squatters showed that neighbors embraced an "ethos of care." As long as squatters positively impacted the physical and social dynamics of the neighborhood, squatting (which is illegal) did not bother residents. Informal practices often gain social legitimacy from residents and authorities in declining neighborhoods. More research can be conducted on how residents cope with and respond to neighborhood decline.

With this agenda in mind, urban decline should not be treated as a niche area within urban sociology, nor as a historical urban process from a long-foregone era. Urban decline remains more common than gentrification within poor urban neighborhoods. As the housing literature has disproportionately focused on gentrification, it has simultaneously understudied contemporary decline. We urge scholars to rectify this lacuna. Rather than a monolithic historical process, urban decline is an ongoing process of urban transformation, shaped by ever-changing institutions, socioeconomic trends, and residential preferences.

16

Learning from Short-Term Rentals' "Disruptions"

Krista E. Paulsen[1]

The emergence of sharing-economy platforms such as Airbnb and VRBO has propelled short-term renting from a strategy that second homeowners employed to earn income on unused vacation properties to a ubiquitous element of communities across the globe. The largest of these platforms, Airbnb, now boasts over seven million listings worldwide, and over two million guests per night (Airbnb n.d.a). An expanding literature examines the potential of short-term rentals (STRs) to "disrupt" the tourism and hospitality industries and explores the nuances of home-sharing market-places (see, e.g., Belarmino and Koh 2020). But STRs also disrupt housing markets and neighborhoods as they introduce a new type of land use into residential areas. The dwellings listed on STR platforms include houses, apartments, and condominiums in tourist destinations, but also in relatively unremarkable urban and suburban neighborhoods. "Guests" are present for less than a month (under thirty days is the common demarcation of a "short-term" rental), enjoying varying levels of contact with and support from property owners. In many locales, STRs are unregulated and unlicensed, appearing with little or no formal announcement. They can also be highly lucrative, providing income to homeowners who rent out a room or accessory dwelling unit (ADU), or, as is increasingly the case, to investors who hold portfolios of multiple STRs and thus expand the financialization of housing (Cócola-Gant and Gago 2019; Grisdale 2019; Hoffman and Heisler 2020). As a result, one dwelling at a time, neighborhoods that were once primarily occupied by long-term residents can become de facto hotel districts.

When occupied by longer-term residents, housing can foster community. Neighborhoods and buildings become sites where individuals see one another routinely, where children play together, and where

---

[1] Kathleen McInally has provided valuable research assistance on this work.

residents support one another through mutual aid or collective action (Kusenbach 2006; Mahmoudi Farahani 2016; McCabe 2016). While some neighborhoods have higher degrees of transience—student districts, for instance—the arrival of STRs takes transience to an extreme. Not only do STR occupants turn over frequently, they are often ignorant of local norms, disconnected from existing residents, and occupied by interests other than community well-being (Gurran and Phibbs 2017; Cócola-Gant 2016). These social and interactional changes within neighborhoods are accompanied by housing market impacts: as STRs increase, rents and home prices typically do as well, while vacancy rates decline (Lee 2016; Barron, Kung, and Proserpio 2021; Grisdale 2019). STRs are particularly common in core neighborhoods and those adjoining tourist districts (Gutiérrez et al. 2017; Pinkster and Boterman 2017; Cócola-Gant and Gago 2019), as well as in neighborhoods experiencing gentrification (Grisdale 2019; Roelofsen 2018), where they may intensify ongoing shifts in housing prices, commercial offerings, and demographic composition. STRs are also proliferating in amenity destinations (Stuber 2021) and in small metros like Boise, Idaho, the site of my research.

This chapter focuses on these two dimensions of STR disruptions—to markets and neighborhoods—in both the emerging literature and in Boise's neighborhoods. By disrupting common social and financial uses of dwellings, examining STR proliferation advances and complicates questions that have long drawn sociologists to housing, such as whether housing is affordable and accessible and how housing potentially organizes social life. STR proliferation also provokes new questions about just how housing is consumed and why, and who profits.

STR Disruptions in a Mountain West City

Boise, Idaho, is in many ways more typical of US cities than the kinds of global capitals and tourist destinations where STRs have been studied. Located in southwestern Idaho, Boise is a fast-growing city of 235,684 (US Census Bureau n.d.) within a metropolitan area about three times that size. It is the capital of Idaho and has a varied economy inclusive of but not dependent upon tourism. Still, by late 2021, Boise was home to 1,368 STRs—up from 488 five years earlier (AirDNA n.d.). This proliferation has become a substantial public concern, as Boise faces an ongoing housing crisis stemming in part from recent growth. Rents in Boise increased 39 percent from March 2020 through July 2021—more than anywhere else in the US—while vacancy rates fell to around 1 percent (Gamboa 2021). Local media have linked the area's housing challenges in part to the spread of STRs (Talerico 2019), a claim consistent with the research on housing market impacts discussed below. In an attempt to add housing inventory, the city eased restrictions on ADU construction in 2019, although some residents feared ADUs would simply become more STRs (Sowell 2019). Following an unsuccessful 2019 regulation push, the city approved licensing of STRs in 2022 (Land 2022). Together, these events have, since 2019, drawn public attention to a conversion of Boise's housing stock that had until then proceeded without official public notice or opportunity for comment.

STRs can be found throughout the city, but their highest density is in neighborhoods surrounding downtown Boise. The research included here focuses on these areas, especially the North End and West Downtown, neighborhoods with a mix of historic homes, apartments, and commercial uses, and which have active neighborhood associations. Residents are highly invested in these neighborhoods. In hearing testimonies, planning-workshop activities, and interviews, participants celebrate their neighborhoods' demographic, aesthetic, and social qualities, including proximity to amenities, diversity, and a strong sense of community. Walkability and abundant front porches facilitate sociability: residents recognize one another's children and pets, and they value local expressions of goodwill and inclusion among both strangers and acquaintances. These qualities of the built and social environments attract newcomers and keep people in place. As one West Downtown resident stated, "Now you can't find houses for sale there, ever, like people just don't sell."

Market Disruptions

Short-term rentals impact housing markets primarily by shifting the use of existing housing stock from long-term occupancy by owners or renters to short-term stays. The types of dwellings used as STRs are reflective of broader housing markets, ranging from large, extravagant homes to small efficiency units. Guests may prefer STRs to hotels for a number of reasons including lower cost and more space, as well as a "homey feel" and the opportunity for a more "authentic local experience" (Guttentag et al. 2018, 349; Paulauskaite et al. 2017). STRs that are entire dwellings (as opposed to a room in a home) offer many appealing features, such as a kitchen or space for children; they can also accommodate large groups. For some STR guests, the opportunity to be situated in a neighborhood may be part of the appeal, particularly for guests in the process of relocating to a new city, or who simply prefer the aesthetics, feel, or scale of neighborhoods over urban convention and hotel districts. STRs also provide lodging options in areas that lack hotels (Gutiérrez et al. 2017; DiNatale, Lewis, and Parker 2018). Regardless of why guests are coming to STRs, the fact is that they are: AirDNA tracked nearly twenty million nights of STR stays in the US in July 2021 (Lane 2021). Demand rebounded after the early months of the pandemic as guests increasingly paired work and vacation stays (Peng and Tobin 2022). For the most part, the units being used as STRs are dwellings that would otherwise be part of long-term housing inventories (Yang and Mao 2019; Rabinowitz 2019; Transparent 2020). Even in vacation and resort communities, it is not just empty second homes being listed on platforms like Airbnb, but increasingly the housing stock once relied upon by local workers (DiNatale, Lewis, and Parker 2018; Stuber 2021).

STRs' effects on housing markets are becoming well known. In cities such as Sydney (Gurran and Phibbs 2017), Berlin (Schäfer and Braun 2016), Toronto (Grisdale 2019), and others, scholars find declining vacancy rates, diminishing inventories, and increasing rents as properties are converted to STRs (Garcia-López et al. 2020; Horn and Merante 2017; Hoffman and Heisler 2020). Describing the relationship of STR use and increasing rents in Los Angeles, Lee observes that "a renter in an Airbnb-saturated neighborhood seeking to occupy one of the handful of available apartments is no longer bidding against the local residential rent price but is instead bidding against the extra profit that STRs can bring" (2016, 238). Importantly, other housing market shifts that co-occur with STR proliferation also impact rents: in London, for instance, both increasing homeownership and STR misuse explain increased rents (Shabrina, Arcaute, and Batty 2021). Studies of STR regulation also demonstrate that the ability to list properties as STRs is associated with increased purchase prices (Valentin 2021; Kim, Leung, and Wagman 2017). While a few reports have found that STR proliferation is *not* associated with increased rents (Levendis and Dicle 2016; Snelling, Colebrook, and Murphy 2016), published studies concur that more STRs generally result in higher long-term housing costs.

Beyond creating housing scarcities, STRs can disrupt typical ways that housing works as a commodity. Housing units are bought, sold, and rented, but other dimensions of housing—its financing and its use as a means of speculation—further establish it as a commodity central to contemporary US and global economies, and one that is particularly reflective of the social and political construction of markets (Pattillo 2013). Financial instruments like mortgage-backed securities created new means of generating wealth from housing; STRs create an opportunity to generate wealth by attracting new types of investors and using dwellings in novel ways. As a result, STR proliferation can extend and intensify housing financialization, or the use of housing as a vehicle to generate wealth (Aalbers 2016; Hoff-man and Heisler 2020). Investors are particularly attracted to STRs, as, compared to long-term tenants, short-term renters may generate more income with less wear on units, allow higher degrees of liquidity and flex-ibility, require less investment, and create opportunities for investment gains in working-class neighborhoods within tourist cities (Gutiérrez and Domènech 2020; Wachsmuth and Weisler 2018). Districts proximate to city centers and to tourist attractions have become particularly desirable sites to offer properties as STRs (Krause and Aschwanden 2020; Gutiérrez and Domènech 2020). As a result, in global capitals in particular, use of residential properties as STRs can reconfigure the rent gap in "culturally desirable and internationally recognizable neighborhoods" (Wachsmuth and Weisler 2018, 1165). STR proliferation can also foil local affordable housing initiatives, such as encouragement of ADU construction (Chap-ple et al. 2017; Ramsey-Musolf 2018). Perhaps the ultimate expression of platform economies' market transformations can be seen in the practice of "Airbnb rental arbitrage," the renting of units with the express intent of re-renting them using STR platforms (AirDNA 2022).

While in many cities investors own and operate multiple STRs, some "hosts" operate just one, often inside or adjacent to a primary residence. These smaller STR operations have their own impacts on housing markets. For instance, the prospect of renting out a room, dwelling, or ADU through STR platforms can alter home buyers' calculations of what they can afford, and income benefits for owner-occupants figure in debates regarding the le-gality of STR regulations (Jefferson-Jones 2015). In cities like Boston, regu-lations allow owner-occupants to rent their properties (or adjacent units) on a short-term basis, while restricting investor-owned properties (Hoffman and Heisler 2020). Airbnb's own materials stress that owner-occupants de-rive meaningful income from renting their properties (e.g., Airbnb n.d.b), deflecting attention away from large-scale investors and toward hosts who are members of the communities where they operate. Empirical explora-tions of owner-occupant hosts are lacking, however. The expansion of STRs thus suggests a research agenda examining this distinct dimension of the financialization of housing, including how it is engaged by investors at a va-riety of scales, and how owner-occupant hosts navigate their multiple roles.

As is the case in many US cities, the proliferation of STRs in Boise has coincided with a broader crisis of housing availability and affordability. It should come as no surprise, then, that residents view STR development in this context. Many residents express concerns that STRs are among the pressures driving up neighborhood housing prices and threatening housing access. STRs are, in their minds, one factor in a broader set of market pressures that include gentrification of core neighborhoods and cash buyers moving to Boise from pricier markets. Together, these forces are transforming a housing market that had long remained affordable relative to other cities in the American West.

Residents of the Boise neighborhoods I study hope these places will remain accessible to residents of varied means, and express sincere, though not unanimous, support for the preservation and development of affordable housing. Here, as in other urban locations, affordable long-term rentals and STRs often compete for the same types of housing stock. Residents of Boise's North End see this competition firsthand and recognize its implications for their neighborhood's demographic makeup and character. The neighborhood includes some of Boise's most expensive real estate, as well as many subdivided older homes, ADUs, and small houses that provide rentals at varying prices. About 44 percent of North End residents rent (City of Boise Planning and Development Services 2019). North End residents value the area's diversity, and in planning activities, advocated a desire to "Keep the North End Weird." They expressed concerns that STRs were "boosting rent and reducing options for folks like college students and middle-income residents" (City of Boise Energize our Neighborhoods 2020). West Downtown residents, too, value their neighborhood's diverse housing stock and can see the local impacts of Boise's changing housing market. There, inventory is low, rental buildings face threats of redevelopment, and the price of single-family homes has increased such that current residents would be priced out. When a developer proposed a new seventeen-unit building to be used *exclusively* for STRs, affordability was "a huge concern" for residents, as the proposal would, in their views, diminish workforce housing in the city's core, leading to both displacement of current residents and sprawl in Boise's more affordable suburbs. In testimony as well as interviews, residents stated a preference for new long-term rentals on this site, including affordable units.

When asked about STRs and affordability, multiple interview subjects related that for property owners, short-term renting makes economic sense. A few supported this claim with some quick arithmetic, explaining how renting an STR for a few nights could be even more profitable than having a long-term tenant. Others spoke of investors who buy houses, offer them as STRs for a year or two, and resell at increased prices—thus profiting doubly from the city's hot housing market. In cases where investors improved neighborhood properties, residents could be appreciative. For instance, one resident praised a West Downtown property that "went from being kind of a rundown turn of the century home, to this actually really cute and very popular Airbnb." But on balance, residents view the profits available through STRs as a threat to their neighborhoods' affordability and stability. They worry that as STRs proliferate, housing costs will increase and residents like them will be priced out—a process Marcuse calls "exclusionary displacement" (1985, 206–07). They also perceive a second impact of this shift, as STRs' value flows from short-term stays. Tenants in long-term rental properties generate income for their landlords while also contributing to social aspects of neighborhoods. When investors use housing as STRs, profits accrue largely without benefit to neighborhoods, and, as detailed below, sometimes at their expense.

Neighborhood Disruptions

At the same time they disrupt housing markets, STRs also have the potential to disrupt taken-for-granted assumptions about neighborhood life, such as who belongs and how dwellings should be used, thus extending sociological understandings of home and neighborhood. Neighboring involves routine and regular interactions that follow predictable local rules. As Kusenbach (2006) details, behaviors such as friendly recognition, providing aid, watching out for neighbors and their property, and managing diversity typify interactions in the "parochial" realm of the neighborhood (distinct from the public realm of the larger city or the private realm of the home). Familiarity with neighbors and their habits, including the norms and expectations of the neighborhood, makes these kinds of interactions possible. As residents stay in place, they form more local social bonds and stronger connections to dwellings as home places (Cuba and Hummon 1993; Sampson 1988).

In neighborhoods where residents turn over quickly, such as areas undergoing "studentification" (Smith 2004), people may be reluctant to form relationships, and behavioral norms are either lacking or difficult to enforce (Hubbard 2008; Powell 2016). The truncated stays of groups like students or STR guests amplify tensions that have long existed between homeowners and renters. As McCabe details, homeowners construct symbolic boundaries between themselves and renters, who are understood as "unprepared or unable to fulfil the obligations of civic life" (McCabe 2016, 115; also see Mayorga 2014). Yet studies of neighborhood social capital indicate that residential stability, rather than homeownership per se, is a greater predictor of important aspects of neighboring such as social interaction and acting in the community's interests (McCabe 2016). Ideally, neighborly relationships provide important sources of social connection, mutual aid, and security and information, and they facilitate action on the neighborhood's behalf, such as participation in neighborhood organizations (Unger and Wandersman 1985; Mahmoudi Farahani 2016).

Importantly, neighborly relationships can also become means of excluding strangers or those perceived as different (Kusenbach 2006).

Emerging scholarship reveals how STR proliferation can disrupt neighborhood social connections. In place of acquaintances and the "familiar strangers" who constitute a reassuring neighborhood presence, long-term residents may see an ever-changing array of tourists and other guests (Pinkster and Boterman 2017, 463). This disruption complicates the routine stock-taking that residents engage in to evaluate neighborhood safety and order (Unger and Wandersman 1985). While STR guests may engage in friendly interactions with long-term residents, not all residents find these interactions satisfying. As Spangler (2020) finds in his research on New Orleans, residents' routine neighborhood activities can begin to feel like uncompensated emotional labor performed for the benefit of strangers. Framing their observations in exchange relationships, Stergiou and Farmaki (2020, 7) observed that residents were thrust into an "involuntary, unintended exchange with Airbnb guests," one that benefits owners and hosts but erodes locals' sense of community and quality of life.

Typically, the introduction of explicitly tourist-serving land uses, such as hotels, in residential neighborhoods would require public notice through a zoning change, conditional use permit, or similar process. But STRs often appear with little fanfare. Unlike major development projects, this type of land use change does not necessarily trigger public notification or comment processes or substantial construction. Instead, residents typically notice small changes, such as lockboxes on doors, people arriving with suitcases, or unfamiliar cars parked overly long on their streets. Disruptions to neighborhood order emerge as STR guests violate local norms around noise, parking, or the treatment of common areas (Stergiou and Farmaki 2020; Gurran and Phibbs 2017). Particularly alarming complaints detail the use of STRs for everything from parties to pornography shoots. But even routine uses introduce serious impacts as the composition and character of neighborhoods change. Examining Airbnb proliferation in Lisbon, Cócola-Gant and Gago (2019) found that within the Alfama neighborhood, about 25 percent of housing units are STRs, including some entire blocks. There, tourist "neighbors" do not speak the language, and their routines are rooted in leisure rather than in work or obligation to the community. Describing tensions between long-term residents and STR guests in Amsterdam, Pinkster and Boterman (2017, 464) observe that tourist activities including drinking and partying were once more contained in the Red Light District, but "with the increasing numbers of visitors and new geographies of tourism—that is, facilitated by AirBnB— the theme park is spilling over" into residential areas of the Canal District.

My own research indicates that neighbors not only worry about problems that might occur at STR properties such as parties, noise, trash, or inappropriate parking, they are also frustrated by limited means of addressing these issues. Most STRs do not have on-site management; and neighbors may not know whom to contact should an emergency or nuisance arise. Residents may fear confronting guests directly or dread the prospect of educating new guests each weekend. Involving the police is unappealing to many, and also raises questions of fairness regarding the costs of maintaining neighborhood order. As one resident testified concerning a proposed STR project that lacked on-site management, "any issues with noise, criminal activity, other nuisances, will become ours, me and my neighbors and the Boise Police Department's to deal with." He continued that the owner effectively proposed to outsource security and management, shifting the cost to taxpayers. This example suggests that for some residents, nonlocal STR investors are a particularly unwelcome variety of absentee landlord.

The "coming and going" of STR guests also raises concerns. Longer-term Boise residents feared strangers near their homes and children who could potentially introduce or increase neighborhood crime. As one interview subject described her neighborhood currently, "we know who's supposed to be here—and so there's a lot of security in that." More STRs would, in her view, introduce more strangers and more uncertainty. Neighborly relationships not only produce a sense of security, they can foster accountability to one's neighbors. Conversely, STR guests may be unaware of local norms and unbeholden to the social connections that encourage compliance. A Boise resident's speculation about STR guests in her quiet condo building illustrates this perceived risk: "They won't know our rules . . . and even worse, they won't care because they're on vacation and they will just leave, and they don't care about the impact." Other residents framed the relationship between STR guests and neighborhoods as potentially extractive. One West Downtown resident testified that long-term residents "contribute to and participate in the community," while STR guests are "basically kind of pulling from the neighborhood, getting all the good things from our neighborhood, but not [giving] much in return." In the neighborhoods that I study, STRs run by nonlocal investors are especially likely to be perceived through this extractive frame.

STRs, Displacement, and Disruption

Two primary concerns regarding the proliferation of STRs—neighborhood changes and decreasing affordability—overlap along a theme of displacement. In Boise, neighborhood residents evince concerns that short-term guests will take the place of full-time residents. Not only does this change create irritations around nuisances, it is perceived as a fundamental shift in the use of housing to foster community. Residents worry that STR guests will not engage in the practices that strengthen the neighborhood's community ties. Guests are simply not in a position to contribute the predictable presence, routine interactions, and organized activism to which residents attribute their neighborhoods' strong senses of community. For these residents, community is rooted in longer tenures, and in the cultivation of a known and predictable set of residents. The presence of STRs appears to bring unwanted changes similar to those seen with housing uses such as studentification (Hubbard 2008; Powell 2016). Disruptions of norms, and transience itself, alter the character of neighborhoods and may lead to direct or symbolic displacement (Atkinson 2015; Powell 2016). Market disruptions amplify this trend: when neighborhoods become more expensive and less socially connected, the rate of turnover and displacement can accelerate as longtime owners opt to sell and tenants leave for other places (Cócola-Gant and Gago 2019).

Concerns that STRs erode community seem to be amplified by their use as an investment opportunity, particularly by nonlocal owners. In considering whether STRs are good or bad for the neighborhood, Boise residents distinguish between STRs that are held by outside investors seeking to speculate or profit in the short term, and those that might be hosted by residents. Their comments suggest different moral orientations toward uses that might benefit a neighbor (i.e., by providing extra income) versus those that take value from the neighborhood while at the same time displacing *would-be* neighbors. Residents might welcome investors renting to long-term tenants who could make valued contributions to the neighborhood. But the combination of short-term guests, who might violate norms and who cannot contribute, and owners engaged in speculation or profit-taking amplifies the perception of STRs as potentially exploitive. It also generates questions regarding the implications of financialization, and what happens if profit generation becomes the primary use of housing stock.

Conclusion

By disrupting both housing markets and neighborhoods, the arrival and proliferation of STRs provides sociologists with new insights into housing markets as well as understandings of neighborhood and community. Short-term uses of residential properties disrupt housing markets as they intensify and lay bare the financialization of housing. While residents might not recognize that term, they do recognize the pattern it describes—particularly when they see the impacts of STR investors in their neighborhoods. They understand the scale of profits available from STR ventures, even relative to other rental properties, and contrast this scale with the limited returns that many STR guests and owners provide to communities. In the variety of places where STRs are proliferating, residents increasingly observe that STR hosts and investors are drawing income from neighborhoods as they profit from, displace, and disrupt long-term residents (Cócola-Gant and Gago 2019; Spangler 2020; Stergiou and Farmaki 2020).

These types of disruptions can lead sociologists to important lines of inquiry. One centers on housing's use and exchange values. As LaBriola explains in this volume, defense of both the use and exchange values of housing motivates political action on the part of homeowners. As STR uses have the potential to shift these values in novel ways, their development and proliferation creates opportunities to better understand just how property values and neighborhood land uses matter for homeowners and residents. A second line of inquiry extends the link between STR proliferation and neighborhood stability. Transience potentially undermines the ability of housing to connect people to places and to one another. In short, if neighbors don't stay around, how can they "do" neighboring (Kusenbach 2006)? Short-term uses of residences, and long-term residents' reactions to these uses, thus provide opportunities for the sociology of housing to better understand how neighboring emerges or fails, how transience relates to social control, and how places do or do not become communities. Distinctions between longer-term residents versus tourists, lodgers, or guests also create opportunities to examine how boundaries are created and maintained and the implications of these boundaries for social inclusion and organizing.

Extending beyond the market and neighborhood disruptions emphasized in this chapter, STRs invite scholars to consider the new ways that housing is being consumed. The dominance of Airbnb in the STR marketplace points to the role of online platforms as a new type of housing intermediary (see Korver-Glenn et al. in this volume). As real estate transactions increasingly rely on apps and online platforms, the design, practices, and uses of platform-based intermediaries merit attention. Finally, sociologists of consumption and tourism might look at what STR usage suggests about people's desire to experience housing and places. Is staying in an authentic dwelling—whatever that might mean—an increasingly important means of consuming a place (Urry 2005), including varied kinds of urban places? And are STR guests merely seeking convenience and space, or are they hoping to experience—if only for a short stay—qualities of housing or neighborhood that their own home places lack?

17

Moving beyond "Good Landlord, Bad Landlord"

A THEORETICAL INVESTIGATION OF EXPLOITATION IN HOUSING

Philip M. E. Garboden

The academic literature on housing is replete with accounts of exploitation. Whether explicitly or implicitly, nearly all housing research in the social sciences confronts cases in which two parties engage in an economic exchange that appears to have unequally and unjustly divided benefits, risks, and costs. It is tempting to interpret these moments as moral rather than social problems, as "bad" actors taking advantage of a situation by profiteering. But such normative perspectives fail to present a valid definition of the problem and are thus incapable of generating solutions. When it comes to housing, the field of sociology provides a unique lens to understand how exploitation operates not just through individual bad actors, but through larger systems of marginalization along intersectional vectors of race, gender, and class, which generate the underlying structural conditions necessary for unequal exchange. Let us consider three illustrative examples.

Beryl Satter's *Family Properties* describes how "speculators exploit[ed] mid-twentieth-century Black Chicagoans' desperate need for housing" (2009, 8) by marketing "contract-for-deed" arrangements to aspiring homeowners. These contracts offered Black families all the responsibilities of homeownership but did not transfer the actual deed until monthly payments had been made for several years (essentially rent-to-own). At the time, Black families had few other options for homeownership. The standard mortgage market largely excluded Black borrowers and refused to underwrite homes in Black neighborhoods. But this new form of homeownership was tenuous. When Black families inevitably missed a payment, they were quickly evicted, and a new household was placed in the unit. The real estate agent thus collected what amounted to rent, while taking no responsibility for maintenance and repairs, including significant structural issues that often predated the contract. Many of the would-be buyers were not informed that they were not true homeowners until the eviction was filed.

More recently, Esther Sullivan's *Manufactured Insecurity* (2018) explores how "markets have arisen to extract profit from poverty" in the case of mobile homes. In her book, Sullivan describes the myriad actors positioned to profit from America's largest source of unsubsidized affordable housing. Numerous stages of vulnerability exist as individual trailers, the lots on which they sit, and the parks in which they are located are all rented, bought, and sold, in each case increasing the likelihood of eviction and displacement. These evictions, in turn, create new opportunities for profit-making in the removal of trailers from the site and other relocation services of affected residents. As with Satter's families, Sullivan's households confront these conditions as both unknown and unavoidable: mobile home parks are often the last and only option for poor rural households.

Third, Desmond and Wilmers (2019) take a direct approach to the question of exploitation in housing by "explor[ing] how tenant exploitation (overcharging renters relative to the market value of their home) and landlord profit margins vary across neighborhood contexts." This article argues that poor and minority households pay more in quality-adjusted rents than more affluent renters due to their limited bargaining positions. Drawing a direct link between exploitation and the reproduction of urban poverty, Desmond and Wilmers advocate for an understanding of poverty that is fundamentally relational and extractive.

All three are cases of exploitation by nearly any definition of the word. And they are just three examples out of many; the issue of exploitation comes up time and again in housing research including work related to eviction (Desmond 2016; Garboden and Rosen 2019; Purser 2016), landlording (Rosen and Garboden 2022; Desmond and Wilmers 2019), foreclosure (Immergluck 2009; Raymond et al. 2018), homelessness (Stuart 2016), and mortgage lending and appraisal (Howell and Korver-Glenn 2018). But this literature rarely addresses the idea of exploitation explicitly, and when it does, it often avoids presenting a formal definition. Thus, the housing sociology lacks a clear explanation of what precisely is meant by "exploitation" and what defines an economic relationship as exploitative.

Unlike the three cases described above, public discussions of exploitation in housing—including some academic accounts—often emphasize normative evaluations of supply-side actors' behavior. If only, the argument goes, landlords, real estate agents, and developers were more empathetic to low-income families, more diverse, more "mission driven," or more willing to embrace a "double bottom line." There is no doubt that the choices made by individuals in any economic system can impact quality of life for traditionally marginalized groups. But focusing on individuals obscures the manner in which an economic system creates opportunities for exploitation that individuals are bound to take advantage of.

Thus, by focusing attention on the adjudication of good versus bad actors, we miss opportunities to understand exploitation in housing in ways that are both relational and structural. As I will argue in this chapter, sociology's ability to view problems across social scales presents enormous opportunities for a rich understanding of exploitation in housing (and, by extension, consumption of many kinds). As evidenced by the examples above, the sociology of housing implicitly views exploitation as occurring on two levels simultaneously. First, there must be an unbalanced moment of exchange—a contract that favors one party over the other, a price that is higher in communities of color than elsewhere, a product of such low quality that it holds null or even negative value to the consumer. But, I will argue, that moment of exchange must occur because one party in the exchange holds a structural vulnerability that prevents them from accessing a more balanced exchange for a similar good or service. Thus, Black home buyers in Chicago are said to be exploited *both* because they sign a bad contract *and* because rampant discrimination in mortgage markets at that time gave them few other options if they wished to become homeowners. Similarly, the tenure insecurity of mobile home residents must be reinforced by policymakers' stigmatization of "trailer parks" and a vastly inadequate social safety net that forces households into untenable situations.

In the rest of the chapter, I consider this definition of exploitation more deeply, drawing on literatures from moral philosophy, Marxism, and critical race theory. Each of these traditions makes important contributions to how we might conceptualize exploitation in housing. In turn, the sociology of housing is in a unique position to provide core insights into the nature of consumption and rental exploitation.

Alternative Accounts of Exploitation

The sociology of housing is far from the first to grapple with the definition of exploitation, and there are a number of key complexities that a close reading of previous work outside sociology can help elucidate. Specifically, the work of moral philosophers has focused on the voluntary nature of exploitation in contemporary society—the question of how an economic exchange can be viewed as exploitative when both parties appear to voluntarily accept the exchange. And while early Marxist economists tended to focus on labor markets, more recent accounts have considered rent relations in ways that clarify the inherent power imbalances of rentier

capitalism. And finally, the work of critical race theorists helps to address
the second component of our definition, how systemic vulnerabilities facilitate economic inequalities. While this is far from an exhaustive summary of these disciplinary approaches to exploitation, I highlight core
texts that address these key contributions.

MORAL PHILOSOPHY DEFINITIONS

Definitions of exploitation from moral philosophy tend to rely on a close
examination of the moments of unbalanced exchange (Vrousalis 2018).
While most authors in this field acknowledge that "there would be much
less micro-level exploitation in a society that is just as the macro level"
(Wertheimer 1999, 9), many of the works of moral philosophy have focused somewhat narrowly on the nature of particular exchanges. While
unbalanced power dynamics are certainly present in these accounts, they
tend to be purely situational—one party has power over the other because
he or she has the good or service that the other party needs and cannot
get elsewhere. The fact that certain groups of people tend to always have
these goods is not of primary interest.

Perhaps the most valuable aspect of this way of thinking is the recognition that an exploitative exchange can be both mutually beneficial
and consensual (Wertheimer 1999). Indeed, many canonical examples
of exploitation in society—the monetization of amateur college athlet-
ics, wage theft by restaurateurs, or the overcharging for shovels during a
snowstorm—do ultimately result in both parties' betterment. For example, while it may be exploitative to charge $75 for water during a disaster,
the exchange is nevertheless technically beneficial to both parties; the
consumer overpays for water but receives more than $75 in benefits by
avoiding dehydration. The key here is that the "mutually beneficial" nature
of these exchanges is conditional on the circumstances under which the
parties enter into an exchange, which define the plausible alternatives to
making the exchange. Under normal conditions, it is not beneficial to pay
$75 for a gallon of water because the alternative is not dehydration, but to
seek out another water dealer.

What appears at first to be a technicality has important implications
for our understanding of exploitation in housing. Nearly all the cases of
exploitation described in the introduction provided goods and services
that are extremely desirable to poor minority communities. Sometimes
this desirability is amplified by deceit—as many families who signed up
for subprime adjustable rate mortgages were misinformed regarding the
payment schedule—but often there is no deceit involved. In the low-end

rental market, for example, most families are fully aware that their housing is not technically worth the price they are paying for it, but they nonetheless consent to paying that higher price because the alternative of homelessness or doubling up with friends or family is worse.

Second, the philosophical literature on exploitation also recognizes that there is insight in the double meaning of the word "exploit," which includes both a benefit that is extracted from the exploited and a vulnerability that the exploiter exploits (Wood 1995). In the context of labor market exploitation, for example, the employer extracts the human capital of the laborer to run his factory, and he does so by taking advantage of the employee's limited bargaining position. The insight here is that exploitation requires both that the exploited have a vulnerability and also that he or she have something of value to the exploiter.

When vulnerability is understood structurally, this double meaning is highly salient to the sociology of housing—a landlord exploits her tenant by overcharging for rent, which is possible both because the tenant has money to spend on somewhere to live (value) and because the tenant cannot find better housing or a subsidy elsewhere (structural vulnerability). But we can also see the limitation of this idea, at least in terms of its relevance for the sociology of housing, when the vulnerability is purely individual. Wood (1995) gives the example of a pilfering butler who is said to "exploit" his employer's trusting nature to deprive him of valuables. In this case, there is nothing inherent about the social position of any party that reinforces the power dynamics. There is nothing particular about being an employer that makes one particularly trusting, nor any aspect of the legal system that systematically advantages butlers. A power dynamic does exist, but it is due to the accidents of personality, not to the larger power relationships that exist within society. Cases such as this one do not rise to the position of a social problem any more than a basketball player "exploiting" a height advantage presents an interesting vector of sociological inquiry. And yet there is a clear difference between using the term "exploitation" to refer to an individual advantage or disadvantage, as compared to a structural one.

MARXIST DEFINITIONS

In contrast, work in the Marxist tradition has historically centered power and social relations in its definition of exploitation, but its focus has been labor relations and the capture of surplus value by the capitalist class. Indeed, the earliest accounts of exploitation in housing explicitly demote the concept as ultimately a manifestation of labor relations (Engels 1872,

1887; see also Castells 1979), insofar as the class antagonisms were largely similar. As capitalism has evolved, however, "housing [has become] implicated in the contemporary capitalist political economy in numerous critical, connected and very contradictory ways" (Aalbers and Christophers 2014), requiring work that considers consumption and rentier relations more directly.

Primary to this project is the work of analytic Marxists to shift the vector of class conflict away from simply who controls the means of production, to who hold assets more generally, including investment capital and rental assets (Roemer 1982, Sørensen 2005)—an important step given the evolution of capitalism since the industrial revolution. Specifically, Roemer argues that exploitation can be identified in any situation in which a group of people (generally employees, consumers, or tenants) engage in some form of market activity despite having "some conditionally feasible alternative under which its members would be better off" (1982, 276). It is important to note Roemer's use of the word "feasible" here as distinct from "available." Going back to the example of selling water in a disaster, it is easy to see how a feasible alternative exists—the merchant does not need to price gouge to ration the consumption of water—but this alternative is not available to the consumer, who must therefore engage in exploitative exchange.

But Roemer's focus is never at the individual level. The exploitation he describes occurs between two groups of people (classes, primarily, but also racial groups, genders, etc.) who are durably positioned in an unbalanced relation. This durability requirement is where the water metaphor breaks down; those lacking water in a disaster constitute an ephemeral category, as does the disaster that makes the category salient. One contribution of the analytic Marxists is to focus the issue of exploitation on groups of people who are stubbornly disadvantaged by a lack of assets. Price gouging for water does not meaningfully reproduce inequality within the American context, while predatory mortgage lending most certainly does.

Moving even closer to a definition of exploitation in housing, Sørensen proposes a class analysis that is rent based, arguing that class is properly based in property rights defined as "the ability to receive the return on the asset, directly or through exchange" (2005, 121). These assets need not be physical, as Sørensen's definition allows for the consideration of intellectual property and human capital as class-defining assets. As profits derived from the ownership of these assets continue to increase as a proportion of economic activity (Christophers 2020), it becomes increasingly important to understand the role they play in defining who is exploited, in what contexts they are exploited, and how antagonisms form across these divides.

It is important to note that rentier capitalism's tendency to generate inequality fits well within neoclassical economics as well (Sørensen 2005). In those terms, the monopolization of rent producing assets, known as "rent seeking," represents a form of market failure because it generates economic profits immune to competition (Lindsey and Teles 2017). While neoclassical economists might avoid the term "exploitation," the behavior evidenced in some sectors of the housing market would be seen as problematic across traditional disciplinary antagonisms.

If, as this work generally suggests, an increasingly salient vector of exploitation is ownership (and ultimately monopolization) of rent producing assets, then housing is replete with potential case studies; mortgage finance and landlording, for example, represent particularly salient examples of asset capitalism. Of particular importance, however, is the question of whether rentier relationships are necessarily exploitative. Certainly the divide between renter and owner is necessarily an asset imbalance and thus produces significant potential for exploitation, but a society in which all property is owned by the current user seems neither viable nor desirable (particularly if the distortionary policy benefits of ownership have been removed). At issue, then, is perpetually Roemer's use of the term "feasibility" and whether the state can effectively structure the housing market in ways that avoid its tendency toward exploitative exchange.

CRITICAL RACE DEFINITIONS

Critical race theorists, particularly those of racial capital, do not reject the material basis of exploitation but instead center structural vulnerability first in racial oppression and subsequently in access to productive assets. As Du Bois noted, "We must remember that the black worker was the ultimate exploited . . . To be sure, the black mass developed again and again, here and there, capitalistic groups . . . groups willing to join white capital in exploiting labor; but they were driven back into the mass by racial prejudice" (1935, 15).

Put another way, whiteness becomes itself the productive asset that facilitates exploitative economic relations (Harris 1993, Mills 2004). But whiteness is a special type of asset, as Dymski (2001) puts it: "Racial domination differs from class domination per se: whereas class domination depends on any one individual's skills and assets, racial domination is ascriptive—it depends on one's given racial classification" (p. 169). Thus, exploitation occurs not simply because one group controls a set of productive assets, but because history aligns multiple institutions (the market, the state, culture, and so forth) to distribute advantages unevenly. As Du Bois points out, even in cases where part of a marginalized group does accumulate assets, the returns on those assets are circumscribed by other inequalities (Baradaran 2019). This perspective greatly complicates our sense of what can be done about exploitation; the wages of whiteness cannot be seized in the traditional sense. They can only be eliminated through concerted reparational justice throughout society's many institutions (Mills 2004).

But despite the practical challenges presented by the definition, it has important value for the sociology of housing. First, it liberates us from an understanding of exploitation that is tied to any particular type of economic transaction, meaning it can apply to multiple pieces of the housing market while *also* accounting for the challenges presented by the labor market. The wages of whiteness are certainly paid out through labor, but they do not stop there. They are paid in a variety of rental transactions, whether in the search for stable rental housing or for a moderately priced loan. Indeed, the form of exploitation articulated by Du Bois and Mills is one that can infuse the entirety of an economic system. Second, as with the Marxist approach, a critical race perspective on exploitation insists on the structural nature of the vulnerability. But it expands the Marxist ideals beyond material vulnerability; racial groups are doubly disadvantaged by white supremacist ideologies, narratives, and logics. Direct discrimination is the most obvious example, but the sociological literature abounds with accounts of other marginalizing processes both visible and invisible. And third, while critical race theory necessarily centers whiteness as the vector for exploitation, its tools and techniques are translatable to other vectors of structural oppression: gender, sexuality, indigeneity, disability, and so forth. Each of these groups faces well-documented discrimination in housing in complex and often intersectional ways.

Toward a Generative Definition of Exploitation in Housing

Of all these definitions, the critical race approach gets us closest to a working definition of exploitation in housing due to two particular insights. First, it embeds the nexus of exploitation not in the specifics of an exchange but in the social relation that frames that exchange. As Du Bois points out in *Black Reconstruction in America*, it is not necessary that a system be perpetually unfair to the oppressed to be rightly labeled as exploitation. But because the harm rests in the social relation (and thus the economic relation), it is always the oppressor who chooses whether or not to manifest his or her power as an unfair exchange. This insight allows sociologists to build past questions regarding whether an exchange is exploitative that benefits both parties, to focus instead on the exploitative economic relations that facilitate unfair exchanges.

By focusing on how racial oppression (a structural phenomenon) drives economic exchange (a relational/micro phenomenon), critical race theory provides a path forward for a broader understanding of exploitation in housing. But despite its importance, race is only one of many intersectional vectors of oppression that serve to unbalance economic exchange in housing. The research summarized in the first section certainly also emphasizes gender and class, but its authors also point to subtler distinctions such as stigma against mobile home parks, spatial stigma, and the myriad distinctions between groups of people delineated by US public policy.

Inspired by both the empirical and theoretical ideas, we can begin to articulate a definition of exploitation that aligns with work in the sociology of housing, namely: *economic relations (in housing and elsewhere) become exploitative when a structural disparity in power (such as racial oppression or class inequality) infuses the process by which a moment of economic exchange is negotiated.*

This definition insists that an unbalanced exchange is necessary but not sufficient for exploitation. There must also be a preexisting structural inequality between the two parties in the exchange. If a gambler takes money from his friend in a game of cards, his superior skill is not structurally defined, and thus the economic benefit he derives from it ought not to be considered exploitation. Even if he is a cheat or a liar who takes advantage of a friend's gullibility, the lack of a relevant power imbalance at a structural level again means his behavior, while perhaps morally deplorable, is not exploitative (at least not in a way relevant to the sociology of housing). At a fundamental level, what matters is the status of the two parties involved, not the amount of money exchanged, the morality of the exchange, or the means of exchanging it.

This first point is on firm ground in a field that has consistently insisted on structural explanations for human behavior. But its inverse implication may be more difficult to stomach. If we should not situate exploitation in the outcome of the specific economic exchange, but in the power imbalance in which the exchange was negotiated, then a low-end landlord who, by altruism or ignorance, charges a discounted price for housing, must be said to remain in an exploitative relationship with his tenant. This is true even if he chooses not to manifest his structural advantage into an exploitative exchange. While it may be expedient politically to praise the altruistic landlord and censor the cruel one, the social problem that the discipline of sociology should concern itself with is the system that permits cruelty to exist.

How does this notion, then, help us understand claims such as Satter's that "Not all slum landlords, for example, were exploiters. Speculators were indeed reaping massive profits and destroying sections of Chicago's West and South sides . . . but there were also some owners who were ruined by their properties" (2009, 10). First and foremost, Satter errs in her conflation of economic viability with exploitation. That a particular landlord was ruined does not provide any evidence regarding whether or not they were exploiting their tenants, only that they were not particularly successful in doing so. Exploitation facilitates profits but it can hardly be thought to guarantee them. But Satter's claim (made in defense of her father) does contain important insights that can help us move beyond notions of exploitation as both totalizing and inevitable.

First, it seems likely from her book that Satter's father had not invested in slum real estate as a profit-making activity. Whether his holdings can be considered to have been truly de-commodified is difficult to answer from her account, but it is possible to avoid exploitation by affording the vulnerable party with rights and resources. Simple altruism does nothing to shift fundamental power dynamics, but providing structurally vulnerable groups with rights that reduce that vulnerability can simultaneously reduce the incidence of exploitation. Those rights can, of course, take many forms including legal protections and guaranteed access to resources.

The second insight from Satter comes from the fact that her father's mission-driven business failed. His failure speaks to the enormous challenges of relying on altruism to reduce exploitation; in a competitive marketplace, individuals who refuse to exploit will become sidelined unless substantial state intervention occurs to reduce the returns to exploitation.

Some might argue that the inherent power dynamics within a renter-rentier relationship mean that all such cases are inevitably exploitative. There is, of course, a philosophical case to be made for such a claim in terms of the specific asset being rented. But participating in a particular consumption relationship does not singularly define one's structural position (here it differs significantly from labor relations). It is true that class in contemporary capitalism is largely defined by the possession of rent generating assets (Christophers 2020), but the choice to rent a particular asset does not necessarily mean that one is not able to own that asset, only that there are transaction and opportunity costs associated with ownership that one may wish to outsource. In this regard, exploitative housing relationships tailored to vulnerable populations (low-end landlording, subprime lending) are qualitatively different from those same types of exchanges in non-vulnerable populations.

Consider the case, for example, of high-end "agritourism" in which wealthy tourists rent space in farming communities in the developing world to expose themselves to authentic agrarian life. Does the Peruvian subsistence farmer "exploit" the wealthy tourist simply because she sits in the rentier's chair? Most would argue that, if anything, the exploitation arrow points the other way as the tourist takes advantage of the global economic forces that threaten the farmer's self-sufficiency.

This example is extreme, but a much more straightforward case comes from interview data from landlords in Washington, DC (Rosen, Garboden, and Cossyleon 2021). In many other cities, the vast majority of rental housing is relegated to populations unable to achieve homeownership. But in DC, the highly transient nature of the young professional population means that large portions of the rental stock are targeted to fairly affluent young people. The interviews with those landlords are fundamentally different from interviews with those who cater to the same city's long-standing low-income Black population. Managers in high-end buildings never even consider evictions and are highly focused on customer service and tenant recruitment. In other words, the landlord-tenant relationship works quite well in a situation where both landlords and tenants have power, just as prime mortgage lending has proven massively profitable to both lender and borrower alike.

By adjudicating the existence of exploitation in a way that insists on a link between structural vulnerability and economic exchange, we should also dispense with the idea that exploitation is simply a function of charging a price above what is "fair." The idea of a "fair" price presupposes a marketplace not only of perfect competition, but also magically untainted by power and social relations. No sociologist (or economist, for that matter) would argue that such a market exists, placing such a definition on unstable ground. Even if one could hypothetically calculate a nonexploitative price (the risk-adjusted cost of goods sold, plus soft costs, plus a profit margin sufficient to maintain production), rents can rise and fall relative to this price in ways that are not necessarily due to structural vulnerabilities. Thus, the sociology of housing should take high profits in particular market segments as strong evidence of exploitation, but then should take the subsequent step of investigating the power dynamics that facilitate these rents and the mechanism that connects the two.

For example, Desmond and Wilmers (2019) argue that quality-adjusted rents are higher in poor communities than in wealthy ones. As the authors note, such an analysis is always vulnerable to claims that they did not properly account for some type of cost, but even if the higher rents were perfectly estimated, it would stretch sociological intuition to argue that if those landlords decided to lower their rents, then the nature of their relationship to their tenants would cease to be exploitative. Unbalanced economic power dynamics can manifest themselves in ways unrelated to price, facilitating, for example, involuntary moves, undermaintenance, and the establishment of sex-for-housing relationships. This flexibility is, after all, why so many attempts to regulate exploitation out of particular markets have failed. Any policy that does not affect the fundamental vulnerabilities of exploited populations will likely fail because the mechanism of exploitation will shift from one arena (rent payments) to another (undermaintenance, eviction, and so forth). Even if all potential mechanisms of exploitation are unrealized, the latent potential of one party to exploit the other would remain an asset. It is for this reason that many of the philosophical attempts to define and understand exploitation become so quickly engrossed in technicalities. My argument is that they are looking for exploitation in the wrong place, as an aspect of a specific extant contractual relationship, where it does not usually reside.

Looking Forward: Exploitation and the Sociology of Housing

Returning to our examples with this definition in mind, it is easy to see why cases of exploitation have dominated previous research and why a careful examination of exploitation presents such generative opportunities. The vast majority of economic relationships within housing are renter-rentier, including the obvious case of landlording, but also the myriad examples of mortgage lending and contract selling. As noted above, we should not understand renter-rentier relationships as necessarily exploitative, but the asset imbalance implied by a renter-rentier relationship increases the likelihood that a structural power imbalance will exist between the two parties in the exchange. When this balance is layered with other forms of structural oppression, it engenders vulnerability in nearly every case. Race, for example, has long been a fundamental component of structuring housing markets in the United States; it has defined where households live, whether or not they own their homes, and the costs of their residential mobility. Given that asset (and thus class) differentials are inherent in most housing-related exchanges, and that many of those exchanges occur in the context of ascriptive oppression, it should be hardly surprising that the sociology of housing so often encounters exploitative relationships.

The development of the sociology of housing as a robust subfield presents enormous opportunity to deepen our understanding of exploitation in arenas beyond the labor market. As argued throughout this chapter, the first step is to move away from a moralistic perspective on housing markets and approaches that center the bad behaviors of some supply-side actors. As with any other system, few landlords or lenders are morally deplorable, and yet deplorable conditions remain within housing systems. It is thus important to understand how structures both within and beyond the housing market lead inexorably to undesirable market outcomes. But the field must also move beyond work that simply describes these deplorable conditions or identifies particular relationships as exploitative.

Instead, two things appear less understood: (1) What is the mechanism by which structural vulnerability translates into unbalanced exchange? And (2), what practical policy interventions can reduce either the incidence or consequences of exploitation?

The first question requires us to focus on the macro-micro link, an area of inquiry with significant precedent in sociology (Coleman 1986). First, we must articulate structural vulnerability in ways that represent the full intersectional nature experienced by a population (Crenshaw 2017). Reducing vulnerability to racial or gender categories does, to be sure, produce vital and important work, but rarely is the situation that simple. By understanding the vulnerabilities of populations in intersectional terms, we are better able to understand the mechanisms by which that vulnerability leads to exploitation. But just as we should not presume to understand a given vulnerability based on a set of reductionist characteristics, nor should we attempt to understand unbalanced exchange based only on categorical relations (landlord-tenant, renter-rentier, lender-borrower, etc.). These larger categories can lead to deterministic thinking that ultimately struggles to inform policy interventions. A sociology of housing gives us the ability to assess the precise mechanisms, down to the contracts themselves, by which the exploiter exploits the exploited.

Finally, the sociology of housing has the potential to make significant contributions to discussions of what ought to be done about exploitation in housing. One of the field's advantages is that it is able to approach social problems with both radical transformative ideas and practical incremental thinking. While the proponents of these approaches like to critique one another, a robust field must do both well if it is to make a difference. Without incremental reforms, we risk not achieving the harm reduction that is possible within existing systems. Without larger structural ideas, we risk assuming that harm reduction is all that is possible and limiting our policy proposals to a narrow window of interventions. By doing both simultaneously, the sociology of housing holds promise to reduce exploitation in both the short and long term.

18

How We Pay to House Each Other

Isaac William Martin

Ask a child in the United States to draw a house, and they are likely to draw you a square with a triangle on top of it. You may find a similar image on the button that represents "home" on the top bar of your web browser, or on a remote control. This iconic shape does not resemble the homes that most Americans actually live in today, but it is a recognizable caricature of the gable-roofed "minimal traditional" houses that dot the landscape of the US. They were constructed by the tens of thousands between 1935 and 1950, and they owe their shape to Federal Housing Administration (FHA) guidelines that provided technical specifications for "the small home of low cost" in which "a maximum amount of usable space, with as much comfort, convenience, and privacy as possible, must be obtained for a minimum amount of money" (Federal Housing Administration 1940, 3; see also McAlester 2013, 588–89). Home builders followed these guidelines because buyers demanded it. Buyers demanded it because lenders favored it. And lenders favored it because the FHA was willing to commit public finances to guarantee them against the risk of default on mortgage loans for homes that conformed to these standardized guidelines.

   Public finance shapes housing. Because housing is a big, fixed investment whose cost exceeds the means of almost any individual person, the cost of housing is almost always shared. The construction and acquisition of housing therefore depends on social relations of obligation—be they the kin ties among relatives who build a backwoods cabin together, or the more impersonal ties among borrowers, lenders, and guarantors who finance the purchase of a suburban home. In a modern market society, some of the most important relations of obligation that affect housing involve obligatory economic transfers between public officials and private persons. We may speak of such relations as relationships between roles—for example, the relationship between the FHA, as a *guarantor* of a mortgage, and a lending institution that is entitled to a payment from the FHA in the event of default; or the relation between that borrower, as a *taxpayer*, and the Internal Revenue Service, to whom they must remit personal income tax—but they are also debts, and they include both durable relationships among people and socially effective obligations to transfer resources. The structure of such relations is important. Who owes tax to which particular public authority, and who is excused from that liability, on what terms; to whom a public payment is owed as a benefit, and under what conditions that benefit may be claimed; who owes *more* to the public sector, so that others may pay less: these are among the most important distributional questions in any modern society. They are also among the most important questions for understanding how we provide housing to each other. Access to housing is embedded in a web of fiscal relations.

The idea that housing markets are embedded in nonmarket relationships is familiar from economic sociology. Exchanges between buyers and sellers often depend on complementary, nonmarket social relations. Polanyi (2001 [1944]), for example, famously argued that any real estate market must be "embedded" in a social safety net: no human population could long endure if it relied exclusively on the market mechanism to allocate land and housing, because even a temporary downturn in the business cycle might in that case threaten the entire working population with death by exposure. DiMaggio and Louch (1998) offered the purchase of homes as a prime example of the "socially embedded consumer transaction." Because houses are so expensive, home purchases are risky, and people therefore often make home purchases from trusted others, such as friends or family members, with whom they have previous, noncommercial relationships. Bourdieu (1999) treated housing as an especially illustrative example of "the social structures of the economy." Because a home is a highly visible and particularly durable symbol of social distinction, housing markets come to be segmented by the occupational status of the buyers, and stratification of housing types conforms to relations of class deference and derogation seen in the workplace. Although these works emphasize different social relations, they all observe that housing markets are embedded in *some* social relations outside of the market.

The claim made in this chapter is more specific: housing markets are embedded in fiscal relations in particular. A *fiscal* relationship is established by the authority of the state and carries an obligation to transfer economic resources without expectation of immediate recompense. Examples of such relationships include tax liabilities, public debts, public loan guarantees, and entitlements to public benefits. A fiscal relationship is not an exchange. Although it may carry a generalized expectation of reciprocity, it does not involve any trade for *specific* goods or services. It may, however, be conditional on a specific behavior or status, as when one's tax liability depends on one's earnings, or when one's entitlement to a public pension is conditional on one's age.

Fiscal relationships matter for housing because we can only meet the expense of constructing and maintaining housing by pooling our resources with others, and fiscal relationships produce the largest collective pool of resources in every rich, democratic country. Public expenditures and loan guarantees are indispensable for housing construction on the scale and of the quality that residents of the US and other rich, democratic countries expect (Potts 2020). Because fiscal relationships involve transfers of enormous sums, they are a particularly important means by which we share the costs of housing with each other, both within and across households. The details concerning *how and with whom* the costs of housing are shared depend on precisely how housing is taxed or exempted from taxation, and how it is subsidized by public spending or public lending. Different answers to these questions may have different consequences for patterns of residential mobility and communal solidarity. A *fiscal sociology* of housing assumes that the qualitative and quantitative details of these fiscal relations may be consequential for where and how we dwell.

This chapter reviews recent scholarship concerning the effects of fiscal relationships on housing, in order to make three arguments. First, the prevalence of any particular form of housing tenure depends directly on the fiscal relationships that make it possible. In the US, for example, the favorable tax treatment of homes relative to other assets makes the purchase of a home into a particularly advantageous way to save for retirement. This fiscal policy may structure social relations by creating a trade-off between *public* old-age pensions and *private* retirement savings that take the form of self-amortizing home mortgages. Some sociologists have called this the "really big trade-off" (Castles 1998; Doling and Horsewood 2011; Kemeny 2005) because the policies are particularly consequential for inequality.

Second, our fiscal relationships, like other social relationships, may impose *conditional* obligations on us, and the specific conditions attached to our fiscal obligations matter a great deal for patterns of residential mobility and housing inequality. The chapter will illustrate this point by comparing three different policy instruments that provide tax privileges for high-income people, conditional on certain expenditures for housing. These are the home mortgage interest deduction (HMID), the low-income housing tax credit (LIHTC), and property assessment limitation (PAL). Although all three policy instruments indirectly subsidize housing and favor high-income people, they have different consequences for such outcomes as housing inequality, residential segregation, and spatial mobility, because they relieve taxpayers from different obligations, conditional on different housing and investment behaviors. A sociology of housing needs to pay attention to the details of whom a given policy obligates, and how.

Third, the effects of fiscal relationships on housing are not only important enough to merit study by sociologists, they are also surprising enough to reward that study. Legislators and courts have attempted to justify some of the policies described here by pointing to their supposed effects on residential patterns: particular policy instruments have been said to encourage homeownership, or produce stable communities, or facilitate integration. The effects of these policies, however, are often different from what their drafters have claimed. Sociologists have much to contribute by studying the effects of various tax and spending policies on such outcomes as housing inequality, residential mobility, and racial segregation.

The Really Big Trade-Off

Because housing is a big, fixed investment, it is also a store of wealth, and the fiscal arrangements by which we finance housing structure transfers of wealth over time and among people (see, e.g., Wolff 2017a). For example, the long-term, fixed-rate, self-amortizing mortgage is subsidized by tax policies, including the deductibility of most mortgage interest for homeowners who itemize their deductions, and the exclusion of imputed rent from the personal income tax base. Thanks to the combination of those subsidies, a homeowner who pays off their mortgage over thirty years may expect reduced housing expenses in retirement; but some of that homeowner's neighbors, including both renters and other homeowners who incurred less mortgage interest, must pay income tax at *higher* rates than would otherwise be necessary to yield the same amount of revenue. Tax breaks for homeowners are social transfers.

Public subsidies for private housing may compete, both fiscally and politically, with other social transfers. That is why, as Castles (1998, 11) summarizes, "high levels of homeownership in Western societies have gone together with weakly developed welfare states." Although Castles observed an apparent trade-off between homeownership and public social expenditures, that negative correlation has attenuated since the 1970s (Van Gunten and Kohl 2020). The enduring trade-off is more specifically between *mortgage-financed* homeownership and spending on publicly financed *old-age* pensions. Figure 18.1 illustrates this really big trade-off with data from nineteen rich democracies circa 2014. Countries in which a greater share of households have mortgage debt tend to spend less on public pensions, as a share of GDP. The overall visual impression is of a

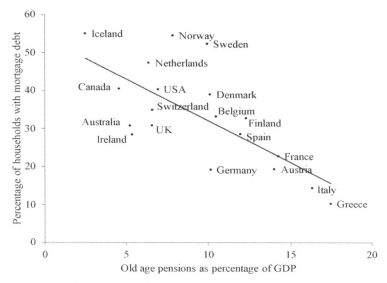

FIGURE 18.1. The really big trade-off: Public pension spending or mortgaged home-
owners, circa 2014
Source: Author's calculations, using data from the OECD Affordable Housing Database and
OECD Social Expenditures Database

continuous trade-off over the domain of observed pension spending. The
United States sits almost exactly on the regression line, suggesting that
it exemplifies a general pattern and that studies of housing policy in the
United States might benefit from a comparative perspective.

Why does this trade-off exist? In the study that is often credited with
first positing the existence of a trade-off between homeownership and welfare spending, Kemeny (1980) hypothesized that homeownership changes
workers' policy preferences. In particular, the expense of saving for private
homeownership might discourage workers from later supporting policies
that would increase their taxes to pay for public pensions. Policies that
encouraged mass homeownership might thereby "act as a strong deterrent
to welfare and social security funded by increasing taxation" (Kemeny
2005, 62). More recent scholarship suggests that it is the economic return
of homeownership, as much as the cost, that creates the trade-off. Ansell
(2014) argues that households treat the mortgage-financed purchase of
appreciating homes as a kind of self-insurance that can undermine their
support for public old-age insurance, and shows that housing price appreciation is associated with reduced support for a social safety net in several
rich, democratic countries. Similarly, Doling and Horsewood (2011) find
a negative association between old-age pension spending and house price

inflation in each of the fourteen richest democratic countries. These studies offer plausible evidence that changes in home prices may cause changes
in the demand for pensions. Changes in pension expenditures also might
affect the demand for owner-occupied homes, as Castles (1998, 17) points
out, "with a weak welfare state providing an incentive to home ownership
as a means of life cycle saving or a well-developed tax state crowding the
possibility of savings for private ownership."

Interest groups and institutional norms of budgeting also may play a role
in reproducing the really big trade-off. Increasing public spending, including
spending on old-age pensions, may be expected to increase political pressure
from business groups and ideological conservatives to constrain the growth
of the public budget. Social policy scholars have pointed out many ways in
which tax breaks can alleviate such political pressure by permitting legislators to disguise or conceal subsidies. Tax breaks such as the HMID permit
Congress to provide benefits without listing those benefits as expenditures
in the formal budget, and therefore without provoking as much public scrutiny to the implied trade-offs as might attend a similarly expensive program
if it were reckoned as a spending program (Howard 1997). The same is
true of the tax exemption for interest on mortgage-backed bonds issued by
government-sponsored entities (see Quinn 2017). Political scientists have
referred to tax breaks like these as a kind of "submerged" (Mettler 2010) or
"hidden" welfare spending. Once such tax breaks have been created, they
also may inspire powerful interest-group constituencies, such as home construction firms, mortgage lending firms, and real estate brokers, to defend
them (Howard 1997; Mettler 2010).

If our aim is to go beyond merely documenting the really big trade-off
to *explaining* it, then sociologists of housing will need to conduct more
research on the causal chain by which public old-age pensions are linked
to mortgage finance. We particularly need studies of how mortgage and
pension policies are made, especially in countries other than the US. It
is important to know precisely how the really big trade-off arises. Public
old-age pensions are among the most effective anti-poverty measures in
modern societies (see, e.g., Korpi and Palme 1998), whereas private mortgage debt is an important source of household financial risk and a reservoir
of wealth inequality (Saez and Zucman 2016; Wolff 2017a). The really big
trade-off is a really big deal.

Tax Breaks for Housing

The really big trade-off is not the only important thing to understand
about the fiscal sociology of housing. Tax and spending policies may have

an important effect on whether we are a society of homeowners or renters, and the *specific design* of those policies also may have many additional consequences for how we dwell together. Consider three tax policy instruments that reduce public revenues and subsidize private housing in the contemporary United States: namely, the home mortgage interest deduction (HMID), the low-income housing tax credit (LIHTC), and property assessment limitation (PAL). Despite their similarities, these three kinds of tax breaks have contrasting effects on social life, including housing inequality, residential mobility, and residential segregation. They affect these outcomes *directly* by allocating resources differentially to different kinds of households and *indirectly* by affecting people's decisions about *whether, where, how,* and *when* to build, buy, or rent housing. Different fiscal policies create different relationships among people, and sociologists must go into the weeds of public policy to understand how.

To begin, the HMID is a provision of federal law that permits personal income tax payers to deduct from their annual income the interest accrued on mortgage debts that were incurred to purchase a first or second home (26 U.S.C. §163). Although some commentators have retrospectively justified this deduction as a way to encourage homeownership, there is no evidence that it was designed for that purpose: the original federal personal income tax law of 1913 permitted deduction of interest on all debts, without any debate or discussion (Howard 1997; Ventry 2010). The specific deduction for mortgage interest grew in importance as more people acquired home mortgages and their income tax increased. The Tax Reform Act of 1986 finally codified the HMID as a separate policy, and it increased the relative value of homeownership by eliminating the deductibility of interest on most other debts (see Ventry 2010). Tax changes since then have changed some of the parameters of the law—at the time of this writing, for example, it only applies on debts up to the first \$750,000 in principal—and recent changes in tax law have decreased its value relative to the standard deduction. It nevertheless remains an important housing policy that subsidizes the housing expenses of 13.7 million households.

Sociologists often have pointed out the regressivity of the HMID. Because the tax rate increases progressively with income, a deduction from income is most valuable to high-income people who purchase the most expensive houses. The fact that it applies also to mortgages on *second* homes makes it especially valuable to the very richest households. For these reasons, Fischer et al. (1996, 136) pointed to the HMID as "a quintessential example of the invisible ways American policy subsidizes the middle class and the wealthy," and Desmond (2017) described it as "what may very well be the most regressive piece of social policy in America."

Quantitative studies have found that the HMID encourages high-income people to purchase larger (Hanson 2012) and more expensive (Martin and Hanson 2016) homes than they would otherwise buy. It thereby increases inequality in housing.

There is no evidence that the HMID has any particular effect on residential mobility (or its converse, residential stability). To be sure, the HMID played an important role in subsidizing the development of suburbs after the Second World War, thereby enabling "white flight" from the urban core (see Jackson 1985, 191). On shorter time scales, however, during which we may take the supply of housing to be more or less fixed, the HMID has no effect on the average household's choice between renting and buying (e.g., Glaeser and Shapiro 2003; Hanson 2012; Hilber and Turner 2014). Because the federal HMID is uniformly available across the United States and the amount of the subsidy is not conditioned on length of housing tenure, it neither encourages nor discourages residential moves among beneficiaries. It is an ineffective subsidy for encouraging the formation of stable residential communities.

When homeowners *do* move, they are more likely to move into economically exclusive enclaves than they might be in the absence of this subsidy. Dwyer (2007) has shown that the construction of new housing focused increasingly on large, expensive single-family homes after the Tax Reform Act of 1986 increased the value of the HMID (Dwyer 2007, 25). She also shows that the construction of these homes increased the residential concentration of high-income households, especially in places with greater household income inequality between Black and white people (2007, 40–42). The HMID appears to increase residential segregation by race and class.

In this respect, the HMID differs from another housing tax break: the LIHTC. This is a credit against corporate or personal income tax liability, offered in exchange for investment in certain qualified low-income housing developments. Like the HMID, the LIHTC was codified in the Tax Reform Act of 1986, and similar policies have been incorporated into many state income tax codes. As a tax policy, the LIHTC is regressive because it is claimed primarily by corporate taxpayers and, to a much lesser degree, personal income tax filers who own financial investment portfolios and itemize their deductions (see Desai, Dharmapala, and Singhal 2010, 188). It also can provide a valuable subsidy to development firms that strategically incorporate low-income housing into their projects (see Robinson III 2020b). The housing that is financed by the credit, however, is targeted to low-income households. The drafters of the LIHTC described it as a policy to increase the supply of low-income housing, among other purposes, and the subsidy provided by the LIHTC indeed appears to provide more and better housing for renters at lower income levels than otherwise would be available (Diamond and McQuade 2019). The LIHTC reduces overall housing inequality.

With respect to residential mobility, the effects of the LIHTC are mixed. To the extent that it encourages new housing development, it encourages moves, but once residents have moved in, the tax credit appears to increase their residential stability. Freeman (2003) found that low-income people were more likely to move into a census tract with LIHTC housing than a similar census tract without it (p. 129). Surveys of LIHTC housing residents often find that many of them report their arrival in LIHTC housing as an improvement over their previous circumstances (e.g., Beck 2019; Massey et al. 2013; Reid 2019). They may enjoy more space, better amenities, and better property management than they would otherwise find for the price they pay, and they may stay put in order to use their savings to invest in education and other long-term projects of economic and social mobility (Reid 2019). Beck (2019) has called this pattern "staying for opportunity," and a recent study by Derby (2020) suggests that it often works. Adults who spent more of their childhoods in LIHTC housing are more likely to attend college and report higher earnings than their peers who merely passed through LIHTC housing as children.

While housing stability provides benefits, there may also be drawbacks to a policy that discourages residents from moving out of low-income communities. Scholars have been particularly concerned with the potential effects of the LIHTC on housing segregation by race and class. Those effects may vary from place to place depending on the "qualified action plans" that states use to allocate the credits to developers. Federal legislation in 1989 expanded bonuses for developers who sited LIHTC housing in historically credit-starved communities, thereby leading some scholars to conclude that the LIHTC reproduced racial and class segregation (see, e.g., Van Zandt 2009; Oakley 2008). Although LIHTC developments are concentrated in high-poverty neighborhoods, some quantitative studies find that they are *less* concentrated in high-poverty neighborhoods than other low-income housing subsidies are (Owens 2015, 240), and that the siting of LIHTC developments has little effect on income segregation at the neighborhood level (Freedman and McGavrock 2015; Won 2020). The role of the state in the allocation of credits has opened up a new opportunity for legal challenges to metropolitan patterns of racial segregation (Robinson III 2019), and there is some evidence that the development of LIHTC housing may, on average, reduce racial segregation at the metropolitan level (Horn and O'Regan 2011). When compared to the patterns of segregation that might arise from the market provision of low-income housing in the absence of any such subsidy, it appears that the LIHTC, in some metro areas, may modestly reduce residential segregation by race and class.

Both the HMID and the LIHTC differ from yet a third kind of tax break, property tax assessment limitation (PAL), which has no federal equivalent. A property tax on the value of real estate is the largest revenue source for local government in the United States, and the property tax bill is among the largest annual housing expenses for most households. Twelve states limit the annual increase in the value of an individual real estate parcel for the purposes of levying local property tax. The savings from this tax break accrue disproportionately to people whose homes are appreciating in value. Many of them may be low-income householders who have simply held onto homes for a long time (O'Sullivan, Sexton, and Sheffrin 1995), but studies of PAL in Michigan (Skidmore, Ballard, and Hodge 2010) and Illinois (Dye, McMillen, and Merriman 2006) have found the tax savings to be proportional or regressive with respect to household income. In eight of the twelve states that currently have a PAL, the limitation applies also to owners of *commercial* real estate, a tax break that produces disproportionate tax savings for upper-income households with real estate portfolio investments (Martin 2020). Like the HMID and the LIHTC, in other words, a PAL is typically a regressive tax break.

Its effects are otherwise distinctive. In contrast with the LIHTC, a PAL reduces residential mobility. Most PAL laws require local governments to reassess property only at the time that it changes hands. The tax savings, which are equivalent to the difference between the property tax that is owed on the home and the tax that *would* be owed if it were taxed at its current market value, increase as long as the home is appreciating in market value—but only until it is sold. The result of this policy is a disincentive to sell. Several studies have documented a substantial "lock-in" effect showing that the longer a homeowner enjoys this tax break, the less likely she is to move (Ferreira 2010; O'Sullivan, Sexton, and Sheffrin 1995). Although there is no evidence that any such overall reduction in residential mobility was intended by the legislative drafters of these state laws, the Supreme Court opined in *Nordlinger v. Hahn*, 505 U.S. 1 (1992), that a state interest in promoting residential stability could be sufficient reason to uphold a PAL that might otherwise be found to violate the Equal Protection Clause of the Constitution.

PAL probably reinforces historical patterns of residential segregation by race and class. The tax savings from PAL accrue disproportionately to white homeowners, who are more likely to have purchased homes decades ago, and to own them in places where values are appreciating rapidly (Martin and Beck 2017). It thereby may create a particularly strong disincentive for homeowners who live in the most segregated, majority-white communities to sell. To the extent that residential integration requires opening opportunities for buyers of color to purchase homes in these communities, PAL impedes progress toward racial integration. Some historians have argued that the desire to preserve racial and class segregation was part of what motivated many suburban voters to approve PAL (e.g., Self 2003). Future research should measure more directly the effects of PAL on race and class segregation.

Although these three regressive tax breaks have similar effects on the income distribution, they have different effects on how we dwell together. All three are tax breaks for housing, but they instantiate different relationships of obligation among the people who are excused from tax liability, those who construct the homes, and the people who live in those homes. These differences should not be dismissed as technocratic details or obvious reflections of legislative intent. In many of these cases, the intent of a fiscal policy may have been contested or unclear. From the standpoint of the sociology of housing, the intent of a policy is less important than its effects on social relations. Fiscal relationships are as real as any other social relation, and more consequential than many.

A Fiscal Sociology of Housing

There is more we can learn about housing and society by attending to fiscal relationships. We need much more comparative research on the policy process in the United States and other rich, democratic countries to understand which policy decisions give rise to the Really Big Trade-Off between private mortgage finance and public pensions. We also need more research on the effects of fiscal policies, including dozens of tax and spending policies that subsidize particular forms of household formation and housing tenure, and that, in doing so, shape the ways that we live together. The examples of such policies described in this chapter barely scratch the surface. Although we know the aggregate budgetary impact of tax expenditures for housing is enormous, we urgently need more research about their effects on housing access, racial and class segregation, and patterns of community interaction.

Sociologists studying housing have long paid special attention to documenting, describing, and theorizing the social relationships among neighbors. In the last decade, we have also expanded the circle of our attention to encompass other relationships outside the immediate neighborhood, including those between landlords and tenants or mortgage lenders and borrowers, that shape the experience of housing. We now have an opportunity to broaden our gaze to encompass some of the most general relationships of obligation required to maintain a modern market society. Fiscal relationships are among the most fundamental *societal* relationships because they connect us all to each other through a common pool of resources to which we all contribute, and on which we all rely to build our homes.

A child may picture a house as a box with a roof, but a house is more than that. It is a concept, and a creature of law and cultural imagination, and the center of a web of relationships (see Lauster 2016). Even the physical structure itself is no more real or concrete than the relationships that maintain it. An individual owner may come and go. A wall may be moved. A roof may rot and require repair. But someone will do those repairs, and someone else will pay for them, and many, many others will help, in one way or another, to finance them. Sometimes the most durable thing about a house is actually the institutionalized social relation by which it is funded. We all share, in some measure, in the expense of housing each other. Precisely *how* we share in that expense makes a big difference for how we live together on earth.

PART IV

Housing, Racial Segregation, and Inequality

19

The Future of Segregation Studies

QUESTIONS, CHALLENGES, AND OPPORTUNITIES

Jacob William Faber

In 2020, the typical white American lived in a neighborhood that was 69 percent white. Black Americans lived, on average, in neighborhoods that were 41 percent Black, while Latinx and Asian Americans lived in neighborhoods that were 45 percent Latinx and 25 percent Asian, respectively. While Black-white segregation has declined since its peak in the 1970s, the segregation of Latinx and Asian Americans has barely budged as those populations have grown (Logan and Stults 2021). While countless social, economic, and political phenomena are responsible for the persistence of the country's uneven racial geography, a "defining feature of the metropolitan United States," in historian Keeanga-Yamahtta Taylor's phrasing (Taylor 2020), housing is at the center. When and where people move, the costs of renting or owning a home, accumulation and intergenerational transfers of wealth in the form of home equity, housing laws, mortgage lending practices, discrimination—these and other aspects of the housing market sort people and families across space in a highly racialized manner.

While there is nothing inherently problematic about people living in racially and ethnically homogenous areas, the layering of opportunity structures (e.g., schools, crime, environmental hazards, political power) on top of segregated neighborhoods, cities, and metropolitan areas means that where you live can have a dramatic impact on your life chances (Sharkey and Faber 2014). Research has identified segregation as detrimental—generally to people of color—to educational opportunity (Reardon, Kalogrides, and Shores 2019; Reardon and Owens 2014; Wodtke, Harding, and Elwert 2011), labor market success (Steil, de la Roca, and Ellen 2015), political efficacy (Ananat and Washington 2009), access to credit (Faber 2018a; Hwang, Hankinson, and Brown 2015; Hyra et al. 2013), home values (Flippen 2004), upward mobility (Chetty et al. 2014a), health (Torrats-Espinosa 2021), and a host of other outcomes (de la Roca, Ellen, and O'Regan 2014).

Sociological interest in segregation has grown over the past half century, likely inspired by the classic works of William Julius Wilson (1987) and Douglas Massey and Nancy Denton (1993). Wilson's *The Truly Disadvantaged* (1987) documented the devastation caused by deindustrialization and disinvestment in America's inner city. Chronic joblessness, crime, and other social ills plagued urban neighborhoods and created a unique form of "social isolation," which limited the life chances of African Americans (Wilson 1987). Massey and Denton's *American Apartheid* (1993) argued that segregation was a core mechanism through which racial inequality reproduced itself. The urban decline and disinvestment documented by Wilson (1987) occurred in parallel with the emergence of booming suburbs rich in financial and social resources. The construction and persistence of the American ghetto, they argued, was "the missing link in prior attempts to understand the plight of the urban poor" (Massey and Denton 1993, 3). Furthermore, the book argued that federal housing policy was primarily responsible for "shoring the bulwarks of segregation" in the mid-twentieth century (Massey and Denton 1993, 42). These two books, as well as important contributions by numerous other scholars (e.g., Hirsch 1983; Jargowsky 1997; Sugrue 1996), spurred interest in the role of geography in racial stratification.

With this scholarly history in mind, this chapter proposes several questions, discusses empirical challenges, and outlines opportunities for future work in the field.[1] The crucial takeaway for sociologists studying segregation, and housing inequality more broadly, is that these are inherently *social* phenomena (Bell 2020b; Krysan and Crowder 2017; Sampson 2012; Sewell 2010). People and institutions are responsible for intentionally creating and perpetuating America's racial geography, and therefore for the resultant consequences. Sociology, with its focus on social interactions, is uniquely positioned to study these relationships.

Emerging Questions

Theories explaining the role of social and economic geographies in shaping life outcomes are as old as sociology itself—as is an understanding of housing as central to these phenomena (Du Bois 1899). However, theoretical and empirical challenges have limited the extent to which scholars have been able to definitively measure the extent to which neighborhood

---

[1] While I focus on the United States because of the limits of my own expertise, much of this chapter is relevant to other contexts.

segregation "matters" (Ellen and Turner 1997; Jencks and Mayer 1990). Scholars have pointed to selection bias as one of the most common difficulties in estimating what are sometimes called "neighborhood effects." This potential source of statistical error refers to the fact that an individual may possess characteristics that affect both the neighborhood an individual *selects* as well as the outcomes we are interested in. For example, our measurement of the statistical relationship between neighborhood affluence and individual income may be *biased* because something akin to motivation (i.e., a difficult-to-measure characteristic) may drive both where someone chooses to live as well as what kind of job someone pursues.

In recent years, scholars have developed a more sophisticated theoretical apparatus to resolve this obstacle to understanding how segregation operates as a social phenomenon. Rather than treating selection bias as a barrier to causal identification, scholars have identified selection as itself a social phenomenon worthy of study (Bell 2020b; Darrah and Deluca 2014; Krysan and Crowder 2017; Sampson 2008, 2012; Sampson and Sharkey 2008). For example, the processes through which individuals select into neighborhoods are shaped by often unconscious preferences, housing supply, landlords, segregation patterns, social networks, macroeconomic conditions, and—importantly—current and past residential contexts. Put another way, the neighborhood someone lives in today will likely help determine the types of neighborhoods someone considers in the future. This insight into neighborhood mobility has opened up a host of new sociological questions about the mechanisms and effects of housing segregation.

WILL SHIFTING SOCIAL DEMOGRAPHY CHANGE THE IMPORTANCE OF PLACE?

The United States is experiencing several dramatic sociodemographic changes including increasing diversity due to rapidly growing Latinx and Asian populations. By midcentury, non-Hispanic whites will no longer be the majority population (Vespa, Medina, and Armstrong 2020). While the history has justifiably focused scholarship on Black-white dynamics, increasing diversity has compelled scholars to broaden theoretical approaches to and analyses of spatial inequality (Hwang 2015; Hwang and McDaniel 2022; Logan and Zhang 2010; Roberto 2018; Rugh 2015; Steil, de la Roca, and Ellen 2015). America is also getting older, with estimates that 22 percent of the country will be sixty-five years of age or older by 2040, up from 17 percent in 2020 (Vespa, Medina, and Armstrong 2020). Overlapping spatial distributions of race/ethnicity and age could predict neighborhood cohesion as well as gentrification (Hwang 2015; Nelson 2022).

Concurrently, income inequality and volatility have increased (Mor-duch and Schneider 2017; Piketty 2014) and upward mobility rates have plummeted (Chetty et al. 2017). This growing financial instability can be directly tied to increasing housing costs (Desmond 2016; Faber 2019; Faber and Rich 2018; Herring, this volume; Lens 2018; Nelson and Lens, this volume). These trends raise questions about the roles geography and housing play in shaping stratification in America. For example, will seg-regation become an even more powerful driver of inequality as the size of marginalized populations grows? Will racially differentiated financial challenges associated with supporting and housing older Americans affect the inheritance of place? Will the economic turmoil of the early twenty-first century shift Americans away from homeownership? Will declining intergenerational mobility increase the extent to which families are "stuck in place" (Sharkey 2013)? How should scholars approach the vast hetero-geneity within traditional racial and ethnic categories (Clerge 2019; Easley 2017; Hamilton 2019; Rugh 2020)?

WILL GENTRIFICATION PLATEAU?

A large body of scholarship has documented an increase in relatively afflu-ent and white residents in many of America's large cities, typically referred to as "gentrification" (Hwang and McDaniel 2022). This phenomenon has transformed notable, historically Black neighborhoods, such as Harlem and Crown Heights in New York (Besbris and Faber 2017; Roberts 2010) and U Street in Washington, DC (Hyra 2017), and may reduce levels of segregation in gentrifying cities. However, if white in-migrants replace Black and Latinx residents, gentrification of one neighborhood may spill over into other neighborhoods. Put another way, reducing segregation in a gentrifying neighborhood may increase segregation in the neighbor-hoods where original residents are compelled to move. Thus, the broad relationship between segregation and gentrification may be ambiguous and/or heterogeneous.

Although the connection between gentrification and displacement is debated (Ding, Hwang, and Divringi 2016; Ellen and O'Regan 2011; Free-man and Braconi 2004), increasing affluence within cities has occurred as suburban poverty (Covington, Freeman, and Stoll 2011; Kneebone and Garr 2010; Lewis-McCoy 2014) and diversity (Douds 2021; Rastogi and Curtis 2020) have increased. In this way, gentrification is a bit of an em-pirical mirage—anyone living in New York, Boston, San Francisco, Los Angeles, or Chicago has seen dramatic neighborhood change. However, the intransigence of spatial inequality is a much broader pattern and arguably a much more serious problem. How can we reconcile these two seemingly contrasting phenomena? Perhaps scholars of segregation and gentrification would benefit from adopting a more flexible and heterogeneous understanding of neighborhoods, one in which racial inequality can manifest in diverse ways.

Another consideration is whether and how a neighborhood's changing racial profile impacts institutions within a neighborhood. Jennifer Candipan (2019), for example, shows that an increasing racial mismatch between public schools and the surrounding neighborhoods correlates with a decline in support for public education. Mahesh Somashekhar (2020) has found that retail development only follows the arrival of white—not Black—gentrifiers. Neighborhood change, therefore, is context-dependent (Hwang and McDaniel 2022; Small 2008; Small and McDermott 2006).

Gentrification has accelerated over the past two decades (Ellen and Torrats-Espinosa 2019; Rucks-Ahidiana 2020), but whether and where this trend is sustainable are open questions. Will gentrification disrupt generations-old patterns of racial isolation (Logan 2016)? Relatedly, it is crucial to understand how city-suburb sorting is related to the increasing importance of municipal boundaries for shaping segregation (Lichter, Parisi, and Taquino 2015; Massey, Rothwell, and Domina 2009). While these topics are often studied as ecological phenomena, they are, ultimately, about people. Sociologists should explore how this shifting geography of affluence and poverty shapes opportunity, especially regarding housing costs and quality.

HOW WILL PLACE MAKE RACE?

Over the course of the twentieth century, suburbanization helped consolidate European ethnic communities into the contemporary white identity by pulling people from urban immigrant enclaves and solidifying the color line between suburb and ghetto (Roediger 2006). Migration, segregation, policy, and housing markets also created a contrasting association between Blackness and urban blight (Hirsch 1983; Wilson 1987). Early in the twenty-first century, racial isolation made Black and Latinx neighborhoods the targets of what subprime mortgage lenders called "ghetto loans" (Massey et al. 2016), in what was effectively a twenty-first century version of redlining (Faber 2020b). These and countless other sociospatial dynamics have made racial and ethnic identities inseparable from place as well as from the types of housing in those places. As George Lipsitz (2011, 5) argues, "race is produced by space, that it takes places for racism to take place." Whiteness is associated not just with suburbs but with the single-family, detached home, while Blackness is associated with apartment living in cities.

Racial and ethnic hierarchies have changed considerably over time (American Sociological Association 2003; Pew Research Center 2020; Wade 2013); there is no reason to assume we have reached a point of stability. Latinx Americans, for example, may increasingly identify as white (Gans 2017). The US Census Bureau continues to debate what categories to include in its surveys (Lo Wang 2019). As the United States becomes more diverse, sociologists should monitor what role segregation plays in the changing racial order. How will municipal, symbolic, and geological borders reinforce the color line? How will housing discrimination shape and be shaped by a shifting, multiethnic population? Will geography play a role in structuring whether and where white identity expands, as it did during the previous century?

THE POST-PANDEMIC HOUSING MARKET

COVID-19 has had a devastating and racially disparate impact on American life, killing over one million people. Black, Latinx, and Indigenous Americans have suffered disproportionately, a suffering made manifest in dramatically higher infection and mortality rates (Chang et al. 2020; COVID Tracking Project 2021) and deteriorating economic conditions (Chetty et al. 2020). Housing and segregation are at the heart of understanding COVID's disparate impact (Torrats-Espinosa 2021). Early in the pandemic, overcrowding (i.e., *not* density) emerged as a powerful predictor of vulnerability (Furman Center 2020). Evictions exacerbated this problem by forcing individuals into ever more crowded housing (Jowers et al. 2021). COVID exposure, as well as subsequent illness, has been driven by concentrated economic disadvantage because of the inability of people of color to work remotely (Chang et al. 2020; Furman Center 2020) or flee to safer geographies (Quealy 2020)—again implicating housing.

It will take years to understand the full impact of this crisis, but the crisis is likely a period of expanding inequality. Research suggests COVID has caused declining housing markets in communities of color, while housing has become more expensive in white neighborhoods (Kuk et al. 2021). Public school systems in large cities, such as New York, NY, are seeing declining enrollment as affluent families flee for suburbs and private schools (Gould and Chang 2021). If the pandemic changes beliefs about what makes places "safe," we may see a reversal of the in-migration many large cities have recently experienced, raising questions about gentrification and city-suburb inequality. The generation of Americans who entered adulthood during the Great Recession are now facing a potentially even greater economic collapse. How will these two back-to-back crises impact housing affordability, wealth accumulation, and opportunities for home-ownership? Given that both periods disproportionately harmed Black and Latinx Americans, it is crucial for sociologists to highlight their implications for long-term racial equality.

BLACK LIVES (AND PLACES) MATTER

The sociopolitical uprising in the wake of the police killings of George Floyd and Breonna Taylor may be the largest movement in American history (Buchanan, Bui, and Patel 2020). At the heart of Black Lives Matter is an understanding that racism is a structural phenomenon. The millions of people pulled into this movement may provide an opportunity for a societal shift in racial attitudes and progressive policy innovation, such as increased density in zoning to address housing affordability. Minneapolis, Minnesota, for example, has tied such changes to histories of racial exclusion. Sociology must take part in understanding this trend as well as the countertrend of white nationalism.

Consistent with the call for appropriately valuing Black lives, it is crucial that sociology move toward a theoretical and empirical valuing of Black places. Too often, scholars pathologize the concentration of Black people (as well as other nonwhite groups) in neighborhoods or schools (Kendi 2016). This logic, Mary Pattillo argues, "stigmatizes Black people and Black spaces and valorizes whiteness as both the symbol of opportunity and the measuring stick for equality" (Pattillo 2019, 29).

Understanding Segregation in an Age of Big Data

Both scholarship on housing and the housing market itself are experiencing a data revolution. Empirical innovations have not only provided evidence supporting what sociologists have argued for over a century, but have highlighted heterogeneity in where, when, why, and for whom neighborhoods matter (Sharkey and Faber 2014). Randomized and natural experiments (Burdick-Will et al. 2011; Chetty, Hendren, and Katz 2016; Schwartz 2010; Sharkey 2010) and statistical tools for handling selection bias (Sampson, Sharkey, and Raudenbush 2008; Burdick-Will et al. 2011; Wodtke, Harding, and Elwert 2011) have expanded our understanding of how the timing and duration of exposure to different neighborhood contexts impact people differently across age, sex, race, income, and other social categories. Meanwhile, the growing ubiquity of algorithmic decision-making, a phenomenon made possible by the arrival of "Big

Data," has the potential to either upend or calcify many traditional practices within the housing market.

LOOKING BACK TO LOOK FORWARD

Recent digitization of archival data has allowed researchers to connect historical policies to contemporary inequalities. The Digital Scholarship Lab (DSL) (Nelson et al. 2022) georeferenced the infamous Home Owners Loan Corporation (HOLC) redlining maps, which influenced mortgage lending for decades, pulling white people and investment out of cities and into suburbs (Massey and Denton 1993). My own work documents that redlined cities became and stayed more segregated than cities that were not redlined (Faber 2020a). Research has shown a similar phenomenon on the neighborhood level: redlined and "yellow lined" neighborhoods became more racially isolated, experienced far less home equity appreciation, and created fewer opportunities for economic mobility than nearby neighborhoods (Aaronson, Hartley, and Mazumder 2020; Aaronson et al. 2021). Housing opportunity is at the center of these intergenerational patterns of inequality. Redlining in the 1930s and 1940s set the groundwork for decades of mortgage exclusion and exploitation (Taylor 2019), including vulnerability to predatory subprime lending during the early years of the first decade of the 2000s (Faber 2020b).

Given the numerous ways that segregation reproduces itself (Krysan and Crowder 2017; Logan 2016), these analyses of HOLC's multigenerational impacts provide an important model for connecting historical policies to contemporary inequalities. DSL has also published data on Urban Renewal projects, which could be used to estimate a range of impacts of the federal program James Baldwin referred to as "Negro Removal." Similar attention should be paid to the evolution of zoning, which has become a favored tool with which municipalities exclude unwanted populations (Hirt 2015; Rothwell and Massey 2009; Shertzer, Twinam, and Walsh 2021).

Big Data and Other Alternative Data Sources

In 2020, the US Census made an important change to ensure that aggregate data cannot be transformed into individually identified data. The Census has "swapped" records such that public data will be unreliable for geographies smaller than congressional districts. This change will likely force scholars to shift to private data sources and/or seek access to restricted census data, both of which increase the costs of research. Making neighborhood-level analyses more difficult may deter future housing scholars and increase inequality in the academy between affluent and relatively underresourced institutions.

The Census, however, is an exception. In general, big data, particularly the sort of big data available from private sources, allow scholars to produce ever more precise analyses. Already scholars have used these data to explore racial geographies and social interactions beyond place of residence (Chang et al. 2020; Wang et al. 2018). With this expanded view of sociospatial dynamics come ethical considerations. Whether and how the field fully embraces, for example, cell phone data, while protecting personally identifiable information is an important and unsettled question.

DOES BIG DATA MEAN BIG DISCRIMINATION?

When scholars consider the forces shaping housing inequality, they often consider what shapes individual preferences. On the other side of the housing search are landlords, mortgage brokers, and others involved in the selling or renting of property. The growing dependence of housing algorithms on extraordinarily granular and sociodemographically rich data may provide expanded opportunities for housing market actors to discriminate, thereby presenting new concerns about the future of fair housing (Barocas and Selbst 2014; Boeing et al. 2021; O'Neil 2016). For example, the adoption of machine-learning models for mortgage lending may exacerbate disparities in credit access (Fuster et al. 2022). Similar practices may allow landlords to evade anti-discrimination laws (Badger 2019; Rosen, Garboden, and Cossyleon 2021; Selbst 2019), in part through microtargeting of advertisements on social media (Benner, Thrush, and Isaac 2019; Lo Wang 2019). Alternatively, algorithmic decision-making could be used to reduce disparities by surfacing previously undetectable patterns and thereby addressing historical injustices (So et al. 2022).

As more Americans rely on online platforms to search for housing (Boeing et al. 2021), it is crucial for researchers to develop empirical and theoretical tools for understanding how racial inequality manifests in big data. Will online unit listings pull down a barrier faced by people of color by expanding choice sets? Or, conversely, will more powerful tools for racial steering exacerbate segregation? Will the covert nature of data collection and use make identifying discrimination more difficult?

Segregation as Social

In *Cycle of Segregation*, Maria Krysan and Kyle Crowder (2017) outline the ways repeated and patterned interactions between individuals create "momentum" that carries inequality forward. A similar theme running through this chapter is the assertion that people must remain at the center of our analyses. Studies repeatedly show the centrality of race within the social practices of effectively all housing market actors. Rich, qualitative research conducted by Max Besbris (Besbris 2020; Besbris and Faber 2017) and Elizabeth Korver-Glenn (Korver-Glenn 2018; 2021), for example, illuminate how real estate agents reinforce inequality through racial steering. Agents have financial and reputational stakes in the neighborhoods they represent and so have strong incentives to "upsell" clients in racialized ways (Besbris 2020). Acting as "race brokers," (Korver-Glenn 2021), they intentionally reproduce inequality in housing.

Similarly, and tragically, an overwhelming body of research into the subprime lending boom and subsequent foreclosure crisis has documented the ways the geography of race created vulnerability to predatory lenders within Black and Latinx communities (Faber 2018b; Hwang, Hankinson and Brown 2015; Hyra et al. 2013; Rugh, Albright, and Massey 2015; Sewell 2016; Steil et al. 2018; Williams, Nesiba, and McConnell 2005). The historical exclusion of these communities from conventional mortgage lending (Taylor 2013) made them easy targets for subprime lenders. The collapse of the housing market that followed widened home equity gaps (Faber and Ellen 2016) and even increased segregation by forcing millions of people to move (Hall, Crowder, and Spring 2015).

This research extends to property appraisers (Howell and Korver-Glenn 2021; Kamin 2020; Korver-Glenn 2021), landlords (Rosen 2020), mobile home park owners (Desmond 2016; Sullivan 2018, this volume), and other housing market intermediaries (Korver-Glenn et al., this volume). These practices are embedded within institutions, creating and created by powerful financial incentives to perpetuate and exploit inequality (Desmond 2016; Garboden, this volume; Taylor 2013, 2019). Thus emerges a pattern of "institutional marginalization" through which segregation limits the economic mobility of people of color (Faber 2018a, 2018b; Small and McDermott 2006).

Segregation's exploitative nature also *benefits* some groups. In addition to the extraction of financial resources described above, segregation creates and protects intergenerational mobility for affluent whites (Massey 1996). One powerful mechanism through which this racial privilege is secured is the uniquely American tie between housing policy and education policy (Lareau and Goyette 2014). Persistent segregation is a determinant of educational opportunity (Johnson 2019; Reardon and Owens 2014; Rich and Jennings 2015), which recent work has shown to benefit wealthy, white Americans (Bischoff and Owens 2019; Howell 2019; Owens 2018).

Thus, policies governing zoning, mortgage allocation, anti-discrimination, building codes, rent subsidies, and other factors ostensibly designed to shape the housing market become school policy through segregation (Schwartz 2010).

Given the countless ways that opportunity is unevenly distributed, sociologists must frame the existence and persistence of segregation as intentional results of historical and contemporary policy and practice. This is certainly not a new idea, but one that recognizes the power of people and interactions between people (i.e., the social) in shaping macro-level phenomena. This conceptual framework also has implications for how we think about solutions to the problems caused by segregation. A commodified housing market motivated primarily by profit will necessarily reproduce inequality (Desmond 2016; Faber 2018b; Pattillo 2013; Rucks-Ahidiana, this volume; Taylor 2013, 2019) because racism continues to be a tool through which white homeowners can increase the value of their property (Kendi 2016). Therefore, the clearest path to equality is through wealth redistribution, which includes repositioning housing as a right. Sociology can—and should—provide the theory and empirical groundwork for this pursuit.

20

Understanding Racial and Ethnic Disparities in Residential Mobility among Housing Choice Voucher Holders

Erin Carll, Hannah Lee, Chris Hess, and Kyle Crowder[1]

Within the sociology of housing, the sources and consequences of persistent racial and ethnic[2] residential stratification have been a major focus of both research and policy. This work is critical in part because racial and ethnic inequality in housing and neighborhood location is an important source of disparities in health and well-being. In the 1970s and 1980s, in response to housing research that emphasized socioeconomic disparities as a source of racial and ethnic stratification, housing policy in the United States embraced Housing Choice Vouchers (HCV) as a vehicle to mitigate racial and ethnically disparate outcomes of residential mobility (e.g., Rosen 2020). This policy assumes vouchers enable greater housing choice across neighborhoods, therefore facilitating mobility into areas with lower poverty and more racial and ethnic integration.

[1] We thank each participant and our partners at the King County and Seattle Housing Authorities. Amal Saleh, Huong Chu, María Vignau Loría, Nadia Herrarte, Najma Osman, Rebece de Buen Kalman, and Samira Farah provided research assistance; Aimée Dechter shared grant-writing advice. The National Science Foundation (Doctoral Dissertation Research Improvement Award #190404), National Poverty Research Center (US Department of Health and Human Services Award #AE00103), and the University of Washington (UW) Department of Sociology provided financial support. The UW Center for Studies in Demography and Ecology provided computing resources, partially funded by Eunice Kennedy Shriver National Institute of Child Health and Human Development funding (#P2CHD042828). The opinions and conclusions expressed herein are ours alone and do not represent any individuals, research centers, universities, or government agencies that have supported this work.
[2] Throughout this chapter, our use of "ethnic" and "racial" should be understood as statuses that people (re)produce and impose on each other to maintain hierarchies, rather than as any sort of essential human characteristic.

Vouchers are now the largest form of tenant-based housing assistance in the United States. Despite vouchers' potential for addressing locational inequalities, voucher recipients in most metropolitan areas are still typically clustered in higher-poverty, relatively ethnically and racially segregated neighborhoods (e.g., DeLuca, Garboden, and Rosenblatt 2013; McClure, Schwartz, and Taghavi 2015). Because the voucher program is only available to individuals and families with marginalized socioeconomic backgrounds, this persistence of residential stratification among voucher holders suggests that socioeconomic disparities are insufficient for explaining racialized differences in voucher recipients' residential outcomes (Walter, Li, and Atherwood 2015; Wang and Walter 2018). Since research about the broader population has yielded similar conclusions, housing sociologists have recently moved beyond attempting to distinguish the relative contributions of socioeconomic inequality, racism in the housing market, and a preference for same-race/ethnicity neighbors in creating racial and ethnic residential segregation (e.g., Faber, this volume; Sewell 2010, cited in Faber, this volume). Instead, researchers are increasingly focusing on how these forces work together with more subtle social processes to reproduce racial and ethnic residential stratification (Krysan and Crowder 2017).

In this chapter, we use findings from a study of voucher holders living in King County, Washington,[3] to explore the implications of this emerging approach for understanding the relationship of residential mobility to racial and ethnic residential stratification. Our discussion applies and builds on Krysan and Crowder's (2017) social structural sorting perspective (SSSP), which contends that members of different racial and ethnic groups draw on knowledge of neighborhood opportunities that emerge from ethnically and racially distinct residential histories (the homes and neighborhoods where individuals have previously lived and their experiences there, including discrimination) and social networks. Having typically spent their lives in segregated spaces, members from different racial and ethnic groups know and develop opinions about different sets of spaces. Some movers, for instance, want to live near their kin for the

---

[3] We analyzed administrative data covering 2008–2019 from the Seattle Housing Authority (SHA) and King County Housing Authority (KCHA), combined with tract-level data from the American Community Survey (Manson et al. 2019) to examine patterns of mobility for households receiving vouchers. We also conducted—in English, Somali, Spanish, and Vietnamese—fifty interviews with voucher holders with children; we analyzed transcripts for themes related to where people lived, housing search processes, and residential satisfaction.

various forms of support they provide (Spring et al. 2017). Others rely on social network connections, who largely have similar racial and ethnic statuses (Smith, McPherson, and Smith-Lovin 2014; Wimmer and Lewis 2010), for advice or leads for homes in similar racial and ethnic spaces.

The SSSP further suggests that economic resources, preferences, discrimination, and additional social factors work in tandem rather than separately. For example, even as people who use vouchers experience source-of-income discrimination across racial and ethnic statuses, despite it being illegal in many municipalities (Tighe, Hatch, and Mead 2017; Reosti 2020; Rosen 2014), racial and ethnic discrimination likely creates a dual disadvantage for Black and Latino movers that reduces their access to integrated and high-opportunity neighborhoods (Faber and Mercier 2018; Rosen, Garboden, and Cossyleon 2021). There is evidence that landlords steer voucher holders into more disadvantaged, segregated neighborhoods (Rosen 2014, 2020; Garboden et al. 2018). But experiences and/ or expectations of discrimination may drive both economic resources and preferences well beyond the mechanism of the vouchers themselves. Housing market discrimination, for instance, influences ethnically and racially disparate home values for property buyers, which induces socioeconomic disparities (here, in the form of wealth) and shapes residential histories. Pager and Shepherd (2008) outline parallel discrimination in the job market, which limits minoritized individuals' access to employment and income. Regarding preferences, Krysan and colleagues (2002, 2009) show how white people often prefer white neighbors based on their own discriminatory avoidance of Black people, while many Black people seek at least some Black neighbors because this signals a lower likelihood of racial discrimination. Accordingly, a long history of racist/ethnocentrist treatment may lead Black and Latino voucher recipients to avoid searching in more advantaged neighborhoods where they may assume discrimination will be more prevalent (Krysan and Crowder 2017).

The voucher program is the biggest tenant-based federal housing subsidy program in the US and deserves to be understood in its own right. At the same time, our results contribute to the sociology of housing by demonstrating the ways that subtle social processes embedded in housing search processes drive broader patterns of segregation and other forms of residential stratification. Specifically, we see racial and ethnic differences in residential outcomes (mobility rates and neighborhood levels of racial/ ethnic segregation and poverty) that especially disadvantage Black people and advantage white people. We find that these disparate outcomes emerge out of racial/ethnic differences in housing search priorities and processes, and that individuals adapt their priorities and approaches based on their residential histories, which are written in the context of widespread, long-standing residential stratification. In short, this study shows how racially and ethnically segregated residential life perpetuates itself by setting people on disparate housing trajectories.

As we describe below, there are reasons to believe these findings are relevant to a sociology of housing more broadly and that racial and ethnic dynamics similar to those we observe for voucher holders operate in other locations and across a wider range of socioeconomic statuses. Therefore, our research aligns with other scholars who argue that an integrated and complex sociological model like the SSSP is necessary to more fully understand and address racial and ethnic residential inequalities (Faber, this volume; Krysan and Crowder 2017; Sewell 2010, cited in Faber, this volume).

The Limits of Mobility

Racial and ethnic residential segregation is an important social challenge in the US regardless of housing voucher status (e.g., Logan 2013; South, Crowder, and Chavez 2005; Wang and Walter 2018). This fact is noteworthy since some policymakers hope housing voucher programs can provide recipients with opportunities for residential mobility (e.g., Rosen 2020), beyond these programs' explicit and primary mandate to help households *pay* for housing, which they do fairly well (Fischer 2015; Shinn and Khadduri 2020). A substantial and growing body of research, including our own, demonstrates that voucher programs struggle to address racial and ethnic segregation despite hopes to the contrary, and regardless of racial and ethnic differences in voucher holders' income.

First, we see racial and ethnic disparities in residential mobility rates. Black voucher participants stand out as having the highest probability of moving each month (see figure 20.1, model 1), despite the inclusion of controls like household income. This finding is contrary to some research about the broader US population that indicates that Black households may move at *lower* rates than other socioeconomically similar non-Black households (e.g., South and Deane 1993). Since many voucher holders move out of necessity rather than desire (DeLuca, Wood, and Rosenblatt 2019), these results may indicate higher levels of housing instability, rather than upward mobility, for Black heads of household.

As found in other research on moving with a voucher (e.g., Basolo and Nguyen 2005; Schwartz, McClure, and Taghavi 2016), racial and ethnic differences in neighborhood outcomes are evident: figure 20.1's model 2 shows that all groups, except white householders, tend to move to neighborhoods

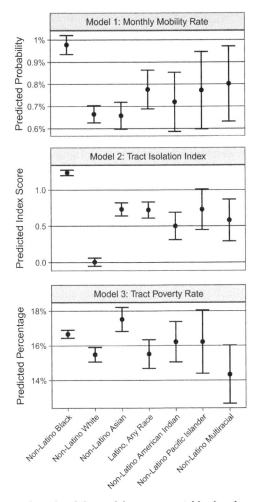

FIGURE 20.1. Residential mobility and destination neighborhood outcomes by race/ ethnicity; models with individual, household, and neighborhood controls

in which their own racial/ethnic group is overrepresented relative to the county level. Black voucher recipients typically move to areas with the greatest representation of Black people within the county. Latino, Asian, and multiracial voucher holders are also likely to move to neighborhoods that have a higher concentration of other same-race/ethnicity households than the King County tract average. In contrast, white voucher holders end up in neighborhoods where the percentage of white residents is roughly equal to the county average (63 percent), demonstrating that, when accounting for controls, white people in King County—who live among more same-race neighbors than any other group—live in neighborhoods with similar racial and ethnic composition regardless of voucher status.

The voucher program struggles to meet its potential to deconcentrate poverty (Eriksen and Ross 2013; Metzger 2014). Regardless of racial and ethnic status, King County voucher holders are socioeconomically segregated, living in neighborhoods with poverty rates roughly double the county average (7.7 percent) (US Census Bureau 2019c). However, there are racial and ethnic disparities, regardless of differences in household income, in neighborhood poverty rates (figure 20.1's model 3), with Asian voucher households living among the most poverty. Other research shows Black, Latino, and Asian voucher recipients as more likely than their white counterparts to live in or move into higher-poverty neighborhoods (Basolo and Nguyen 2005; McClure 2010; McClure, Schwartz, and Taghavi, 2015; Schwartz, McClure, and Taghavi 2016; Wang and Walter 2018). That Asian people with vouchers stand out as living in the highest-poverty neighborhoods may reflect the composition of the Asian population in Seattle, which has more relatively disadvantaged Asian groups than the US overall. Nationally, Asian people as a whole face substantially less neighborhood disadvantage than Black and Latino people (e.g., Timberlake 2002).

These findings suggest that voucher holders' moves reinforce patterns of inequality and segregation that housing voucher programs hope to eliminate. Moreover, they imply that additional factors are at play beyond those we can capture in a regression model (such as annual income). The interviews provide evidence that such factors include racial and ethnic variation in neighborhood priorities and residential mobility processes that are shaped by residential histories, discrimination, and the influence of social networks.

Residential Histories Shape Residential Priorities

In our qualitative interviews, some US-born Black participants reported hesitance in or avoidance of areas with more white people, despite a draw to the schools in some of these areas, which also have lower poverty rates. Instead, the potential of racial and source-of-income discrimination in those spaces made them undesirable for these movers. For example, Latiya[4] is a Black woman in her early thirties who would not search for housing in a predominantly white area where Black people make up only

---

[4] All participant names are pseudonyms.

2 percent of the population. The location, she reported, would have been convenient because her daughter's father lives there and her daughter goes to school there. However, the racial climate is uncomfortable, and she finds herself avoiding shopping in this town. "Something about the atmosphere is different. Something about when I step outside, I feel different and I don't know if it's the color of my skin. I don't know if it's the way I dress [. . .] I don't know what it is, but I know that I don't even go to the Dollar Tree there and I'm a Dollar Tree lover, you know? I prefer to go to the Dollar Tree in my neighborhood strangely." This finding aligns with other research documenting how some Black people avoid predominantly white neighborhoods (e.g., Krysan and Farley 2002; Lee 2000), stores (Lee 2000), and higher education institutions (Hotchkins and Dancy 2015) in order to avoid discrimination.

We also see that avoidance of white spaces arises differently based on participants' residential backgrounds. For example, a small number of US-born Black women who had spent ample time in segregated King County neighborhoods reported feeling geographically stuck and expecting racist and/or voucher-based exclusion in predominantly white and affluent areas of the county. Each of these individuals had substantial direct or vicarious experiences of neighborhood violence. Importantly, these women's expectations of exclusion shaped *where* they searched for housing, avoiding certain neighborhoods or towns. With rare exception, this pattern did not arise within other groups, which may not have had such close contact with this kind of neighborhood violence.

Jennifer, an African American woman in her fifties who has spent her life in Seattle and broader King County, reports experiencing a variety of forms of residential exclusion. When asked what she looks for in a neighborhood beyond proximity to her church, she said the following: "No drugs. I wanted it to be no drugs and no violence and that's all you have up here on this hill. Is you have so much . . . I don't know the word for it . . . So much crap. Once you go up to [a nearby city] it's a lot better. But right here on this hill? I don't want to raise my son over here." Jennifer expressed an interest in moving to a safe neighborhood, but her choices were tempered by her expectation that she would face strong discrimination based not only on her race, but also on having a child and using a voucher as part of her rent payment. Accordingly, when asked if she looked in a nearby "better" area that might have fit her housing and neighborhood needs, but that has a high concentration of white people, she replied, "I didn't look in [that city], because I already knew . . . that there wasn't gonna be no doors open. . . . I knew that no one was going to rent to an African American woman and her single self with her son and her Section 8 voucher. I just didn't even take myself there. Why? Why get disappointed on purpose?" Voucher holders of color already face multiple forms of discrimination (Faber and Mercier 2018); perhaps for some US-born Black participants, the prospect of moving to a potentially racist white neighborhood or town is simply too much.

In contrast to those, like Jennifer, who grew up in segregated King County, some participants who grew up in the rural South compared King County favorably, in terms of sustained and overt racism, to their childhoods in Louisiana or Mississippi. These individuals identified race as a salient factor in determining where to live, but they did not report feelings of geographic restrictions within King County.

Racial and Ethnic Preferences Shape Residential Priorities

Throughout our research, and consistently with broader research on racialized housing priorities (Krysan and Farley 2002), voucher holders described their neighborhood priorities in ways that invoked race and ethnicity. For example, some white interview participants talked about wanting to avoid areas that have historically been predominantly Black (for example, Rainier Beach and the Central District prior to recent gentrification), though they typically voiced this opposition in terms other than race. Such reasons include being too far from their current lives (e.g., their kid's school) or were expressed in more obviously racially coded comments (for instance, that a neighborhood has too much violence) (Hurwitz and Peffley 2005). Perhaps given the consistently high representation of white people across most King County neighborhoods, white respondents did not explicitly mention a preference for living among same-race neighbors. Explicit anti-Black sentiment came up in several interviews, especially with Latino and Vietnamese migrants, some of whom suggested that they might avoid a neighborhood because of the presence of many Black people.

Some people of color did report that they purposely sought out areas with greater racial and ethnic diversity or concentrations of in-group neighbors, which were often also higher-poverty areas. In-group affinity was explicitly salient for some Latino people in terms of their level of satisfaction within the neighborhood. Perhaps as a result of their being relatively spread out across Seattle, some Latino people expressed a desire to live among more co-ethnic neighbors than they did at the time of the interview. Many foreign-born Somali and Vietnamese individuals similarly preferred areas in which their communities also lived, despite relatively high poverty rates in those areas. Because we know that family and friends are typically ethnically and racially similar (Smith, McPherson, and Smith-Lovin 2014; Wimmer and Lewis 2010), and because many of the Somali and Vietnamese participants' language communities are fairly homogeneous in terms of race/ethnicity, their preferences for living among friends, family, and amenities where they can speak their language likely means a preference for at least some same-race/ethnicity neighbors.

It is notable that these priorities were rarely articulated in terms of neighborhood racial and ethnic composition. The Somali women we spoke with, for example, emphasized the importance of the people in their lives and proximity to the institutions and amenities they frequented, rather than the characteristics of the home or neighborhood. Nasra is a Somali woman in her thirties who lived with her husband and five children in a house in Seattle. She moved to the US more than a decade ago, after having spent several years in a refugee community in Kenya. She suggested that her home and neighborhood are not particularly important to her, so long as she lives among people who share her language and religion and who frequently visit and drink tea together. This mirrors literature about the US population more generally, which shows that neighborhood priorities favoring ties to family, friends, and broader social networks can be an important part of Black and Latino households' mobility decisions and need to be addressed in theory and practice about household mobility strategies and outcomes (Charles 2003; Havekes, Bader, and Krysan 2016).

The Vietnamese women we spoke with highlighted proximity to amenities. Annie, Nancy, and Tam are three Vietnamese women in their forties who have lived in South Seattle since arriving in the US or shortly thereafter. They live across two census tracts in which over one in four people are Asian and more than one in five are in poverty. While Nancy also raised proximity to a mutual aid network as a preference, all three prioritized the convenience of the areas in which they lived, citing for example the desirability of being close to markets and doctor's offices where they could conduct their business in Vietnamese. Nancy and Tam also appreciated being close to the bus line for easy access to transit.

Reflections from Nasra, Annie, Nancy, and Tam, which demonstrate preferences for geographically situated communities and amenities, also speak to long-standing questions about "person-based" and "place-based" housing policies and programs (see Galster 2017 for a literature review). Specifically, these individuals' stories raise questions about the potential racial and ethnic inequities that will result if programs facilitate moves into lower-poverty neighborhoods (so-called person-based programs) without also addressing the structural causes of local poverty in the neighborhoods they leave behind (so-called place-based programs). Person-based

programs like the Creating Moves to Opportunity (CMTO) demonstration have had substantial success leveraging mobility counseling, financial
help with moving costs, and other supports to increase the rate of moves
into "high-opportunity" neighborhoods for both Black and white householders, as well as for a third "other race/ethnicity" category (Bergman et
al. 2019). However, it appears that there are racial and ethnic differences
in neighborhood priorities that may make some groups more willing and
able than others to leave their current neighborhood for a "higher opportunity" area. While place-based investments in affordable housing are one
potential way policymakers can help assisted households avoid a zero-sum
game between choosing community and "high-opportunity" neighborhood contexts, other research highlights that such interventions need
to be crafted in an equitable manner to avoid gentrification and instead
preserve ethnic, racial, and socioeconomic diversity as greater economic
resources flow into the neighborhood (Ellen and Torrats-Espinosa 2019).

Social Networks Shape Racial and Ethnic Outcomes

Beyond playing an important role in shaping residential priorities, especially for the Somali and Vietnamese people we talked with, social network dynamics contributed to neighborhood outcomes in additional
racial and ethnic ways. For example, a small number of participants,
particularly Black and Vietnamese householders, reportedly found their
homes through a personal connection, a finding in line with prior studies
of housing voucher households (Ellen, Suher, and Torrats-Espinosa 2019).
Similarly, other Somali and Vietnamese movers received successful leads
from a friend, family member, or acquaintance who helped them find a
home within the same zip code in which they had already been living.
For example, Leylo, a Somali woman in her twenties who had come to
the US as a child, moved within the same zip code, into a home after her
mother moved out of it. Tam, whose last five moves had been spurred by
the sale of her homes in South Seattle, felt so pressured to find a place that
she asked everyone she knew, as well as people she did not know—for
example, people she passed on the street—about whether they knew of a
place she might move into. Eventually, somebody she asked referred her to
the landlord of the apartment she moved into, a mile from her last home.

The US-born Black respondents generally moved across zip codes
when they learned about a home or neighborhood through a personal
connection. Each of these contacts had a residential or professional connection to the place they recommended. This finding may reflect the geographic splintering of King County's Black community; networks of Black

individuals may now be more dispersed in the Seattle area than they were in prior decades. The conditions of the destination neighborhoods for those finding a place through a personal contact varied for this group. Mia and Mz. C are Black women in their thirties and fifties whose family members pointed them to areas that are either higher in poverty and/or have a disproportionately Black population. In contrast, Sam is a Black man in his sixties who found an apartment in a very low-poverty area with a disproportionately white population because he had a professional connection to the property manager there. In each of these cases, respondents' networks were important in facilitating moves to new neighborhoods, but there were material differences in neighborhood outcomes to the extent that networks reflected existing patterns of segregation by race and ethnicity across neighborhoods, workplaces, and other social institutions (Hall, Iceland, and Yi 2019). Overall, these findings suggest that knowledge and information from social networks help explain racial and ethnic differences in residential outcomes for voucher recipients and households more generally (Krysan and Crowder 2017).

Implications for Future Research and Policy

In this chapter, we document significant racial and ethnic stratification in residential mobility and neighborhood outcomes for housing voucher households in Seattle and King County, Washington, and connect this stratification to the literature on residential dynamics for the broader US population. By doing so, we outline how studying residential dynamics among voucher holders can provide policy insights and contribute to a thriving sociology of housing.

Our research is among the first to apply the SSSP framework. We show that housing outcomes, including residential stratification, emerge out of ethnically and racially differentiated residential histories, social networks, and related social dynamics. These histories, social networks, and additional dynamics at least partly shape residential outcomes by influencing residential priorities and the housing search process. We also incorporate into our model the experiences of internal and international migration, which constitute important aspects of residential history that may moderate how ethnicity and/or race relate to socioeconomic status, exposure to discrimination, and social networks.

Our research suggests that addressing residential stratification through residential mobility may not be an appropriate goal for every household, since some may want to remain where they are even if that area has a high level of poverty. People of color often have to choose between lower poverty rates and living among many same-race neighbors, further limiting choices for groups that have been historically marginalized. Even if, as Darrah and DeLuca show (2014), voucher holders' residential preferences can change once they move into lower-poverty neighborhoods, our findings highlight three ongoing challenges for person-based approaches to housing policy. First, it is unlikely that we can move everyone into low-poverty neighborhoods without creating more low-poverty areas. Second, our study and others show that lower-poverty neighborhoods are less accessible and welcoming to people of color, so they may enjoy fewer benefits to their well-being by moving there. Third, some residential priorities we discuss above are tied to specific communities, so additional information may not be enough to encourage a move. People have built communities in the spaces they have lived in, however they ended up there. While many people are eager to move to a "higher opportunity" neighborhood (e.g., Bergman et al. 2019), our research suggests that the desirability and feasibility of moving into these areas may be shaped by racial and ethnic experiences.

It is important to note that our research is specific to King County, Washington, home to Seattle, a large city in the western US with a tight and fast-growing housing market that has seen declining rates of racial and ethnic residential segregation and a substantial out-migration of some people of color in recent decades (Beason 2016; Krysan and Crowder 2017; Rosenberg 2018; US Census Bureau 2019b). We may not see the precise dynamics we describe here in other parts of the country. For example, research in Baltimore, which has a weaker housing market, has found landlord discrimination in *favor* of voucher holders, varying by neighborhood (Rosen 2014, 2020; Garboden et al. 2018). Indeed, our emphasis on variation in residential priorities based on differing residential histories means that we expect differences across geographic contexts that systematically influence our residential trajectories. Still, there is no reason to believe the presence of subtle racial and ethnic dynamics would be limited to the voucher holders in our study (e.g., Lee 2021). However, we encourage readers to exercise caution in applying our specific findings to other metros, given the peculiarities of Seattle and the nonrepresentative interview data. Future research should consider how the web of dynamics we discuss manifests in other geographies and for additional racial and ethnic and socioeconomic groups.

The SSSP fundamentally argues for a structural analysis of racial and ethnic inequalities. While it relies on individual residential histories, social networks, and housing search processes as contributing to racial/ethnic residential stratification, it also emphasizes that these individual-level dynamics are influenced by the larger set of structural conditions in which they emerge. The dynamics we discuss emphasize the need for policy and subsidy program responses that are attuned to variation in mobility processes across racial and ethnic statuses, to ensure that resources and services provide equitable support across the board.

Our arguments have implications for thinking about racial and ethnic disparities in residential patterns broadly, as well as for other social systems and for how various systems feed each other. It is arguably unsurprising that addressing racial and ethnic disparities requires a systematic approach. Critical race theory contends that racism is ubiquitous within society and that laws and policies that claim "colorblindness" cannot be so because social institutions, structures, and rules have been built within a legacy of racial discrimination (Delgado and Stefancic 2013). As such, "race-neutral" programs are not sufficient to address racial inequalities because they do not directly address racial bias. Yet federal law requires ostensible "colorblindness" in its housing and other programs. Given that voucher programs were developed partly in response to racial segregation resulting from the mid-twentieth century's housing projects, it is crucial to question the appropriateness of "race-neutral" approaches.

21

All in the Family

SOCIAL CONNECTIONS AND THE
CYCLE OF SEGREGATION

Maximilian Cuddy, Amy Spring,
Maria Krysan, and Kyle Crowder

Many of the most important impacts of housing on people's lives—its
capacity for providing safety, economic security, a sense of well-being,
and access to resources—are dependent on the broader neighborhood
in which their housing is embedded. For this reason, housing sociologists have long been interested in understanding the processes upholding
persistent neighborhood stratification. This research focuses on patterns
and drivers of residential segregation by race—the tendency for members of different racialized groups to occupy separate and qualitatively
distinct neighborhoods. It identifies racial residential segregation as a key
mechanism of systemic racial inequality in the United States, giving rise
to dramatic racial inequities in wealth, education, criminal justice, health,
and exposure to crime (Bell 2020b; Massey and Denton 1993; Reardon,
Kalogrides, and Shores 2019; Reskin 2012; Shapiro 2017; Taylor 2019;
Williams and Collins 2001). These processes allow resources and opportunities to accumulate in spaces occupied by white residents, and to be
withheld or extracted from areas occupied by people of color.

In this chapter we provide an overview of core theoretical debates related to the persistence of residential segregation by race. We begin the
chapter with an overview of the three theoretical traditions informing
research on the topic and provide a basic outline of the evidence related to
these arguments. While these traditional arguments have dominated the
study of residential segregation for decades, they each suffer from a weak
engagement with insights into how people search for housing. Accordingly, we also offer an overview of more contemporary theoretical frames
that explicitly conceive of segregation as emerging from stratified housing
searches and underlying social dynamics. We illustrate these efforts by
exploring the diverse effects of one social realm—family—on housing
searches and segregation. Rather than providing an exhaustive treatment
of prevailing theoretical arguments, the chapter highlights opportunities

for housing scholars to further conceptualize housing search processes as a crucial lens through which discrimination, economic stratification, and more subtle social processes shape residential outcomes.

Traditional Explanations

While the impacts of segregation are well documented, our understanding of its primary drivers is still underdeveloped. Most research on the drivers of segregation has been informed by some combination of three traditional explanations (Krysan and Crowder, 2017). Each of these perspectives receives some support in research on residential segregation, but each also falls short of offering a complete explanation for racial differences in neighborhood sorting processes that constantly reinforce segregation.

The first of these explanations sees segregation as a function of racial differences in economic resources, with limited income and wealth preventing many people of color from gaining access to the most advantaged neighborhoods occupied by whites (Crowder, South, and Chavez 2006; South and Crowder 1997). This argument is supported by the positive association between household resources and the likelihood of gaining access to more advantaged neighborhoods occupied by white populations (Crowder, South, and Chavez 2006; Krysan and Crowder 2017). Levels of segregation are highest in metropolitan areas in which economic disparities between racial groups are most pronounced (Farley and Frey 1994; Logan, Stults, and Farley 2004). However, pronounced racial differences in residential outcomes remain even after controlling for income, wealth, and a wide range of sociodemographic characteristics (Crowder, South, and Chavez 2006; Krysan and Crowder 2017). Aggregate income inequality explains just a small part of the overall variation in segregation between groups (Bayer, McMillan, and Rueben 2004; Jargowsky 2014).

A second traditional perspective suggests that segregation stems from racial and ethnic differences in residential preferences. Members of most groups are presumed to be strongly inclined toward sharing residential areas with neighbors from their own racial group and disinclined to live in areas containing large shares of other groups. This argument is supported by the frequent observation that survey respondents identifying as white, Black, Asian, and Latino/a all express relatively strong preferences for hypothetical neighborhoods containing large numbers of neighbors from their own racial group (Charles 2006; Krysan and Bader 2007; Zubrinsky and Bobo 1996). At the same time, this basic argument is challenged by the fact that members of all four groups tend to describe their "ideal" neighborhood as containing substantial levels of integration (Charles 2006).

Black survey respondents in particular tend to report the strongest preferences for neighborhoods with levels of integration that far exceed those
present in the neighborhoods occupied by average Black families (Krysan
and Bader 2007).

Finally, the third traditional argument, often couched in terms of the
place stratification perspective (Charles 2003; Logan and Molotch 2007),
suggests that policy makers, white residents, and residential gatekeepers
(e.g., real estate agents, landlords, and mortgage lenders) erect a variety
of discriminatory barriers that relegate people of color to relatively isolated and devalued residential areas (Roscigno, Karafin, and Tester 2009;
Ross and Turner 2005; Rothstein 2017). While racial discrimination
remains deeply ingrained in all kinds of housing processes (Flage 2018;
Korver-Glenn 2021; Gaddis and DiRago, this volume), the most overt
exclusionary forms appear to be declining more rapidly than are levels of
segregation (Ross and Turner 2005). Moreover, variations in measurable
levels of discrimination appear to explain little of the racial variation in
mobility patterns that shape segregation (South and Crowder 1998). Thus,
the available evidence suggests that, while housing markets are highly
stratified in ways that severely disadvantage people of color, it is not clear
that the eradication of exclusionary discrimination would, by itself, spell
the end of residential segregation.

Challenging Tradition

Krysan and Crowder (2017) developed the social structural sorting perspective (SSSP) as a complement to these traditional perspectives. This
approach focuses attention on underappreciated social forces upholding
residential segregation by race. The SSSP argues that segregation persists
as a function of dynamic reinforcement in which our residential histories, social networks, and daily experiences lead to patterns of residential
mobility dominated by short distance moves between racially similar
neighborhoods. As these social dynamics are all themselves racially circumscribed by the separation of racial groups across space, and because
segregation is at the root of massive racial differences in economic resources and inter-group dynamics, the SSSP highlights the ways in which
residential segregation has generated a self-reinforcing cycle.

While recognizing the importance of stratified economic resources,
racial attitudes, and persistent discrimination in housing and other arenas, the SSSP addresses several key shortcomings of traditional theoretical arguments and brings the study of segregation more firmly into the
realm of the sociology of housing. First, while most research on residential

segregation reflects an acknowledgment that segregation is maintained by racially differentiated patterns of mobility, examination of the processes through which families search for housing and make decisions about where to live are rare (Clark 1982). By bringing the search process more explicitly into the study of segregation, the SSSP provides an opportunity for research into residential decision-making as a driver of segregation (Bruch and Swait 2019; DeLuca, Wood, and Rosenblatt 2019; Harvey et al. 2020).

Traditional explanations of segregation are also based on the implicit assumption that individuals possess uniformly strong knowledge about the residential opportunities available in their area. The assumption is that families utilize this broad knowledge of residential options to sort themselves into the most desirable neighborhoods as dictated by their race-specific preferences, economic resources, and ability to avoid exclusionary forms of discrimination. The SSSP draws attention to the fact that knowledge about, and impressions of, neighborhood options vary significantly by race in ways that likely produce highly disparate residential outcomes. For example, available evidence suggests that Black, white, and Latino/a residents of Chicago reported significantly more awareness of neighborhoods in which their own racial/ethnic group was overrepresented and less awareness about areas populated by other groups (Krysan and Bader 2009). Moreover, perceptions of the social, physical, and economic characteristics of specific neighborhoods likely vary sharply by race (Jones and Dantzler 2021).

The search for housing is likely to be shaped by residential histories in similar ways. Housing and neighborhood experiences during childhood and adolescence, for example, significantly affect the likelihood of moving to relatively advantaged and integrated neighborhoods, in part because these early residential exposures shape perceptions of residential opportunities and expectations for conditions in specific neighborhoods (Huang et al. 2020; Leibbrand et al. 2020). This shaping has important implications for patterns of segregation. Existing research indicates that racial differences in early-life residential exposures help explain racial disparities in neighborhood racial isolation and socioeconomic advantage in adulthood (South et al. 2016). The point here is that lived experiences and residential histories produce highly stratified levels of knowledge and perceptions of neighborhoods that are likely to have a large impact on housing searches. The racial stratification of these social dynamics is likely to reinforce segregation in ways missed by traditional explanations of segregation.

According to Krysan and Crowder (2017), social networks are likely to shape housing outcomes by providing an important source of direct and indirect information about housing options and neighborhood characteristics. This information allows individuals to develop strong impressions of the composition and social conditions in a specific neighborhood or area of the metropolis, even in the absence of personal exposure to that area. To a large extent, these impressions may rest on neighborhood stereotypes emanating from what we refer to as correlated characteristics. Individuals use what they assume about the racial composition of an area to make further assumptions about other characteristics of the neighborhood. In this way, perceptions of residential spaces tend to be highly racialized. White residents interviewed by Krysan and Crowder (2017) tended to assume that areas with relatively high Black concentrations have high levels of crime, poor property values, and ineffective schools, while simultaneously reporting that they know little about these places. Similarly, Black respondents often report spending little time in, and knowing little about, areas with high white concentrations, but they still assume that these places would be unaffordable and/or unwelcoming to Black residents. According to the SSSP, these inferences, while not rooted in direct experience of specific areas, are clearly rooted in direct and indirect experiences of racism and have substantial impacts on the search for housing. They create sharp racial differences in the sets of places that individuals consider during their search and ultimately circumscribe residential outcomes.

These search-altering impressions and knowledge patterns are likely shaped by a wide range of forces, but social networks are likely to be especially influential. The residents interviewed by Krysan and Crowder (2017) often reported learning about neighborhoods from friends, coworkers, and family members who lived or worked in these places. Because the size and content of social networks vary so sharply by race (Alwin, Thomas, and Sherman-Wilkins 2018), members of different racialized groups are likely to have access to pools of information about housing options and specific neighborhoods that differ sharply in terms of quantity and content. The resulting group differences in levels of knowledge about, and perceptions of conditions in, various neighborhoods are likely to produce residential outcomes that are also quite distinct. In this way, the SSSP conceives of racially circumscribed social networks as an important underlying driver of residential segregation and racialized differences in housing outcomes. And because social networks remain racially circumscribed, their connection to segregation can be thought of as reciprocal and deeply ingrained in the cycle of segregation.

The reciprocal nature of the effects of social networks is illustrative of a central theme of the SSSP. While past research hints at the influence of several social factors explicitly described in the SSSP, their effects on housing outcomes remain largely hidden from view because they shape segregation indirectly through other, seemingly benign, features of residential sorting. According to Krysan and Crowder (2017), residential segregation is so deeply embedded in the operation of our housing markets and metropolitan areas that it has become self-reinforcing. More specifically, the separation of different racial and ethnic groups into distinct and qualitatively different residential spaces produces sharp racial differences not only in the composition of social networks but also in economic resources and life experiences that, in turn, exacerbate the effects of discrimination to produce profound racial differences in residential search processes and neighborhood outcomes. These racialized patterns of mobility and immobility continually reinforce segregation; the cycle continues through subsequent generations. Developing stronger explanations of residential stratification and its repercussions requires careful attention to these subtle, self-reinforcing features of housing segregation.

A Key Component of the Social Network: Family

While the SSSP introduces interpersonal networks and other social forces into explanations of persistent segregation, many aspects of the theoretical frame remain underdeveloped. For example, while Krysan and Crowder (2017) emphasize the role of social networks as a source of indirect knowledge about housing options and neighborhoods, connections to other people have important impacts on multiple parts of the housing search process. Indeed, sociology teaches us that understanding most social phenomenon, including residential mobility, requires engaging with the idea of "linked lives" (Coulter, van Ham, and Findlay 2016). In this section we illustrate this point by delving into the variety of ways that housing searches may be influenced by one particularly important component of the social network: family.

Existing research documents the importance of social networks for mobility, yet tends to frame the role of social networks on mobility decisions in a fairly restricted way. For example, proximity to family is often presented as one of many amenities households consider as they decide whether and where to move (Dawkins 2006; Clark and Maas 2015; Mulder 2018; Spring et al. 2017). We draw on interviews with forty-four Black and forty-one white families who had school-aged children, conducted as part of the Chicago Neighborhood-Schools Connections study (where Krysan served as co-PI). We demonstrate a broad range of ways that social networks shape residential decisions, some of which are not fully articulated by Krysan and Crowder's initial exposition of the SSSP. In what follows, we define family fairly broadly, including extremely close friends who might be considered "fictive kin" (Nelson 2013). We illustrate four different types of family impact: (1) family as necessity; (2) family as amenity; (3) family as facilitator; and (4) the invisible hand of the family. We also highlight more distant friends as an alternative influence that can disrupt the impact of family on residential decision-making.

FAMILY AS NECESSITY

Research that points to the role of family in shaping housing outcomes often frames the impact in terms of necessity, in which someone moves to a unit or neighborhood to either give or receive support from their family members (Spring et al. 2017). This dynamic was evident in our interviews with some households, as was the role of this dynamic in shaping racially stratified residential outcomes. For some of the people we interviewed, proximity to family was clearly motivated by an ability to have access to low-cost housing, childcare, and other family supports. For others, the choice of housing near family was rooted in the need to care for aging parents, support younger siblings, or provide other assistance *for* family.

In many cases, this instrumental family support overrode other prerogatives of the housing search process. For example, Cynthia, a Black mother, had a strong preference for living in a racially integrated space, having experienced such conditions in college. However, lacking strong contacts in other areas and facing the high cost of housing, Cynthia found it necessary to move in with her mother in the racially isolated neighborhood in which she grew up. Facing similar needs, many of the white mothers we interviewed found themselves moving into predominantly white spaces because of the need to be near family. These outcomes sometimes contradicted other residential priorities, but they always helped to reinforce racial residential segregation.

FAMILY AS AMENITY

For other respondents, proximity to family simply represented one piece of the bundle of locational amenities that drew them to a location. Indeed, many of these respondents would not have chosen to live near family if several other amenities—the architecture of the housing in the area, the proximity to work or school, or other locational features—had not also been present in the neighborhood. For instance, Michael, a Black father, and his wife lived downtown until they wanted to start a family. They listed proximity to family as one of several amenities, including a house with a yard, more space, and a house with "character." Indeed, Michael later mentioned that Niles, a nearby suburb, was ruled out as an option *not* because of being too far from family, but because they preferred to be closer to downtown.

In many cases, proximity to family serves as tiebreaker in choosing between otherwise similar neighborhoods. Because of relative racial homogeneity within families, such dynamics help to reinforce patterns of segregation as householders of different races tend to end up in neighborhoods that already contain members of their own family and racial group.

FAMILY AS FACILITATOR

Of particular relevance to housing scholars, family can also impact housing outcomes by facilitating direct access to, or information about, specific units. For example, Kelly, a white mother, was geographically expansive in her housing search. Affordability drove her search, coupled with an attempt (which ultimately failed) to find a place near her son's school. While she was conducting this expansive search and struggling to find something affordable, Kelly's mother-in-law directed her to apartments she had seen advertised in her local paper. While Kelly came to appreciate the proximity to family, her residential outcome was shaped more by the information she received from her mother-in-law than by the desire to be near family.

Especially in the context of low housing affordability (see part II of this volume), family can also provide crucial information about affordable units in a building or home occupied by the family member. Similarly, an endorsement from a tenant might convince a landlord to rent to an individual with a criminal record, a past eviction, or some other negative credential. The availability of such an endorsement might facilitate a move toward a building or area already occupied by family members. In these situations, family impacts the housing outcome by making the pathway of movement to a particular neighborhood easier. The magnitude of the impact on housing outcomes is not always clear, and the counterfactual is impossible to know. Nevertheless, providing information and access is clearly one way that family shapes the mobility process.

THE INVISIBLE HAND OF FAMILY

The previous examples show how family has an overt impact on mobility decisions. Sometimes, however, family's impact is considerably subtler. In the language of the SSSP, family interactions may help to shape the information people have about communities and neighborhoods, affecting the mental maps of potential housing options. These mental maps then help to define the parameters of housing searches. In this way, family and other components of a person's social network serve as a kind of invisible hand in shaping residential outcomes.

Ellen, a white mother, illustrates this dynamic. When asked how she ended up in her neighborhood, she offered a list of friends and family members, including her mother, who lived in the neighborhood. She knew the area well, having spent time at friends' houses when she was growing up. She found her current home when she "stumbled upon" a "For Sale" sign on one of the many days that she happened to be in the neighborhood.

Ellen's residential outcome was not directly influenced by a family member. No one person in her life pointed her to a location or offered a specific amenity. Instead, family indirectly impacted Ellen's basic knowledge about a set of locations—before and during the search itself. Revealing the invisibility of this impact, when asked by the interviewer whether her contact had good things to say about the neighborhood, Ellen didn't see the point of the question: "There really wasn't anything to say."

This example reveals how family shapes our mental maps—how we come to understand residential spaces—and how these maps then impact the set of residential options that we consider during a search. This dynamic was apparent in the residential experiences of the vast majority of people we interviewed, regardless of their racial identity. Yet few of these respondents consciously recognized the impact of family on their residential decisions. Their reflections nevertheless made it apparent that their housing choices were highly influenced by where they grew up and the residential decisions their parents and guardians made during their formative years. When we consider the ways that family can shape residential outcomes, in addition to those routinely described in existing research (c.f., Clark and Maas 2015; Spring et al. 2017), we must pay attention to these more nuanced ways families set the stage for a housing search. This influence is so subtle that it is often overlooked in explanations of residential mobility and stratification, but it is crucial for understanding where people end up living and—though we cannot test for this using our qualitative data—likely contributes to the perpetuation of segregation.

FRIENDS AS DISRUPTORS: AN ALTERNATIVE INFLUENCE

Our focus on the family illustrates the variety of complex and nuanced ways that a single component of the social network can shape housing processes. It is likely that other social relations have similar effects. For example, some of our interviewees moved closer to their friends because they liked where their friends lived or wanted to be near their social contacts. One respondent reported that a friend influenced his perception of his neighborhood when he was looking to buy a house. While the respondent had not grown up in the area, his friend had, and he liked what his friend had to say about it, and liked what he saw when he visited.

Interactions with friends also help to shape the mental map of the city. One respondent described how they started searching for housing in their current neighborhood after attending a coworker's birthday party, while another described how visiting a coworker in a different neighborhood had changed her impression of the area and convinced her to look for housing nearby. Friends also provided leads on specific housing units for many of our respondents.

Our qualitative research indicates that friends, acquaintances, and coworkers often disrupted the effects of past residential experiences and the subtle pulls of family by introducing respondents to neighborhoods they did not know about previously. If families made neighborhoods "familiar" for respondents, friends were more likely to be a gateway into the unfamiliar. For many of our respondents, friends created an opportunity to break out of one's regular activity space and provide a reason to travel to another part of the city. Often, friendship ties were established at workplaces, which may tend to draw from a wider swath of the metropolitan area. The experience of seeing where a friend or acquaintance lives can inspire others to want a similar arrangement. In this way, friends can serve as unintentional ambassadors for their neighborhoods.

Without information about where people's friends live and their level of interaction with them, sources of data traditionally used to study residential decision-making leave potential friend effects unmeasured. Friends are an underrecognized feature in the housing search, but according to our interviews, their influence can be dramatic. In most cases, friends play a role in disrupting the impacts of lived experiences and family ties, introducing people to places they would not have considered otherwise.

Future Directions for the Sociology of Housing

Krysan and Crowder's (2017) social structural sorting perspective (SSSP) reorients explanations for racial residential segregation to encompass the dynamic reinforcement of segregation that operates through social networks and lived experiences—which themselves have developed in racially circumscribed ways because of residential segregation. Our goal in this chapter was to take stock of *how* one component of social networks—the family—operates in residential decisions and, in light of the SSSP, contributes to larger patterns of residential segregation.

Our qualitative interviews demonstrate the multiple ways in which residential decision-making can be influenced by social networks. Family enters the housing search in a variety of often interlocking ways (that are not mutually exclusive). We conceptualized four versions of family impact: (1) family as necessity; (2) family as amenity; (3) family as facilitator; and (4) family as the invisible hand. The latter, as the name suggests, captures a subtler but important way that family operates in the background to shape our residential outcomes beyond the traditional assumptions that we are drawn to live by family because they can support us (or we can support them). Family shapes knowledge, experience, and our personal notions of which neighborhoods are "good," "safe," and "familiar." In many cases, the "pull" toward family—and toward neighborhoods similar to those occupied by family—ends up reinforcing existing racial segregation (see Carll et al., this volume).

Our research also offers new insights into how nonfamily social networks can influence moves. When friends and coworkers play a role, they seem to facilitate "bigger" moves—moves that take respondents further out of the areas they already know. These moves led some respondents into more racially integrated neighborhoods. Thus, friends add additional complexity to our understanding of the dynamic reinforcement implicated by the SSSP. Differences in the effects of *family ties* and *friend ties* is a refinement to the SSSP that still needs to be undertaken. Research by sociologists on *strong ties* versus *weak ties* could provide an important frame of reference for this exploration, pointing to ways that different types of ties facilitate the flow of different types of information (Granovetter 1973; Henning and Lieberg 1996).

While these findings point to surprisingly diverse effects of social connections on residential decision-making, they raise many questions worthy of attention in future research. For example, which types of family influence are most common across different racialized groups (Carll 2021), across the adult life course, and across housing market conditions? In the context of stratified, family-affected mobility dynamics, how will the continued "graying" of America (Achenbaum 2020) reshape residential choices and resulting patterns of segregation by age and race? How will the continued financial strain on younger people—higher debt amounts, stagnant wages in many industries, a weakened social safety net, decreasing housing affordability—alter patterns of residential choices, not just in terms of the likelihood of returning home, but also in terms of the need to locate near family? How will the increased rates of white-Latina/o and, to a lesser extent, white-Asian intermarriage reshape future residential-family trajectories (Gabriel 2016; Lichter and Qian 2018)? How do the multifaceted influences of families relate to the influence of broader social networks that include acquaintances, close confidants, coworkers, and other nonfamily connections that may shape perceptions of residential spaces and access to housing opportunities? And how might the continued proliferation of social media alter the structure of social networks and the complexity of their effects on housing decisions?

In addition to fleshing out the complex effects of social networks, future research should more fully investigate other social dynamics implicated in the SSSP. For example, researchers will need to attend to how media depictions of residential spaces trigger assumptions of correlated characteristics in ways that shape home searchers' perceptions of residential options. Future research should also focus on how mundane, but racially stratified, experiences in different areas of the metropolis and residential exposures over the life course shape both our knowledge of residential opportunities and the filters through which we assess the information about places that we receive from friends, family, media, and other sources. Addressing the full complexity of these social dynamics will be important for the sociology of housing and the development of a fuller understanding of the forces that perpetuate residential stratification.

22

Policing, Property, and the Production of Racial Segregation

Rahim Kurwa

In 1882, James Falloon of Hiawatha, Kansas, sued his neighbor Adam Schilling to stop him from building a new home on his property and renting it to a Black family. Over the prior decade, as Jim Crow's ascendance was felt across the country, the Black population of Kansas had doubled due to out-migration from the South. Falloon was one of many white Kansans searching for new ways to maintain the racial order amid these changes. His strategy revolved around nuisance property law, which states that a person should use his or her property in a way that doesn't injure their neighbor's property. This stipulation is generally interpreted to refer to acts that reach over the property line in some way—like causing pollution, uprooting trees, or disrupting the water supply. Falloon extended this argument to cast race as a nuisance, arguing that Schilling renting his property to a Black family would damage the value and enjoyment of Falloon's property.

Despite the relative flexibility of nuisance law, *Falloon v. Schilling*, which was identified by Godsil (2006) as the first "race nuisance" case, failed. The court ruled that Falloon's claim was too aggressive, stating that nuisance law should be used to respond to, rather than preempt, other homeowners' actions, and that limiting the defendant's ability to construct a lawful addition would infringe on the defendant's own property rights. The court added that the mere presence of Black renters was not enough to substantiate a nuisance claim, although it took pains to describe the family in question as an upstanding one headed by a preacher, suggesting the conditionality of its recognition of Black status.

Although Falloon and many subsequent plaintiffs lost these race nuisance cases, his claim merits attention. By seeking to bar his neighbor from renting or selling to a Black occupant, he asked for the right to use law enforcement to enforce that ruling if it was violated. In effect, he was asking the court to recognize property rights as including the right to maintain racial segregation.

Such a claim was not unique to Falloon or the other race nuisance plaintiffs. Eighty years later, California property owners and the California Real Estate Association (CREA) mobilized against the Rumford Fair Housing Act, a bill that would bar racial discrimination in the sale and rental of residential property. CREA described the Rumford bill as a diminishment of the "right to discriminate," which it saw as one of the constituent parts of property rights. As Slater (2021) documents, CREA proposed a "Property Owners' Bill of Rights" to enshrine the right to discriminate as a property right. While CREA and the state's white property owners were successful in passing Proposition 14 and overturning the Rumford Act, their victory was undone when the courts struck down the proposition and the federal government obviated it through the 1968 Fair Housing Act.

And yet today, the descendants of Falloon's era have acquired, through policing, powerful versions of the powers and rights Falloon asked for. In gaining powers to preempt, police, and evict their neighbors, they have expanded their property rights in the ways that prior generations had unsuccessfully demanded.

While conducting fieldwork in the Antelope Valley, the northernmost region of Los Angeles, I asked private renters and homeowners how they felt about tenants moving into their neighborhood through the Housing Choice Voucher program. They saw this trend as just the latest sign that the once entirely white, upper-middle class area was changing for the worse. While many private-market residents gave subsidized tenants the cold shoulder, some also spoke about how they used a variety of powerful tools to confront and turn back this trend. Among these tools are crime-free and nuisance housing ordinances. First, crime-free housing ordinances allow neighborhoods to—as Falloon had once hoped— preemptively exclude people from residency based on criminal legal system involvement (Archer 2019). This system ensures that crime-free ordinances have disparate impacts on Black renters. Second, nuisance property ordinances create pathways for individuals to use law enforcement to evict their neighbors. Although the rules vary across jurisdictions, they generally encourage or force landlords to evict tenants once they are the subject of some number of nuisance complaints or police visits— both of which can be initiated by neighbors filing complaints or making police calls.

How did this generation of property owners obtain powers of segregation that their predecessors in the Jim Crow South could not? To answer this question, I consider the role of policing in the production and

maintenance of racial residential segregation. In my view, property owners have regained the right to discriminate in housing through participatory forms of policing—programs that allow individuals to surveil their
neighbors and use complaints to evict them. Cities employ participatory
policing because it moves the locus of discrimination down from local
government to individuals. The state reifies discrimination by enforcing
the complaints it receives, knowing full well they are racially biased. People participate in policing by surveilling others in their community, sharing information with others for the purposes of control and punishment,
and calling in complaints to municipal governments or law enforcement.
They do so because it gives them the power to maintain domination of
neighborhoods. In the process, following Harris (1993), policing becomes
a sort of property: usable for those empowered to engage in it, excludable
in that others cannot meaningfully participate, and valuable in that it confers an elevated social status upon its user, while subordinating its targets.

It's not just that the contemporary merger of policing and housing has
produced legal realities that echo a moment deep in the nation's past.
Rather, between Falloon and the present lie multiple moments in which
the carceral state has been used to racially segregate. Much of this history
involves law enforcement actions substituting for other mechanisms of
segregation, all of which rise and fall in ways that fit the social and political landscape of the time. Seeing policing as one of the many substituting
technologies of racial segregation expands the sociology of housing in
important and productive ways. In contemporary society, participatory
forms of policing represent a break with the past. This form of policing
synthesizes individual and state action—enfolding private individuals
into activity traditionally carried out by the government. This shift poses
a challenge to fair-housing jurisprudence, which has traditionally not seen
policing as something that could violate fair housing.

Participatory policing illustrates the material stakes that may be motivating the broad expansion of neighborhood policing through both
municipal ordinances and digital platforms such as Nextdoor, Ring, and
Citizen. In the classic model of racial segregation, inequality is produced
from the geographic separation of groups. Policing plays a key role in this
process, allowing some to attain status through the subordination of others (or through their expulsion).

Substituting Policies to Maintain Racial Segregation

The substitution framework posits that when one mode of achieving segregation becomes ineffective, it can be replaced by another. In the early

Jim Crow era, for example, white communities in the American South often used collective action to enforce and maintain racial segregation. Whites discouraged each other from renting or selling property to Black residents, and often used violence to enforce this expectation. But as white society's capacity to police itself waned, they turned to their local governments to pass municipal segregation ordinances to codify preferences they could no longer enforce on their own. Troesken and Walsh (2019) find that white communities whose ability to establish and enforce segregation had declined were most likely to turn to their municipal governments to pass segregation ordinances. Starting with Baltimore in 1910, twenty-four cities in or bordering the South passed segregation ordinances prohibiting whites in white neighborhoods from selling or renting to nonwhites (and vice versa).

After the 1917 *Buchanan v. Warley* ruling invalidated municipal segregation ordinances, other strategies (violence, restrictive covenants, real estate association policies, redlining, etc.) emerged to reproduce segregation. In this way, the substitution framework accounts for shifts in the production of racial segregation over time and de-exceptionalizes white violence by situating it within the ebbs and flows of a broader array of forces of segregation. Substitution also helps us to understand the role of policing in maintaining racial residential segregation, suggesting that when existing modes of creating racial segregation are insufficient, both the formal actions of police agencies and the informal acts of individuals and groups policing their communities might substitute for them.

Sociologists and economists have documented the role policing played as part of the bulwark against racial integration. Between 1880 and 1950, Muller (2012) finds that northern states receiving Black migrants from the South increased their policing and incarceration of Black residents. This increase drove a significant share of the growth of racial disparities in incarceration in the North. Extending Muller's analysis to 1970, Derenoncourt (2022) shows that municipalities across the North responded to Black mobility by increasing spending on policing and raising incarceration rates. These findings frame the growth of policing and punishment in the North not just as a general process of mass incarceration but as specifically responsive to Black migration.

But it was not just the amount of policing in response to Black migration that mattered. It was also the tactics police used to concretize segregation. Chicago is a useful case study here. A key moment in the city's segregation was the 1919 riot, which was the largest of several episodes of white violence against the city's growing Black population. During the riot, white violence pushed Black residents into the Black Belt and punished those outside it. At the time, police abetted the violence, but as Balto (2019) chronicles, over time they continued to encourage racial segregation, corralling vice in the Black Belt, allowing drug markets to operate in Black neighborhoods, and abetting white mob violence aimed at preventing Black Chicagoans from renting or purchasing homes in white neighborhoods. That law enforcement has historically abetted and assisted white violence and vigilantism illustrates the limits of the substitution framework. And as policy has evolved through crime-free and nuisance housing ordinances, we can see something more akin to synthesis occurring.

The Shift to Crime-Free and Nuisance Housing Ordinances

As collective action against racial residential integration waned in the aftermath of the civil rights movement, individual acts of violence grew to replace it. Bell (2013) documents 455 incidents of move-in violence around the country. These took the form of vandalism, harassment, verbal threats, cross burnings, arson, physical attacks, shootings, and homicides when a Black family moved into a predominantly or all-white neighborhood (p. 68). Mass resistance to racial integration in housing was ripe for substitution by government policy. Rather than substitute vigilante violence with public policy, public policy has absorbed and codified vigilantism. The origins of this shift can be traced to the nation's cruel policy innovations in public housing.

When Congress passed the Anti-Drug Abuse Act of 1988, it pushed the War on Drugs into the welfare state by authorizing local housing authorities to employ lease terms that empowered the government to evict public housing tenants based on suspected criminal activity. Eight years later, President Clinton rebranded Reagan's eviction law as an even crueler "one strike policy." Instead of allowing housing authorities to evict tenants based on criminal activity, Clinton's 1996 Housing Opportunity Extension Act mandated eviction. And rather than require a conviction, Clinton's legislation allowed eviction to occur based on the mere belief that a tenant had violated the law. In advocating for these rules, Clinton declared, "If you break the law, you no longer have a home in public housing, one strike and you're out. That should be the law everywhere in America" (Clinton 1996). Through municipal ordinances that deny renters leases based on criminal background and empower individuals to evict their neighbors through even unproven law enforcement and nuisance complaints, Clinton's wish has come true (Ramsey 2018).

Through organizations like the International Crime Free Association, these ordinances have spread throughout the country. According to the organization, roughly two thousand ordinances have been passed in municipalities (International Crime Free Association 2003). Just as policing in northern cities grew in response to Black movement, the adoption of these ordinances grew in response to the demographic threat of Black migration. In California, journalists Dillon, Poston, and Barajas (2020) investigate the timing of the adoption of crime-free ordinances by municipalities in California. They find that one in four California municipalities have adopted crime-free housing ordinances, but among the twenty cities with the largest growth in Black residency since 1990, that rate jumps to 85 percent. A somewhat smaller rate of adoption holds for cities experiencing rapid growth of Latino residents (75 percent). They also report that Black and Latino tenants and other tenants of color are more likely to be evicted through crime-free ordinances than white tenants. A similar pattern holds in Illinois, where the adoption of crime-free housing ordinances in suburbs around Chicago closely mirrors the distribution of the Black population across those suburbs (Mason 2020). That these policies further racial exclusion likely blunts the reality that they are also restrictions on the rights of property owners to rent to whom they please. Several case studies from around the country illustrate how these policies gain traction, how individuals act to take advantage of these policies, and how these policies affect Black tenants.

City officials in Lancaster, California, built a legal apparatus that fulfills both the preemption and eviction components of the early race nuisance cases. Although these moves occurred in the context of significant growth of the city's Black population, the proximate reason stated by public officials was the rising number of tenants—most of whom were also Black—moving to the city through the Housing Choice Voucher program. The city mandated that residential rental properties deny housing to rental applicants with prior criminal legal system involvement. And they passed a chronic nuisance housing ordinance that levied fines and penalties on owners of rental properties whose tenants were subject to multiple complaints by neighbors. In this manner, the city used the racialized nature of American policing to prevent many Black renters from moving into the city and created a pathway for anti-Black neighbors to file complaints that would evict those who managed to move in.

Turning their focus to Black tenants in the Housing Choice Voucher program, Lancaster Mayor Rex Parris "specifically asked the City Council to . . . look into a means for making it very easy for neighbors to file nuisance lawsuits with the assistance of the City against . . . Section 8 housing."[1] The Council obliged, passing an ordinance defining nuisance designations broadly and tying them to police calls. Alongside the Housing Authority's fraud reporting hotline, Lancaster residents now had the power to evict their neighbors at their fingertips (Ocen 2012; Hayat 2016; Kurwa 2020a).

Lancaster was not alone. During the 2005 City Council meeting in which Bedford, Ohio, passed its nuisance ordinance, the mayor was asked to "address" the "mixture of community" and responded by tying the adoption of a nuisance ordinance to changes associated with the city's shifting demography (Mead et al. 2017). Presiding over an all-white Council governing a suburb whose Black population had quadrupled over the past ten years, the mayor reassured his constituents that he was acting to prevent integration. "We believe in neighborhoods not hoods" he said. "We will do everything we can to maintain those quality of life issues . . . That is one of the reasons we passed that nuisance law tonight" (Mead et al. 2017). Later, he described his policies as a quest to preserve his suburb's quality of life, which necessitated curtailing "urban immigration," and he bragged to the neighboring city's mayor that Bedford's nuisance ordinance had solved the city's "Section 8" problem.[2]

Peoria, Illinois, passed a chronic nuisance ordinance that established a rule mandating the eviction of tenants in "chronic nuisance" properties—a definition triggered by three or more police calls tied to a property within a 365-day span (or two calls for "serious crimes"). Once these thresholds are met, the police department may compel a landlord to propose a solution (generally, eviction) that would abate the nuisance. The rules only apply to rental property, and do not distinguish between properties with few or many units. Despite evidence that more than ten thousand properties across the city would qualify for nuisance abatement under the city's chronic nuisance ordinance, HOPE Fair Housing Center alleged that Peoria only enforced the rule on roughly 1 percent of those properties, mostly located in neighborhoods with high rates of Black residency.[3] This evidence further supports Henderson and Jefferson-Jones's (2019) argument that the law is used to cast "Blackness as nuisance."

Peoria police went out of their way to reinforce this understanding. In 2008, it took an armored truck donated by a local bank and converted it

[1] The Community Action League et al. v. City of Lancaster and City of Palmdale, CV 11-4817 ODW (VBKx) (C.D. Cal. Feb. 8, 2012).
[2] Somai v. City of Bedford, 1:19-cv-373:526 (2019) (N.D. OH).
[3] HOPE Fair Housing Center v. City of Peoria, 1:17-cv-1360 (C.D. Ill.). NB: The author served as an expert witness in this case.

into what it called a "nuisance abatement vehicle." They painted it black and affixed it with police logos, cameras, speakers, and lights, creating a tool of intimidation for property owners to deploy. As the city's website told residents, "If you feel that a property in your neighborhood may qualify for the Nuisance Property Surveillance Vehicle, email your request to the Nuisance Abatement Officer at nuisanceprop@peoriagov.org" ("Nuisance Property" n.d.). As officers wrote in a report about the program, "It says to the law abiding, good people in the area, 'we have heard your complaints and we want to help you stop the chaos.' It says to the thugs and the miscreants, 'You have dedicated your time to make life miserable for your neighbors we will now dedicate our time to give you a taste of what that feels like'" (Peoria Police Department n.d., 7). The truck, now called an "Armadillo," served multiple expressive functions, and residents were eager to deploy it against neighbors. As the officers wrote, "The department received many emails and phone calls endorsing the Armadillo as well as requesting immediate placement in front of a problem property" (Peoria Police Department n.d., 8).

Back in Lancaster, I interviewed private-market residents who said they were familiar with the tools at their disposal and used them to evict Black Housing Choice Voucher tenants. One described a sense of pride and empowerment from having a sheriff's phone number and his encouragement to call. Others justified the surveillance and policing of voucher tenants based on contradictory explanations only made consistent when considered as coded expressions of race and gender prejudice. Individuals purporting to be from the city posted on public message boards encouraging residents to use these policing pathways and assuring skeptics that the program was working. Within a three-year span, Lancaster and its neighbor city, Palmdale, evicted more Housing Choice Voucher renters than the rest of Los Angeles County combined.[4]

The consequences in other cities are similar. In Faribault, Minnesota, Selma Jones was evicted by her landlord on the instruction of the police after they sought to enforce the city's crime-free housing ordinance. Her white neighbors, one of whom had told her to "go back to where [she] came from," had leveraged their ability to make police calls to force her eviction. They summoned the police to her home eighty-two times, not to report criminal activity but rather to complain about barbecues, birthday parties, and her children playing on the trampoline. But because police responded to the calls, Jones was in violation of the crime-free ordinance's

<hr />

4 Community Action League et al. v. City of Lancaster et al., 2:11-cv-04817 (C.D. CA).

ban on having too many police visits. Unless the landlord evicted Jones and her family, the police could enforce the ordinance by suing the landlord for maintaining a nuisance property (Archer 2019).

Policing as Property

While interviewing private renters and homeowners in Lancaster about their hostility toward the voucher program, I asked what they thought of their neighbors who had moved out of the city and either rented their homes through the voucher program or sold them to new owners who did so. As it turns out, they did not begrudge their neighbors. They too would have left for wealthier, whiter cities if they could. Here lies a second function of crime-free and nuisance housing ordinances. For white residents unable to leave what, in their parents' generation, was a destination for white flight, policing serves to re-establish a racialized status gradient within a diversifying neighborhood. Here, policing is a form of political and racial subjectivity itself. To engage in policing is to create and occupy a different social position. If we consider policing as property in the same manner that Harris (1993) theorizes whiteness as property, we can recognize the characteristics of policing that fit common definitions of property.

In arguing that whiteness is a form of property, Harris (1993) measures whiteness against metrics that have historically been used to define property. The first of these states that something is property if one has the right to use it. As videos of white individuals confronting Black counterparts in public space have made clear, policing is as usable as a tool in a tool belt. Examples of this deployment abound in the genre of what McNamarah (2018) calls "white caller crime." In weaponizing the ability to dispatch police, these individuals implicitly acknowledge and explicitly demonstrate the usability of policing. They do not have to call the police and often know their calls are legally unsupportable, but they do so because policing is theirs.

The second metric in defining property is conference of status: something might be property if owning it confers a different status upon its owner. To participate in policing is to embody a meaningfully different status. One who can engage in policing is recognizably different than, and in this context, elevated above, one who is policed or who can neither engage in policing nor rely upon formal police services. To police is to acquire that status, and it is perhaps for this reason that so many incidents of white use of policing appear to confer a psychic reward upon the one doing the policing. The act of policing one's neighbor produces and communicates a subordinate status to the policed while simultaneously producing and confirming one's own superordinate status. In both the case of whiteness (Harris 1993) and policing, the conference of status as a marker of property harkens back to Du Bois's (1935) notion of the public and psychological wage. Du Bois lists a series of ways that whites of the time enjoyed social benefits that outweighed their class interests, among them the fact that "the police were drawn from their ranks." Today, as the ability to engage in policing has diffused in ways that make private participation possible, Du Bois's mechanism merits the corollary that the ranks themselves can engage in policing, and that this participation may generate its own psychological wages. Thus, through crime-free and nuisance housing ordinances, policing reasserts a status hierarchy eroded by neighborhood integration.

Third, something might be property if one can exclude others from its use. One of the most important consequences of nuisance ordinances has been the eviction of women experiencing domestic violence after making calls to the police for protection (Desmond and Valdez 2013). They deny tenants the ability to seek police assistance because they do not distinguish between reasons for police visits when utilizing the number of police visits as evidence of nuisance. And when tenants in Lancaster and Palmdale told me that they felt they could not call the police as it would render them on the precipice of "too many police visits" and trigger their potential eviction, they too demonstrated their exclusion from the ability to use or rely upon the police (Kurwa 2020b). That a city has rendered some of its residents unable to access policing is evidence of the right to exclude. This exclusion creates a gradient between those empowered and able to police and those subject to and unable to access policing. A fourth traditional marker of property is disposability—the ability to give or sell a thing. Although this marker has declined in relevance, policing fits this definition as well: for example, the ability to police is often given to people who are appointed captains of neighborhood watch groups.

This property interpretation of policing helps us bridge *Falloon v. Schilling* and today. Then, the case was about both racial segregation and the boundaries of property rights. Did a white homeowner's property rights extend far enough to allow him to prevent a nonwhite person from living next door? At the time, the answer was no, partly because the issue was framed as a balance between the interests of two white property owners. But the contemporary function of nuisance and crime-free ordinances today is to enlarge the property rights of white homeowners. Their property rights have expanded to give them a say over who can live next door. To be able to police while others cannot, to degrade through policing, and to acquire a superior social status through policing—these rewards illustrate the stakes, beyond attitudes, that motivate participation in policing.

Conclusion

Though this chapter has focused on participatory forms of policing in neighborhoods, these forms constitute only one pathway by which policing can segregate, and only one part of the larger interactions between the carceral state and housing, as Bryan and Alao elaborate in the next chapter. Herbert (1996) illustrates how officers threaten or force targets out of neighborhoods, individual acts guided by department efforts to categorize and mark spaces to govern. Gordon (2022) theorizes this spatial governance as place consolidation, showing how a midwestern city redrew its patrol-district boundaries to enable police to enact either service-oriented or repressive policing tactics within race-class homogenous districts. Along these lines, in San Diego, Welsh, Chanin, and Henry (2020) document how police use traffic stops to harass drivers based on racialized assumptions of who belongs in each neighborhood. Laniyonu (2018) and Beck (2020) find positive relationships between gentrification and real estate growth, respectively, and police deployment of harsh tactics like order maintenance and broken-windows policing, while Johnson and Patterson (2022) show similar findings in the gentrification-oriented policing of mass transit in Los Angeles. Lautenschlager (2022) argues that patterns of proactive police stops show that they are drivers of urban race-class transformation. And Muñiz (2015) uses the case of gang injunctions to show how policing strategies deployed by the Los Angeles City Attorney banish Black and Brown men from once-redlined neighborhoods (Bloch and Phillips 2022). Concurrently, the city is using nuisance property ordinances to force evictions from low-income housing in gentrifying South Los Angeles (Roy, Graziani, and Stephens 2020). Finally, Bell (2020b) shows the iterative nature of these policing practices—finding that Black residents account for the geography of policing when making housing decisions and avoid moving to neighborhoods where they understand they will be racially profiled and repressively policed. Thus, in multiple, interactive ways, the law and order enforced by police includes the spatial order of racial segregation. And this segregation only empowers vicious policing tactics in segregated neighborhoods that would not be viable under more power-balanced conditions, illuminating what Bell (2020a) describes as the "mutually constitutive" nature of policing and segregation. The result of this interrelation, as Simes (2021) documents, is that incarceration and its community-level effects are part of the legacy of racial segregation.

While conventional perspectives on policing situate it as a mechanism of protecting property values and reducing crime, thinking of policing as itself a form of property can illuminate its role in both building and negating social status in neighborhoods. That policing and punishment are part of a hostile reaction to Black movement should shift how we understand sociological frameworks that envision neighborhoods as places of opportunity accessible to those historically blocked from them. Neighborhood attainment, for example, deserves scrutiny when framed as a concrete goal: moving to a neighborhood does not guarantee being able to enjoy its opportunities. Participation in digital neighborhood surveillance and communication platforms like Nextdoor, Ring, and Citizen illustrates the enormous interest and material stakes involved in participatory policing, as well as the community-building function of policing (Kurwa 2020a; Bloch 2022; Bridges 2021).

As such, the sociology of housing has a stake in the fate of social movements challenging the carceral state. Existing campaigns against the nation's vast systems of criminalization, policing, and punishment may have knock-on effects on segregation. The fewer people who have criminal records, for example, the less that housing exclusions based on such records can have an effect. Similarly, today's campaigns to shift funding away from police and toward social services could cut police programs that cater to homeowner complaints, like Peoria's Armadillos. And efforts to create nonpolice responses to nonviolent emergency calls might lessen individuals' power to weaponize police deployment. De-policing housing might mean taking sheriff enforcement out of evictions, ending crime-free and nuisance ordinances, removing barriers to housing for formerly incarcerated persons, ending app-based policing of individuals deemed "suspicious" or "out of place," and ending the policing and punitive regulation of subsidized housing.

None of these efforts would be easy. If policing has become a sort of property for homeowners today, then removing such a power is a challenge to property itself. But it is worth noting that challenges to the policing-segregation nexus are not without precedent. Recall the landmark restrictive-covenants case *Shelley v. Kraemer*. Had the Shelley family lost their appeal to the Supreme Court and nevertheless refused to vacate their home, "the sheriff would have enforced the covenant by physically removing the family and their possessions from the property" (Saidel-Goley and Singer 2018, 467). The Shelley family's victory did not bring an end to restrictive covenants, but it did end the state's police power to enforce them.

The sociology of housing can produce research that investigates the segregating effects of policing programs. It can help lawyers and courts see policing as part of the panoply of forces that violate fair-housing law, and existing efforts around the country have made important gains on this front. It can provide evidence used to stave off the growth of those programs under the rubric of "community policing." And it can argue for ending nuisance enforcement programs altogether rather than criminalizing their misuse (Har 2020). In all these ways, sociologists can highlight contexts in which the removal of police would constitute a tremendous advancement of housing justice.

23

Criminal Justice Contact and Housing Inequality

Brielle Bryan and Temi Alao

Though not typically considered in conversations about American housing policy, prisons and jails house more than two million people every day (Minton, Beatty, and Zeng 2021). For most, this housing situation is temporary: fewer than one in ten incarcerated Americans are serving life or long-term sentences (Nellis 2017). Yet this temporary experience represents a disruption that may derail subsequent housing outcomes through its effects on other domains crucial to achieving stability: namely, employment, financial well-being, relationships, and health. Likewise, far more prevalent noncustodial sentences, like probation and parole, may also disrupt housing stability. While sociologists widely acknowledge the American criminal justice system as a stratifying institution, one reifying inequality along both race and class lines, the sociology of housing has largely overlooked the role of criminal justice contact. We argue that to fully understand important housing outcomes (e.g., homelessness, home-ownership, neighborhood attainment) and disparities in these outcomes, we must consider the consequences of justice system contact.

This chapter explores the interplay between criminal justice contact and subsequent housing outcomes in modern America, laying out what we know and what we still need to know. We begin by outlining mechanisms through which criminal justice contact may affect subsequent individual housing opportunities, particularly focusing on finances, relationships, mental health, and discrimination. We next review the limited existing literature on housing outcomes following criminal justice contact, then proceed to illustrate the likely implications for racial inequality in housing, given stark racial disparities in criminal justice system contact. We conclude by outlining a research agenda for moving forward, emphasizing the necessity of investigating how criminal justice contact shapes the places individuals reside and, accordingly, the resources and opportunities available to them.

The Growing American Criminal Justice System and Its Consequences

Over the past five decades, the American criminal justice system has grown to a scale unprecedented in both historical and global perspective. The share of Americans under correctional supervision on any given day rose from 1.1 percent of the adult population in 1980 to 2.5 percent in 2019 (Minton, Beatty, and Zeng 2021; Snell 1995). Consequently, the number of Americans who have passed through and been marked by the criminal justice system has also climbed sharply. Recent estimates indicate that the number of Americans with a felony conviction record rose from approximately five million in 1980 to more than nineteen million—8 percent of the US population—in 2010 (Shannon et al. 2017).

In response to this growth, a robust literature has developed around the "collateral consequences" of criminal justice system contact. This work has established justice system contact, particularly incarceration, as a destabilizing event leading to greater disadvantage in domains ranging from employment to health to relationship stability (Bushway 1998; Sugie and Turney 2017; Lopoo and Western 2005). The implications of criminal justice contact for housing, however, have been relatively understudied. A handful of papers have considered the consequences of incarceration and felony conviction for residential mobility, homeownership, and discrimination in the rental housing market (Geller and Curtis 2011; Warner 2015; Bryan 2020a, 2022; Leasure and Martin 2017; Evans and Porter 2015),

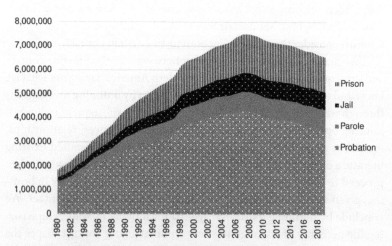

FIGURE 23.1. United States correctional population, 1980–2019
Source: Authors' calculations, using Bureau of Justice statistics

suggesting that criminal justice contact is detrimental for both housing instability and housing market prospects. Still, there is much work to be done to understand how various forms of criminal justice contact shape not just how often individuals move and whether they own their homes, but where they live, with whom they live, and for how long.

Mechanisms Linking Criminal Justice Contact and Housing Outcomes

Qualitative studies following individuals recently released from prison identify multiple barriers to stable housing, including poor employment history, diminished financial resources, strained relationships, and substance abuse or mental health issues (Harding, Morenoff, and Wyse 2019; Petersilia 2003; Western 2018). Though formerly incarcerated individuals have received the bulk of scholarly attention in recent decades, these same mechanisms may also shape housing opportunities for the millions of Americans who interact with the criminal justice system through arrest and conviction, even without incarceration.

FINANCIAL

Perhaps the most immediate way criminal justice system contact may influence housing outcomes is through its effect on financial resources: limiting how much income individuals have to expend on housing, increasing income volatility, diminishing savings available for security deposits and down payments, and generating additional expenses as a direct result of justice system contact. Prior research suggests that criminal justice contact may affect both income (i.e., flow of financial resources) and assets (i.e., stock of financial resources). Formerly incarcerated individuals face extensive labor market discrimination (Pager 2007), and when they do find work they are often channeled into lower quality, more precarious jobs (Bumiller 2015; Sugie 2018) and receive lower wages than they did before incarceration (Apel and Sweeten 2010; Western 2002).

Even low-level justice system contact may affect one's access to well-paying, stable work, given the occupational licensure restrictions that accompany former felon status in many states (Samuels and Mukamal 2004) and the ease with which employers can access criminal background checks with arrest records (Lageson 2016; Uggen et al. 2014). Time lost to arrest processing, pretrial detention, court appearances, and/or probation and parole meetings may cause justice-system-involved individuals to miss out on work shifts or even lose their jobs entirely. Harding, Siegel, and Morenoff (2017), for example, find that short-term custodial parole sanctions—that is, brief jail stays resulting from a parole violation—negatively impact earnings in the year following.

Justice system contact may also be detrimental for one's stock of financial resources. Asset levels, as well as ownership of assets (i.e., bank accounts, vehicles), decrease markedly following incarceration. Turney and Schneider (2016) find that recent incarceration is associated with lower likelihood of owning a vehicle or having a bank account, and Maroto (2015) finds that individual net worth decreases by $42,000, on average, following incarceration. Arrest, independent of conviction or incarceration, is also associated with asset and debt declines in early adulthood (Maroto and Sykes 2019).

The financial costs of criminal justice system interaction in the form of court fines, fees, restitution orders, and other financial obligations to criminal justice agencies may also affect individuals' savings and, hence, their ability to find and maintain desirable stable housing (Pattillo et al. 2022). Finally, incarceration brings with it the potential of significant child support arrearage debt accrual, which may affect not only asset levels but employment (Haney 2018). These additional debts and diminished savings can create difficulty in affording housing-related start-up costs like security deposits and down payments, as well as in covering unexpected expenses, jeopardizing the ability to continue paying monthly rent or mortgages.

RELATIONSHIPS

In addition to having trouble affording independent housing, justice-system-involved individuals may struggle to maintain stable cohabiting housing arrangements. Incarceration weakens romantic partnerships (Apel 2016; Lopoo and Western 2005; Turney 2015) and strains broader family relationships (Western 2018; Harding, Morenoff, and Wyse 2019). Ethnographic work highlights how justice system involvement may promote unpredictable behavior among young men, destabilizing their romantic relationships (Goffman 2009). Thus, the deleterious relationship consequences of criminal justice system contact may reduce the probability that justice-system-involved individuals reside with relatives and/or romantic partners.

MENTAL HEALTH

Mental health challenges stemming from justice system contact may further undermine one's ability to find and maintain stable, secure housing.

While psychiatric disorders largely predate criminal justice system contact, incarceration and even arrest alone can increase the prevalence of mood disorders and depression (Turney, Wildeman, and Schnittker 2012; Sugie and Turney 2017). Increased mental health challenges following criminal justice contact may contribute to subsequent housing challenges for this population, given the link between mental health and chronic homelessness (Lippert and Lee 2015).

HOUSING MARKET PROHIBITIONS AND DISCRIMINATION

Prohibitions on where one can live and discrimination from wary landlords are well known in the case of registered sex offenders (Williams 2018), but there are numerous reasons to believe that everyone with criminal records, particularly those convicted of felony offenses, may encounter market-based hurdles to housing. Many public housing authorities reject applicants with felony convictions who apply for subsidized units or vouchers (Curtis, Garlington, and Schottenfeld 2013; Tran-Leung 2015), and in many cities, individuals already living in subsidized housing can lose their housing assistance for allowing someone with a felony conviction to move in with or even visit them (Blidner 2014; GAO 2005). In the private housing market, landlords in all states but New Jersey are permitted to ask applicants about their criminal history and run criminal records checks when deciding whether to rent to prospective tenants. Indeed, a survey of large apartment management companies found that 80 percent reported screening applicants on criminal history (Delgado 2005), and qualitative work reveals that even smaller landlords who rely on "gut feelings" frequently run criminal background checks (Rosen, Garboden, and Cossyleon 2021). Experimental audit studies find that both landlords and real estate agents in New York discriminate against renters who disclose felony records (Evans 2016; Evans and Porter 2015). Bryan (2020b) finds that such discrimination prevails across housing markets, with prospective renters who reveal a felony conviction record receiving positive responses one-third (Detroit, Milwaukee) to half as often (DC, Houston) as prospective tenants who do not reveal a conviction history.

This type of screening may affect the duration of the housing search process but also, presumably, the quality and cost of housing for renters with criminal histories. Indeed, this type of discrimination is more likely among landlords of higher priced rental units (Bryan 2020b). And while felony convictions have been the focus of experimental studies of housing discrimination, low-level arrests may also be detrimental thanks to the ready availability of criminal background checks online (Uggen et al. 2014).

How Housing Impacts Criminal Justice Contact

Despite the mechanisms potentially linking criminal justice system contact to individual housing prospects, little empirical research has directly considered this relationship. We first briefly review research examining how housing shapes criminal justice contact risk, then turn to what we know about how justice system contact shapes subsequent housing-related outcomes.

In an effort to drive visible homeless populations out of urban areas, cities have criminalized homelessness by applying "nuisance" laws that subject homeless individuals to citations, fines, and even jail time (Amster 2003; Stuart 2015; Robinson 2019). Such efforts have ramped up in recent years as cities attempt to draw tourists and higher status residents back into urban cores, but the criminalization of homelessness can be traced back to vagrancy laws passed during Reconstruction to perpetuate social control by imprisoning unemployed African Americans (Blackmon 2008). While some police officers enforcing these laws report that their ultimate goal is to help individuals find appropriate services, not punish or jail them (Stuart 2014), research shows that citation or arrest is far more common than provision of social services (Robinson 2019).

Early-life housing experiences also appear to play a role in shaping the probability of subsequent criminal justice system contact. Housing assistance program participation (i.e., voucher receipt, public housing residence) during childhood is associated with small but significant reductions in arrest and incarceration by early adulthood, largely for girls (Kling, Ludwig, and Katz 2005; Andersson et al. 2016). On the other hand, residential instability during adolescence is associated with higher risk of arrest in early adulthood (Fowler, Henry, and Marcal 2015).

The interplay between criminal justice system interactions and housing has been most explored in the context of individuals returning from prison. Despite the protective benefits of stable housing for promoting independence and reducing arrest and reincarceration (Harding, Morenoff, and Wyse 2019; Petersilia 2003; Western 2018), residential instability is the norm for this population (Harding, Morenoff, and Herbert 2013; Western et al. 2015; Steiner, Makarios, and Travis 2015). Studies of post-incarceration neighborhood quality indicate that parolees tend to return to disadvantaged neighborhoods when exiting prison (Lee, Harding, and Morenoff 2017).

Housing challenges appear to last well beyond the reentry period, however. Studies using longitudinal survey data show greater residential instability and housing insecurity among formerly incarcerated individuals relative to their pre-incarceration experiences and relative to similar never-incarcerated individuals (Geller and Curtis 2011; Warner 2015). The detrimental impacts extend to homeownership, as well, with the probability of homeownership decreasing by 28 percentage points following incarceration (Maroto 2015). Examinations of neighborhood quality suggest that incarceration pushes individuals, particularly whites, into poorer and more disadvantaged neighborhoods than they resided in before incarceration (Massoglia, Firebaugh, and Warner 2013); though the negative effect on neighborhood quality for whites appears to wear off with time (Warner 2016).

More recent studies consider the consequences of arrest and conviction, finding that arrest incidents contribute to residential instability by prompting moves into and out of parental households (Warner and Remster 2021) and that even felony convictions that do not result in prison or jail time increase residential instability and risk of residence in temporary housing (Bryan 2022). Lower-level forms of criminal justice contact also appear to affect homeownership prospects: arrest, being charged with a crime, and conviction each independently delay entry into homeownership and help to explain a substantial portion of the association between incarceration and lower likelihood of homeownership (Bryan 2020a).

Least studied of all is the question of what criminal justice system interactions mean for the housing experiences of those who reside with or around justice-system-involved individuals. At the household level, Wildeman (2014) finds that paternal incarceration, but not maternal, increases the risk of homelessness among Black children, contributing to growing Black-white disparities in child homelessness. At the neighborhood level, there are strong theoretical reasons to believe the spatial concentration of incarceration will have important implications for the strength and safety of communities most affected by mass incarceration, yet there is relatively little empirical evidence on this question (Morenoff and Harding 2014). Clear's (2007) study of Tallahassee neighborhoods, however, highlights the community-level harm caused by the churning of residents in and out of prison in the already disadvantaged neighborhoods where incarceration rates are highest. We know even less about how broader forms of justice system contact—e.g., police stops, arrest, probation, parole—shape housing experiences for the household members and neighbors of those subject to these interactions, but recent work highlights the role policing plays in perpetuating patterns of residential segregation (Bell 2020a; Kurwa, this volume). Future work examining these relationships will be critical to developing a fuller understanding of the role criminal justice system institutions play in the stratification and segregation of American society and spaces.

Criminal Justice System Racial Disparities
and Inequalities in Housing

While the massive growth of the US criminal justice system is alarming in its own right, this phenomenon is of concern to sociologists of stratification and race because of the disproportionate concentration of this growth among Black and brown Americans. The prevalence of felony conviction, for example, rose from 3 percent in 1980 to 8 percent in 2010 among all US adults but increased from 8 percent to 23 percent among Black adults over the same period (Shannon et al. 2017). Among Black men, a full third have been convicted of a felony (Shannon et al. 2017), and incarceration is now a more common life event than college completion or marriage (Pettit and Western 2004). These racial disparities exist in lower-level criminal justice contacts, as well. By age thirty, more than half of Black men (54 percent) have been arrested compared to just 42 percent of white men (table 23.1).

Disparities in criminal justice contact by ethnicity have been less studied, but the available evidence suggests that Hispanic men also experience disproportionate contact relative to non-Hispanic white men. Table 23.1 displays the proportion of young adults born between 1980 and 1984 who report having been arrested, charged with a crime, convicted of a crime, or incarcerated by age thirty. While Hispanic women report lower levels of each form of criminal justice contact than non-Hispanic white and non-Hispanic Black women, Hispanic men report 17 percent higher arrest rates and 28 percent higher incarceration rates than non-Hispanic white men.

Racial disparities in criminal justice contact mean that the housing consequences of justice system contact are concentrated among Black and brown Americans. Thus, the increased risk of homelessness and housing instability and the decreased chances of homeownership outlined above will be more often borne by nonwhite Americans—particularly Black Americans—simply because they are more likely to have criminal justice system interactions. Consequently, unexplained racial differences in outcomes like homelessness (Fusaro, Levy, and Shaefer 2018) and homeownership (Rucks-Ahidiana, this volume) may well be driven in part by racial disparities in justice system contact.

Given enduring racial segregation, racial disparities in justice system contact may reinforce preexisting racial disparities at the neighborhood level (Faber, this volume). The spatial concentration of arrests and imprisonment in Black neighborhoods (Simes 2018a; Soss and Weaver 2017) means that the individual-level consequences of criminal justice system contact will accumulate within these communities. Moreover, because of racial disparities in justice system contact, discrimination against

TABLE 23.1. Criminal justice contact by age 30, by race and gender

	Arrested	Charged	Convicted	Incarcerated
Male				
White (non-Hispanic)	41.7%	36.3%	28.2%	11.9%
Black (non-Hispanic)	54.0%	44.1%	36.0%	22.0%
Hispanic	48.8%	41.3%	31.6%	15.3%
Female				
White (non-Hispanic)	24.4%	19.1%	13.0%	3.9%
Black (non-Hispanic)	25.3%	16.8%	10.8%	3.8%
Hispanic	21.1%	15.9%	11.5%	3.7%
Full sample	34.4%	28.1%	21.0%	9.0%

Source: Authors' calculations from National Longitudinal Survey of Youth 1997 data
Note: Weighted values

prospective tenants on the basis of criminal history may serve as de facto racial discrimination via disparate impact—a possibility highlighted by HUD's Office of General Counsel at the end of the Obama presidency (2016). Further, landlord prohibitions against renters with criminal histories may end up concentrating these individuals in the most disadvantaged neighborhoods and/or lowest-quality units if those are the only places willing to rent to individuals with records. Experimental research suggests that discrimination against individuals with felony records increases as the rent value increases (Bryan 2020b).

Evidence of racial variation in the effect size of criminal justice contact has been mixed. Recent scholarship suggests white individuals may be less able to rely on friends and family for housing assistance following release from prison than Black or Hispanic individuals (Western 2018; Western et al. 2015); that criminal justice contact appears to be slightly less detrimental to subsequent homeownership prospects for Hispanics than whites (Bryan 2020a); and that whites, but not Blacks or Hispanics, experience downward mobility in neighborhood quality following incarceration because whites reside in more advantaged neighborhoods prior to incarceration (Massoglia, Firebaugh, and Warner 2013).

Other research suggests that the negative consequences may be larger for Black and Hispanic individuals than whites. A study of Massachusetts parolees, for example, found that recently released Black and Hispanic individuals lived in more disadvantaged neighborhoods after release than their white counterparts, even after accounting for differences in pre-incarceration neighborhood quality (Simes 2018b). Similarly, longitudinal analysis of formerly incarcerated individuals suggests that while individuals of all races experience higher residential instability following incarceration, this pattern fades over time for whites and, to a lesser extent, Hispanics, but does not fade for Blacks (Warner 2015).

Despite uncertain evidence of racial differences in the effects of justice system contact, the vast racial disparities in the American criminal justice system still suggest that criminal justice contact likely reinforces ongoing racial inequity in housing, homelessness, and neighborhoods.

Outlining a Path Forward for Researchers

While existing evidence provides ample reason to believe that criminal justice contact affects individual housing opportunities, racial inequalities in these outcomes, and larger phenomena like racial segregation, many of these hypotheses have not been sufficiently tested. Below we outline a research agenda for moving forward, focusing on three key lines of research: (1) deeper exploration of the implications of various forms of justice system contact for individual housing outcomes, (2) examinations of how local policy context shapes these relationships, and (3) investigations that reveal how the criminal justice system contributes to macro-level racial disparities in housing-related outcomes. Sociology's focus on mechanisms and the variety of methods that sociologists employ make our discipline uniquely well suited to answering these questions.

FURTHER EXPLORATION OF INDIVIDUAL-LEVEL HOUSING OUTCOMES

Existing research suggests that incarceration increases residential instability, reduces homeownership, and diminishes one's neighborhood quality. The evidence on implications of lower-level criminal justice contact for housing-related outcomes is far more limited but suggests that less intensive forms of justice system contact (e.g., arrest, conviction without incarceration, legal debts) might also increase residential instability and decrease likelihood of homeownership (Bryan 2020a; 2022; Pattillo et al. 2022). Given the prevalence of these other forms of criminal justice system contact, an important first step will be building on the existing literature to consider the implications of noncustodial contact with the justice system. Research testing whether lower-level forms of justice system contact are also associated with changes in neighborhood quality would be especially helpful given the importance of place for shaping health, safety, and access to resources.

One line of inquiry should investigate the types of households and housing situations in which justice-system-involved individuals reside. Qualitative studies suggest that recently released individuals are often dependent on others (e.g., family, friends, charitable organizations) for housing in the years immediately following release (Western 2018; Harding, Morenoff, and Wyse 2019), but how long such dependent housing situations last and whether lower-level forms of criminal justice contact similarly increase one's odds of depending on others for housing is unknown. This question is particularly significant given the prevalence and implications of shared-housing situations (see Hope and Perkins, this volume).

Given prohibitions and discrimination faced by justice-system-involved individuals, important questions also arise about the quality and safety of both units and neighborhoods that such individuals live in and whether they pay fair market rent when they are able to establish independent households. Qualitative research investigating the types of households, housing, and neighborhoods to which individuals involved with the criminal justices system *aspire* might be most helpful in understanding where policy interventions may best be targeted.

EXAMINING THE ROLE OF POLICY CONTEXT

Comparative policy analysis work that investigates how local policies shape housing outcomes for individuals with criminal records is also sorely needed. Such analyses should consider policies specifically framed around individuals with a criminal history, as well as more general housing policies, particularly renter protections.

A clear place to start would be in comparing outcomes across cities with and without "One Strike" public housing rules that bar individuals with drug convictions or whom public housing authorities simply suspect as being involved in drug use or sales (HUD 1997). Such policies—which affect both one's ability to access individual housing assistance and one's ability to reside with friends or family living in subsidized units—could conceivably affect residential mobility, probability of establishing independent households, and rent paid relative to area fair market rent for individuals with drug-related charges or convictions.

Another important line of inquiry will be investigating whether current efforts to prohibit the consideration of criminal history in screening prospective tenants (e.g., Seattle's Fair Chance Housing Ordinance) will improve housing options for justice-system-involved individuals or may backfire and lead to greater discrimination against Black applicants who may be suspected of having criminal histories in the absence of direct information, as seems to have happened with employment-focused "ban the box" efforts (Doleac and Hansen 2020).

Similarly, we hope to see researchers investigate how the presence and strength of local renter protection laws shape housing outcomes among individuals with criminal justice histories. If the presence of such laws makes landlords reticent to rent to prospective tenants with criminal histories, whom they may consider riskier applicants, then such laws may inadvertently harm an already marginalized subset of the renter population. Multicity audit studies designed to test the extent of discrimination that individuals with criminal histories face in the rental market may be a particularly fruitful channel for testing this hypothesis.

MAKING CONNECTIONS TO MACRO-LEVEL RACIAL INEQUALITIES

Beyond thinking through the implications of criminal justice contact for individual-level outcomes, sociologists are particularly well suited to make larger connections between the individual-level consequences of criminal justice system contact and macro-level racial disparities in American society. Similar work has examined how racial disparities in felony conviction have affected voting and the outcome of federal elections (Uggen and Manza 2002), and we see great opportunity for sociologists to similarly investigate what the unequal distribution of justice system punishments across racial and ethnic lines means for housing-related outcomes at the community, city, and population levels. Analyses that decompose the contribution of racial disparities in criminal justice system contact to macro-level racial disparities in outcomes like homeownership rates and risk of homelessness would be a great contribution to the field. Likewise, once we know more about how local policies shape outcomes and whether discrimination against individuals with criminal histories is more common in some types of communities, we hope to see simulation-based studies that produce estimates of residential segregation under alternative policy scenarios (e.g., reduced racial disparities in criminal justice system contact, a shrunken correctional population, etc.).

Conclusion

In recent decades, sociologists have widely accepted the perspective that the American criminal justice system is a stratifying institution, reifying inequality along both race and class lines. This line of empirical and theoretical work has not yet been well integrated with the sociology of housing, however. We call for sociologists to join these lines of research not only because housing is another domain in which formerly incarcerated and convicted individuals may experience disadvantage but because doing so may help explain enduring phenomena like the racial homeownership gap, residential segregation, and racial disparities in homelessness, particularly child homelessness. Moreover, as America stares down a nationwide affordable housing crisis, understanding how the penal state interacts with the housing market—altering who can access affordable housing and where—should be a priority for sociologists of all stripes. We see great opportunity to unite sociologists studying housing, stratification, race/ethnicity, and criminology in these investigations, and we hope future research in this area will yield fruitful collaborations across subdisciplines.

24

The Housing Divide in the Global South

Marco Garrido

The housing situation in much of the Global South is different from the situation in the United States.[1] As the chapters in this volume attest, the housing problem in the US is usually articulated in terms of economic and social barriers, such as affordability, racial discrimination, and eviction. In many southern cities, the issue of access tends to be framed in terms of exclusion from the formal housing market, informality, and insecurity of tenure. Racial discrimination is seen as restricting access to housing in the US, whereas in many Global South cities housing status—specifically, hailing from a slum—is itself a powerful source of discrimination, even more powerful than skin color (Perlman 2010). Finally, eviction is not an individual affair but a collective one (Weinstein 2021). We see the demolition of entire communities happen all at once as part of a systematic effort to expurgate "slums." These differences underscore the inadequacy of simply generalizing a conceptual framework developed with reference to the US and applying it to other parts of the world. Doing so risks misrepresenting the reality of these places (Garrido, Ren, and Weinstein 2021).

In this chapter I will argue that a sociology of housing in the Global South needs to go beyond the scholarship's traditional focus on housing low-income residents and issues of housing need and access. It is not enough to focus on just one type of housing or another, whether slums or

---

[1] The term "Global South" is imprecise and can be troublesome because of its ambiguity. It is simply a way of referring to what used to be called the Third World and is sometimes called the developing world; that is, it gets at the distance between one set of countries, the West broadly, and another set in terms of economic and political "development" (another fraught term). In using the term Global South, I have in mind countries in Latin America, South Asia, Southeast Asia, and Africa—the old Third World, basically (developing-country market economies, and so not China), save for the few that have "ascended" since the 1960s, e.g., South Korea, Hong Kong, Taiwan, and Singapore.

upper- and middle-class enclaves. We also need to understand how these settlements and their residents relate to one another, because their relationship is productive of urban space and social relations. In other words, we need to focus on the divide between formal and informal housing. In many cities in the Global South, the housing divide is a social structure of exceptional power. It distinguishes urban space in terms of quality of housing, population density, and the provision of infrastructure and services. It also serves to distinguish people categorically into unequally valued social groups. This divide has become more salient in the neoliberal era with the proliferation of industrial, commercial, and residential enclaves. Today, the class-cum-housing divide defines many Global South cities in the same way the racial divide defines many American ones. Taking it into account is essential to building a sociology of housing that is truly global in scope.

The aim of this chapter is to do some of this accounting. First, I will review key works and new directions in the sociology of housing in the Global South in an effort to demarcate the subfield. Second, I will trace the development of the housing divide in Metro Manila specifically, underscoring its significance as a social boundary. Finally, I will make the case for globalizing the sociology of housing by putting housing scholars of the Global North and South in conversation.

The Sociology of Housing in the Global South: Demarcating a Burgeoning Field

There is a longer tradition than we might suppose of sociologists writing about housing in the Global South. Pierre Bourdieu, Kingsley Davis, Bryan Roberts, Alejandro Portes, Janet Abu-Lughod, Manuel Castells, Josef Gugler, and others helped lay the foundation of the subfield. In demarcating a sociology of housing in the Global South, I highlight work by sociologists primarily, distinguish between "classic" work largely published in the mid- to late twentieth century and contemporary work produced in the twenty-first, and focus mainly on books.

Bourdieu (1979) situated the housing problem in the context of modernization, a process of rapid and profoundly unsettling social change accelerated, in Algeria, by war. Hence the title of the essay in which this discussion appears, "The Disenchantment of the World," and of a recent book on Bourdieu's fieldwork in Algeria, *Uprooting* (Bourdieu and Sayad 2020). The demographer Paul Bairoch (1988) provides an indispensable account of the runaway population growth in Third World cities. He situates the experience historically and in comparison to urbanization in the

First World. A series of texts published in the 1970s through the 1990s set out to describe and explain the emerging Third World city (Abu-Lughod and Hay 1977; Roberts 1978; Bromley and Gerry 1979; Gugler 1988, 1997; Gilbert and Gugler 1992; Roberts 1995). These volumes covered topics like urbanization, migration, precarious work, informal housing, and the politics of the urban poor.

The topic of housing received considerable attention. One branch of this scholarship focused on the problem of squatting and policy solutions (Abrams 1964; Leeds 1969; Grimes 1976; Mangin 1967). A second branch focused on the social organization and lifeworlds of the poor in slums (Hollnsteiner 1972; Roberts 1973; Perlman 1976). Inspired by Chicago school–type ethnographies of slum and "ghetto" areas in US cities, this work sought to describe the slum as "a way of life" with distinct associations, customs, and norms (Jocano 1975). Unlike the American scholarship, however, the urban poor were portrayed as integral, not marginal, to the emerging city, given their number and the indispensability of their labor.

A third branch of the housing scholarship on the Global South focused on the politics of the urban poor. While scholars in the 1960s observed the spectacular growth of slums with alarm, they concluded that the urban poor were generally conservative, preoccupied with making a living, and apt to view radical political activity as too risky (Cornelius 1976; Nelson 1979; Portes and Walton 1976). The urban poor became less uniformly conservative and parochial by the late 1970s. Castells (1983) and Stokes (1995) document squatter movements taking shape in Santiago and Lima under the pressure of military rule and through the efforts of radical unions, political parties, and church organizations. Research in the 1990s and early in the first decade of the 2000s by Gay (1994), Auyero (2000), and Shefner (2001) considered the politics of the urban poor in greater depth by providing on-the-ground accounts of political organizing and clientelism.

Finally, a fourth branch of the housing scholarship on the Global South focused on the ecology of urban poverty and its implications for collective action. Portes and colleagues documented the changing urban form of Latin American cities with the adoption of free market or neoliberal reforms in the 1980s, noting, in particular, that the housing settlements of the urban rich and poor have drawn closer together, resulting in a kind of "perverse integration" (Portes 1989; Portes, Dore-Cabral, and Landolt 1997; Portes and Roberts 2005; and Roberts and Portes 2006).

The contemporary work on housing in the Global South takes up topics both familiar and new. Informal or slum housing continues to be an area of interest. Weinstein (2014) examines how the residents of the Dharavi settlement managed to secure semipermanent housing on some of Mumbai's most valuable real estate. Her forthcoming book compares informal settlements in several Indian cities and identifies various "logics of dispossession." Ren (2011) distinguishes between territorial and associational forms of governance in Chinese and Indian cities, respectively, illustrating these logics with regard to the regulation of land, housing, and air pollution. Other research considers social class (or more precisely, group formation) in the context of housing status. Harms (2016) argues that the development of a land market in Vietnam has led to the urban rich and poor becoming more conscious of property rights. Both groups have become more likely to articulate issues of inequality, injustice, and social distinction or "civility" in terms of homeownership and housing status. Zhang (2001) examines the plight of migrant workers in Beijing. This "floating population" is denied urban citizenship (*hukou*) and forced to settle along the urban periphery. Zhang (2010) explores the formation of a Chinese middle-class identity through residence in exclusive housing estates. My own work seeks to connect the housing divide with the formation of social groups and political dispositions. In *The Patchwork City* (2019), I argue that class boundaries are clarifying along the housing divide and that the urban poor and middle class are emerging as class actors—not as labor and capital but as squatters and "villagers" (in Manila, residential subdivisions are called villages).

Contemporary scholars remain very interested in the politics of housing but are looking beyond the urban poor and questions of political mobilization. Today there is greater interest in the implications of the housing divide for populism, citizenship, and democracy. Holston (2008) views encroachment, territorial mobilization, and spatial contention by the urban poor as a form of "insurgent citizenship." Caldeira (2000) spotlights the privately provisioned, physically enclosed, and socially exclusive housing of the urban rich and middle class. She attributes the proliferation of fortified enclaves in São Paulo to upper-class fear of crime and social contamination by the masses—and also to status anxiety prompted by democratization. She argues that walls have become a way to preserve social hierarchy at a time when Brazilians are putatively equal politically. In Garrido (2021), I suggest that enclaves have played a role in fostering antidemocratic politics. Housing segregation makes it easier to see the lower class as socially inferior and unfit to participate in politics, and the concentration of the urban rich in enclaves makes it easier for them to believe in top-down, private-sector fixes to public problems.

We see junior scholars taking up established topics as well as branching off in new directions. There is brand new work on the politics of housing in Capetown (Levenson 2021) and Santiago (Koppelman 2021); on the use of natural disasters to justify slum clearance (Diwakar 2019); on the conditions underlying the effective distribution of housing in São Paulo (Bradlow 2021); on policing favelas in Rio de Janeiro (Fahlberg 2018; de Souza 2019); on the emergence of a gated *city* in Monterrey, Mexico, in response to cartel violence (Villarreal 2021); and on the racialization of gentrification processes in Cartagena, Colombia (Valle 2018). The sociology of housing in the Global South is clearly vibrant and growing. Indeed, there is enough good work to merit its own edited volume.

The Housing Divide

I focus on the housing divide because of the powerful role it plays in structuring urban space, social relations, and politics in many Global South cities. The housing divide as a framework trains our attention on the *relationship* between different housing types. While there is a lot of work on slums and enclaves individually, their meaning in the urban fabric is constituted by their relation to one another. Slums are stigmatized in relation to formal housing. They are taken as abnormal despite their modality. Second, the framework enables us to articulate housing with other topics, including segregation, social organization, political mobilization, and citizenship. Third, the housing divide represents an urban structure that is particular to, indeed, has become emblematic of, Third World cities and a process of late urbanization, as I discuss below.

THE PROBLEM OF SLUMS

A number of so-called Third World countries urbanized rapidly in the mid-twentieth century. Their urbanization differed markedly from the process that shaped European and North American cities a century earlier, however. It was distinguished by, one, the greater scale and speed of urban population growth and, two, the smaller role played by industrialization. These dynamics led to precarious work and informal settlement becoming major urban forms. A housing divide took shape as a result and became an important and durable social boundary. Scholars in the 1950s and 1960s diagnosed cities in developing countries as being "overurbanized." By this they meant that urban growth had "run ahead" of the city's capacity to absorb the population (Davis and Golden 1954; Gugler and Flanagan 1976).

There was not enough industrialization or economic development relative to urban population growth; specifically, there were not enough jobs, housing, or services. This situation came to define the social landscape of these cities for decades to come.

Overurbanization manifests in the growth of slums.[2] The UN Habitat (2003) uses the word "slum" as a general term for low-income settlement distinguished by some combination of the following characteristics: inadequate infrastructure and services, substandard housing, overcrowding, and tenure insecurity. In many Third World cities, slums became a major urban form, comprising 35–40 percent of urban populations in the 1970s (Bairoch 1988, 473). Slums were growing at a much faster rate than the cities themselves, which were already growing fast. In some cities, the growth rate was 12–15 percent compared to 3–4 percent for the city as a whole (Turner 1967). Slums were a general problem. They affected Third World cities across the board. They are, moreover, a persistent problem. A third of the urban population in developing countries continues to live in slums. This figure represents a decline proportionally but a breathtaking increase in absolute numbers. The slum population in Third World cities grew from one hundred million in 1960 to nearly nine hundred million in 2014 (UN Habitat 2016).

Slums stood out for their irregularity and density, the quality of housing materials and construction, and deficiencies in infrastructure and services. Paved roads, electrical power, plumbing, and garbage pickup stopped where the worst slums started, although most acquired basic services over time. Life chances in slum areas, as indicated by levels of mortality, morbidity, and malnutrition, differed starkly from neighboring non-slum areas. Slums formed distinct communities. A web of associations organized to protect against eviction, fire, and other disasters, and to promote economic security and community life. In addition, various informal networks developed, of kinship, *compadrazgo* (fictive kinship), friendship, and acquaintance. Strong patterns of "neighboring"—borrowing and lending, sharing news, and passing leisure time together—were established. Norms of mutual aid and support provided a measure of shelter from the rules of the market (Lomnitz 1988). Slums were not at all anomic or impersonal but were thickly, if sometimes oppressively, social environments. Strong ties furnished a means of social control particularly through gossip and jokes (Hollnsteiner 1972). These patterns of interaction bred "a

---

[2] The term "slum" is controversial (see Gilbert 2007), and I use it advisedly.

closeness beyond mere sociability" (p. 32), a solidarity or "we consciousness" coincident with the slum's territorial boundaries (Leeds 1974).

Slums, finally, represented a discontinuity in urban meaning. They were
seen as ugly, unsanitary, unsafe, and obstructions to urban development.
They were described in pathological terms as an "urban sickness" in need
of immediate remediation lest it spread (Juppenplatz 1970, 3). The distinction between normal and abnormal housing underlay a moral valuation
of the residents of each type. The housing divide traced a social boundary, and relations across it took a definite form. Residents were not just
unequal but categorically unequal. They were seen as belonging to different and differentially valued social groups. Slum dwellers were "squatters"
and, as such, second-class citizens. They were backward: deficient in terms
of housing quality, tenure security, income, and education but, above all,
in *civilization*.

Bourdieu (1979) described formal housing as a "poisoned gift." On the
one hand, it represented a step up in one's material situation; on the other,
it required developing an appropriate economic disposition, in particular,
being able to keep up with the costs associated with the new space: rent,
utilities, furniture, upkeep, and transportation. It also required adopting a
new approach to social life by accepting a more circumscribed definition
of family and community, maintaining the boundaries between public and
private space, and learning to appreciate isolation as "privacy." Bourdieu's
informants—Algerians relocated from shantytowns to government flats—
quickly discovered that being poor in formal housing was not the same
thing as being poor in a slum. Formality exacted an unforeseen psychological toll. "There is an abyss," Bourdieu wrote, "between not having gas
when you live in a shanty town and being obliged to turn it off, when it
is there, inside your own flat, and to go back to the *kanun* (terracotta bra-
zier), so as to save money" (p. 82). Adapting to modern housing from slum
life meant learning "a new art of living," he argued, and thus described
the housing divide as "a boundary between classes" and "the threshold
of modernity" (p. 91).

THE PATCHWORK CITY

The housing problem in many Global South countries is often reduced
to a problem of slums. But there is more to it than that. The real issue is
the sociospatial divide between formal and informal housing. In recent
decades, the housing divide has become more pronounced mainly as a
result of neoliberal economic restructuring. Slums remain as integral to

the city as ever, but now we are seeing the proliferation of upper- and middle-class enclaves—gated subdivisions and condominiums, upscale commercial centers, and exclusive compounds. Cities like Manila are being transformed from a collection of hodgepodge areas, as Simone (2014) characterized neighborhoods in Jakarta, to more of a patchwork of classed spaces. And it is not just urban space being transformed but urban social relations. As the residents of slums and enclaves are more sharply distinguished, a class division is crystallizing around the housing divide. I discuss these changes below as they affect Metro Manila.

In Manila in the 1950s through the 1970s, as the slum population became entrenched (accounting for nearly 40 percent of the metro population today (Ballesteros 2011), the middle class lived in mixed neighborhoods and in subdivisions along the metropolitan outskirts. Hollnsteiner (1969) characterized middle-class households as atomized and disconnected from their locality. Although middle-class subdivisions were generally not gated, each house constituted a "self-contained, independent unit"; "high walls with glass on top and an occasional ferocious watchdog below mark the middle-class block" (p. 182). This state of affairs changed in the late 1980s with democratization. Existing subdivisions put up gates and posted guards while new subdivisions were constructed with gates and guards. These changes enabled the middle class to react to the greater presence of slums in the city. They were reacting to the increased legal protection afforded the urban poor through the Urban Development and Housing Act of 1992, which made it harder to dislodge squatters. Gating was also a response to crime, or at least to the perception of crime. While the crime rate spiked in the early years of democracy, it declined sharply throughout the 1990s (PSA 1991–2000). Despite the falling crime rate, the gates stayed up.

The pace of enclavization accelerated quickly in the 1990s, driven largely by demand from a growing middle class and overseas Filipino workers (Ortega 2016). The real estate industry helped to create this demand by marketing gated communities and "closed" condominiums (heavily guarded high-rises) as the very definition of modern housing (Connell 1999). In the 1970s, there were 750 subdivisions in all of Metro Manila registered with the now defunct Department of Local Government and Community Development (Keyes 1976). Between 1981 and 2013, the Housing and Land Use Regulatory Board (2014) documented the construction of 3,837 private residential subdivisions and condominiums. The new subdivisions were built in the south of Metro Manila and outlying provinces alongside corporate offices, call centers, export processing zones, and industrial parks. At the same time, new condominiums proliferated around Manila's multiple central business districts (Reyes 1998).

By the 2000s, enclavization had reached a point where observers could speak of a "private city" having seceded from the public one (Muijzenberg and Naerssen 2005; Shatkin 2008; Rimmer and Dick 2009). Enclaves had become both more numerous and larger in scale. Corporate "cities" were being built—megaprojects that bundled several facilities within the same complex, including office buildings, condominiums, malls, sports clubs, schools, hospitals, and even consulates. These spaces came equipped with premium, privately provisioned infrastructure and services. One such project, Bonifacio Global City, is equipped with a dual piping system that allows residents to distinguish between water for drinking, cooking, and bathing and water for flushing, irrigation, and outdoor washing. Just outside the development, many of the nearby neighborhoods cannot rely on a steady supply of water for any purpose.

Different kinds of enclaves grew more connected. Real estate developers partnered with the government to build transportation infrastructure, including light rail and expressways, motivated by the opportunity to connect their various residential and commercial properties. Shatkin (2008) describes the resulting pattern of private-sector-led urban development as "bypass-implant urbanism." Private developers would implant new spaces for production and consumption—business districts, technoparks, commercial centers, and housing developments—and connect them through transportation infrastructure. This strategy helped give shape to the private city as a network of corporate, commercial, and residential enclaves.

Enclavization is worsening the segmentation of the upper and middle classes. These groups are withdrawing from the public city. They are opting out of public services including public schools and hospitals, and shunning public spaces like parks, walkways, and déclassé malls. Upper- and middle-class social life is increasingly taking place in various kinds of enclaves encapsulating nearly every aspect of their lives. They live in gated subdivisions and condominiums. They study in private schools. They work in office buildings in one of several central business districts around the metro. They shop in mid- to high-end malls. They go out to clubs, cafés, and bars located inside commercial compounds. They even attend mass at the churches within these compounds. They move in private cars from one enclave to another and travel through toll roads too expensive for the general public to use.

By the end of the twentieth century, the spatial division between slums and enclaves had become the most important social division in Metro Manila. These divisions subsumed other significant lines of differentiation, including social divisions based on provincial origin, ethnicity, and occupational status. "What is taking place," Berner (1998) wrote, "is the

exhaustive emergence of enclaves, a de-differentiation of the city's population [into rich and poor] due to the social differentiation of urban space
[into enclaves and slums]" (p. 8).

Toward a Global Sociology of Housing

The housing divide is a significant social structure in many cities of the
Global South. A sociology of housing needs to take it into account. Moreover, it needs to understand it on its own terms; that is, without trying to
assimilate it into a framework conceived with US cities in mind. The common project ahead of us is to create a framework able to accommodate
urban situations around the world without losing sight of or glossing over
their differences while at the same time being able to identify and cata-
log continuities. Doing so requires putting scholars of the Global North
and South in conversation and getting them to talk to and not past one
another. To date, the conversation has been largely one-sided. Scholars
of the Global South draw upon, adapt, and revise the US scholarship but
remain peripheral to the field, their own scholarship neglected, regarded as
empirically interesting perhaps but theoretically mute. This state of affairs
appears to be changing, however.

A global sociology of housing is essentially comparative. We might
compare gated communities in Los Angeles and São Paulo; public housing
in Chicago and Singapore; regimes of housing provision and governance
in China and India with the American regime; the stigma of ghettos and
banlieues with the stigma of slums; segregation distinguished by inter-
spersion rather than concentration; social divisions cutting along class,
versus racial, versus religious lines; and so on. Making these comparisons
is productive. It leads to new questions, new ideas, and new directions
for further research. It is not just that we learn more about other parts of
the world, but that, in situating ourselves within the world at large, we
are forced to question our assumptions about the small parts of the world
we study. We are forced to rethink how we approach these sites, and to
check the parochial bias of our theories. We develop a more sophisticated
understanding of cities and housing as a result.

Consider the following circuit of influence. In *City of Walls*, a book
about São Paulo, Teresa Caldeira adapts some of Mike Davis's ideas in *City
of Quartz* (1990), a book about Los Angeles. For example, she applies ideas
about a climate of fear, the "securitized" landscape, and the built environment as a condition of possibility for public life. She also extends these
ideas in ways suggested by her case—for example, articulating segregation
and citizenship or walling and democracy. My own work is indebted to

Caldeira's research, but also to the Chicago school tradition and its central interest in both the role of spatial boundaries in group-making and social boundaries in demarcating urban space. Given my own interest in political dissensus between the urban poor and middle class in the Philippines, I bring this sociospatial dialectic to bear on the formation of political dispositions for and against a populist leader. Notably, this thread began with questions about the implications of housing inequality on public life and has ended up, thus far, with questions about the disjunctive experience of democracy in parts of the Global South—the greater political freedom afforded by democracy contradicted by increasing unfreedom in social intercourse and the built environment. As new topics are pulled into the conversation, its scope expands. We become attuned to a wider set of issues and come to articulate housing not just to the market and state as usual but to culture, contentious politics, citizenship, and democracy. We are able to recognize more clearly that the sociology of housing is about more than just housing.

Hopefully the circuit will complete. Just as work on Chicago and Los Angeles has informed analyses of São Paulo and Manila, the latter work may yet inform the former, providing scholars of Chicago, LA, and other US cities new ways to frame the housing situation in their cities. Of course, the condition is that this work be included in the conversation, that it be seen as relevant and useful rather than discounted as foreign and unrelated. That is to say, the sociology of housing becomes more global the more it is able to hold differences in the housing situations around the world within the same framework. We need a broader framework.

Works Cited

Aalbers, Manuel B. 2016. *The Financialization of Housing: A Political Economy Approach.* London: Routledge.

Aalbers, Manuel B. 2019. "Financial Geography II: Financial Geographies of Housing and Real Estate." *Progress in Human Geography* 43: 376–87.

Aalbers, Manuel B., and B. Christophers. 2014. "Centring Housing in Political Economy." *Housing, Theory and Society* 31, no. 4: 373–94.

Aaronson, Daniel, Jacob Faber, Daniel Hartley, Bhashkar Mazumder, and Patrick Sharkey. 2021. "The Long-Run Effects of the 1930s HOLC 'Redlining' Maps on Place-Based Measures of Economic Opportunity and Socioeconomic Success." *Regional Science and Urban Economics* 86 (November): 103622.

Aaronson, Daniel, Daniel Hartley, and Bhashkar Mazumder. 2020. "The Effects of the 1930s HOLC 'Redlining' Maps." Working paper, Federal Reserve Bank of Chicago, August.

Abdi, Fadumo M., and Kristine Andrews. 2018. "Redlining Has Left Many Communities of Color Exposed to Lead." *Child Trends*, February 13. https://www.childtrends.org/blog/redlining-left-many-communities-color-exposed-lead.

Abramovitz, Mimi, and Richard J. Smith. 2020. "The Persistence of Residential Segregation by Race, 1940 to 2010: The Role of Federal Housing Policy." *Families in Society* 102, no. 1: 5–32.

Abrams, Charles. 1964. *Man's Struggle for Shelter in an Urbanizing World.* Cambridge, MA: MIT Press.

Abu-Lughod, Janet, and Richard Hay Jr., eds. 1977. *Third World Urbanization.* Chicago: Maaroufa Press.

Achenbaum, W. Andrew. 2020. *Old Age in the New Land: The American Experience Since 1790.* Baltimore, MD: Johns Hopkins University Press.

Aguilera, Thomas, and Alan Smart. 2016. "Squatting, North, South, and Turnabout: A Dialogue Comparing Illegal Housing Research." In *Public Good versus Economic Interests: Global Perspectives on the History of Squatting*, edited by Freia Anders and Alexander Sedlmaier, 29–55. New York: Routledge.

Ahmed, Ali M., and Mats Hammarstedt. 2008. "Discrimination in the Rental Housing Market: A Field Experiment on the Internet." *Journal of Urban Economics* 64, no. 2: 362–72.

Aiello, Daniela, Lisa Bates, Terra Graziani, Christopher Herring, Manissa Maharawal, Erin McElroy, Pamela Phan, and Gretchen Purser. 2018. "Eviction Lab Misses the Mark." *Shelterforce*, August 22. https://shelterforce.org/2018/08/22/eviction-lab-misses-the-mark.

Aikau, Hokulani. 2012. *A Chosen People, a Promised Land*. Minneapolis: University of Minnesota Press.

Airbnb. n.d.a. "Fast Facts." *Airbnb Newsroom*. Retrieved February 19, 2020. https://news.airbnb.com/fast-facts.

Airbnb. n.d.b. "How Tessa Hosts." Airbnb. Retrieved January 30, 2021. https://www.airbnb.com/d/host_testimonial_tessa.

AirDNA. n.d. Airbnb and MarketMinder data overview for vacation rentals in Boise, Idaho. AirDNA—MarketMinder. Retrieved December 11, 2019, and May 31, 2022. https://www.airdna.co/vacation-rental-data/app/us/idaho/boise/overview.

AirDNA. 2022. "Airbnb Rental Arbitrage: A Data-Driven Guide for 2022 and 2023." AirDNA (blog), November 15. https://www.airdna.co/blog/airbnb-rental-arbitrage.

Akee, Randall. 2017. "Land Titles and Dispossession: Allotment on American Indian Reservations." Unpublished manuscript, March 30. Retrieved October 2021. https://ucla.app.box.com/s/77wcbkvegg1rqdcyt645mws7kpj8u2ml.

Alatorre, L., Bilal Ali, Jennifer Friedenbach, Chris Herring, T. J. Johnston, and Dilara Yarbrough. 2020. "Fighting Anti-Homeless Laws through Participatory Action Research: Reflections from the San Francisco Coalition on Homelessness' Criminalization Study." In *Collaborating for Change: A Casebook of Participatory Action Research*, edited by Susan D. Greenbaum, Glenn Jacobs, and Prentice Zinn, 33–46. New Brunswick, NJ: Rutgers University Press.

Alba, Richard D. 2009. *Blurring the Color Line: The New Chance for a More Integrated America*. Cambridge, MA: Harvard University Press.

Alba, Richard D., and John R. Logan. 1992. "Assimilation and Stratification in the Homeownership Patterns of Racial and Ethnic Groups." *International Migration Review* 26: 1314–41.

Alba, Richard D., John R. Logan, and Brian J. Stults. 2000. "The Changing Neighborhood Contexts of the Immigrant Metropolis." *Social Forces* 79, no. 2: 587–621.

Aliprantis, Dionissi, and Daniel Carroll. 2019. "What Is behind the Persistence of the Racial Wealth Gap?" Economic commentary 2019-03, February 28, Federal Reserve Bank of Cleveland. https://www.clevelandfed.org/publications/economic-commentary/2019/ec-201903-what-is-behind-the-persistence-of-the-racial-wealth-gap.

Aliprantis, Dionissi, Hal Martin, and David Phillips. 2022. "Landlords and Access to Opportunity." *Journal of Urban Economics* 129: 0094–1190.

Almaguer, Tomás. 2016. "Race, Racialization, and Latino Populations in the United States." In *The New Latino Studies Reader*, edited by Ramon A. Gutierrez and Tomas Almaguer, 210–28. Los Angeles: University of California Press.

Almeida, Joanna, Ichiro Kawachi, Beth E. Molnar, and S. V. Subramanian. 2009. "A Multilevel Analysis of Social Ties and Social Cohesion among Latinos and Their Neighborhoods: Results from Chicago." *Journal of Urban Health* 86: 745–59.

Alwin, Duane F., Jason R. Thomas, and Kyler J. Sherman-Wilkins. 2018. "Race, Social Relations and the Life Course." In *Social Networks and the Life Course: Integrating the Development of Human Lives and Social Relational Networks*, edited by Duane F. Alwin, Diane H. Felmlee, and Derek A. Kreager, 285–314. Cham, Switzerland: Springer International Publishing.

Ameri, Mason, Sean Edmund Rogers, Lisa Schur, and Douglas Kruse. 2019. "No Room at the Inn? Disability Access in the New Sharing Economy." *Academy of Management Discoveries* 6, no. 2: 176–205.

American Sociological Association. 2003. "The Importance of Collecting Data and Doing Social Scientific Research on Race." Washington, DC: American Sociological Association.

Amorim, Mariana. 2019. "Are Grandparents a Blessing or a Burden? Multigenerational Coresidence and Child-Related Spending." *Social Science Research* 80 (February): 132–44.

Amorim, Mariana, Rachel Dunifon, and Natasha Pilkauskas. 2017. "The Magnitude and Timing of Grandparental Coresidence during Childhood in the United States." *Demographic Research* 37 (December): 1695–706.

Amster, Randall. 2003. "Patterns of Exclusion: Sanitizing Space, Criminalizing Homelessness." *Social Justice* 30, no. 1 (91): 195–221.

Amuedo-Dorantes, Catalina, and Cynthia Bansak. 2006. "Money Transfers among Banked and Unbanked Mexican Immigrants." *Southern Economic Journal* 73, no. 2: 374–401.

Ananat, Elizabeth Oltmans, and Ebonya Washington. 2009. "Segregation and Black Political Efficacy." *Journal of Public Economics* 93, no. 5–6: 807–22.

Anderson, Elijah. 1990. *Streetwise: Race, Class, and Change in an Urban Community*. Chicago: University of Chicago Press.

Anderson, Elijah. 2003. *A Place on the Corner*. Chicago: University of Chicago Press.

Anderson, Nels. 1967. *The Hobo*. Chicago: University of Chicago Press

Andersson, Fredrik, John C. Haltiwanger, Mark J. Kutzbach, Giordano E. Palloni, Henry O. Pollakowski, and Daniel H. Weinberg. 2016. "Childhood Housing and Adult Earnings: A Between-Siblings Analysis of Housing Vouchers and Public Housing." Working paper 22721, October, National Bureau of Economic Research. https://www.nber.org/papers/w22721.

Andrade, Troy. 2016. "Changing Tides: A Political and Legal History of the Office of Hawaiian Affairs." PhD diss., University of Hawai'i at Mānoa. https://scholarspace.manoa.hawaii.edu/items/075cb841-b8b5-4b18-a912-675c2c421b25.

Andrews, Jeff. 2020. "Affordable Housing Is in Crisis. Is Public Housing the Solution?" *Curbed*, January 13. https://archive.curbed.com/2020/1/13/21026108/public-housing-faircloth-amendment-election-2020.

Ansell, Ben. 2014. "The Political Economy of Homeownership: Housing Markets and the Welfare State." *American Political Science Review* 108, no. 2: 383–402.

Apel, Robert. 2016. "The Effects of Jail and Prison Confinement on Cohabitation and Marriage." *Annals of the American Academy of Political and Social Science* 665, no. 1: 103–26.

Apel, Robert, and Gary Sweeten. 2010. "The Impact of Incarceration on Employment during the Transition to Adulthood." *Social Problems* 57, no. 3: 448–79.

Apgar, William, Allegra Calder, Michael Collins, and Mark Duda. 2002. "An Examination of Manufactured Housing as a Community- and Asset-Building Strategy." Working paper W02-11, November 30, Neighborhood Reinvestment Corporation with the Joint Center for Housing Studies of Harvard University. https://www.jchs.harvard.edu/research-areas/working-papers/examination-manufactured-housing-community-and-asset-building-strategy.

Applied Survey Research (ASR). 2019. *San Francisco Homeless Point in Time Count.* San Jose, CA: ASR. https://hsh.sfgov.org/wp-content/uploads/2020/01/2019 HIRDReport_SanFrancisco_FinalDraft-1.pdf.

Aquilino, William S. 1996. "The Life Course of Children Born to Unmarried Mothers: Childhood Living Arrangements and Young Adult Outcomes." *Journal of Marriage and the Family* 58, no. 2: 293–310.

Archer, Deborah N. 2019. "The New Housing Segregation: The Jim Crow Effects of Crime-Free Housing Ordinances." *Michigan Law Review* 118: 173–231.

Arvin, Maile. 2019. *Possessing Polynesians: The Science of Settler Colonial Whiteness in Hawai'i and Oceania.* Durham, NC: Duke University Press.

Asquith, Brian, Evan Mast, and Davin Reed. 2020. "Supply Shock Versus Demand Shock: The Local Effects of New Housing in Low-Income Areas." Working paper 20-07, Federal Reserve Board of Philadelphia, February. https://www.philadelphiafed .org/-/media/frbp/assets/working-papers/2020/wp20-07.pdf.

Atkinson, Rowland. 2015. "Losing One's Place: Narratives of Neighbourhood Change, Market Injustice and Symbolic Displacement." *Housing, Theory and Society* 32, no. 4: 373–88.

Atlas, John. 2010. *Seeds of Change: The Story of ACORN, America's Most Controversial Anti-Poverty Community Organizing Group.* Nashville, TN: Vanderbilt University Press.

Atuahene, Bernadette, and Christopher Berry. 2019. "Taxed Out: Illegal Property Tax Assessments and the Epidemic of Tax Foreclosures in Detroit." *UC Irvine Law Review* 9, no. 4: 847–86.

Augustine, Jennifer March, and R. Kelly Raley. 2013. "Multigenerational Households and the School Readiness of Children Born to Unmarried Mothers." *Journal of Family Issues* 34, no. 4: 431–59.

Aulette, Judy, and Albert Aulette. 1987. "Police Harassment of the Homeless: The Political Purpose of the Criminalization of Homelessness." *Humanity and Society* 11, no. 2: 244–56.

Auspurg, Katrin, Andreas Schneck, and Thomas Hinz. 2019. "Closed Doors Every-where? A Meta-Analysis of Field Experiments on Ethnic Discrimination in Rental Housing Markets." *Journal of Ethnic and Migration Studies* 45, no. 1: 95–114.

Auyero, Javier. 2000. *Poor People's Politics: Peronist Survival Networks and the Legacy of Evita.* Durham, NC: Duke University Press.

Avery, Robert B., and Michael S. Rendall. 2002. "Lifetime Inheritances of Three Generations of Whites and Blacks." *American Journal of Sociology* 107, no. 5: 1300–46.

Badger, Emily. 2019. "Who's to Blame When Algorithms Discriminate?" *New York Times*, August 23, section B: 7.

Bailey, Everton, Jr. 2018. "Portland Changes Zoning Rules to Allow Duplexes, Triplexes, Fourplexes in Areas Previously Reserved for Single-Family Homes." *Oregonian*, August 13. https://www.oregonlive.com/portland/2020/08/portland-changes -zoning-code-to-allow-duplexes-triplexes-fourplexes-in-areas-previously-reserved -for-single-family-homes.html.

Bairoch, Paul. 1988. *Cities and Economic Development: From the Dawn of History to the Present.* Chicago: University of Chicago Press.

Baker, Mary Tuti. 2018. "Waiwai (Abundance) and Indigenous Futures." In *Routledge Handbook of Postcolonial Politics*, edited by Olivia Rutazibwa and Robbie Shilliam. New York: Routledge.

Balderrama, Francisco E., and Raymond Rodríguez. 2006. *Decade of Betrayal: Mexican Repatriation in the 1930s*. Albuquerque: University of New Mexico Press.

Ballesteros, Marife M. 2011. *Why Slum Poverty Matters*. Policy notes 2011-02, Philippine Institute for Development Studies. https://www.pids.gov.ph/publication/policy-notes/why-slum-poverty-matters.

Baltimore, Maryland, Commission on City Plan. 1945. *Redevelopment of Blighted Residential Areas in Baltimore: Conditions of Blight Some Remedies and Their Relative Cost*. Baltimore, MD: Commission on City Plan, July 1. http://jhir.library.jhu.edu/handle/1774.2/59079.

Balto, Simon. 2019. *Occupied Territory: Policing Black Chicago from Red Summer to Black Power*. Chapel Hill: University of North Carolina Press.

Balzarini, John, and Melody L. Boyd. 2021. "*Working with Them*: Small-Scale Landlord Strategies for Avoiding Evictions." *Housing Policy Debate* 31, no. 3–5: 425–45.

Baradaran, Mehrsa. 2019. *The Color of Money: Black Banks and the Racial Wealth Gap*. Cambridge, MA: Harvard University Press.

Barocas, Solon, and Andrew D. Selbst. 2014. "Big Data's Disparate Impact." *California Law Review* 104, no. 671: 671–732.

Barr, Donald A. 2019. *Health Disparities in the United States: Social Class, Race, Ethnicity, and the Social Determinants of Health*. Baltimore, MD: Johns Hopkins University Press.

Barron, Kyle, Edward Kung, and Davide Proserpio. 2021. "The Effect of Home-Sharing on House Prices and Rents: Evidence from Airbnb." *Marketing Science* 40, no. 1: 23–47.

Bartlett, Robert, Adair Morse, Richard Stanton, and Nancy Wallace. 2017. "Consumer Lending Discrimination in the FinTech Era." Working paper 25943, June, UC Berkeley. https://www.nber.org/papers/w25943.

Bartram, Robin. 2019. "Going Easy and Going After: Building Inspections and the Selective Allocation of Code Violations." *City and Community* 18: 594–617.

Bartram, Robin. 2021. "Cracks in Broken Windows: How Objects Shape Professional Evaluation." *American Journal of Sociology* 126, no. 5: 759–94.

Bartram, Robin. 2022. *Stacked Decks: Building Inspectors and the Reproduction of Urban Inequality*. Chicago: University of Chicago Press.

Bartram, Robin. Forthcoming. *Cities of Stacked Decks: Code Enforcement, Inequality, and Frontline Justice*. Chicago: University of Chicago Press.

Bashi, Vilna. 2007. *Survival of the Knitted: Immigrant Social Networks in a Stratified World*. Stanford, CA: Stanford University Press.

Basolo, Victoria, and Mai Thi Nguyen. 2005. "Does Mobility Matter? The Neighborhood Conditions of Housing Voucher Holders by Race and Ethnicity." *Housing Policy Debate* 16: 297–324.

Bauman, John F. 1987. *Public Housing, Race, and Renewal: Urban Planning in Philadelphia, 1920–1974*. Philadelphia, PA: Temple University Press.

Bayat, Asef. 1997. *Street Politics: Poor People's Movements in Iran*. New York: Columbia University Press.

Bayat, Asef. 2000. "From 'Dangerous Classes' to 'Quiet Rebels': The Politics of the Urban Subaltern in the Global South." *International Sociology* 15, no. 3: 533–57.

Bayer, Patrick, Robert McMillan, and Kim S. Rueben. 2004. "What Drives Racial Segregation? New Evidence Using Census Microdata." *Journal of Urban Economics* 56, no. 3: 397–407.

Beamer, Kamanamaikalani, and N. Wahine'aipohaku Tong. 2016. "The Māhele Did
    What? Native Interest Remains." *Hūlili: Multidisciplinary Research on Hawaiian
    Wellbeing* 10: 125–45.

Beason, Tyrone. 2016. "Central District's Shrinking Black Community Wonders
    What's Next." *Seattle Times*, May 28. https://www.seattletimes.com/seattle-news
    /central-districts-shrinking-black-community-wonders-whats-next.

Bécares, Laia. 2014. "Ethnic Density Effects on Psychological Distress among Latino
    Ethnic Groups: An Examination of Hypothesized Pathways." *Health and Place* 30:
    177–86.

Becher, Debbie. 2014. *Private Property and Public Power: Eminent Domain in Philadelphia.*
    New York: Oxford University Press.

Beck, Brenden. 2020. "Policing Gentrification: Stops and Low–Level Arrests during
    Demographic Change and Real Estate Reinvestment." *City and Community* 19, no. 1:
    245–72.

Beck, Kevin R. 2019. "Staying for Opportunity: Residential Mobility, Neighborhood
    Effects, and Assisted Housing." PhD diss., University of California—San Diego.
    https://escholarship.org/content/qt0hb6g10b/qt0hb6g10b_noSplash_eea6bda
    7ba05e546c8337cb317450fc0.pdf.

Beckett, Katherine, and Steve Herbert. 2009. *Banished: The New Social Control in Urban
    America.* New York: Oxford University Press.

Been, Vicki, Ingrid Ellen, and Josiah Madar. 2009. "The High Cost of Segregation:
    Exploring Racial Disparities in High-Cost Lending." *Fordham Urban Law Journal* 36,
    no. 3: 361–93.

Been, Vicki, Ingrid Gould Ellen, and Katherine O'Regan. 2019. "Supply Skepticism:
    Housing Supply and Affordability." *Housing Policy Debate* 29, no. 1: 25–40.

Been, Vicki, Josiah Madar, and Simon McDonnell. 2014. "Urban Land-Use Regulation:
    Are Homevoters Overtaking the Growth Machine?" *Journal of Empirical Legal
    Studies* 11, no. 2: 227–65.

Belarmino, Amanda, and Yoon Koh. 2020. "A Critical Review of Research Regarding
    Peer-to-Peer Accommodations." *International Journal of Hospitality Management* 84
    (January): 102315.

Bell, Jeannine. 2013. *Hate Thy Neighbor: Move-In Violence and the Persistence of Racial
    Segregation in American Housing.* New York: NYU Press.

Bell, Monica C. 2020a. "Anti-Segregation Policing." *New York University Law Review* 95,
    no. 3: 650–765.

Bell, Monica C. 2020b. "Located Institutions: Neighborhood Frames, Residential
    Preferences, and the Case of Policing." *American Journal of Sociology* 125, no. 4:
    917–73.

Benfer, Emily A. 2017. "Contaminated Childhood: How the United States Failed to
    Prevent the Chronic Lead Poisoning of Low-Income Children and Communities of
    Color." *Harvard Environmental Law Review* 41, no. 2: 493–561.

Benites-Gambirazio, Eliza. 2020. "Working as a Real Estate Agent: Bringing Clients In
    Line with the Market." *Journal of Cultural Economy* 13: 153–68.

Benner, Katie, Glenn Thrush, and Mike Isaac. 2019. "U.S. Claims Ad Practices by
    Facebook Discriminate." *New York Times*, March 29, section B: 1.

Bennett, Larry, and Adolph Reed, Jr. 1999. "The New Face of Urban Renewal: The Near
    North Redevelopment and the Cabrini-Green Neighborhood." In *Without Justice*

for All: The New Liberalism and Our Retreat from Racial Equality, edited by Adolph Reed, Jr., 175–211. Boulder, CO: Westview Press.

Bergman, Peter, Raj Chetty, Stefanie DeLuca, Nathaniel Hendren, Lawrence F. Katz, and Christopher Palmer. 2019. "Creating Moves to Opportunity: Experimental Evidence on Barriers to Neighborhood Choice." Working paper 26164, August, National Bureau of Economic Research. https://www.nber.org/papers/w26164.

Berner, Erhard. 1998. "Globalization, Fragmentation, and Local Struggles." *Philippine Sociological Review* 46, no. 3–4: 121–42.

Bernhardt, A. 1981. *Building Tomorrow: The Mobile/Manufactured Housing Industry.* Cambridge, MA: MIT Press.

Besbris, Max. 2016. "Romancing the Home: Emotions and the Interactional Creation of Demand in the Housing Market." *Socio-Economic Review* 14: 461–82.

Besbris, Max. 2020. *Upsold: Real Estate Agents, Prices, and Neighborhood Inequality.* Chicago: University of Chicago Press.

Besbris, Max, and Jacob W. Faber. 2017. "Investigating the Relationship between Real Estate Agents, Segregation, and House Prices: Steering and Upselling in New York State." *Sociological Forum* 32, no. 4: 850–73.

Besbris, Max, and Elizabeth Korver-Glenn. 2022. "Value Fluidity and Value Anchoring: Race, Intermediaries and Valuation in Two Housing Markets." *Socio-Economic Review.*

Besbris, Max, John Kuk, Ann Owens, and Ariela Schachter. 2022. "Predatory Inclusion in the Market for Rental Housing: A Multicity Empirical Test." *Socius* 8: 1–16.

Besbris, Max, Ariela Schachter, and John Kuk. 2021. "The Unequal Availability of Rental Housing Information Across Neighborhoods." *Demography* 58: 1197–221.

Bessy, Christian, and Pierre-Marie Chauvin. 2013. "The Power of Market Intermediaries: From Information to Valuation Processes." *Valuation Studies* 1: 83–117.

Bezalel, Ronit, dir. 2014. *70 Acres in Chicago: Cabrini Green.* Ronit Films. DVD. https://70acresinchicago.com/.

Bezdek, Barbara. 1992. "Silence in the Court: Participation and Subordination of Poor Tenants' Voices in Legal Process." *Hofstra Law Review* 20, no. 3: 553–608.

Bickford, Adam, and Douglas Massey. 1991. "Segregation in the Second Ghetto: Racial and Ethnic Segregation in American Public Housing 1977." *Social Forces* 69: 1011–36.

Bischoff, Kendra, and Ann Owens. 2019. "The Segregation of Opportunity: Social and Financial Resources in the Educational Contexts of Lower- and Higher-Income Children, 1990–2014." *Demography* 56, no. 5: 1635–64.

Bittner, Egon. 1967. "The Police on Skid-Row: A Study of Peace Keeping." *American Sociological Review* 32, no. 5: 699.

Blackmon, Douglas A. 2008. *Slavery by Another Name: The Re-Enslavement of Black People in America from the Civil War to World War II.* New York: Doubleday.

Blalock, Hubert M. 1967. *Toward a Theory of Minority-Group Relations.* New York: Wiley.

Blatto, Anna. 2018. "A City Divided: A Brief History of Segregation in Buffalo." Buffalo, NY: Partnership for the Public Good, May 7. https://ppgbuffalo.org/buffalo-commons/library/resource:a-city-divided-a-brief-history-of-segregation-in-buffalo-1/.

Blau, Joel. 1993. *The Visible Poor: Homelessness in the United States.* New York: Oxford University Press.

Blidner, Rachelle. 2014. "Public Housing Safety Policy Can Hit Whole Family." Associated Press, September 14. https://archive.sltrib.com/article.php?id=58413084&itype=CMSID.

Bloch, Stefano. 2022. "Aversive Racism and Community-Instigated Policing: The Spatial Politics of Nextdoor." *Environment and Planning C: Politics and Space* 40, no. 1: 260–78.

Bloch, Stefano, and Susan A. Phillips. 2022. "Mapping and Making Gangland: A Legacy of Redlining and Enjoining Gang Neighbourhoods in Los Angeles." *Urban Studies* 59, no. 4: 750–70.

Blosser, Jamie, Nathaniel Corum, Daniel Glenn, Joseph Kunkel, and Ed Rosenthal. 2014. "Best Practices in Tribal Housing: Case Studies 2013." Sustainable Native Communities Collaborative, November. https://dx.doi.org/10.2139/ssrn.2563139.

Bobo, Lawrence, and Camille L. Zubrinsky. 1996. "Attitudes on Residential Integration: Perceived Status Differences, Mere In-Group Preference, or Racial Prejudice?" *Social Forces* 74, no. 3: 883–909.

Boeing, Geoff, Max Besbris, Ariela Schachter, and John Kuk. 2021. "Housing Search in the Era of Big Data: Smarter Cities or Same Old Blind Spots?" *Housing Policy Debate* 31: 112–26.

Boen, Courtney, Lisa Keister, and Brian Aronson. 2020. "Beyond Net Worth: Racial Differences in Wealth Portfolios and Black–White Health Inequality across the Life Course." *Journal of Health and Social Behavior* 61, no. 2: 153–69.

Boen, Courtney, and Y. Claire Yang. 2016. "The Physiological Impacts of Wealth Shocks in Late Life: Evidence from the Great Recession." *Social Science and Medicine* 150: 221–30.

Bogardus, Emory S. 1916. "The House-Court Problem." *American Journal of Sociology* 22, no. 3: 391–99.

Bogardus, Emory S. 1930. "The Mexican Immigrant and Segregation." *American Journal of Sociology* 36, no. 1: 74–80.

Bogardus, Emory S. 1934. *The Mexican in the United States*. Los Angeles: University of California Press.

Bonilla-Silva, Eduardo. 2003. *Racism without Racists: Color-Blind Racism and the Persistence of Racial Inequality in the United States*. Lanham, MD: Rowman and Littlefield.

Bourdieu, Pierre. 1979. *Algeria 1960: The Disenchantment of the World, the Sense of Honor, the Kabyle House or the World Reversed: Essays*. Cambridge: Cambridge University Press.

Bourdieu, Pierre. 1984. *Distinction: A Social Critique of the Judgement of Taste*. Cambridge, MA: Harvard University Press.

Bourdieu, Pierre. 1999. *The Weight of the World: Social Suffering in Contemporary Society*. Stanford, CA: Stanford University Press.

Bourdieu, Pierre, and Abdelmayek Sayad. 2020. *Uprooting: The Crisis of Traditional Agriculture in Algeria*. Cambridge: Polity.

Boustan, Leah Platt. 2010. "Was Postwar Suburbanization 'White Flight'? Evidence from the Black Migration." *Quarterly Journal of Economics* 125, no. 1: 417–43.

Boyle, Kevin. 2007. *Arc of Justice: A Saga of Race, Civil Rights, and Murder in the Jazz Age*. New York: Henry Holt and Company.

Bradlow, Benjamin H. 2021. "Embeddedness and Cohesion: Regimes of Urban Public Goods Distribution." *Theory and Society* 51, no. 1: 1–28.

Brady, Henry E., Sidney Verba, and Kay Lehman Schlozman. 1995. "Beyond SES: A Resource Model of Political Participation." *American Political Science Review* 89, no. 2: 271–94.

Brenner, Neil. 2017. *Critique of Urbanization: Selected Essays.* Berlin: Bauverlag Gütersloh.

Brenner, Neil, and Nik Theodore. 2002. "Cities and the Geographies of 'Actually Existing Neoliberalism.'" In *Spaces of Neoliberalism: Urban Restructuring in North American and Western Europe*, edited by Neil Brenner and Nik Theodore, 1–32. New York: Blackwell Publishing.

Bridges, Lauren. 2021. "Infrastructural Obfuscation: Unpacking the Carceral Logics of the Ring Surveillant Assemblage." *Information, Communication and Society* 24, no. 6: 830–49.

Bromley, Ray, and Chris Gerry. 1979. "Who are the Casual Poor?" In *Casual Work and Poverty in Third World Cities*, edited by Ray Bromley and Chris Gerry, 3–23. New York: John Wiley and Sons.

Brooks-Gunn, Jeanne, Greg J. Duncan, and J. Lawrence Aber. 1997. *Neighborhood Poverty.* New York: Russell Sage Foundation.

Brown, Anne, Vinit Mukhija, and Donald Shoup. 2020. "Converting Garages into Housing." *Journal of Planning Education and Research* 40, no. 1: 56–68.

Brown, David L., and Glenn V. Fuguitt. 1972. "Percent Nonwhite and Racial Disparity in Nonmetropolitan Cities in the South." *Social Science Quarterly* 53: 573–82.

Brown, Rebecca T., Leah Goodman, David Guzman, Lina Tieu, Claudia Ponath, and Margot B. Kushel. 2016. "Pathways to Homelessness among Older Homeless Adults: Results from the HOPE HOME Study." *PloS One* 11, no. 5: e0155065.

Brown, Susan K. 2007. "Delayed Spatial Assimilation: Multigenerational Incorporation of the Mexican-Origin Population in Los Angeles." *City and Community* 6, no. 3): 193–209.

Brown-Saracino, Japonica. 2010. *A Neighborhood That Never Changes: Gentrification, Social Preservation, and the Search for Authenticity.* Chicago: University of Chicago Press.

Brown-Saracino, Japonica. 2017. "Explicating Divided Approaches to Gentrification and Growing Income Inequality." *Annual Review of Sociology* 43, no. 1: 515–39.

Bruch, Elizabeth, and Joffre Swait. 2019. "Choice Set Formation in Residential Mobility and Its Implications for Segregation Dynamics." *Demography* 56, no. 5: 1665–92.

Brueckner, Jan K. 2000. "Urban Sprawl: Diagnosis and Remedies." *Land Economics* 23, no. 2: 160–71.

Brunsma, David L., and Jennifer Padilla Wyse. 2019. "The Possessive Investment in White Sociology." *Sociology of Race and Ethnicity* 5, no. 1: 1–10.

Buchanan, Larry, Quoctrung Bui, and Jugal K. Patel. 2020. "Black Lives Matter May Be the Largest Movement in U.S. History." *New York Times*, July 3. https://www.nytimes.com/interactive/2020/07/03/us/george-floyd-protests-crowd-size.html.

Burawoy, Michael. 2017. "On Desmond: The Limits of Spontaneous Sociology." *Theory and Society* 46, no. 4: 261–84.

Burdick-Will, Julia, Jens Ludwig, Stephen W. Raudenbush, Robert J. Sampson, Lisa Sanbonmatsu, and Patrick Sharkey. 2011. "Converging Evidence for Neighborhood Effects on Children's Test Scores: An Experimental, Quasi-Experimental, and Observational Comparison." In *Whither Opportunity: Rising Inequality, Schools, and Children's Life Chances*, edited by Greg J. Duncan and Richard J. Murnane, 255–76. New York: Russel Sage Foundation.

Bryan, Brielle. 2020a. "Homeownership Experiences Following Criminal Justice Contact." *Cityscape* 22, no. 1: 103–46.

Bryan, Brielle. 2020b. "Locked Out of Place: How Felony Conviction History Shapes Residential Opportunity and Racial Segregation." Presented at the Association for Public Policy Analysis and Management Annual Meeting, Washington, DC, November 11–13.

Bryan, Brielle. 2022. "Housing Instability Following Felony Conviction and Incarceration: Disentangling Being Marked from Being Locked Up." *Journal of Quantitative Criminology* (June).

Bumiller, Kristin. 2015. "Bad Jobs and Good Workers: The Hiring of Ex-Prisoners in a Segmented Economy." *Theoretical Criminology* 19, no. 3: 336–54.

Burrows, Lawrence B. 1978. *Growth Management: Issues, Techniques, and Policy Implications*. New Brunswick, NJ: Center for Urban Policy Research.

Bush, Hannah, and Marybeth Shinn. 2017. "Families' Experiences of Doubling Up After Homelessness." *Cityscape* 19, no. 3: 331.

Bushway, Shawn D. 1998. "The Impact of an Arrest on the Job Stability of Young White American Men." *Journal of Research in Crime and Delinquency* 35, no. 4: 454–79.

Byrne, Thomas, Ellen A. Munley, Jamison D. Fargo, Ann E. Montgomery, and Dennis P. Culhane. 2013. "New Perspectives on Community-Level Determinants of Homelessness." *Journal of Urban Affairs* 35, no. 5: 607–25.

Caldeira, Teresa P. R. 2000. *City of Walls: Crime, Segregation, and Citizenship in São Paulo*. Berkeley: University of California Press.

Camarillo, Albert. 1979. *Chicanos in a Changing Society: From Mexican Pueblos to American Barrios in Santa Barbara and Southern California, 1848–1930*. Cambridge, MA: Harvard University Press.

Candipan, Jennifer. 2019. "Neighbourhood Change and the Neighbourhood-School Gap." *Urban Studies* 56, no. 15: 3308–33.

Carll, Erin. 2021. "How Ethno-Racialized Residential Histories and Support Networks Shape Residential Stratification for Housing Voucher Holders." PhD diss., University of Washington. https://digital.lib.washington.edu/researchworks/handle/1773/47132.

Carlson, Leonard A. 1983. "Federal Policy and Indian Land: Economic Interests and the Sale of Indian Allotments, 1900–1934." *Agricultural History* 57, no. 1: 33–45.

Carpusor, Adrian G., and William E. Loges. 2006. "Rental Discrimination and Ethnicity in Names." *Journal of Applied Social Psychology* 36, no. 4: 934–52.

Castellow, Jennifer, Bret Kloos, and Greg Townley. 2015. "Previous Homelessness as a Risk Factor for Recovery from Serious Mental Illnesses." *Community Mental Health Journal* 51, no. 6: 674–84.

Castells, Manuel. 1979. *The Urban Question: A Marxist Approach*. London: E. Arnold.

Castells, Manuel. 1983. *The City and the Grassroots: A Cross-Cultural Theory of Urban Social Movements*. Berkeley: University of California Press.

Castells, Manuel, and Alejandro Portes. 1989. "World Underneath: The Origins, Dynamics and Effects of the Informal Economy." In *The Informal Economy: Studies in Advanced and Less Developed Countries*, edited by Manuel Castells, Alejandro Portes, and Laura Benton, 11–40. Baltimore, MD: Johns Hopkins University Press.

Castles, Francis G. 1998. "The Really Big Trade-Off: Home Ownership and the Welfare State in the New World and the Old." *Act Politica* 33, no. 1: 5–19.

Cavanagh, Shannon E., and Paula Fomby. 2019. "Family Instability in the Lives of American Children." *Annual Review of Sociology* 45, no. 1: 493–513.

Centers for Disease Control and Prevention. 2022. "Sources of Lead Exposure." Last reviewed January 13. https://www.cdc.gov/nceh/lead/prevention/sources.htm.

Chang, David A. 2010. *The Color of the Land: Race, Nation, and the Politics of Landownership in Oklahoma, 1832–1929.* Chapel Hill: University of North Carolina Press.

Chang, Serina, Emma Pierson, Pang Wei Koh, Jaline Gerardin, Beth Redbird, David Grusky, and Jure Leskovec. 2020. "Mobility Network Models of COVID-19 Explain Inequities and Inform Reopening." *Nature* 589 (January): 82–87.

Chapple, Karen, Jake Wegmann, Farzad Mashhood, and Rebecca Coleman. 2017. "Jumpstarting the Market for Accessory Dwelling Units: Lessons Learned from Portland, Seattle, and Vancouver." San Francisco: Urban Land Institute. https://escholarship.org/uc/item/4b9836bh.

Charles, Camille Zubrinsky. 2003. "The Dynamics of Racial Residential Segregation." *Annual Review of Sociology* 29: 167–207.

Charles, Camille Zubrinsky. 2006. *Won't You Be My Neighbor? Race, Class, and Residence in Los Angeles.* New York: Russell Sage Foundation.

Chaskin, Robert J., and Mark L. Joseph. 2015. *Integrating the Inner City: The Promise and Perils of Mixed-Income Public Housing Transformation.* Chicago: University of Chicago Press.

Cheng, Mingming, and Carmel Foley. 2018. "The Sharing Economy and Digital Discrimination: The Case of Airbnb." *International Journal of Hospitality Management* 70 (March): 95–98.

Cherry, Frances, and Marc Bendick. 2018. "Making It Count: Discrimination Auditing and the Activist Scholar Tradition." In *Audit Studies: Behind the Scenes with Theory, Method, and Nuance*, edited by S. Michael Gaddis, 45–62. Cham, Germany: Springer International Publishing.

Chetty, Raj, John N. Friedman, Nathaniel Hendren, and Michael Stepner. 2020. "The Economic Impacts of COVID-19: Evidence from a New Public Database Built Using Private Sector Data." Working paper 27431, June, National Bureau of Economic Research. https://www.nber.org/papers/w27431.

Chetty, Raj, David Grusky, Maximilian Hell, Nathaniel Hendren, Robert Manduca, and Jimmy Narang. 2017. "The Fading American Dream: Trends in Absolute Income Mobility since 1940." *Science* 356, no. 6336: 398–406.

Chetty, Raj, Nathaniel Hendren, and Lawrence F. Katz. 2016. "The Effects of Exposure to Better Neighborhoods on Children: New Evidence from the Moving to Opportunity Experiment." *American Economic Review* 106, no. 4: 855–902.

Chetty, Raj, Nathaniel Hendren, Patrick Kline, and Emmanuel Saez. 2014a. "Where Is the Land of Opportunity? The Geography of Intergenerational Mobility in the United States." *Quarterly Journal of Economics* 129, no. 4: 1553–623.

Chetty, Raj, Nathaniel Hendren, Patrick Kline, Emmanuel Saez, and Nicholas Turner. 2014b. "Is the United States Still a Land of Opportunity? Recent Trends in Intergenerational Mobility." *American Economic Review* 104, no. 5: 141–47.

Choi, Jung Hyun, and Laurie Goodman. 2020. "22 Million Renters and Owners of Manufactured Homes Are Mostly Left Out of Pandemic Assistance." *Urban Wire*, August 21. https://www.urban.org/urban-wire/22-million-renters-and-owners-manufactured-homes-are-mostly-left-out-pandemic-assistance.

Choi, Jung Hyun, Alanna McCargo, Caitlin Young, Michael Neal, and Laurie Goodman. 2019. "Explaining the Black-White Homeownership Gap." Washington, DC: Urban Institute, October 10.

"Cholo Invasion and Its Bad Results." 1902. *Los Angeles Herald* XXX, no. 31(October 31): 9.

Christophers, Brett. 2020. *Rentier Capitalism: Who Owns the Economy, and Who Pays for It?* London: Verso.

Cisneros, Henry, and Lora Engdahl. 2009. *From Despair to Hope: HOPE VI and the New Promise of Public Housing in America's Cities.* Washington, DC: Brookings Institution Press.

City of Boise Energize our Neighborhoods. 2020. *North End Workshop 2 Survey All Responses—Raw Data.* Boise, ID: City of Boise. https://www.cityofboise.org/media/9880/northend_workshop2_survey_all-responses.pdf.

City of Boise Planning and Development Services. 2019. *City of Boise Neighborhood Data Almanac.* Boise, ID: City of Boise. https://www.cityofboise.org/programs/energize/neighborhood-almanac/.

Clampet-Lundquist, Susan. 2003. "Finding and Keeping Affordable Housing: Analyzing the Experiences of Single-Mother Families in North Philadelphia." *Journal of Sociology and Social Welfare* 30, no. 4: 123–40.

Clark, Anna. 2018. *The Poisoned City: Flint's Water and the American Urban Tragedy.* New York: Metropolitan.

Clark, William A. V., ed. 1982. *Modelling Housing Market Search.* London, UK: Croom Helm.

Clark, William A. V. 2013. "The Aftermath of the General Financial Crisis for the Ownership Society: What Happened to Low-Income Homeowners in the US?" *International Journal of Housing Policy* 13: 227–46.

Clark, William A. V., and Sarah A. Blue. 2004. "Race, Class, and Segregation Patterns in US Immigrant Gateway Cities." *Urban Affairs Review* 39: 667–88.

Clark, William A. V., and Regan Maas. 2015. "Interpreting Migration through the Prism of Reasons for Moves." *Population, Space and Place* 21, no. 1: 54–67.

Clear, Todd R. 2007. *Imprisoning Communities: How Mass Incarceration Makes Disadvantaged Neighborhoods Worse.* New York: Oxford University Press.

Clement, Daniel, and Miguel Kanai. 2015. "The Detroit Future City: How Pervasive Neoliberal Urbanism Exacerbates Racialized Spatial Injustice." *American Behavioral Scientist* 59, no. 3: 369–85.

Clerge, Orly. 2019. *The New Noir: Race, Identity, and Diaspora in Black Suburbia.* Oakland: University of California Press.

Clift, Theresa. 2021. "Sacramento Moves Forward with Controversial Zoning Change Designed to Address Housing Crisis." *Sacramento Bee,* January 19. https://www.sacbee.com/news/local/article248544635.html.

Clinton, Bill. 1996. "Remarks Announcing the 'One Strike and You're Out' Initiative in Public Housing." White House Office of the Press Secretary, March 28. Posted online by Gerhard Peters and John T. Woolley, American Presidency Project. https://www.presidency.ucsb.edu/documents/remarks-announcing-the-one-strike-and-youre-out-initiative-public-housing.

Cloke, Paul J., Jon May, and Sarah Johnsen. 2011. *Swept up Lives? Re-Envisioning the Homeless City.* New York: John Wiley and Sons.

Cócola-Gant, Agustín. 2016. "Holiday Rentals: The New Gentrification Battlefront." *Sociological Research Online* 21, no. 3: 1–9.

Cócola-Gant, Agustín, and Ana Gago. 2019. "Airbnb, Buy-to-Let Investment and Tourism-Driven Displacement: A Case Study in Lisbon." *Environment and Planning A: Economy and Space* 53, no. 7: 1671–88. https://doi.org/10.1177/0308518X19869012.

Cohen, Philip N., and Lynne M. Casper. 2002. "In Whose Home? Multigenerational Families in the United States, 1998–2000." *Sociological Perspectives* 45, no. 1: 1–20.

Colburn, Gregg, and Clayton Page Aldern. 2022. *Homelessness Is a Housing Problem: How Structural Factors Explain U.S. Patterns.* Los Angeles: University of California Press.

Coleman, J. S. 1986. "Social Theory, Social Research, and a Theory of Action." *American Journal of Sociology* 91, no. 6: 1309–35.

Collyer, Sophie, Katherine Friedman, and Christopher Wimer. 2021. "Comparing Methods for Measuring the Prevalence of Evictions and Forced Moves on the Poverty Tracker and the American Housing Survey: What Can Be Learned?" *Cityscape* 23, no. 2: 269–77.

Collyer, Sophie, Christopher Wimer, Megan Curran, Katherine Friedman, Robert Paul Hartley, David Harris, and Andrew Hinton. 2020. *Housing Vouchers and Tax Credits.* Vol. 4, no. 9. New York: Center on Poverty and Social Policy at Columbia University.

Conley, Dalton. 1999. *Being Black, Living in the Red: Race, Wealth, and Social Policy in America.* Berkeley: University of California Press.

Connell, John. 1999. "Beyond Manila: Walls, Malls, and Private Spaces." *Environment and Planning A* 31, no. 3: 417–39.

Connolly, N. D. B. 2014. *A World More Concrete: Real Estate and the Remaking of Jim Crow South Florida.* Chicago: University of Chicago Press.

Consumer Financial Protection Bureau (CFPB). 2014. *Manufactured-Housing Consumer Finance in the United States.* Washington, DC: Consumer Financial Protection Bureau, September 30. https://www.consumerfinance.gov/data-research/research -reports/manufactured-housing-consumer-finance-in-the-u-s/.

Consumers Union. 2001. *Manufactured Homeowners Who Rent Lots Lack Security of Basic Tenants Rights.* Austin, TX: Consumers Union, February. https://inspectapedia.com /Manufactured_Homes/Manufactured-Home-Tenants-Rights.pdf.

Cooke, Sophie. 2012. "Half of Native Hawaiians Awarded Homesteads under Lingle Lack Homes." *Honolulu Civil Beat,* May 19.

Cooper, George, and Gavan Daws. 1990. *Land and Power in Hawaii: The Democratic Years.* Honolulu: University of Hawai'i Press.

Cooper-McCann, Patrick, Meagan Elliott, Eric Seymour, Matthew Weber, and Margaret Dewar. 2017. "Learning from Detroit: How Research on a Declining City Enriches Urban Studies." In *Reinventing Detroit,* edited by Michael Peter Smith and L. Owen Kirkpatrick, 37–56. New York: Routledge.

Corey, Kristen, Jennifer Biess, Nancy Pindus, and Doray Sitko. 2017. *Housing Needs of Native Hawaiians: A Report from the Assessment of American Indian, Alaska Native, and Native Hawaiian Housing Needs.* Washington, DC: Department of Housing and Urban Development, Office of Policy Development and Research.

Cornelissen, Sharon. 2022. "Remember This Is Brightmoor:' Historical Violence, Neighborhood Experiences, and the Hysteresis of Street Life." *Urban Affairs Review* 58, no. 3: 832–60.

Cornelissen, Sharon. Forthcoming. *Cutting the Tall Grass: Hardship and Privilege in the Depopulated City.* Chicago: University of Chicago Press.

Cornelius, Wayne. 1976. "The Impact of Cityward Migration on Urban Land and Housing Markets." In *The City in Comparative Perspectives: Cross-National Research and New Directions in Theory*, edited by John Walton and Louis Masotti, 249–70. New York: Sage Publications.

Corntassel, Jeff. 2008. "Toward Sustainable Self-Determination: Rethinking the Contemporary Indigenous-Rights Discourse." *Alternatives* 33, no. 1:105–32.

Corporation for Enterprise Development (CFED). 2010. *Promoting Resident Ownership of Communities*. Washington, DC: CFED.

Cotera, María Eugenia, and María Josefina Saldaña-Portillo. 2015. "Indigenous but not Indian? Chicana/os and the Politics of Indigeneity." In *The World of Indigenous North America*, edited by Robert Warrior, 549–68. New York: Routledge.

Coulson, N. Edward. 1999. "Why Are Hispanic- and Asian-American Homeownership Rates So Low? Immigration and Other Factors." *Journal of Urban Economics* 45, no. 2: 209–27.

Coulter, Rory, Maarten van Ham, and Allan M. Findlay. 2016. "Re-thinking Residential Mobility: Linking Lives through Time and Space." *Progress in Human Geography* 40, no. 3: 352–74.

COVID Tracking Project. 2021. "Racial Data Dashboard." Retrieved January 27, 2021. https://covidtracking.com/race/dashboard.

Covington, Kenya, Lance Freeman, and Michael A. Stoll. 2011. *The Suburbanization of Housing Choice Voucher Recipients*. Washington, DC: Brookings.

Crabtree, Charles, S. Michael Gaddis, John B. Holbein, and Edvard N. Larsen. 2021. "Changes in the Amount and Type of Social Science Research on Discrimination: 1950 to 2015." Working paper 3977169, December 1, Social Science Research Network. https://dx.doi.org/10.2139/ssrn.3977169.

Crabtree, Charles, S. Michael Gaddis, John B. Holbein, and Edvard N. Larsen. 2022. "Racially Distinctive Names Signal Both Race/Ethnicity and Social Class." *Sociological Science* 9: 454–72.

Cramer, Renee Ann. 2006. "The Common Sense of Anti-Indian Racism: Reactions to Mashantucket Pequot Success in Gaming and Acknowledgment." *Law and Social Inquiry* 31, no. 2: 313–41.

Crane, Maureen, and Anthony Warnes. 2000. "Evictions and Prolonged Homelessness." *Housing Studies* 15: 757–73.

Crenshaw, K. W. 2017. *On Intersectionality: Essential Writings*. New York: New Press.

Cross, Christina. 2018. "Extended Family Households among Children in the United States: Differences by Race/Ethnicity and Socio-Economic Status." *Population Studies* 72, no. 2: 235–51.

Crowder, Kyle, Scott South, and Erick Chavez. 2006. "Wealth, Race, and Inter-Neighborhood Migration." *American Sociological Review* 71, no. 1: 72–94.

Crowell, Amber R., and Janine Nkosi. 2020. "Evicted in the Central Valley: The Avoidable Crisis and Systemic Injustice of Housing Displacement." *Boom California*, November 29. https://boomcalifornia.org/2020/11/29/evicted-in-the-central -valley-the-avoidable-crisis-and-systemic-injustice-of-housing-displacement/.

Crowley, Martha, Daniel T. Lichter, and Zhenchao Qian. 2006. "Beyond Gateway Cities: Economic Restructuring and Poverty among Mexican Immigrant Families and Children." *Family Relations* 55, no. 3: 345–60.

Crump, Jeff. 2002. "Deconcentration by Demolition: Public Housing, Poverty, and Urban Policy." *Environment and Planning D* 20, no. 5: 581–96.

Cuba, Lee, and David M. Hummon. 1993. "A Place to Call Home: Identification with Dwelling, Community, and Region." *Sociological Quarterly* 34, no. 1: 111–31.

Cui, Ruomeng, Jun Li, and Dennis J. Zhang. 2020. "Reducing Discrimination with Reviews in the Sharing Economy: Evidence from Field Experiments on Airbnb." *Management Science* 66, no. 3: 1071–94.

Culhane, Dennis. 2008. "The Cost of Homelessness: A Perspective from the United States." *European Journal of Homelessness* 2 (January): 97–114.

Cunningham, Mary K., Martha Galvez, Claudia L. Aranda, Robert Santos, Doug Wissoker, Alyse Oneto, Rob Pitingolo, and James Crawford. 2018. "A Pilot Study of Landlord Acceptance of Housing Choice Vouchers." Washington, DC: US Department of Housing and Urban Development. https://www.huduser.gov /portal/pilot-study-landlord-acceptance-hcv.html.

Curtis, Marah, Sarah Garlington, and Lisa Schottenfeld. 2013. "Alcohol, Drug, and Criminal History Restrictions in Public Housing." *Cityscape* 15, no. 3: 37–52.

Damiano, Anthony, and Chris Frenier. 2020. "Build Baby Build? Housing Submarkets and the Effects of New Construction on Existing Rents." Working paper, University of Minnesota Center for Urban and Regional Affairs, October 16. https://www .tonydamiano.com/project/new-con/bbb-wp.pdf.

Daniel, William Wentworth. 1968. *Racial Discrimination in England: Based on the PEP Report.* New York: Penguin.

Dantzler, Prentiss. 2021. "The Urban Process under Racial Capitalism: Race, Anti-Blackness, and Capital Accumulation." *Journal of Race, Ethnicity and the City* 2, no. 2: 113–34.

Dantzler, Prentiss, Elizabeth Korver-Glenn, and Junia Howell. 2022. "Introduction: What Does Racial Capitalism Have to Do with Cities and Communities?" *City and Community* 21, no. 3: 163–72.

Darrah, Jennifer, and Stefanie DeLuca. 2014. "'Living Here has Changed My Whole Perspective': How Escaping Inner-City Poverty Shapes Neighborhoods and Housing Choice." *Journal of Policy Analysis and Management* 33: 350–84.

Darrah-Okike, Jennifer. 2019a. "'The Decision You Make Today Will Affect Many Generations to Come': Environmental Assessment Law and Indigenous Resistance to Urbanization." *Environment and Planning E: Nature and Space* 2, no. 4: 807–30. https://doi.org/10.1177/2514848619861043.

Darrah-Okike, Jennifer. 2019b. "Disrupting the Growth Machine: Evidence from Hawai'i." *Urban Affairs Review* 55, no. 2: 428–61.

Darrah-Okike, Jennifer, Sarah Soakai, Susan Nakaoka, Tai Dunson-Strane, and Karen Umemoto. 2018. "'It Was Like I Lost Everything': The Harmful Impacts of Homeless-Targeted Policies." *Housing Policy Debate* 28, no. 4: 635–51.

Davis, Kingsley, and Hilda Hertz Golden. 1954. "Urbanization and the Development of Pre-Industrial Areas." *Economic Development and Cultural Change* 3, no. 1: 6–26.

Davis, Mike. 1990. *City of Quartz: Excavating the Future in Los Angeles.* London: Verso.

Dawkins, Casey J. 2006. "Are Social Networks the Ties That Bind Families to Neighborhoods?" *Housing Studies* 21, no. 6: 867–81.

Dawkins, Casey J., and Theodore Koebel. 2010. "Overcoming Barriers to Placing Manufactured Housing in Metropolitan Communities." *Journal of the American Planning Association* 76, no. 1: 73–88.

De la Roca, Jorge, Ingrid Gould Ellen, and Katherine M. O'Regan. 2014. "Race and Neighborhoods in the 21st Century: What Does Segregation Mean Today?" *Regional Science and Urban Economics* 47, no. 1: 138–51.

De Souza, Stefanie Israel. 2019. "Pacification of Rio's Favelas and the 'Pacification of the Pacification Police': The Role of Coordinating Brokerage in Police Reform." *Sociological Forum* 34, no. 2: 458–82.

Dear, Michael. 1992. "Understanding and Overcoming NIMBY Syndrome." *Journal of the American Planning Association* 58, no. 3: 288–300.

Dear, Michael J., and Jennifer R. Wolch. 1987. *Landscapes of Despair: From Deinstitutionalization to Homelessness*. Princeton, NJ: Princeton University Press.

Deitz, Shiloh, and Katie Meehan. 2019. "Plumbing Poverty: Mapping Hot Spots of Racial and Geographic Inequality in U.S. Household Water Insecurity." *Annals of the American Association for Geographers* 109, no. 4: 1092–109.

DeLeire, Thomas, and Ariel Kalil. 2002. "Good Things Come in Threes: Single-Parent Multigenerational Family Structure and Adolescent Adjustment." *Demography* 39, no. 2: 93–413.

Delgado, Jeanne. 2005. "Security Survey Shows Current Premise-Protection Practices of M-H Owners." *Multi-Housing News* 40, no. 6: 9.

Delgado, Richard, and Jean Stefancic, eds. 2013. *Critical Race Theory: The Cutting Edge*. Philadelphia, PA: Temple University Press.

DeLuca, Stefanie, Philip M. E. Garboden, and Peter Rosenblatt. 2013. "Segregating Shelter: How Housing Policies Shape the Residential Locations of Low-Income Minority Families." *Annals of the American Academy of Political and Social Science* 647, no. 1: 268–99.

DeLuca, Stefanie, and Eva Rosen. 2022. "Housing Insecurity among the Poor Today." *Annual Review of Sociology* 48: 343–71.

DeLuca, Stefanie, Holly Wood, and Peter Rosenblatt. 2019. "Why Poor Families Move (and Where They Go): Reactive Mobility and Residential Decisions." *City and Community* 18, no. 2: 556–93.

Demsas, Jerusalem. 2021a. "How to Convince a NIMBY to Build More Housing." *Vox*, February 24. https://www.vox.com/22297328/affordable-housing-nimby-housing-prices-rising-poll-data-for-progress.

Demsas, Jerusalem. 2021b. "Covid-19 Caused a Recession. So Why Did the Housing Market Boom?" *Vox*, February 5. https://www.vox.com/22264268/covid-19-housing-insecurity-housing-prices-mortgage-rates-pandemic-zoning-supply-demand.

Derby, Elena. 2020. "Does Growing Up in Tax-Subsidized Housing Lead to Higher Earnings and Educational Attainment?" Working paper 3491787, December 10, Social Science Research Network. https://ssrn.com/abstract=3491787.

Derenoncourt, Ellora. 2022. "Can You Move to Opportunity? Evidence from the Great Migration." *American Economic Review* 112, no. 2: 369–408.

Desai, Mihir, Dhammika Dharmapala, and Monica Singhal. 2010. "Tax Incentives for Affordable Housing: The Low Income Housing Tax Credit." In *Tax Policy and the Economy*, vol. 24, edited by Jeffrey R. Brown, 181- 205. Chicago: University of Chicago Press.

DeSilva, Sanjaya, and Yuval Elmelech. 2012. "Housing Inequality in the United States: Explaining the White-Minority Disparities in Homeownership." *Housing Studies* 27, no. 1: 1–26.

Desilver, Drew, and Kristen Bialik. 2017. "Blacks and Hispanics Face Extra Challenges in Getting Home Loans." Pew Research Center Fact Tank, January 10. https://www.pewresearch.org/fact-tank/2017/01/10/blacks-and-hispanics-face-extra-challenges-in-getting-home-loans.

Desjarlais, Robert R. 1997. *Shelter Blues: Sanity and Selfhood among the Homeless.* Philadelphia: University of Pennsylvania Press.

Desmond, Matthew. 2012. "Eviction and the Reproduction of Urban Poverty." *American Journal of Sociology* 118, no. 1: 88–133.

Desmond, Matthew. 2016. *Evicted: Poverty and Profit in the American City.* New York: Crown.

Desmond, Matthew. 2017. "How Homeownership Became the Engine of American Inequality." *New York Times Magazine*, May 9.

Desmond, Matthew. 2018. "Heavy Is the House: Rent Burden among the American Urban Poor." *International Journal of Urban and Regional Research* 42, no. 1:160–70.

Desmond, Matthew, Weihua An, Richelle Winkler, and Thomas Ferriss. 2013. "Evicting Children." *Social Forces* 92, no. 1: 303–27.

Desmond, Matthew, and Monica Bell. 2015. "Housing, Poverty, and the Law." *Annual Review of Law and Social Science* 11: 15–35

Desmond, Matthew, and Carl Gershenson. 2016. "Housing and Employment Insecurity among the Working Poor." *Social Problems* 63, no. 1: 46–67.

Desmond, Matthew, and Carl Gershenson. 2017. "Who Gets Evicted? Assessing Individual, Neighborhood, and Network Factors." *Social Science Research* 62: 362–77.

Desmond, Matthew, Carl Gershenson, and Barbara Kiviat. 2015. "Forced Relocation and Residential Instability among Urban Renters." *Social Service Review* 89, no. 2: 227–62.

Desmond, Matthew, Ashley Gromis, Lavar Edmonds, James Hendrickson, Katie Krywokulski, Lillian Leung, and Adam Porton. 2018. Eviction Lab National Database. Princeton, NJ: Princeton University. https://www.evictionlab.org.

Desmond, Matthew, and Rachel Tolbert Kimbro. 2015. "Eviction's Fallout: Housing, Hardship, and Health." *Social Forces* 94, no. 1: 295–324.

Desmond, Matthew, and Kristin L. Perkins. 2016a. "Housing and Household Instability." *Urban Affairs Review* 52, no. 3: 421–36.

Desmond, Matthew, and Kristin L. Perkins. 2016b. "Are Landlords Overcharging Housing Voucher Holders?" *City and Community* 15: 137–62.

Desmond, Matthew, and Tracey Shollenberger. 2015. "Forced Displacement from Rental Housing: Prevalence and Neighborhood Consequences." *Demography* 52, no. 5: 1751–72.

Desmond, Matthew, and Nicol Valdez. 2013. "Unpolicing the Urban Poor: Consequences of Third-Party Policing for Inner-City Women." *American Sociological Review* 78, no. 1: 117–41.

Desmond, Matthew, and Nathan Wilmers. 2019. "Do the Poor Pay More for Housing? Exploitation, Profit, and Risk in Rental Markets." *American Journal of Sociology* 124, no. 4: 1090–124.

Detroit Blight Removal Task Force. 2014. *Every Neighborhood Has a Future . . . And It Doesn't Include Blight.* Detroit, MI: Detroit Blight Removal Task Force, May. https://www.documentcloud.org/documents/1173946-detroit-blight-removal-task-force-plan-may-2014.

Devlin, Ryan Thomas. 2019. "A Focus on Needs: Toward a More Nuanced Understanding of Inequality and Urban Informality in the Global North." *Journal of Cultural Geography* 36, no. 2: 121–43.

Dewar, Margaret, Eric Seymour, and Oana Druță. 2015. "Disinvesting in the City: The Role of Tax Foreclosure in Detroit." *Urban Affairs Review* 51, no. 5: 587–615.

Dewar, Margaret, and June Manning Thomas. 2012. *The City after Abandonment.* Philadelphia, PA: University of Pennsylvania Press.

Diamond, Rebecca, and Tim McQuade. 2019. "Who Wants Affordable Housing in Their Backyard? An Equilibrium Analysis of Low-Income Property Development." *Journal of Political Economy* 127, no. 3: 1063–117.

Diaz, David, and Rodolfo Torres. 2012. *Latino Urbanism: The Politics of Planning, Policy, and Redevelopment.* Edited by David R. Diaz and Rodolfo D. Torres. New York: NYU Press.

Diaz, David R., and Rodolfo D. Torres. 2012. *Latino Urbanism: The Politics of Planning, Policy, and Redevelopment.* New York: NYU Press.

Dillon, Liam, Ben Poston, and Julia Barajas. 2020. "Black and Latino Renters Face Eviction, Exclusion amid Police Crackdowns in California." *Los Angeles Times,* November 19.

DiMaggio, Paul, and Hugh Louch. 1998. "Socially Embedded Consumer Transactions: For What Kinds of Purchases Do People Most Often Use Networks?" *American Sociological Review* 63, no. 5: 619–37.

DiNatale, Sadie, Rebecca Lewis, and Robert Parker. 2018. "Short-Term Rentals in Small Cities in Oregon: Impacts and Regulations." *Land Use Policy* 79 (December): 407–23.

Ding, Lei, Jackelyn Hwang, and Eileen Divringi. 2016. "Gentrification and Residential Mobility in Philadelphia." *Regional Science and Urban Economics* 61 (July): 38–51.

Diwakar, Pranathi. 2019. "A Recipe for Disaster: Framing Risk and Vulnerability in Slum Relocation Policies in Chennai, India." *City and Community* 18, no. 4: 1314–37.

Doleac, Jennifer L., and Benjamin Hansen. 2020. "The Unintended Consequences of 'Ban the Box': Statistical Discrimination and Employment Outcomes When Criminal Histories Are Hidden." *Journal of Labor Economics* 38, no. 2: 321–74.

Doling, John, and Nick Horsewood. 2011. "Home Ownership and Pensions: Causality and the Really Big Trade-Off." *Housing, Theory and Society* 28, no. 2: 166–82.

Donato, Rubén, and Jarrod Hanson. 2012. "Legally White, Socially 'Mexican': The Politics of De Jure and De Facto School Segregation in the American Southwest." *Harvard Educational Review* 82, no. 2: 202–25.

Douds, Kiara Wyndham. 2021. "The Diversity Contract: Constructing Racial Harmony in a Diverse American Suburb." *American Journal of Sociology* 126, no. 6: 1347–88.

Dougherty, Conor. 2017. "The Great American Single-Family Home Problem." *New York Times,* December 1. https://www.nytimes.com/2017/12/01/business/economy /single-family-home.html.

Dougherty, Conor. 2020. *Golden Gates: Fighting for Housing in America.* New York: Penguin.

Douglas, Gordon C. C. 2018. *The Help-Yourself City: Legitimacy and Inequality in DIY Urbanism.* New York: Oxford University Press.

Du Bois, William Edward Burghardt. 1899. *The Philadelphia Negro: A Social Study.* Philadelphia: University of Pennsylvania.

Du Bois, William Edward Burghardt. 1903. *The Souls of Black Folk.* Chicago: A. C. McClurg and Co.

Du Bois, William Edward Burghardt. 1935. *Black Reconstruction in America, 1860–1880.* New York: Atheneum.

Duke, Joanna. 2010. "Exploring Homeowner Opposition to Public Housing Developments." *Journal of Sociology and Social Welfare* 37, no. 1: 49–74.

Dum, Christopher P. 2016. *Exiled in America: Life on the Margins in a Residential Motel.* New York: Columbia University Press.

Duneier, Mitchell. 1999. *Sidewalk.* New York: Farrar, Straus and Giroux.

Dunifon, Rachel, Kathleen Ziol-Guest, and Kimberly Kopko. 2014. "Grandparent Coresidence and Family Well-Being: Implications for Research and Policy." *Annals of the American Academy of Political and Social Science* 654, no. 1: 110–26.

Durst, Noah J. 2015. "Second-Generation Policy Priorities for Colonias and Informal Settlements in Texas." *Housing Policy Debate* 25, no. 2: 395–417.

Durst, Noah J. 2018. "Informal and Ubiquitous: Colonias, Premature Subdivisions and Other Unplanned Suburbs on America's Urban Fringe." *Urban Studies* 56, no. 4: 722–40.

Durst, Noah J., and Esther Sullivan. 2019. "The Contribution of Manufactured Housing to Affordable Housing in the United States: Assessing Variation among Manufactured Housing Tenures and Community Types." *Housing Policy Debate* 29, no. 6: 880–98.

Durst, Noah J., Esther Sullivan, Huiqing Huang, and Hogeun Park. 2021. "Building Footprint-Derived Landscape Metrics for the Identification of Informal Subdivisions and Manufactured Home Communities: A Pilot Application in Hidalgo County, Texas." *Land Use Policy* 101: 1–16.

Durst, Noah J., and Peter M. Ward. 2015. "Colonia Housing Conditions in Model Subdivisions: A Déjà Vu for Policy Makers." *Housing Policy Debate* 26, no. 2: 316–33.

Durst, Noah J., and Jake Wegmann. 2017. "Informal Housing in the United States." *International Journal of Urban and Regional Research* 41, no. 2: 282–97.

Dwyer, Rachel. 2007. "Expanding Homes and Increasing Inequalities: U.S. Housing Development and the Residential Segregation of the Affluent." *Social Problems* 54, no. 1: 23–46.

Dye, Richard F., Daniel P. McMillen, and David F. Merriman. 2006. "Illinois's Response to Rising Residential Property Values: An Assessment Growth Cap in Cook County." *National Tax Journal* 59, no. 3: 707–16.

Dymski, G. 2001. "Racial Inequality and Capitalist Exploitation." In *Philosophy and the Problems of Work: A Reader*, edited by Kory Schaff, 165–74. Lanham, MD: Rowman and Littlefield.

Eagan-Smith, Courtney. 2008. "A House with No Walls: The Federal Government's Role in Indian Housing." *Tulsa Law Review* 44, no. 2: 447–65.

Easley, Janeria. 2017. "Spatial Mismatch beyond Black and White: Levels and Determinants of Job Access among Asian and Hispanic Subpopulations." *Urban Studies* 55, no. 8: 1800–20.

Edelman, Benjamin, Michael Luca, and Dan Svirsky. 2017. "Racial Discrimination in the Sharing Economy: Evidence from a Field Experiment." *American Economic Journal: Applied Economics* 9, no. 2: 1–22.

Edin, Kathryn, and Laura Lein. 1997. "Work, Welfare, and Single Mothers' Economic Survival Strategies." *American Sociological Review* 62, no. 2: 253–66.

Edin, Kathryn, and H. Luke Shaefer. 2015. *$2.00 a Day: Living on Almost Nothing in America.* Boston, MA: Houghton Mifflin Harcourt.

Einstein, Katherine Levine, David M. Glick, and Maxwell Palmer. 2019. *Neighborhood Defenders: Participatory Politics and America's Housing Crisis.* Cambridge: Cambridge University Press.

Ellen, Ingrid Gould, and Katherine M. O'Regan. 2011. "How Low Income Neighborhoods Change: Entry, Exit, and Enhancement." *Regional Science and Urban Economics* 41, no. 2: 89–97.

Ellen, Ingrid Gould, Katherine O'Regan, Sophia House, and Ryan Brenner. 2021. "Do Lawyers Matter? Early Evidence on Eviction Patterns After Rollout of Universal Access to Counsel in New York City." *Housing Policy Debate* 31, no. 3–5: 540–61.

Ellen, Ingrid Gould, Michael Suher, and Gerard Torrats-Espinosa. 2019. "Neighbors and Networks: The Role of Social Interactions on the Residential Choices of Housing Choice Voucher Holders." *Journal of Housing Economics* 43: 56–71.

Ellen, Ingrid Gould, and Gerard Torrats-Espinosa. 2019. "Gentrification and Fair Housing: Does Gentrification Further Integration?" *Housing Policy Debate* 29, no. 5: 835–51.

Ellen, Ingrid Gould, and Margery Austin Turner. 1997. "Does Neighborhood Matter? Assessing Recent Evidence." *Housing Policy Debate* 8, no. 4: 833–66.

Engels, Friedrich. 1872. *The Housing Question*. New York: International Publishers

Engels, Friedrich. 1887. *The Condition of the Working-Class in England: From Personal Observation and Authentic Sources*. London: Panther Books.

Engels, Friedrich. 1935. *The Housing Question*. New York: International Publishers.

Engler, Russell. 2009. "Connecting Self-Representation to Civil Gideon: What Existing Data Reveal About When Counsel Is Most Needed." *Fordham Urban Law Journal* 37, no. 1: 37–92.

Entwisle, Doris R., and Karl L. Alexander. 1996. "Family Type and Children's Growth in Reading and Math over the Primary Grades." *Journal of Marriage and the Family* 58, no. 2: 341–55.

Eriksen, Michael D., and Amanda Ross. 2013. "The Impact of Housing Vouchers on Mobility and Neighborhood Attributes." *Real Estate Economics* 41, no. 2: 255–77.

Eriksson, Katherine, and Zachary Ward. 2019. "The Residential Segregation of Immigrants in the United States from 1850 to 1940." *Journal of Economic History* 79, no. 4: 989–1026.

Esposito, Emiliano, and Francesco Chiodelli. 2021. "Beyond Proper Political Squatting: Exploring Individualistic Need-Based Occupations in a Public Housing Neighbourhood in Naples." *Housing Studies*. https://www.tandfonline.com/doi/full/10.1080/02673037.2021.1946017.

Estes, Nick. 2019. *Our History Is the Future: Standing Rock versus the Dakota Access Pipeline, and the Long Tradition of Indigenous Resistance*. Brooklyn, NY: Verso.

Evans, Douglas N. 2016. "The Effect of Criminal Convictions on Real Estate Agent Decisions in New York City." *Journal of Crime and Justice* 39, no. 3: 363–79.

Evans, Douglas N., Kwan-Lamar Blount-Hill, and Michelle A. Cubellis. 2019. "Examining Housing Discrimination across Race, Gender and Felony History." *Housing Studies* 34, no. 5: 761–78.

Evans, Douglas N., and Jeremy R. Porter. 2015. "Criminal History and Landlord Rental Decisions: A New York Quasi-Experimental Study." *Journal of Experimental Criminology* 11, no. 1: 21–42.

Ewens, Michael, Bryan Tomlin, and Liang Choon Wang. 2014. "Statistical Discrimination or Prejudice? A Large Sample Field Experiment." *Review of Economics and Statistics* 96, no. 1: 119–34.

Ewing, Eve L. 2018. *Ghosts in the Schoolyard: Racism and School Closings on Chicago's South Side*. Chicago: University of Chicago Press.

Ewing, Reid, and Robert Cervero. 2017. " 'Does Compact Development Make People Drive Less?' The Answer Is Yes." *Journal of the American Planning Association* 83, no. 1: 19–25.

Faber, Jacob W. 2019. "Segregation and the Cost of Money: Race, Poverty, and the Prevalence of Alternative Financial Institutions." *Social Forces* 98, no. 2: 819–48.

Faber, Jacob W. 2020a. "We Built This: Consequences of New Deal Era Intervention in America's Racial Geography." *American Sociological Review* 85, no. 5: 739–75.

Faber, Jacob W. 2020b. "Contemporary Echoes of Segregationist Policy: Spatial Marking and the Persistence of Inequality." *Urban Studies* 58, no. 5: 1067–86.

Faber, Jacob W., and Marie-Dumesle Mercier. 2022. "Multidimensional Discrimination in the Online Rental Housing Market: Implications for Families with Young Children." *Housing Policy Debate.* https://doi.org/10.1080/10511482.2021.2010118.

Faber, Jacob W., and Peter M. Rich. 2018. "Financially Over-Extended: College Attendance as a Contributor to Foreclosures during the Great Recession." *Demography* 55: 1727–48

Faber, Jacob William. 2013. "Racial Dynamics of Subprime Mortgage Lending at the Peak." *Housing Policy Debate* 23, no. 2: 328–49.

Faber, Jacob William. 2018a. "Cashing in on Distress: The Expansion of Fringe Financial Institutions During the Great Recession." *Urban Affairs Review* 54, no. 4: 663–96.

Faber, Jacob William. 2018b. "Segregation and the Geography of Creditworthiness: Racial Inequality in a Recovered Mortgage Market." *Housing Policy Debate* 28, no. 2: 215–47.

Faber, Jacob William, and Ingrid Gould Ellen. 2016. "Race and the Housing Cycle: Differences in Home Equity Trends among Long-Term Homeowners." *Housing Policy Debate* 26, no. 3: 456–73. https://doi.org/10.1080/10511482.2015.1128959.

Faber, Jacob William, and Terri Friedline. 2020. "The Racialized Costs of 'Traditional' Banking in Segregated America: Evidence from Entry-Level Checking Accounts." *Race and Social Problems* 12, no.4: 344–61.

Faber, Jacob William, and Marie-Dumesle Mercier. 2018. "Multidimensional Discrimination in the Online Rental Housing Market: Implications for Families with Young Children." Paper presented at APPAM: Association for Public Policy Analysis and Management annual conference, Washington, DC, November 9. https://appam.confex.com/appam/2018/webprogram/Paper27008.html.

Fahlberg, Anjuli N. 2018. " 'It Was Totally Different Than What We Had Before': Perceptions of Urban Militarism under Rio de Janeiro's Pacifying Policing Units." *Qualitative Sociology* 41, no. 4: 303–24.

Fairbanks, Robert P., II. 2009. *How It Works: Recovering Citizens in Post-Welfare Philadelphia.* Chicago: University of Chicago Press.

Fang, Albert H., Andrew M. Guess, and Macartan Humphreys. 2019. "Can the Government Deter Discrimination? Evidence from a Randomized Intervention in New York City." *Journal of Politics* 81, no. 1: 127–41.

Fannie Mae. 2019. *Duty to Serve Underserved Markets Plan for the Manufactured Housing Market.* Washington, DC: Fannie Mae, December 20. https://www.fanniemae.com/media/33491/display.

Farley, Reynolds, and William H. Frey. 1994. "Changes in the Segregation of Whites from Blacks during the 1980s: Small Steps Toward a More Integrated Society." *American Sociological Review* 59, no. 1: 23–45.

Farley, Reynolds, Charlotte Steeh, Maria Krysan, Tara Jackson, and Keith Reeves. 1994. "Stereotypes and Segregation: Neighborhoods in the Detroit Area." *American Journal of Sociology* 100, no. 3: 750–80.

Federal Housing Administration. 1940. *Principles of Planning for Small Houses: Technical Bulletin No. 4.* Washington, DC: Federal Housing Administration.

Fedorowicz, Martha, Joe Schilling, and Emily Bramhall. 2020. *Leveraging the Built Environment for Health Equity. Promising Interventions for Small- and Medium-Size Cities.* Washington, DC: Urban Institute, July 14. https://www.urban.org/research /publication/leveraging-built-environment-health-equity.

Feige, Edgar L. 1990. "Defining and Estimating the Underground and Informal Economies: The New Institutional Economics Approach." *World Development* 18, no. 7: 989–1002.

Fenelon, James V. 2014. *Culturicide, Resistance, and Survival of the Lakota (Sioux Nation).* New York: Routledge.

Fenelon, James V. 2016. "Critique of Glenn on Settler Colonialism and Bonilla-Silva on Critical Race Analysis from Indigenous Perspectives." *Sociology of Race and Ethnicity* 2, no. 2: 237–42.

Fennelly, Katherine. 2008. "Prejudice Toward Immigrants in the Midwest." In *New Faces in New Places: The Changing Geography of American Immigration*, edited by D. S. Massey, 206–43. New York: Russell Sage Press.

Fernald, Maria, ed. 2020. *The State of the Nation's Housing: 2020.* Cambridge, MA: Harvard Joint Center for Housing Studies. https://www.jchs.harvard.edu/sites /default/files/reports/files/Harvard_JCHS_The_State_of_the_Nations_Hous ing_2020_Report_Revised_120720.pdf.

Ferreira, Fernando. 2010. "You Can Take It with You: Proposition 13 Tax Benefits, Residential Mobility, and Willingness to Pay for Housing Amenities." *Journal of Public Economics* 94: 661–73.

Ferrer, Alexander. 2021. *Beyond Wall Street Landlords: How Private Equity in the Rental Market Makes Housing Unaffordable, Unstable, and Unhealthy.* Los Angeles: Strategic Actions for a Justice Economy.

Fields, Desiree. 2018. "Constructing a New Asset Class: Property-Led Financial Accumulation after the Crisis." *Economic Geography* 94, no. 2: 118–40.

Fischel, William A. 2001. *The Homevoter Hypothesis.* Cambridge, MA: Harvard University Press.

Fischel, William A. 2004. "An Economic History of Zoning and a Cure for its Exclusionary Effects." *Urban Studies* 41, no. 2: 317–40.

Fischel, William A. 2008. "Political Structure and Exclusionary Zoning: Are Small Suburbs the Big Problem?" In *Fiscal Decentralization and Land Policies*, edited by Gregory K. Ingram and Yu-Hung Hong, 111–36. Cambridge, MA: Lincoln Institute of Land Policy.

Fischer, Claude, Michael Hout, Martín Sánchez-Jankowski, Samuel R. Lucas, Ann Swidler, and Kim Voss. 1996. *Inequality by Design: Cracking the Bell Curve Myth.* Princeton, NJ: Princeton University Press.

Fischer, Mary J. 2008. "Shifting Geographies: Examining the Role of Suburbanization in Black's Declining Segregation." *Urban Affairs Review* 43: 475–96.

Fischer, Mary J., and Marta Tienda. 2006. "Redrawing Spatial Color Lines: Hispanic Metropolitan Dispersal, Segregation, and Economic Opportunity." In *Hispanics and the Future of America*, edited by M. Tienda and F. Mitchell. Washington, DC: National Academies Press.

Fischer, Will. 2015. *Research Shows Housing Vouchers Reduce Hardship and Provide Platform for Long-Term Gains among Children*. Washington, DC: Center on Budget and Policy Priorities, updated October 7. https://www.cbpp.org/sites/default/files /atoms/files/3-10-14hous.pdf.

Fisher, Marina, Nathaniel Miller, Lindsay Walter, and Jeffrey Selbin. 2018. "California's New Vagrancy Laws: The Growing Enactment and Enforcement of Anti-Homeless Laws in the Golden State." *SSRN Electronic Journal* (January). http://dx.doi.org/10 .2139/ssrn.2558944.

Fitchen, Janet M. 1992. "On the Edge of Homelessness: Rural Poverty and Housing Insecurity." *Rural Sociology* 57, no. 2: 173–93.

Fix, Michael, and Raymond J. Struyk. 1993. *Clear and Convincing Evidence: Measurement of Discrimination in America*. Washington, DC: Urban Institute Press.

Flage, Alexandre. 2018. "Ethnic and Gender Discrimination in the Rental Housing Market: Evidence from a Meta-Analysis of Correspondence Tests, 2006–2017." *Journal of Housing Economics* 41: 251–73.

Flanagan, Barry, Edward Gregory, Elaine Hallisey, Janet Heitgerd, and Brian Lewis. 2011. "A Social Vulnerability Index for Disaster Management." *Journal of Homeland Security and Emergency Management* 8, no. 1: 1–22.

Fletcher, Matthew L. M. 2012. "Tribal Membership and Indian Nationhood." *American Indian Law Review* 37, no. 1: 1–18.

Flippen, Chenoa A. 2004. "Unequal Returns to Housing Investments? A Study of Real Housing Appreciation among Black, White, and Hispanic Households." *Social Forces* 82, no. 4: 1523–51.

Flippen, Chenoa A. 2010. "The Spatial Dynamics of Stratification: Metropolitan Context, Population Redistribution, and Black and Hispanic Homeownership." *Demography* 47, no. 4: 845–68. http://doi.org/10.1007/BF03214588.

Fogelson, Robert M. 1967. *The Fragmented Metropolis: Los Angeles, 1850–1930*. Berkeley: University of California Press.

Foley, Donald L. 1980. "The Sociology of Housing." *Annual Review of Sociology* 6: 457–78.

Fomby, Paula, and Stefanie Mollborn. 2017. "Ecological Instability and Children's Classroom Behavior in Kindergarten." *Demography* 54, no. 5: 1627–51.

Fowler, Patrick J., David B. Henry, and Katherine E. Marcal. 2015. "Family and Housing Instability: Longitudinal Impact on Adolescent Emotional and Behavioral Well-Being." *Social Science Research* 53 (September): 364–74.

Fox, Cybelle. 2012. *Three Worlds of Relief: Race, Immigration, and the American Welfare State from the Progressive Era to the New Deal*. Princeton, NJ: Princeton University Press.

Fox, Cybelle, and Thomas A Guglielmo. 2012. "Defining America's Racial Boundaries: Blacks, Mexicans, and European Immigrants, 1890–1945." *American Journal of Sociology* 118, no. 2: 327–79.

Freeman, Lance. 2003. "The Impact of Assisted Housing Developments on Concentrated Poverty." *Housing Policy Debate* 14, no. 1–2: 103–41.

Freeman, Lance, and Frank Braconi. 2004. "Gentrification and Displacement New York City in the 1990s." *Journal of the American Planning Association* 70, no. 1: 39–52.

Freeman, Lisa. 2017. "Governed through Ghost Jurisdictions: Municipal Law, Inner Suburbs and Rooming Houses." *International Journal of Urban and Regional Research* 41, no. 2: 298–317.

Freedman, Matthew, and Tamara McGavrock. 2015. "Low-Income Housing Development, Poverty Concentration, and Neighborhood Inequality." *Journal of Policy Analysis and Management* 34, no. 4: 805–34.

Frey, William H. 2020. "The Nation Is Diversifying Even Faster Than Predicted, According to New Census Data." *Brookings*, July 1. https://www.brookings.edu/research/new -census-data-shows-the-nation-is-diversifying-even-faster-than-predicted/.

Friedman, Samantha, and Emily Rosenbaum. 2007. "Does Suburban Residence Mean Better Neighborhood Conditions for All Households? Assessing the Influence of Nativity Status and Race/Ethnicity." *Social Science Research* 36: 1–27.

Friedman, Samantha, Hue-Shien Tsao, and Cheng Chen. 2013. "Housing Tenure and Residential Segregation in Metropolitan America." *Demography* 50, no. 4: 1477–98.

Freund, David. 2006. "Marketing the Free Market: State Intervention and the Politics of Prosperity in Metropolitan America." In *The New Suburban History*, edited by Kevin M. Kruse and Thomas J. Sugrue, 11–32. Chicago: University of Chicago Press.

Fry, Richard, and Paul Taylor. 2013. *Hispanic High School Graduates Pass Whites in Rate of College Enrollment*. Washington, DC: Pew Research Center, May 9. https://www .pewresearch.org/hispanic/2013/05/09/hispanic-high-school-graduates-pass-whites -in-rate-of-college-enrollment/.

Fujikane, Candace, and Jonathan Okamura. 2008. *Asian Settler Colonialism: From Local Governance to the Habits of Everyday Life in Hawai'i*. Honolulu: University of Hawai'i Press.

Fullilove, Mindy Thompson. 2016. *Root Shock: How Tearing Up City Neighborhoods Hurts America, and What We Can Do about It*. New York: New Village Press.

Furman Center. 2020. "COVID-19 Cases in New York City, a Neighborhood-Level Analysis." *Stoop* (blog), April 10. https://furmancenter.org/thestoop/entry /covid-19-cases-in-new-york-city-a-neighborhood-level-analysis.

Fusaro, Vincent A., Helen G. Levy, and H. Luke Shaefer. 2018. "Racial and Ethnic Disparities in the Lifetime Prevalence of Homelessness in the United States." *Demography* 55, no. 6: 2119–28.

Fuster, Andreas, Paul Goldsmith-Pinkham, Tarun Ramadorai, and Ansgar Walther. 2022. "Predictably Unequal? The Effects of Machine Learning on Credit Markets." *Journal of Finance* 77, no. 1: 5–47.

Gabriel, Ryan. 2016. "A Middle Ground? Residential Mobility and Attainment of Mixed-Race Couples." *Demography* 53, no. 1: 165–88.

Gaddis, S. Michael. 2017. "How Black Are Lakisha and Jamal? Racial Perceptions from Names Used in Correspondence Audit Studies." *Sociological Science* 4: 469–89.

Gaddis, S. Michael. 2018a. "An Introduction to Audit Studies in the Social Sciences." In *Audit Studies: Behind the Scenes with Theory, Method, and Nuance*, edited by S. Michael Gaddis, 3–44. Cham, Germany: Springer International Publishing.

Gaddis, S. Michael, ed. 2018b. *Audit Studies: Behind the Scenes with Theory, Method, and Nuance*. Cham, Germany: Springer International Publishing.

Gaddis, S. Michael. 2019a. "Signaling Class: An Experiment Examining Social Class Perceptions from Names Used in Correspondence Audit Studies." Working paper 3350739, March 8, Social Science Research Network. https://ssrn.com /abstract=3350739.

Gaddis, S. Michael. 2019b. "Understanding the 'How' and 'Why' Aspects of Racial-Ethnic Discrimination: A Multimethod Approach to Audit Studies." *Sociology of Race and Ethnicity* 5, no. 4: 443–55.

Gaddis, S. Michael, and Raj Ghoshal. 2015. "Arab American Housing Discrimination, Ethnic Competition, and the Contact Hypothesis." *Annals of the American Academy of Political and Social Science* 660, no. 1: 282–99.

Gaddis, S. Michael, and Raj Ghoshal. 2020. "Searching for a Roommate: A Correspondence Audit Examining Racial/Ethnic and Immigrant Discrimination among Millennials." *Socius* 6 (December). https://journals.sagepub.com/doi/full/10.1177/2378023120972287.

Gaddis, S. Michael, A. Nicole Kreisberg, and Charles Crabtree. 2021. "Assessing Immigrant Generation and Citizenship Status from Names." Working paper 3022217, August 1, Social Science Research Network. https://ssrn.com/abstract=3022217.

Galster, George. 1990a. "Racial Steering by Real Estate Agents: Mechanisms and Motives." *Review of Black Political Economy* 19, no. 1: 39–63.

Galster, George. 1990b. "Racial Discrimination in Housing Markets during the 1980s: A Review of the Audit Evidence." *Journal of Planning Education and Research* 9, no. 3: 165–75.

Galster, George. 2017. "The Geography of Opportunity 20 Years Later." *Housing Policy Debate* 27, no. 6: 941–43.

Galster, George. 2019. "Why Shrinking Cities Are Not Mirror Images of Growing Cities: A Research Agenda of Six Testable Propositions." *Urban Affairs Review* 55, no. 1: 355–72.

Galster, George, and Peter Constantine. 1991. "Discrimination Against Female-Headed Households in Rental Housing: Theory and Exploratory Evidence." *Review of Social Economy* 49, no. 1: 76–100.

Galster, George, and Erin Godfrey. 2005. "By Words and Deeds: Racial Steering by Real Estate Agents in the US in 2000." *Journal of the American Planning Association* 71, no. 3: 251–68.

Gamboa, Anna Daly. 2021. "Boise Rent Prices Continue to Increase Faster Than Anywhere Else in the US." *BoiseDev*, July 28. https://boisedev.com/news/2021/07/28/boise-rent-prices-up-39-percent-since-last-march/.

Gamio, Manuel. 1930. *Mexican Immigration to the US: A Study of Human Migration and Adjustment.* Chicago: University of Chicago Press.

Ganong, Peter, and Daniel Shoag. 2017. "Why Has Regional Income Divergence in the U.S. Declined?" *Journal of Urban Economics* 102: 76–90.

Gans, Herbert. 2017. "The Census and Right-Wing Hysteria." *New York Times*, May 11, 2017.

Gans, Herbert J. 1962. *The Urban Villagers: Group and Class in the Life of Italian-Americans.* New York: Free Press.

Gans, Herbert J. 1972. "The Positive Functions of Poverty." *American Journal of Sociology* 78, no. 2: 275–89.

Garboden, Philip M. E., and Eva Rosen. 2018. "Talking to Landlords." *Cityscape* 20: 281–91.

Garboden, Philip M. E., and Eva Rosen. 2019. "Serial Filing: How Landlords Use the Threat of Eviction." *City and Community* 18, no. 2: 638–61.

Garboden, Philip M. E., Eva Rosen, Stefanie DeLuca, and Kathryn Edin. 2018. "Taking Stock: What Drives Landlord Participation in the Housing Choice Voucher Program." *Housing Policy Debate* 28, no. 6: 979–1003.

Garcia-López, Miquel-Àngel, Jordi Jofre-Monseny, Rodrigo Martínez-Mazza, and Mariona Segú. 2020. "Do Short-Term Rental Platforms Affect Housing Markets? Evidence from Airbnb in Barcelona." *Journal of Urban Economics* 119 (September): 103278.

Garfinkel, Harold. [1967] 1999. *Studies in Ethnomethodology*. Malden, MA: Blackwell Publishers, Ltd.

Garrido, Marco. 2019. *The Patchwork City: Class, Space, and Politics in Metro Manila*. Chicago: University of Chicago Press.

Garrido, Marco. 2021. "Disciplining Democracy: How the Middle Class in Metro Manila Envision Democratic Order." *Qualitative Sociology* 44, no. 3: 419–35.

Garrido, Marco, Xuefei Ren, and Liza Weinstein. 2021. "Towards a Global Urban Sociology: Keywords." *City and Community* 20, no. 1: 4–12.

Garroutte, Eva. 2003. *Real Indians: Identity and the Survival of Native America*. Berkeley: University of California Press.

Gay, Robert. 1994. *Popular Organization and Democracy in Rio de Janeiro: A Tale of Two Favelas*. Philadelphia, PA: Temple University Press.

Geller, Amanda, and Marah A. Curtis. 2011. "A Sort of Homecoming: Incarceration and the Housing Security of Urban Men." *Social Science Research* 40, no. 4: 1196–213.

George, Samuel, Amber Hendley, Jack Macnamara, Jasson Perez, and Alfonso Vaca-Loyola. 2019. *The Plunder of Black Wealth in Chicago: New Findings on the Lasting Toll of Predatory Housing Contracts*. Durham, NC: Samuel DuBois Cook Center on Social Equity at Duke University, May. https://socialequity.duke.edu/wp-content/uploads/2019/10/Plunder-of-Black-Wealth-in-Chicago.pdf.

Gerardi, Kristopher, Lauren Lambie-Hanson, and Paul Willen. 2022. "Lessons Learned from Housing Policy during COVID-19." In *Recession Remedies: Lessons Learned from the Economic Policy Response to COVID-19*, edited by Wendy Edelberg, Louise Sheiner, and David Wessel, 163–213. Washington, DC: Brookings Institute.

Gilbert, Alan. 2007. "The Return of the Slum: Does Language Matter?" *International Journal of Urban and Regional Research* 31, no. 4: 697–713.

Gilbert, Alan, and Josef Gugler. 1992. *Cities, Poverty, and Development: Urbanization in the Third World*. Oxford: Oxford University Press.

Glaeser, Edward, and Jesse M. Shapiro. 2003. "The Benefits of the Home Mortgage Interest Deduction." *Tax Policy and the Economy* 17: 37–82.

Glenn, Evelyn Nakano. 2015. "Settler Colonialism as Structure: A Framework for Comparative Studies of US Race and Gender Formation." *Sociology of Race and Ethnicity* 1, no. 1: 52–72.

Glick, Jennifer E., and Jennifer Van Hook. 2011. "Does a House Divided Stand? Kinship and the Continuity of Shared Living Arrangements." *Journal of Marriage and Family* 73, no. 5: 1149–64.

Glynn, Chris, Thomas H. Byrne, and Dennis P. Culhane. 2018. *Inflection Points in Community-Level Homeless Rates*. Seattle, WA: Zillow.

Godsil, Rachel D. 2006. "Race Nuisance: The Politics of Law in the Jim Crow Era." *Michigan Law Review* 105: 505–58.

Goetz, Edward G. 2003. *Clearing the Way: Deconcentrating the Poor in Urban America*. Washington, DC: Urban Institute Press.

Goetz, Edward G. 2013. *New Deal Ruins: Race, Economic Justice, and Public Housing Policy*. Ithaca, NY: Cornell University Press.

Goffman, Alice. 2009. "On the Run: Wanted Men in a Philadelphia Ghetto." *American Sociological Review* 74, no. 3: 339–57.

Gómez, Laura E. 2018. *Manifest Destinies: The Making of the Mexican American Race*. New York: NYU Press.

Gong, Neil. 2019. "Between Tolerant Containment and Concerted Constraint: Managing Madness for the City and the Privileged Family." *American Sociological Review* 84, no. 4: 664–89.

Gonzalez, Gilbert G. 1994. *Labor and Community: Mexican Citrus Worker Villages in a Southern California County, 1900–1950*. Vol. 43. Champaign: University of Illinois Press.

Goodman, Catherine, and Merril Silverstein. 2002. "Grandmothers Raising Grandchildren: Family Structure and Well-Being in Culturally Diverse Families." *Gerontologist* 42, no. 5: 676–89.

Goodyear-Kaʻōpua, Noelani. 2013. "The Seeds We Planted: Portraits of a Native Hawaiian Charter School." Minneapolis: University of Minnesota Press.

Goodyear-Kaʻōpua, Noelani, Ikaika Hussey, and Erin Kahunawaikaʻala Wright, eds. 2014. *A Nation Rising: Hawaiian Movements for Life, Land, and Sovereignty*. Durham, NC: Duke University Press.

Gordon, Adam. 2005. "The Creation of Homeownership: How New Deal Changes in Banking Regulation Simultaneously Made Homeownership Accessible to Whites and Out of Reach for Blacks." *Yale Law Journal* 115: 186–226.

Gordon, Daanika. 2022. *Policing the Racial Divide: Urban Growth Politics and the Remaking of Segregation*. New York: NYU Press.

Gormory, Henry. 2021. "Social and Institutional Contexts Underlying Landlords' Eviction Practices." *Social Forces* 100, no. 4 (June): 1774–805.

Gotham, Kevin Fox. 2002. *Race, Real Estate, and Uneven Development: The Kansas City Experience, 1900–2000*. Albany: State University of New York Press.

Gotham, Kevin Fox. 2006. "The Secondary Circuit of Capital Reconsidered: Globalization and the U.S. Real Estate Sector." *American Journal of Sociology* 112, no. 1: 231–75.

Gotham, Kevin Fox. 2009. "Creating Liquidity out of Spatial Fixity: The Secondary Circuit of Capital and the Subprime Mortgage Crisis." *International Journal of Urban and Regional Research* 33: 355–71.

Gould, Jessica, and Sophia Chang. 2021. "Decline in NYC Public School Enrollment Brings Budget Worries for Educators." *Gothamist*, January 30. https://gothamist .com/news/decline-nyc-public-school-enrollment-brings-budget-worries-educators.

Gowan, Teresa. 2002. "The Nexus: Homelessness and Incarceration in Two American Cities." *Ethnography* 3, no. 4: 500–34.

Gowan, Teresa. 2010. *Hobos, Hustlers, and Backsliders: Homeless in San Francisco*. Minneapolis: University of Minnesota Press.

Granovetter, Mark S. 1973. "The Strength of Weak Ties." *American Journal of Sociology* 78, no. 6: 1360–80.

Granovetter, Mark. 1985. "Economic Action and Social Structure: The Problem of Embeddedness." *American Journal of Sociology* 91, no. 3: 481–510.

Grebler, Leo, John W. Moore, and Ralph C. Guzman. 1970. *The Mexican-American People: The Nation's Second Largest Minority*. New York: Free Press.

Greenberg, Deena, Carl Gershenson, and Matthew Desmond. 2016. "The Disparate Impact of Eviction." *Harvard Civil Rights-Civil Liberties Law Review* 51: 115–58.

Greif, Meredith J. 2018. "Regulating Landlords: Unintended Consequences for Poor Tenants." *City and Community* 17, no. 3: 658–74.

Greif, Meredith J. 2022. *Collateral Damages: Landlords and the Urban Housing Crisis.* New York: Russell Sage Foundation.

Greiner, D. James, Cassandra Wolos Pattanayak, and Jonathan Hennessy. 2013. "The Limits of Unbundled Legal Assistance: A Randomized Study in a Massachusetts District Court and Prospects for the Future." *Harvard Law Review* 126, no. 4: 901–89.

Griffith, David. 2005. "Rural Industry and Mexican Immigration and Settlement in North Carolina." In *New Destinations: Mexican Immigration in the United States,* edited by V. Zúñiga and R. Hernández-León, 50–75. New York: Russell Sage Foundation.

Grimes, Orville F. 1976. *Housing for Low-Income Urban Families: Economics and Policy in the Developing World.* Baltimore, MD: Johns Hopkins University Press.

Grisdale, Sean. 2019. "Displacement by Disruption: Short-Term Rentals and the Political Economy of 'Belonging Anywhere' in Toronto." *Urban Geography* 42, no. 5: 654–80.

Griswold del Castillo, Richard. 1979. *The Los Angeles Barrio, 1850–1890: A Social History.* Berkeley: University of California Press.

Gromis, Ashley, and Matthew Desmond. 2021. "Estimating the Prevalence of Eviction in the United States: New Data from the 2017 American Housing Survey." *Cityscape* 23, no. 2: 279–90.

Gromis, Ashley, James R. Hendrickson, and Matthew Desmond. 2022. "Eviction from Public Housing in the United States." *Cities* 127: 1–13.

Groth, Paul. 1999. *Living Downtown: The History of Residential Hotels in the United States.* Los Angeles: University of California Press.

Gugler, Josef, ed. 1988. *The Urbanization of the Third World.* Oxford: Oxford University Press.

Gugler, Josef. 1997. *Cities in the Developing World: Issues, Theory, and Policy.* Oxford: Oxford University Press.

Gugler, Josef, and William G. Flanagan. 1976. "On the Political Economy of Urbanization in the Third World." *International Journal of Urban and Regional Research* 1, no. 1–4: 272–92.

Gurran, Nicole, and Peter Phibbs. 2017. "When Tourists Move In: How Should Urban Planners Respond to Airbnb?" *Journal of the American Planning Association* 83, no. 1: 80–92.

Gurusami, Susila, and Rahim Kurwa. 2021. "From Broken Windows to Broken Homes: Homebreaking as Racialized and Gendered Poverty Governance." *Feminist Formations* 33, no. 1: 1–32.

Gutiérrez, Aaron, and Antoni Domènech. 2020. "Understanding the Spatiality of Short-Term Rentals in Spain: Airbnb and the Intensification of the Commodification of Housing." *Geografisk Tidsskrift—Danish Journal of Geography* 120, no. 2: 98–113.

Gutiérrez, Javier, Juan Carlos García-Palomares, Gustavo Romanillos, and María Henar Salas-Olmedo. 2017. "The Eruption of Airbnb in Tourist Cities: Comparing Spatial Patterns of Hotels and Peer-to-Peer Accommodation in Barcelona." *Tourism Management* 62 (October): 278–91.

Gutierrez, Maria Paz, Gene Demby, and Kara Frame. 2018. "Housing Segregation in Everything." *Code Switch,* April 11. NPR video, 6:37. https://www.npr.org/sections /codeswitch/2018/04/11/601494521/video-housing-segregation-in-everything.

Guttentag, Daniel. 2015. "Airbnb: Disruptive Innovation and the Rise of an Informal Tourism Accommodation Sector." *Current Issues in Tourism* 18, no. 12: 1192–217.

Guttentag, Daniel. 2019. "Progress on Airbnb: A Literature Review." *Journal of Hospitality and Tourism Technology* 10, no. 4: 814–44.

Guttentag, Daniel, Stephen Smith, Luke Potwarka, and Mark Havitz. 2018. "Why Tourists Choose Airbnb: A Motivation-Based Segmentation Study." *Journal of Travel Research* 57, no. 3: 342–59.

Gyourko, Joseph, Jonathan Hartley, and Jacob Krimmel. 2019. "The Local Residential Land Use Regulatory Environment Across U.S. Housing Markets: Evidence from a New Wharton Index." Working paper 26573, December, National Bureau of Economic Research. https://www.nber.org/papers/w26573.

Gyourko, Joseph, and Raven Molloy. 2015. "Regulation and Housing Supply." In *Handbook of Regional and Urban Economics*, vol. 5B, edited by Gilles Duranton, J. Vernon Henderson, and William C. Strange, 1289–338. Amsterdam, ND: North-Holland.

Hackworth, Jason R. 2007. *The Neoliberal City: Governance, Ideology, and Development in American Urbanism*. Ithaca, NY: Cornell University Press.

Hackworth, Jason R. 2016. "Why There Is No Detroit in Canada." *Urban Geography* 37, no. 2: 272–95.

Hackworth, Jason R. 2019. *Manufacturing Decline: How Racism and the Conservative Movement Crush the American Rust Belt*. New York: Columbia University Press

Hall, Andrew B., and Jesse Yoder. 2022. "Does Homeownership Influence Political Behavior? Evidence from Administrative Data." *Journal of Politics* 84, no. 1: 351–66.

Hall, Matthew. 2013. "Residential Integration on the New Frontier: Immigrant Segregation in Established and New Destinations." *Demography* 50, no. 5: 1873–96.

Hall, Matthew, Kyle D. Crowder, and Amy Spring. 2015. "Neighborhood Foreclosures, Racial/Ethnic Transitions, and Residential Segregation." *American Sociological Review* 80, no. 3: 526–49.

Hall, Matthew, and Emily Greenman. 2013. "Housing and Neighborhood Quality among Undocumented Mexican and Central American Immigrants." *Social Science Research* 42, no. 6: 1712–25.

Hall, Matthew, John Iceland, and Youngmin Yi. 2019. "Racial Separation at Home and Work: Segregation in Residential and Workplace Settings." *Population Research and Policy Review* 38, no. 5: 671–94.

Hamilton, Tod G. 2019. *Immigration and the Remaking of Black America*. New York: Russell Sage Foundation.

Haney, Lynne. 2018. "Incarcerated Fatherhood: The Entanglements of Child Support Debt and Mass Imprisonment." *American Journal of Sociology* 124, no. 1: 1–48.

Hankinson, Michael. 2018. "When Do Renters Behave Like Homeowners? High Rent, Price Anxiety, and NIMBYism." *American Political Science Review* 112, no. 3: 473–93.

Hanratty, Maria. 2017. "Do Local Economic Conditions Affect Homelessness? Impact of Area Housing Market Factors, Unemployment, and Poverty on Community Homeless Rates." *Housing Policy Debate* 27, no. 4: 640–55.

Hanson, Andrew. 2012. "Size of Home, Homeownership, and the Mortgage Interest Deduction." *Journal of Housing Economics* 21: 195–201.

Hanson, Andrew. 2017. "Do College Admissions Counselors Discriminate? Evidence from a Correspondence-Based Field Experiment." *Economics of Education Review* 60 (October): 86–96.

Hanson, Andrew, and Zackary Hawley. 2011. "Do Landlords Discriminate in the Rental Housing Market? Evidence from an Internet Field Experiment in US Cities." *Journal of Urban Economics* 70: 99–114.

Hanson, Andrew, Zackary Hawley, Hal Martin, and Bo Liu. 2016. "Discrimination in Mortgage Lending: Evidence from a Correspondence Experiment." *Journal of Urban Economics* 92: 48–65.

Hanson, Andrew, Zackary Hawley, and Aryn Taylor. 2011. "Subtle Discrimination in the Rental Housing Market: Evidence from Email Correspondence with Landlords." *Journal of Housing Economics* 20: 276–84.

Hao, Lingxin, and Mary C. Brinton. 1997. "Productive Activities and Support Systems of Single Mothers." *American Journal of Sociology* 102, no. 5: 1305–44.

Har, Janie. 2020. "San Francisco Officials Let People Sue over Racist 911 Calls." *Associated Press*, October 20. https://apnews.com/article/race-and-ethnicity-san-francisco-legislation-crime-a130bb0f8d13b46dacf58ed8fa8a3169.

Harding, David J., Jeffrey D. Morenoff, and Claire W. Herbert. 2013. "Home Is Hard to Find: Neighborhoods, Institutions, and the Residential Trajectories of Returning Prisoners." *Annals of the American Academy of Political and Social Science* 647, no. 1: 214–36.

Harding, David J., Jeffrey D. Morenoff, and Jessica J. B. Wyse. 2019. *On the Outside: Prisoner Reentry and Reintegration.* Chicago: University of Chicago Press.

Harding, David J., Jonah A. Siegel, and Jeffrey D. Morenoff. 2017. "Custodial Parole Sanctions and Earnings after Release from Prison." *Social Forces* 96, no. 2: 909–34.

Harms, Erik. 2016. *Luxury and Rubble: Civility and Dispossession in the New Saigon.* Oakland: University of California Press.

Harris, Cheryl I. 1993. "Whiteness as Property." *Harvard Law Review* 106, no. 8: 1707–91.

Harris, Richard. 2018. "Modes of Informal Urban Development: A Global Phenomenon." *Journal of Planning Literature* 33, no. 3: 267–86.

Harrison, Austin, Dan Immergluck, Jeff Ernsthausen, and Stephanie Earl. 2021. "Housing Stability, Evictions, and Subsidized Rental Properties: Evidence from Metro Atlanta, Georgia." *Housing Policy Debate* 31, no. 3–5: 411–24.

Hartman, Chester, and David Robinson. 2003. "Evictions: The Hidden Housing Problem." *Housing Policy Debate* 14, no. 4: 461–501.

Hartt, Maxwell. 2021. *Quietly Shrinking Cities: Canadian Urban Population Loss in an Age of Growth.* Vancouver: University of British Columbia Press.

Harvey, David. 1982. *The Limits to Capital.* Chicago: University of Chicago Press.

Harvey, Hope. 2018a. "Economic Exchange and Relational Work within Doubled-Up Households." Presented at the American Sociological Association Annual Meeting, Philadelphia, PA, August.

Harvey, Hope. 2018b. "Experiences of Doubling-Up among American Families with Children." PhD diss., Harvard University. https://dash.harvard.edu/handle/1/39947157.

Harvey, Hope. 2020a. "When Mothers Can't 'Pay the Cost to Be the Boss': Roles and Identity within Doubled-Up Households." *Social Problems* 69, no. 1: 261–81.

Harvey, Hope. 2020b. "Cumulative Effects of Doubling Up in Childhood on Young Adult Outcomes." *Demography* 57, no. 2: 501–28.

Harvey, Hope. 2020c. "Becoming Doubled-Up: The Formation of Shared Households." Presented at the Association for Public Policy Analysis and Management Annual Meeting, Washington, DC, November.

Harvey, Hope, Rachel Dunifon, and Natasha Pilkauskas. 2021. "Under Whose Roof? Understanding the Living Arrangements of Children in Doubled-Up Households." *Demography* 58, no. 3: 821–46.

Harvey, Hope, Kelley Fong, Kathryn Edin, and Stefanie DeLuca. 2020. "Forever Homes and Temporary Stops: Housing Search Logics and Residential Selection." *Social Forces* 98, no. 4: 1498–523.

Hasager, Ulla, and Marion Kelly. 2001. "Public Policy of Land and Homesteading in Hawaiʻi." *Social Process in Hawaiʻi* 40: 190232. http://www2.hawaii.edu/~aoude/ES350/SPIH_vol40/10HasagerKelly2001.pdf.

Hatch, Megan. 2017. "Statutory Protection for Renters: Classification of State Landlord-Tenant Policy Approaches." *Housing Policy Debate* 27, no. 1: 98–119.

Havekes, Esther, Michael Bader, and Maria Krysan. 2016. "Realizing Racial and Ethnic Neighborhood Preferences? Exploring the Mismatches between What People Want, Where They Search, and Where They Live." *Population Research and Policy Review* 35, no. 1: 101–26.

Hayat, Norrinda Brown. 2016. "Section 8 Is the New N-Word: Policing Integration in the Age of Black Mobility." *American University Journal of International Law and Policy* 51, no. 1: 61–93.

Healthy Children. 2019. "Lead Exposure: Steps to Protect Your Family." American Academic of Pediatrics, last updated September 9, 2021. https://www.healthychildren.org/English/safety-prevention/all-around/Pages/Lead-Screening-for-Children.aspx.

Helper, Rose. 1969. *Racial Policies and Practices of Real Estate Brokers*. Minneapolis: University of Minnesota Press.

Henderson, Peter. 1993. "Local Deals and the New Deal State: Implementing Public Housing in Baltimore, 1933–1968." PhD diss., Johns Hopkins University. https://www.proquest.com/openview/f8660b1b56b275eff23c9deba6dc66df/.

Henderson, Taja-Nia Y., and Jamila Jefferson-Jones. 2019. "# LivingWhileBlack: Blackness as Nuisance." *American University Law Review* 69: 863–914.

Henkels, Jacob. 2020. "Housing Discrimination at the Intersection of Health Condition, Race and Felony Status." Honors thesis, University of North Carolina at Chapel Hill. https://doi.org/10.17615/fmre-cr57.

Hennigan, Brian. 2017. "House Broken: Homelessness, Housing First, and Neoliberal Poverty Governance." *Urban Geography* 38, no. 9: 1418–40.

Henning, Cecilia, and Mats Lieberg. 1996. "Strong Ties or Weak Ties? Neighbourhood Networks in a New Perspective." *Scandinavian Housing and Planning Research* 13, no. 1: 3–26.

Hepburn, Peter, Renee Louis, and Matthew Desmond. 2020. "Racial and Gender Disparities among Evicted Americans." *Sociological Science* 7: 649–62.

Herbert, Claire W. 2018a. "Like a Good Neighbor, Squatters Are There: Property and Neighborhood Stability in the Context of Urban Decline." *City and Community* 17, no. 1: 236–58.

Herbert, Claire W. 2018b. "Squatting for Survival: Precarious Housing in a Declining U.S. City." *Housing Policy Debate* 28, no. 5: 797–813.

Herbert, Claire W. 2021. *A Detroit Story: Urban Decline and the Rise of Property Informality.* Oakland: University of California Press.

Herbert, Steve. 1996. "The Normative Ordering of Police Territoriality: Making and Marking Space with the Los Angeles Police Department." *Annals of the Association of American Geographers* 86: 567–82.

Hernandez, Jesus. 2009. "Redlining Revisited: Mortgage Lending Patterns in Sacramento 1930–2004." *International Journal of Urban and Regional Research* 33, no. 2: 291–313.

Herring, Chris. 2014. "The New Logics of Homeless Seclusion: Homeless Encampments in America's West Coast Cities." *City and Community* 13, no. 4: 285–309.

Herring, Chris. 2019a. "Between Street and Shelter: Seclusion, Exclusion, and the Neutralization of Poverty." In *Class, Ethnicity and State in the Polarized Metropolis,* edited by John Flint and Ryan Powell, 281–305. New York: Springer.

Herring, Chris. 2019b. "Complaint-Oriented Policing: Regulating Homelessness in Public Space." *American Sociological Review* 84, no. 5: 769–800.

Herring, Chris, and Manuel Lutz. 2015. "The Roots and Implications of the USA's Homeless Tent Cities." *City* 19, no. 5: 689–701.

Herring, Chris, and Dilara Yarbrough. 2015. *Punishing the Poorest: How San Francisco's Criminalization of Homelessness Perpetuates Poverty.* Berkeley, CA: UC Berkeley Human Rights Center and the San Francisco Coalition on Homelessness.

Herring, Chris, Dilara Yarbrough, and Lisa Marie Alatorre. 2020. "Pervasive Penalty: How the Criminalization of Poverty Perpetuates Homelessness." *Social Problems* 67, no. 1: 131–49.

Herring, Chris, Dilara Yarbrough, Jamie Chang, Jenny Friedenbach, Olivia Glowacki, Christoph Hansmann, Sam Lew, Pike Long, and Kelsey Ludwig. 2020. *Stop the Revolving Door: A Street Level Framework for a New System.* San Francisco: San Francisco Coalition on Homelessness.

Hilber, Christian A., and Tracy M. Turner. 2014. "The Mortgage Interest Deduction and Its Impact on Homeownership Decisions." *Review of Economics and Statistics* 96, no. 4: 618–37.

Hillabrant, Walter, Judy Earp, Mack Rhoades, and Nancy Pindus. 2004. *Overcoming Challenges to Business and Economic Development in Indian Country.* Washington, DC: US Department of Health and Human Services. https://www.urban.org/sites /default/files/publication/42846/411104-Overcoming-Challenges-to-Business-and -Economic-Development-in-Indian-Country.PDF.

Hirsch, Arnold R. 1983. *Making the Second Ghetto: Race and Housing in Chicago 1940– 1960.* Chicago: University of Chicago Press.

Hirsch, Arnold R. 2003. *Public Policy and Racial Segregation in Baltimore 1900–1968.* Expert report in *Thompson v. HUD,* MJG 95–309 (1995).

Hirsch, Arnold R. 2006. "Less Than Plessy: The Inner City, Suburbs, and State-Sanctioned Residential Segregation in the Age of Brown." In *The New Suburban History,* edited by Kevin M. Kruse and Thomas J. Sugrue, 33–56. Chicago: University of Chicago Press.

Hirt, Sonia. 2015. *Zoned in the USA: The Origins and Implications of American Land use Regulation.* Ithaca, NY: Cornell University Press.

Hitchens, Brooklynn K., Patrick J. Carr, and Susan Clampet-Lundquist. 2018. "The Context for Legal Cynicism: Urban Young Women's Experiences with Policing in Low-Income, High-Crime Neighborhoods." *Race and Justice* 8, no. 1: 27–50.

Hoffman, Abraham. 1974. *Unwanted Mexican Americans in the Great Depression: Repatriation Pressures, 1929–1939.* Tucson: University of Arizona Press.

Hoffman, Lily M., and Barbara Schmitter Heisler. 2020. *Airbnb, Short-Term Rentals and the Future of Housing.* London: Routledge.

Hogan, Bernie, and Brent Berry. 2011. "Racial and Ethnic Biases in Rental Housing: An Audit Study of Online Apartment Listings." *City and Community* 10, no. 4: 351–72.

Hollnsteiner, Mary R. 1969. "The Urbanization of Metro Manila." In *Modernization: Its Impact in the Philippines IV*, edited by Walden Bello and Alfonso de Guzman, 147–74. Quezon City: Ateneo de Manila University Press.

Hollnsteiner, Mary R. 1972. "Becoming an Urbanite: The Neighborhood as a Learning Environment." In *The City as a Centre of Change in Asia*, edited by D. J. Dwyer, 29–40. Hong Kong: Hong Kong University Press.

Holm, Andrej, and Armin Kuhn. 2017. "Squatting and Gentrification in East Germany since 1989." In *Public Goods versus Economic Interests*, edited by Freia Anders and Alexander Sedlmaier. New York: Routledge.

Holston, James. 2008. *Insurgent Citizenship: Disjunctions of Democracy and Modernity in Brazil.* Princeton, NJ: Princeton University Press.

Holt, Thomas C. 2000. *The Problem of Race in the Twenty-First Century.* Cambridge, MA: Harvard University Press.

Hong, Seunghye, Wei Zhang, and Emily Walton. 2014. "Neighborhoods and Mental Health: Exploring Ethnic Density, Poverty, and Social Cohesion among Asian Americans and Latinos." *Social Science and Medicine* 111: 117–24.

Hopper, Kim. 2003. *Reckoning with Homelessness.* Ithaca, NY: Cornell University Press.

Horn, Keren, and Mark Merante. 2017. "Is Home Sharing Driving up Rents? Evidence from Airbnb in Boston." *Journal of Housing Economics* 38 (December): 14–24.

Horn, Keren M., and Katherine O'Regan. 2011. "The Low Income Housing Tax Credit and Racial Segregation." *Housing Policy Debate* 21. no. 3: 443–73.

Hornstein, Jeffrey M. 2005. *A Nation of Realtors: A Cultural History of the Twentieth-Century American Middle Class.* Durham, NC: Duke University Press.

Horsman, Reginald. 1981. *Race and Manifest Destiny.* Cambridge, MA: Harvard University Press.

Hotchkins, Bryan K., and T. Dancy. 2015. "Black Male Student Leaders in Predominantly White Universities: Stories of Power, Preservation, and Persistence." *Western Journal of Black Studies* 39, no. 1: 30–44.

Houle, Jason N., and Cody Warner. 2017. "Into the Red and Back to the Nest? Student Debt, College Completion, and Returning to the Parental Home among Young Adults." *Sociology of Education* 90, no. 1: 89–108.

Housing and Land Use Regulatory Board (HLURB). 2014. "Residential Licenses to Sell, National Capital Region, 1981–2013." Unpublished data. Quezon City: HLURB.

Housing Assistance Council (HAC). 2011. *Preserving Affordable Manufactured Home Communities in Rural America: A Case Study.* Washington, DC: Housing Assistance Council. https://ruralhome.org/wp-content/uploads/2009/06/rcbi_manu factured.pdf.

Housing Assistance Council (HAC). 2012. *Taking Stock: Rural People, Poverty, and Housing in the 21st Century*. Washington, DC: Housing Assistance Council. https://ruraldataportal.org/docs/HAC_Taking-Stock-Full.pdf.

Housing Commission of the City of Los Angeles. 1909. *Report of the Housing Commission of the City of Los Angeles: February 20, 1906, to March 31st, 1913*. Los Angeles, CA: n.p. Print.

Howard, Christopher. 1997. *The Hidden Welfare State: Tax Expenditures and Social Policy in the United States*. Princeton, NJ: Princeton University Press.

Howell, Junia. 2019. "The Truly Advantaged: Examining the Effects of Privileged Places on Educational Attainment." *Sociological Quarterly* 60, no. 3: 420–38.

Howell, Junia, and Elizabeth Korver-Glenn. 2018. "Neighborhoods, Race, and the Twenty-First-Century Housing Appraisal Industry." *Sociology of Race and Ethnicity* 4, no. 4: 473–90.

Howell, Junia, and Elizabeth Korver-Glenn. 2021. "The Increasing Effect of Neighborhood Racial Composition on Housing Values, 1980–2015." *Social Problems* 68, no. 4:1051–70.

Hsieh, Chang-Tai, and Enrico Moretti. 2019. "Housing Constraints and Spatial Misallocation." *American Economic Journal: Macroeconomics* 11, no. 2: 1–39.

Huang, Ying, Scott South, Amy Spring, and Kyle Crowder. 2020. "Life-Course Exposure to Neighborhood Poverty and Migration between Poor and Non-poor Neighborhoods." *Population Research and Policy Review* 40: 401–19.

Hubbard, Phil. 2008. "Regulating the Social Impacts of Studentification: A Loughborough Case Study." *Environment and Planning A: Economy and Space* 40, no. 2: 323–41.

Human Impact Partners and Community Advocates Public Policy Institute. 2020. *Lead-Safe Certification for Rental Units*. Milwaukee, WI: Community Advocates Public Policy Institute. https://ppi.communityadvocates.net/file_download/8d96efe7-d8fa-4a83-acdd-024ed98fde18.

Hunt, D. Bradford. 2009. *Blueprint for Disaster: The Unraveling of Chicago Public Housing*. Chicago: University of Chicago Press.

Hurwitz, Jon, and Mark Peffley. 2005. "Playing the Race Card in the Post-Willie Horton Era: The Impact of Racialized Code Words on Support for Punitive Crime Policy." *Public Opinion Quarterly* 69, no. 1: 99–112.

Hwang, Jackelyn. 2015. "Pioneers of Gentrification: Transformation in Global Neighborhoods in Urban America in the Late Twentieth Century." *Demography* 53, no. 1: 189–213.

Hwang, Jackelyn, and Lei Ding. 2020. "Unequal Displacement: Gentrification, Racial Stratification, and Residential Destinations in Philadelphia." *American Journal of Sociology* 126, no. 2: 354–406.

Hwang, Jackelyn, Michael Hankinson, and Kreg Steven Brown. 2015. "Racial and Spatial Targeting: Segregation and Subprime Lending within and across Metropolitan Areas." *Social Forces* 93, no. 3: 1081–108.

Hwang, Jackelyn, and Jeffrey Lin. 2016. "What Have We Learned About the Causes of Recent Gentrification?" *Cityscape* 18, no. 3: 9–26.

Hwang, Jackelyn, and Tyler W. McDaniel. 2022. "Racialized Reshuffling: Urban Change and the Persistence of Segregation in the Twenty-First Century." *Annual Review of Sociology* 48, no. 1: 1–23.

Hwang, Jackelyn, and Robert J. Sampson. 2014. "Divergent Pathways of Gentrification: Racial Inequality and the Social Order of Renewal in Chicago Neighborhoods." *American Sociological Review* 79, no. 4: 726–51.

Hyde, Allen, and Mary J. Fischer. 2021. "Neighborhood Attainment for White and Latino Homebuyers during the Housing Boom and Bust." *City and Community* 20, no. 2: 99–120.

Hyra, Derek S. 2017. *Race, Class, and Politics in the Cappuccino City.* Chicago: University of Chicago Press.

Hyra, Derek S., Gregory D. Squires, Robert N. Renner, and David S. Kirk. 2013. "Metropolitan Segregation and the Subprime Lending Crisis." *Housing Policy Debate* 23 (March): 37–41.

Immergluck, Daniel. 2009. *Foreclosed: High-Risk Lending, Deregulation, and the Undermining of America's Mortgage Market.* Ithaca, NY: Cornell University Press.

Immergluck, Daniel. 2018. "Old Wine in Private Equity Bottles? The Resurgence of Contract-for-Deed Home Sales in US Urban Neighborhoods." *International Journal of Urban and Regional Research* 42, no. 4: 651–65.

Immergluck, Daniel, Jeff Ernstausen, Stephanie Earl, and Allison Powell. 2020. "Evictions, Large Owners, and Serial Filings: Findings from Atlanta." *Housing Studies* 35, no. 5: 903–24.

Indiana Advisory Committee. 2020. *Environmental Injustice: Lead Poisoning in Indiana.* Washington, DC: US Commission on Civil Rights, November. https://www.usccr .gov/files/2020-11-12-Report-Lead-Poisoning-in-Indiana.pdf.

International Crime Free Association. 2003. "Crime Free Multi-Housing: Keep Illegal Activity Off Rental Property." International Crime Free Association. http://www .crime-free-association.org/multi-housing.htm.

Jackson, Kenneth T. 1985. *Crabgrass Frontier: The Suburbanization of the United States.* New York: Oxford University Press.

Jacob, John S., and Ricardo Lopez. 2009. "Is Denser Greener? An Evaluation of Higher-Density Development as an Urban Stormwater-Quality Best Management Practice." *Journal of the American Water Resources Association* 45, no. 3: 687–701.

James, Franklin J., Betty J. McCummings, and Eileen A. Tynan. 1984. *Minorities in the Sunbelt.* New Brunswick, NJ: Rutgers University Center for Urban Policy Research.

Jang-Trettien, Christine. 2022. "House of Cards: Informal Housing Markets and Precarious Pathways to Homeownership in Baltimore." *Social Problems* 69, no. 4: 928–51.

Jargowsky, Paul A. 1997. *Poverty and Place: Ghettos, Barrios, and the American City.* New York: Russell Sage Foundation.

Jargowsky, Paul A. 2014. "Segregation, Neighborhoods, and Schools." In *Choosing Homes, Choosing Schools,* edited by Annette Lareau and Kimberly Goyette, 97–136. New York: Russell Sage Foundation.

Jefferson-Jones, Jamila. 2015. "Can Short-Term Rental Arrangements Increase Home Values? A Case for Airbnb and Other Home Sharing Arrangements." *Cornell Real Estate Review* 13, no. 1: 12–19.

Jelleyman, T., and N. Spencer. 2008. "Residential Mobility in Childhood and Health Outcomes: A Systematic Review." *Journal of Epidemiology and Community Health (1979–)* 62, no. 7: 584–92.

Jencks, Christopher. 1995. *The Homeless.* Cambridge, MA: Harvard University Press.

Jencks, Christopher, and Susan E. Mayer. 1990. "The Social Consequences of Growing Up in a Poor Neighborhood." In *Inner-City Poverty in the United States,* edited by Laurence E. Lynn Jr. and Michael G. H. McGeary, 111–86. Washington, DC: National Academy Press.

Jepson, Wendy, and Emily Vandewalle. 2016. "Household Water Insecurity in the Global North: A Study of Rural and Periurban Settlements on the Texas-Mexico Border." *Professional Geographer* 68, no. 1: 66–81.

Jindrich, Jason. 2017. "Squatting in the US: What Historians Can Learn from Developing Countries." In *Public Goods versus Economic Interests*, edited by Freia Anders and Alexander Sedlmaier. New York: Routledge.

Jocano, F. Landa. 1975. *Slum as a Way of Life*. Diliman: University of the Philippines Press.

Johnson, Lallen T., and Evelyn J. Patterson. 2022. "The Policing of Subway Fare Evasion in Postindustrial Los Angeles." *Punishment and Society* 24, no. 3: 457–76.

Johnson, Rucker C. 2019. *Children of the Dream: Why School Integration Works*. New York: Hachette UK.

Joint Center for Housing Studies. 2018. *The State of the Nation's Housing 2018*. Cambridge, MA: Harvard University. http://www.jchs.harvard.edu/state-nations -housing-2018.

Jones, Antwan, and Prentiss Dantzler. 2021. "Neighbourhood Perceptions and Residential Mobility." *Urban Studies* 58, no. 9: 1792–810.

Jones, Richard C. 2008. "The Ambiguous Roles of Suburbanization and Immigration in Ethnic Segregation: The Case of San Antonio." *Urban Geography* 29, no. 3:196–223.

Jowers, Kay, Christopher Timmins, Nrupen Bhavsar, Qihui Hu, and Julia Marshall. 2021. "Housing Precarity and the COVID-19 Pandemic: Impacts of Utility Disconnection and Eviction Moratoria on Infections and Deaths Across US Counties." Working paper 28394, National Bureau of Economic Research. https:// www.nber.org/papers/w28394.

Jung, Moon-Kie. 2015. *Beneath the Surface of White Supremacy*. Stanford, CA: Stanford University Press.

Juppenplatz, Morris. 1970. *Cities in Transformation: The Urban Squatter Problem of the Developing World*. Queensland: University of Queensland Press.

Kameʻeleihiwa, Lilikalā. 1992. *Native Land and Foreign Desires: How Shall We Live in Harmony?* Honolulu, HI: Bishop Museum Press.

Kamin, Debra. 2020. "Black Homeowners Face Discrimination in Appraisals." *New York Times*, August 25.

Kanaʻiaupuni, Shawn Malia, and Carolyn Liebler. 2005. "Pondering Poi Dog: Place and Racial Identification of Multiracial Native Hawaiians." *Ethnic and Racial Studies* 28, no. 4: 687–721.

Kanahele, George S. 1986. "The Dynamics of Aloha." In *Kū Kanaka, Stand Tall: A Search for Hawaiian Values*, edited by George S. Kanahele, 375–494. Honolulu: University of Hawaiʻi Press.

Kandel, William, and John Cromartie. 2004. *New Patterns of Hispanic Settlement in Rural America*. Rural Development Research report no. RDRR-99. Washington, DC: US Department of Agriculture, Economic Research Service, May. https://www .ers.usda.gov/publications/pub-details/?pubid=47091.

Kandel, William, and Emilio Parrado. 2005. "Restructuring of the U.S. Meat Processing Industry and New Hispanic Migrant Destinations." *Population and Development Review* 31: 447–71.

Kang, Jeehye, and Philip N. Cohen. 2017. "Extended Kin and Children's Behavioral Functioning: Family Structure and Parental Immigrant Status." *Social Science and Medicine* 186: 61–69.

Karn, Valerie Ann, Jim Kemeny, and Peter Williams. 1985. *Home Ownership in the Inner City: Salvation or Despair?* Brookfield, VT: Gower.

Kauanui, J. Kēhaulani. 2008. *Hawaiian Blood: Colonialism and the Politics of Sovereignty and Indigeneity.* Durham, NC: Duke University Press.

Kauanui, J. Kēhaulani. 2016. "'A Structure, Not an Event': Settler Colonialism and Enduring Indigeneity." *Lateral* 5, no. 1.

Kearns, Kevin C. 1979. "Intraurban Squatting in London." *Annals of the Association of American Geographers* 69, no. 4: 589–98.

Keeler, Kasey. 2016. "Putting People Where They Belong: American Indian Housing Policy in the Mid-Twentieth Century." *Native American and Indigenous Studies* 3, no. 2:70–104.

Kelly, Anne Keala. 2014. "Portrait. Marie Beltran and Annie Pau: Resistance to Empire, Erasure, and Selling Out." In *A Nation Rising: Hawaiian Movements for Life, Land, and Sovereignty*, edited by Noelani Goodyear-Kaʻōpua, Ikaika Hussey, and Erin Kahunawaikaʻala Wright, 36–47. Durham, NC: Duke University.

Kemeny, Jim. 1980. "Home Ownership and Privatisation." *International Journal of Urban and Regional Research* 4, no. 3: 372–88.

Kemeny, Jim. 2005. "'The Really Big Trade-Off' between Home Ownership and Welfare: Castles' Evaluation of the 1980 Thesis, and a Reformulation 25 Years On." *Housing, Theory and Society* 22, no. 2: 59–75.

Kendi, Ibram X. 2016. *Stamped from the Beginning: The Definitive History of Racist Ideas in America.* New York: Nation Books.

Kennedy, Ian, Chris Hess, Amandalynne Paullada, and Sarah Chasins. 2021. "Racialized Discourse in Seattle Rental Ad Text." *Social Forces* 99: 1432–56.

Keyes, William J. 1976. "Land Use—and Abuse." *Philippine Studies* 24, no. 4: 381–98.

Khare, Amy T. 2018. "Privatization in an Era of Economic Crisis: Using Market-Based Policies to Remedy Market Failures." *Housing Policy Debate* 28, no. 1: 6–28.

Kim, Jin-Hyuk, Tin Cheuk Leung, and Liad Wagman. 2017. "Can Restricting Property Use Be Value Enhancing? Evidence from Short-Term Rental Regulation." *Journal of Law and Economics* 60, no. 2: 309–34. doi.org/10.1086/694415.

Kim, Keuntae, Ivis Garcia, and Simon Brewer. 2021. "Spatial Relationship between Eviction Filings, Neighborhood Characteristics, and Proximity to the Central Business District: A Case Study of Salt Lake County, Utah." *Housing Policy Debate* 31, no. 3–5: 601–26.

Kimelberg, Shelley McDonough. 2011. "Inside the Growth Machine: Real Estate Professionals on the Perceived Challenges of Urban Development." *City and Community* 10: 76–99.

Kinder, Kimberley. 2016. *DIY Detroit: Making Do in a City without Services.* Minneapolis: University of Minnesota Press.

King, Tiffany Lethabo. 2010. "One Strike Evictions, State Space and the Production of Abject Black Female Bodies." *Critical Sociology* 36, no. 1: 45–64.

Kitsuse, John I., and Aaron V. Cicourel. 1963. "A Note on the Uses of Official Statistics." *Social Problems* 11, no. 2: 131–39.

Kleysteuber, Rudy. 2006. "Tenant Screening Thirty Years Later: A Statutory Proposal to Protect Public Records Note." *Yale Law Journal* 116, no. 6: 1344–88.

Kline, Patrick M., Evan K. Rose, and Christopher R. Walters. 2021. "Systemic Discrimination among Large U.S. Employers." Working paper 29053, National

Bureau of Economic Research. https://eml.berkeley.edu//~crwalters/papers/ran
dres.pdf.

Kline, Patrick M., and Christopher Walters. 2021. "Reasonable Doubt: Experimental
Detection of Job-Level Employment Discrimination." *Econometrica* 89, no. 2:
765–92.

Kling, Jeffrey R., Jens Ludwig, and Lawrence F. Katz. 2005. "Neighborhood Effects on
Crime for Female and Male Youth: Evidence from a Randomized Housing Voucher
Experiment." *Quarterly Journal of Economics* 120, no. 1: 87–130.

Kneebone, Elizabeth, and Emily Garr. 2010. *The Suburbanization of Poverty: Trends in
Metropolitan America, 2000 to 2008.* Washington, DC: Brookings Institute, January 20.
https://www.brookings.edu/research/the-suburbanization-of-poverty-trends-in
-metropolitan-america-2000-to-2008/.

Kneebone, Elizabeth, and Natalie Holmes. 2015. *The Growing Distance between People
and Jobs in Metropolitan America.* Washington, DC: Metropolitan Policy Program
at Brookings, March. https://www.brookings.edu/wp-content/uploads/2016/07
/Srvy_JobsProximity.pdf.

Kneebone, Elizabeth, and Mark Trainer. 2019. *How Housing Supply Shapes Access to
Entry-Level Homeownership.* Berkeley, CA: UC Berkeley Terner Center.

Kochhar, Rakesh, Ana Gonzalez-Barrera, and Daniel Dockterman. 2009. *Through
Boom and Bust: Minorities, Immigrants and Homeownership.* Washington, DC: Pew
Research Center, May 12. https://www.pewresearch.org/hispanic/2009/05/12
/through-boom-and-bust/.

Kohl, Sebastian. 2020. "Too Much Mortgage Debt? The Effect of Housing
Financialization on Housing Supply and Residential Capital Formation."
Socio-Economic Review 19, no. 2: 413–40.

Koppelman, Carter M. 2021. "Inclusion in Indignity: Seeing the State and Becoming
Citizens in Chile's Social Housing." *Qualitative Sociology* 44, no. 1: 385–402.

Korfmacher, Katrina S., and Michael L. Hanley. 2013. "Are Local Laws the Key to
Ending Childhood Lead Poisoning?" *Journal of Health Politics, Policy, and Law* 38,
no. 4: 757–813.

Korpi, Walter, and Joakim Palme. 1998. "The Paradox of Redistribution and Strategies of
Equality: Welfare State Institutions, Inequality, and Poverty in Western Countries."
American Sociological Review 63, no. 5: 661–87.

Korver-Glenn, Elizabeth. 2018. "Compounding Inequalities: How Racial Stereotypes
and Discrimination Accumulate Across the Stages of the Housing Exchange."
American Sociological Review 83: 627–56.

Korver-Glenn, Elizabeth. 2020. "Property Manager-Produced Precarity in U.S. Rental
Markets." Virtual presentation at the Annual Meetings of the American Sociological
Association, August 8–11.

Korver-Glenn, Elizabeth. 2021. *Race Brokers: Housing Markets and Segregation in
21st Century Urban America.* Oxford, UK: Oxford University Press.

Kosack, Edward, and Zachary Ward. 2018. "El Sueño Americano? The Generational
Progress of Mexican Americans Prior to World War II." *Journal of Economic History*
80: 961–95.

Krause, Andy, and Gideon Aschwanden. 2020. "To Airbnb? Factors Impacting Short-
Term Leasing Preference." *Journal of Real Estate Research* 42, no. 2: 261–84.

Kreider, R., and Renee Ellis. 2011. *Living Arrangements of Children: 2009. Current
Population Reports.* Washington, DC: US Census Bureau, US Department of

Commerce: 70–126. https://www.census.gov/library/publications/2011/demo/p70-126.html.

Krieger, James, and Donna L. Higgins. 2002. "Housing and Health: Time Again for Public Health Action." *American Journal of Public Health* 92, no. 5: 758–68.

Krysan, Maria, and Michael Bader. 2007. "Perceiving the Metropolis: Seeing the City through a Prism of Race." *Social Forces* 86, no. 2: 699–733.

Krysan, Maria, and Michael D. M. Bader. 2009. "Racial Blind Spots: Black-White-Latino Differences in Community Knowledge." *Social Problems* 56, no. 4: 677–701.

Krysan, Maria, Mick P. Couper, Reynolds Farley, and Tyrone A. Forman. 2009. "Does Race Matter in Neighborhood Preferences? Results from a Video Experiment." *American Journal of Sociology* 115, no. 2: 527–59.

Krysan, Maria, and Kyle Crowder. 2017. *Cycle of Segregation: Social Processes and Residential Stratification.* New York: Russell Sage Foundation.

Krysan, Maria, and Reynolds Farley. 2002. "The Residential Preferences of Blacks: Do They Explain Persistent Segregation?" *Social Forces* 80, no. 3: 937–80.

Kuebler, Meghan. 2013. "Closing the Wealth Gap: A Review of Racial and Ethnic Inequalities in Homeownership." *Sociology Compass* 7, no. 8: 670–85.

Kuebler, Meghan, and Jacob S. Rugh. 2013. "New Evidence on Racial and Ethnic Disparities in Homeownership in the United States from 2001 to 2010." *Social Science Research* 42, no. 5:1357–74.

Kuhn, Moritz, Moritz Schularick, and Ulrike I. Steins. 2020. "Income and Wealth Inequality in America, 1949–2016." *Journal of Political Economy* 128, no. 9: 3469–519.

Kuk, John, Ariela Schachter, Jacob William Faber, and Max Besbris. 2021. "The COVID-19 Pandemic and the Rental Market: Evidence from Craigslist." *American Behavioral Scientist* 65, no. 12: 1623–48.

Kurashige, Scott. 2010. "Between 'White Spot' and 'World City': Racial Integration and the Roots of Multiculturalism." In *A Companion to Los Angeles*, edited by William Deverell and Greg Hise, 56–71. New York: Wiley-Blackwell.

Kurashima, Natalie, Jason Jeremiah, A. Nāmaka Whitehead, Jon Tulchin, Mililani Browning, and Trever Duarte. 2018. " 'Āina Kaumaha: The Maintenance of Ancestral Principles for 21st Century Indigenous Resource Management." *Sustainability* 10, no. 11: 3975–96.

Kurwa, Rahim. 2015. "Deconcentration without Integration: Examining the Social Outcomes of Housing Choice Voucher Movement in Los Angeles County." *City and Community* 14, no. 4: 364–91.

Kurwa, Rahim. 2020a. "Opposing and Policing Racial Integration: Evidence from the Housing Choice Voucher Program." *Du Bois Review: Social Science Research on Race* 17, no. 2: 363–87.

Kurwa, Rahim. 2020b. "The New Man in the House Rules: How the Regulation of Housing Vouchers Turns Personal Bonds into Eviction Liabilities." *Housing Policy Debate* 30, no. 6: 926–49.

Kusenbach, Margarethe. 2006. "Patterns of Neighboring: Practicing Community in the Parochial Realm." *Symbolic Interaction* 29, no. 3: 279–306. doi.org/10.1525/si.2006.29.3.279.

Kusenbach, Margarethe. 2009. "Salvaging Decency: Mobile Home Residents' Strategies of Managing the Stigma of 'Trailer' Living." *Qualitative Sociology* 32, no. 4: 399–428.

Kusenbach, Margarethe. 2017. "'Look at My House!' Home and Mobile Home Ownership among Latino/a Immigrants in Florida." *Journal of Housing and the Built Environment* 32, no. 1: 29–47.

LaBriola, Joe. 2022. "The Race to Exclude: Residential Growth Controls in California Cities, 1970–1992." SocArXiv, October 6. https://osf.io/preprints/socarxiv/nqvfa.

LaBriola, Joe. 2023. "Housing Market Dynamics and the White-Black Wealth Gap." SocArXiv, February 10. https://osf.io/preprints/socarxiv/rp3ed.

Lageson, Sarah Esther. 2016. "Digital Punishment's Tangled Web." *Contexts* 15, no. 1: 22–27. https://doi.org/10.1177/1536504216628841.

Lai, Clement. 2012. "The Racial Triangulation of Space: The Case of Urban Renewal in San Francisco's Fillmore District." *Annals of the Association of American Geographers* 102, no. 1: 151–70.

Lamont, Michele. 2000. *The Dignity of Working Men: Morality and the Boundaries of Race, Class, and Immigration.* New York: Russell Sage.

Lancione, Michele. 2014. "Assemblages of Care and the Analysis of Public Policies on Homelessness in Turin, Italy." *City* 18, no. 1: 25–40.

Land, Joni Auden. 2022. "Boise Council Narrowly Passes Short-Term Rental Ordinance. Here's What You Need to Know." *Idaho Statesman*, March 16. https://www.idahostatesman.com/news/local/community/boise/article259444344.html.

Lands, LeeAnn. 2009. *The Culture of Property: Race, Class, and Housing Landscapes in Atlanta, 1880–1950.* Athens: University of Georgia Press.

Lane, Jamie. 2021. "AirDNA Market Review: U.S. July 2021." AirDNA—Short-Term Vacation Rental Data and Analytics, August 17. https://www.airdna.co/blog/airdna-market-review-us-july-2021.

Laniyonu, Ayobami. 2018. "Coffee Shops and Street Stops: Policing Practices in Gentrifying Neighborhoods." *Urban Affairs Review* 54, no. 5: 898–930.

Lareau, Annette, and Kimberly Goyette. 2014. *Choosing Homes, Choosing Schools.* New York: Russell Sage Foundation.

Larson, Erik. 2006. "Case Characteristics and Defendant Tenant Default in a Housing Court." *Journal of Empirical Legal Studies* 3, no. 1: 121–44.

Larson, Jane E. 2002. "Informality, Illegality, and Inequality." *Yale Law and Policy Review* 20, no. 1: 137–82.

Lauff, Erich, and Steven J. Ingels. 2013. *Education Longitudinal Study of 2002 (ELS: 2002): A First Look at 2002 High School Sophomores 10 Years Later.* NCES 2014–363. Washington, DC: National Center for Education Statistics.

Lauster, Nathanael. 2016. *The Death and Life of the Single-Family House: Lessons from Vancouver on Building a Livable City.* Philadelphia, PA: Temple University Press.

Lautenschlager, Rachel. 2022. "Urban Revitalization and the Policing of Racial Territoriality." *Race and Justice* (June 14). https://doi.org/10.1177/21533687221107807.

Leasure, Peter, and Tara Martin. 2017. "Criminal Records and Housing: An Experimental Study." *Journal of Experimental Criminology* 13, no. 4: 527–35.

Ledward, Brandon C. 2007. "On Being Hawaiian Enough: Contesting American Racialization with Native Hybridity." *Hūlili: Multidisciplinary Research on Hawaiian Well-Being* 4, no. 1: 107–43.

Lee, Barrett A., Townsand Price-Spratlen, and James W. Kanan. 2003. "Determinants of Homelessness in Metropolitan Areas." *Journal of Urban Affairs* 25, no. 3: 335–56.

Lee, Barrett A., Kimberly Tyler, and James Wright. 2010. "The New Homelessness Revisited." *Annual Review of Sociology* 36: 501–21.

Lee, C. Aujean. 2021. "'Working towards a Better Future for Ourselves': Neighborhood Choice of Middle-Class Latino and Asian Homeowners in Los Angeles." *Journal of Urban Affairs* 43, no. 7: 941–59.

Lee, Caroline, Michael McQuarrie, and Edward Walker. 2015. *Democratizing Inequalities: Pitfalls and Unrealized Promises of the New Public Participation*. New York: NYU Press.

Lee, Dayne. 2016. "How Airbnb Short-Term Rentals Exacerbate Los Angeles's Affordable Housing Crisis: Analysis and Policy Recommendations." *Harvard Law and Policy Review* 10, no. 1: 229–53.

Lee, Hyojung. 2017. "Who Owns Rental Properties, and Is It Changing?" *Housing Perspectives: Joint Center for Housing Studies of Harvard University* (blog), August 18. https://www.jchs.harvard.edu/blog/who-owns-rental-properties-and-is-it-changing/.

Lee, Jennifer. 2000. "The Salience of Race in Everyday Life: Black Customers' Shopping Experiences in Black and White neighborhoods." *Work and Occupations* 27, no. 3: 353–76.

Lee, Keunbok, David J. Harding, and Jeffrey D. Morenoff. 2017. "Trajectories of Neighborhood Attainment after Prison." *Social Science Research* 66 (August): 211–33.

Leeds, Anthony. 1969. "The Significant Variables Determining the Character of Squatter Settlements." *America Latina* 12, no. 3: 44–86.

Leeds, Anthony. 1974. "Housing Settlement Types, Arrangements for Living, Proletarianization and the Social Structure of the City." *Latin American Urban Research* 4: 67–99.

Leibbrand, Christine, Ryan Gabriel, Chris Hess, and Kyle Crowder. 2020. "Is Geography Destiny? Disrupting the Relationship between Segregation and Neighborhood Outcomes." *Social Science Research* 86.

Lens, Michael C. 2018. "Extremely Low-Income Households, Housing Affordability and the Great Recession." *Urban Studies* 55, no. 8: 1615–35.

Lens, Michael C., and Paavo Monkkonen. 2016. "Do Strict Land Use Regulations Make Metropolitan Areas More Segregated by Income?" *Journal of the American Planning Association* 82, no. 1: 6–21.

Lens, Michael C., Kyle Nelson, Ashley Gromis, and Yiwen Kuai. 2020. "The Neighborhood Context of Eviction in Southern California." *City and Community* 19, no. 4: 912–32.

Leopold, Josh. 2012. "The Housing Needs of Rental Assistance Applicants." *Cityscape* 14, no. 2: 275–98.

Leung, Lillian, Peter Hepburn, and Matthew Desmond. 2021. "Serial Eviction Filing: Civil Courts, Property Management, and the Threat of Displacement." *Social Forces* 100, no. 1: 316–44.

Levendis, John, and Mehmet F. Dicle. 2016. "The Neighborhood Impact of Airbnb on New Orleans." Working paper 2855771, October 24, Social Science Research Network. https://papers.ssrn.com/abstract=2856771.

Levenson, Zachary. 2021. "Becoming a Population: Seeing the State, Being Seen by the State, and the Politics of Eviction in Capetown." *Qualitative Sociology* 44, no. 3: 367–84.

Levine, Jeremy. 2017. "The Paradox of Community Power: Cultural Processes and Elite Authority in Participatory Governance." *Social Forces* 95, no. 3: 1155–79.

Levy, Diane K., Margery Austin Turner, Robert Santos, Doug Wissoker, Claudia L. Aranda, Rob Pitingolo, and Helen Ho. 2015. *Discrimination in the Rental Housing Market against People Who Are Deaf and People Who Use Wheelchairs: National Study Findings*. Washington, DC: Urban Institute.

Lewis-McCoy, R. L'Heureux. 2014. *Inequality in the Promised Land: Race, Resources, and Suburban Schooling*. Palo Alto, CA: Stanford University Press.

Lewis, Valerie A., Michael O. Emerson, and Stephen L. Klineberg. 2011. "Who We'll Live With: Neighborhood Racial Composition Preferences of Whites, Blacks and Latinos." *Social Forces* 89, no. 4: 1385–407.

Li, Xiaodi. 2019. "Do New Housing Units in Your Backyard Raise Your Rents?" Working paper, December 16. https://blocksandlots.com/wp-content/uploads/2020/02/Do-New-Housing-Units-in-Your-Backyard-Raise-Your-Rents-Xiaodi-Li.pdf.

Lichter, Daniel T., Domenico Parisi, and Michael C. Taquino. 2015. "Toward a New Macro-Segregation? Decomposing Segregation within and between Metropolitan Cities and Suburbs." *American Sociological Review* 80, no. 4: 843–73.

Lichter, Daniel T., Domenico Parisi, Michael C. Taquino, and Steven Michael Grice. 2010. "Residential Segregation in New Hispanic Destinations: Cities, Suburbs, and Rural Communities Compared." *Social Science Research* 392: 215–30.

Lichter, Daniel T., and Zhenchao Qian. 2018. "Boundary Blurring? Racial Identification among the Children of Interracial Couples." *Annals of the American Academy of Political and Social Science* 677, no. 1: 81–94.

Liévanos, Raoul S. 2019. "Green, Blue, Yellow, and Red: The Relational Racialization of Space in the Stockton Metropolitan Area." In *Relational Formations of Race: Theory, Method, and Practice*, edited by Natalia Molina, Daniel Martinez HoSang, and Ramón A. Gutiérrez, 224–54. Los Angeles: University of California Press.

Lin, Jan. 2008. "Los Angeles Chinatown: Tourism, Gentrification, and the Rise of an Ethnic Growth Machine." *Amerasia Journal* 34, no. 3: 110–25.

Lin, Ken-Hou, and Megan Tobias Neely. 2020. *Divested: Inequality in the Age of Finance*. Oxford: Oxford University Press.

Lin, Ken-Hou, and Donald Tomaskovic-Devey. 2013. "Financialization and U.S. Income Inequality, 1970–2008." *American Journal of Sociology* 118, no. 5: 1284–329.

Lindsey, Brink, and Steven M. Teles. 2017. *The Captured Economy: How the Powerful Enrich Themselves, Slow Down Growth, and Increase Inequality*. Oxford: Oxford University Press.

Lippert, Adam M., and Barrett A. Lee. 2015. "Stress, Coping, and Mental Health Differences among Homeless People." *Sociological Inquiry* 85, no. 3: 343–74.

Lipsitz, George. 2011. *How Racism Takes Place*. Philadelphia, PA: Temple University Press.

Lo, Lydia, Megan Gallagher, Rolf Pendall, Ananya Hariharan, and Christopher Davis. 2019. "National Longitudinal Land Use Survey." Washington, DC: Urban Institute. https://datacatalog.urban.org/node/6082/revisions/13825/view.

Lo Wang, Hansi. 2019. "On Census, Facebook and Instagram to Ban Disinformation and False Ads." *NPR*, December 19. https://news.wfsu.org/2019-12-19/on-census-facebook-and-instagram-to-ban-disinformation-and-false-ads.

Logan, John R. 1978. "Growth, Politics, and the Stratification of Places." *American Journal of Sociology* 84, no. 2: 404–16.

Logan, John R. 2002. *Hispanic Populations and Their Residential Patterns in the Metropolis*. Albany, NY: Lewis Mumford Center for Comparative Urban and Regional Research.

Logan, John R. 2013. "The Persistence of Segregation in the 21st Century Metropolis." *City and Community* 12, no. 2: 160–68.

Logan, John R. 2016. "As Long as There Are Neighborhoods." *City and Community* 15, no. 1: 23–28.

Logan, John R., Richard D. Alba, Tom McNulty, and Brian Fisher. 1996. "Making a Place in the Metropolis: Locational Attainment in Cities and Suburbs." *Demography* 33: 443–53.

Logan, John R., and Harvey Luskin Molotch. 2007 (1987). *Urban Fortunes: The Political Economy of Place*. Los Angeles: University of California Press.

Logan, John R., and Brian J. Stults. 2021. "The Persistence of Segregation in the Metropolis: New Findings from the 2020 Census." Diversity and Disparities Project, Brown University, Providence, RI. https://s4.ad.brown.edu/Projects/Diversity.

Logan, John R., Brian Stults, and Reynolds Farley. 2004. "Segregation of Minorities in the Metropolis: Two Decades of Change." *Demography* 41: 1–22.

Logan, John R., and Charles Zhang. 2010. "Global Neighborhoods: New Pathways to Diversity and Separation." *American Journal of Sociology* 115, no. 4: 1069–109.

Logan, John R., and Min Zhou. 1990. "The Adoption of Growth Controls in Suburban Communities." *Social Science Quarterly* 71, no. 1: 118–29.

Lomnitz, Larissa. 1988 (1974). "The Social and Economic Organization of a Mexican Shanty Town." In *The Urbanization of the Third World*, edited by Josef Gugler, 242–63. Oxford: Oxford University Press.

Lopez, Ian Haney. 1997. *White by Law: The Legal Construction of Race*. Vol. 21. New York: NYU Press.

Lopoo, Leonard M., and Bruce Western. 2005. "Incarceration and the Formation and Stability of Marital Unions." *Journal of Marriage and Family* 67, no. 3: 721–34.

Lundberg, Ian, and Louis Donnelly. 2019. "A Research Note on the Prevalence of Housing Eviction among Children Born in U.S. Cities." *Demography* 56, no. 1: 391–404.

Lundberg, Ian, Sarah L. Gold, Louis Donnelly, Jeanne Brooks-Gunn, and Sara S. McLanahan. 2020. "Government Assistance Protects Low-Income Families from Eviction." *Journal of Policy Analysis and Management* 40, no. 1 (Winter): 107–27. 10.1002/pam.22234.

Lyon-Callo, Vincent. 2008. *Inequality, Poverty, and Neoliberal Governance: Activist Ethnography in the Homeless Sheltering Industry*. 2nd ed. Toronto: University of Toronto Press, Higher Education Division.

Lytle Hernández, Kelly. 2017. *City of Inmates: Conquest, Rebellion, and the Rise of Human Caging in Los Angeles, 1771–1965*. Chapel Hill: University of North Carolina Press.

MacDonald, Christine. 2019. "Detroit Push Fails to Boost Rental Inspections." *Detroit News*, January 14. https://www.detroitnews.com/story/news/local/detroit-city/2019/01/14/detroit-push-rental-inspections-fails-increase-compliance/2473755002/.

MacKenzie, Melody Kapilialoha. 1991. *Native Hawaiian Rights Handbook*. Honolulu: University of Hawaiʻi Press.

Magavern, Sam. 2018. "Policies to Reduce Lead Exposure: Lessons from Buffalo and Rochester." *International Journal of Environmental Research and Public Health* 15, no. 10: 2197–205.

Mahmoudi Farahani, Leila. 2016. "The Value of the Sense of Community and Neighbouring." *Housing, Theory and Society* 33, no. 3: 357–76.

Mallach, Alan. 2014. "Lessons from Las Vegas: Housing Markets, Neighborhoods, and Distressed Single-Family Property Investors." *Housing Policy Debate* 24, no. 4: 769–801.

Mallach, Alan. 2018. *The Divided City: Poverty and Prosperity in Urban America.* Washington, DC: Island Press.

Mandelker, Daniel R. 2016. "Zoning Barriers to Manufactured Housing." *Urban Lawyer* 48, no. 2: 233–78.

Manduca, Robert, and Robert J. Sampson. 2019. "Punishing and Toxic Neighborhood Environments Independently Predict the Intergenerational Social Mobility of Black and White Children." *Proceedings of the National Academy of Sciences* 116, no. 16: 7772–77.

Mangin, William. 1967. "Latin American Squatter Settlements: A Problem and a Solution." *Latin American Research Review* 2, no. 3: 65–98.

Manson, Steven, Jonathan Schroeder, David Van Riper, and Steven Ruggles. 2019. "2016 American Community Survey: 5-Year Data (2012–2016, Block Groups and Larger Areas)." IPUMS National Historical Geographic Information System: Version 14.0 [Database]. Minneapolis, MN: IPUMS. http://doi.org/10.18128/D050.V14.0.

Manufactured Housing Institute (MHI). 2012. "Manufactured Housing: An Industry Overview." Presentation to the National Association of Counties Rural Housing Forum, Western Interstate Region Conference, Santa Fe, New Mexico, May 16.

Manufactured Housing Institute (MHI). 2020. *Manufactured Housing Facts: Industry Overview.* Arlington, VA: MHI, May. https://www.manufacturedhousing.org/wp-content/uploads/2020/07/2020-MHI-Quick-Facts-updated-05-2020.pdf.

Manville, Michael, and Paavo Monkkonen. 2021. "Unwanted Housing: Localism and Politics of Housing Development." *Journal of Planning Education and Research.*

Marble, William, and Clayton Nall. 2021. "When Self-Interest Trumps Ideology: Liberal Homeowners and Local Opposition to Housing Development." *Journal of Politics* 83, no. 4: 1747–63.

Marcuse, Peter. 1985. "Gentrification, Abandonment, and Displacement: Connections, Causes, and Policy Responses in New York City." *Washington University Journal of Urban and Contemporary Law* 28: 195–240.

Marcuse, Peter. 1988. "Neutralizing Homelessness." *Socialist Review* 18, no. 1: 69–96.

Marina, Peter J. 2017. *Down and Out in New Orleans: Transgressive Living in the Informal Economy.* New York: Columbia University Press.

Markley, Scott N., Taylor J. Hafley, Coleman A. Allums, Steven R. Holloway, and Hee Cheol Chung. 2020. "The Limits of Homeownership: Racial Capitalism, Black Wealth, and the Appreciation Gap in Atlanta." *International Journal of Urban and Regional Research* 44, no. 2: 310–28.

Maroto, Michelle. 2015. "The Absorbing Status of Incarceration and Its Relationship with Wealth Accumulation." *Journal of Quantitative Criminology* 31, no. 2: 207–36.

Maroto, Michelle, and Bryan L. Sykes. 2019. "The Varying Effects of Incarceration, Conviction, and Arrest on Wealth Outcomes among Young Adults." *Social Problems* 67, no. 4 (November): 698–718.

Marr, Matthew D. 2015. *Better Must Come: Exiting Homelessness in Two Global Cities.* Cornell University Press.

Marrow, Helen B. 2011. *New Destination Dreaming: Immigration, Race, and Legal Status in the Rural American South.* Stanford, CA: Stanford University Press.

Martin, Hal, and Andrew Hanson. 2016. "Metropolitan Area Home Prices and the Mortgage Interest Deduction: Estimates and Simulations from Policy Change." *Regional Science and Urban Economics* 59: 12–23.

Martin, Isaac William. 2020. "Commercial Assessment Inequality and Income Inequality among Racial Groups." Working paper, August 12, Silicon Valley Community Foundation. https://www.siliconvalleycf.org/sites/default/files /documents/scf/scf-martin-report.pdf.

Martin, Isaac William, and Kevin Beck. 2017. "Property Tax Limitation and Racial Inequality in Effective Tax Rates." *Critical Sociology* 43, no. 2: 221–36.

Martinez, Brandon P., and Alan A. Aja. 2021. "How Race Counts for Latinx Homeownership." *Critical Sociology* 47, no. 6: 993–1011.

Martínez, Miguel A. 2020. *Squatters in the Capitalist City: Housing, Justice, and Urban Politics*. New York: Routledge.

Marx, Karl. 2000 (1887). *Capital*. Vol. 1. Moscow: Progress Publishers. https://www .marxists.org/archive/marx/works/1867-c1/.

Maryland State Advisory Board of the Federal Emergency Administration of Public Works, W. W. Emmart, Chairman. 1934. *Report of the Joint Committee on Housing in Baltimore*. Baltimore, MD: Joint Committee on Housing in Baltimore.

Mason, Katherine Ramsey. 2020. *Crime-Free Housing Ordinances and Eviction*. Madison: University of Wisconsin Institute for Research on Poverty, December. https://www .irp.wisc.edu/resource/crime-free-housing-ordinances-and-eviction/.

Massey, Douglas S. 1996. "The Age of Extremes: Concentrated Affluence and Poverty in the Twenty-First Century." *Demography* 33, no. 4: 395–412.

Massey, Douglas. 2005. "Racial Discrimination in Housing: A Moving Target." *Social Problems* 52, no. 2: 148–51.

Massey, Douglas S. 2007. *Categorically Unequal: The American Stratification System*. New York: Russell Sage Foundation.

Massey, Douglas S. 2008. *New Faces, New Places: The Changing Geography of American Immigration*. New York: Russell Sage Foundation.

Massey, Douglas S., and Nancy A. Denton. 1988. "Suburbanization and Segregation in U.S. Metropolitan Areas." *American Journal of Sociology* 94: 592–626.

Massey, Douglas S., and Nancy A. Denton. 1993. *American Apartheid: Segregation and the Making of the Underclass*. Cambridge, MA: Harvard University Press.

Massey, Douglas S., and Mary J. Fischer. 1999. "Does Rising Income Bring Integration? New Results for Blacks, Hispanics, and Asians in 1990." *Social Science Research* 28: 316–26.

Massey, Douglas S., and Brendan P. Mullan. 1984. "Processes of Hispanic and Black Spatial Assimilation." *American Journal of Sociology* 89, no. 4: 836–73.

Massey, Douglas S., Len Albright, Rebecca Casciano, Elizabeth Derickson, and David N. Kinsey. 2013. *Climbing Mount Laurel: The Struggle for Affordable Housing and Social Mobility in an American Suburb*. Princeton, NJ: Princeton University Press.

Massey, Douglas S., Jonathan Rothwell, and Thurston Domina. 2009. "The Changing Bases of Segregation in the United States." *Annals of the American Academy of Political and Social Science* 626 (November): 74–90.

Massey, Douglas S., Jacob S. Rugh, Justin P. Steil, and Len Albright. 2016. "Riding the Stagecoach to Hell: A Qualitative Analysis of Racial Discrimination in Mortgage Lending." *City and Community* 15: 118–36.

Massoglia, Michael, Glenn Firebaugh, and Cody Warner. 2013. "Racial Variation in the Effect of Incarceration on Neighborhood Attainment." *American Sociological Review* 78, no. 1: 142–65.

Mast, Evan. 2019. "The Effect of New Market-Rate Construction on the Low-Income Housing Market." Working paper 19-307, July 1, Upjohn Institute. https://research.upjohn.org/up_workingpapers/307/.

Mayorga, Sarah. 2014. *Behind the White Picket Fence: Power and Privilege in a Multiethnic Neighborhood.* Chapel Hill, NC: UNC Press.

McAlester, Virginia Savage. 2013. *A Field Guide to American Houses: The Definitive Guide to Identifying and Understanding America's Domestic Architecture.* New York: Knopf.

McAllister, Tara G., Jacqueline R. Beggs, Shaun Ogilvie, Rauru Kirikiri, Amanda Black, and Priscilla M. Wehi. 2019. "Kua Takoto Te Mānuka: Mātauranga Māori in New Zealand Ecology." *New Zealand Journal of Ecology* 43, no. 3: 1–7.

McCabe, Brian. 2013. "Are Homeowners Better Citizens? Homeownership and Community Participation in the United States." *Social Forces* 91, no. 3: 929–54.

McCabe, Brian J. 2016. *No Place Like Home: Wealth, Community, and the Politics of Homeownership.* New York: Oxford University Press.

McCabe, Brian J. 2018. "Why Buy a Home? Race, Ethnicity, and Homeownership Preferences in the United States." *Sociology of Race and Ethnicity* 4: 452–72.

McCabe, Brian J., and Eva Rosen. 2020. *Eviction in Washington, D.C.: Racial and Geographic Disparities in Housing Instability.* Washington, DC: Georgetown University. https://georgetown.app.box.com/s/df0d4mruf59wcvqm6cqo9a8pyu8ukeuk.

McCarthy, Daniel J. 1979. "Housing Courts Bibliography." *Urban Law Annual* 17: 371–98.

McClure, Kirk. 2010. "The Prospects for Guiding Housing Choice Voucher Households to High-Opportunity Neighborhoods." *Cityscape* 25: 101–22.

McClure, Kirk, Alex F. Schwartz, and Lydia B. Taghavi. 2015. "Housing Choice Voucher Location Patterns a Decade Later." *Housing Policy Debate* 25, no. 2: 215–33.

McConnell, Eileen D. 2015. "Hurdles or Walls? Nativity, Citizenship, Legal Status and Latino Homeownership in Los Angeles." *Social Science Research* 53: 19–33.

McCormack, Karen, and Iyar Mazar. 2015. "Understanding Foreclosure Risk: The Role of Nativity and Gender." *Critical Sociology* 41: 115–32.

McGregor, Davianna Pomaika'i. 2007. *Na Kua 'Aina: Living Hawaiian Culture.* Honolulu: University of Hawai'i Press.

McKay, Dwanna L. 2019. "Real Indians: Policing or Protecting Authentic Indigenous Identity?" *Sociology of Race and Ethnicity* 7, no. 1: 12–25. https://doi.org/10.1177/2332649218821450.

McKernan, Signe-Mary, Caroline Ratcliffe, Margaret Simms, and Sisi Zhang. 2014. "Do Racial Disparities in Private Transfers Help Explain the Racial Wealth Gap? New Evidence from Longitudinal Data." *Demography* 51, no. 3: 949–74.

McLafferty, Sara, and Valerie Preston. 2019. "Who Has Long Commutes to Low-Wage Jobs? Gender, Race, and Access to Work in the New York Region." *Urban Geography* 40, no. 9: 1270–90.

McLanahan, Sara, Laura Tach, and Daniel Schneider. 2013. "The Causal Effects of Father Absence." *Annual Review of Sociology* 39, no. 1: 399–427.

McNamarah, Chan Tov. 2018. "White Caller Crime: Racialized Police Communication and Existing While Black." *Michigan Journal of Race and Law* 24: 335–415.

McWilliams, Carey. 1948. *North from Mexico: The Spanish-Speaking People of the United States*. Santa Barbara, CA: ABC-CLIO.

Mead, Joseph, Megan Hatch, J. Rosie Tighe, Marissa Pappas, Kristi Andrasik, and Elizabeth Bonham. 2017. "Who Is a Nuisance? Criminal Activity Nuisance Ordinances in Ohio." Working paper 3067028, November 10, Social Science Research Network. https://ssrn.com/abstract=3067028.

Meehan, Katie, Jason R. Jurjevich, Nicholas M. J. W. Chun, and Justin Sherrill. 2020. "Geographies of Insecure Water Access and the Housing-Water Nexus in US Cities." *Proceedings of the National Academy of Sciences of the United States of America* 117, no. 46: 28700–07.

Menchaca, Martha. 1995. *The Mexican Outsiders: A Community History of Marginalization and Discrimination in California*. Austin: University of Texas Press.

Menchaca, Martha. 2001. *Recovering History, Constructing Race: The Indian, Black and White Roots of Mexican Americans*. Austin: University of Texas Press.

Menchik, Paul L., and Nancy Ammon Jianakoplos. 1997. "Black-White Inequality: Is Inheritance the Reason?" *Economic Inquiry* 35, no. 2: 428–42.

Menjívar, Cecilia. 2000. *Fragmented Ties: Salvadoran Immigrant Networks in America*. Berkeley: University of California Press.

Mervosh, Sarah. 2018. "Minneapolis, Tackling Housing Crisis and Equity, Votes to End Single-Family Zoning." *New York Times*, December 13. https://www.nytimes.com/2018/12/13/us/minneapolis-single-family-zoning.html.

Mettler, Suzanne. 2010. "Reconstituting the Submerged State: The Challenges of Social Policy Reform in the Obama Era." *Perspectives on Politics* 8, no. 3: 803–24.

Metzger, Molly. 2014. "The Reconcentration of Poverty: Patterns of Housing Voucher Use 2000 to 2008." *Housing Policy Debate* 24, no. 3: 544–67.

MH Action. 2021. "Displacement, Inc.: How Havenpark Capital and Enterprise Community Partners Are Eroding Affordable Housing and How Residents Are Fighting Back." San Francisco, CA: MH Action. https://mhaction.org/wp-content/uploads/2021/05/MHAction-DIsplacement-Inc-English.pdf.

Migration Policy Institute. 2019. "Profile of the Unauthorized Population: United States." Migration Policy Institute. https://www.migrationpolicy.org/data/unauthorized-immigrant-population/state/US.

Mills, C. Wright. 1959. *The Sociological Imagination*. New York: Oxford University Press.

Mills, Charles W. 2004. "Racial Exploitation and the Wages of Whiteness." In *The Changing Terrain of Race and Ethnicity*, edited by Maria Krysan and Amanda Lewis, 235–62. New York: Russell Sage Foundation.

Minton, Todd D., Lauren G. Beatty, and Zhen Zeng. 2021. *Correctional Populations in the United States, 2019—Statistical Tables*. NCJ 300655, July. Washington, DC: Bureau of Justice Statistics. https://bjs.ojp.gov/sites/g/files/xyckuh236/files/media/document/cpus19st.pdf.

Mitchell, Don. 1997. "The Annihilation of Space by Law: The Roots and Implications of Anti-Homeless Laws in the United States." *Antipode* 29, no. 3: 303–35.

Molina, Natalia. 2006. *Fit to be Citizens? Public Health and Race in Los Angeles, 1879–1939*. Vol. 20. Los Angeles: University of California Press.

Molina, Natalia. 2010. "'In a Race All Their Own': The Quest to Make Mexicans Ineligible for US Citizenship." *Pacific Historical Review* 79, no. 2: 167–201.

Molina, Natalia. 2014. *How Race Is Made in America: Immigration, Citizenship, and the Historical Power of Racial Scripts*. Vol. 38. Los Angeles: University of California Press.

Mollborn, Stefanie. 2012. "Extended Household Transitions, Race/Ethnicity, and Early Childhood Cognitive Outcomes." *Social Science Research* 41, no. 5: 1152–65.

Mollborn, Stefanie. 2016. "Young Children's Developmental Ecologies and Kindergarten Readiness." *Demography* 53, no. 6: 1853–82.

Mollborn, Stefanie, Paula Fomby, and Jeff A. Dennis. 2011. "Who Matters for Children's Early Development? Race/Ethnicity and Extended Household Structures in the United States." *Child Indicators Research* 4, no. 3: 389–411.

Molotch, Harvey. 1976. "The City as a Growth Machine: Toward a Political Economy of Place." *American Journal of Sociology* 82, no. 2: 309–32.

Monkkonen, Paavo. 2016. "Understanding and Challenging Opposition to Housing Construction in California's Urban Areas." White paper, UC Center Sacramento, Housing, Land Use, and Development Lectureship and White Paper Award, December 1. https://dx.doi.org/10.2139/ssrn.3459823.

Monkkonen, Paavo, and Michael Manville. 2019. "Opposition to Development or Opposition to Developers? Experimental Evidence on Attitudes toward New Housing." *Journal of Urban Affairs* 41, no. 8: 1123–41.

Moody, Heather, Joe T. Darden, and Bruce William Pigozzi. 2016. "The Racial Gap in Childhood Blood Levels Related to Socioeconomic Position of Residence in Metropolitan Detroit." *Sociology of Race and Ethnicity* 2, no. 2: 200–18.

Moore, M. Kathleen. 2016. "Lists and Lotteries: Rationing in the Housing Choice Voucher Program." *Housing Policy Debate* 26, no. 3: 474–87.

Moore, M. Kathleen. 2018. " 'I Don't Do Vouchers': Experimental Evidence of Discrimination against Housing Voucher Recipients across Fourteen Metro Areas." Working paper. Institute for Research on Poverty, University of Wisconsin–Madison.

Morduch, Jonathan, and Rachel Schneider. 2017. *The Financial Diaries: How American Families Cope in a World of Uncertainty*. Princeton, NJ: Princeton University Press.

Morenoff, Jeffrey D., and David J. Harding. 2014. "Incarceration, Prisoner Reentry, and Communities." *Annual Review of Sociology* 40, no. 1: 411–29.

Morris, Aldon. 2015. *The Scholar Denied: W. E. B. Du Bois and the Birth of Modern Sociology*. Oakland: University of California Press.

Morrow, Betty Hearn. 1999. "Identifying and Mapping Social Vulnerability." *Disasters* 23, no. 1: 1–18.

Motel, Seth, and Eileen Patten. 2013. "Statistical Portrait of Hispanics in the United States, 2011." Pew Research Center, February 15. https://www.pewresearch.org/hispanic/2013/02/15/2011-statistical-information-on-hispanics-in-united-states/.

Muijzenberg, Otto van den, and Ton van Naerssen. 2005. "Metro Manila: Designers or Directors of Urban Development?" In *Directors of Urban Change in Asia*, edited by Peter J. M. Nas, 126–47. New York: Routledge.

Mulder, Clara H. 2018. "Putting Family Centre Stage: Ties to Nonresident Family, Internal Migration, and Immobility." *Demographic Research* 39: 1151–80.

Muller, Christopher. 2012. "Northward Migration and the Rise of Racial Disparity in American Incarceration, 1880–1950." *American Journal of Sociology* 118, no. 2: 281–326.

Muller, Christopher, Robert J. Sampson, and Alix S. Winter. 2018. "Environmental Inequality: Causes and Consequences of Lead Exposure." *Annual Review of Sociology* 44: 263–82.

Muñiz, Ana. 2015. *Police, Power, and the Production of Racial Boundaries*. New Brunswick, NJ: Rutgers University Press.

Murchie, Judson, and Jindong Pang. 2018. "Rental Housing Discrimination across Protected Classes: Evidence from a Randomized Experiment." *Regional Science and Urban Economics* 73 (November): 170–79.

Murchie, Judson, Jindong Pang, and David J. Schwegman. 2021. "Can Information Help Lakisha and Jamal Find Housing? Evidence from a Low-Cost Online Experiment of Landlords." *Regional Science and Urban Economics* 90 (September): 103712.

Murphy, Laura W. 2016. *Airbnb's Work to Fight Discrimination and Build Inclusion: A Report Submitted to Airbnb*. San Francisco, CA: Airbnb.

Musick, Kelly, and Larry Bumpass. 2012. "Reexamining the Case for Marriage: Union Formation and Changes in Well-Being." *Journal of Marriage and Family* 74, no. 1: 1–18.

Mutchler, Jan E., and Lindsey A. Baker. 2009. "The Implications of Grandparent Coresidence for Economic Hardship among Children in Mother-Only Families." *Journal of Family Issues* 30, no. 11: 1576–97.

Mykyta, Larissa, and Suzanne Macartney. 2012. *Sharing a Household: Household Composition and Economic Well-Being: 2007–2010*. Current Population Report P60–24. Washington, DC: US Census Bureau.

Nagel, Joane. 1997. *American Indian Ethnic Renewal: Red Power and the Resurgence of Identity and Culture*. New York: Oxford University Press.

National Alliance to End Homelessness. 2020. *State of Homelessness: 2020 Edition*. Washington, DC: National Alliance to End Homelessness. https://endhome lessness.org/homelessness-in-america/homelessness-statistics/state-of -homelessness/.

National Association of Realtors. 2021. *Snapshot of Race and Home Buying in America*. Washington, DC: National Association of Realtors. https://cdn.nar.realtor/sites /default/files/documents/2021-snapshot-of-race-and-home-buyers-in-america -report-02-19-2021.pdf.

National Center for Healthy Housing. 2021. "Lead Resources." https://nchh.org /information-and-evidence/healthy-housing-policy/state-and-local/lead/.

National Center for Homeless Education. n.d. "Understanding Doubled-Up." National Center for Homeless Education. PowerPoint presentation. Retrieved October 4, 2019. https://nche.ed.gov/understanding-doubled-up/.

National Housing Law Project. 2002. *False HOPE: A Critical Assessment of the HOPE VI Public Housing Redevelopment Program*. Oakland, CA: National Housing Law Project.

National Law Center on Homelessness and Poverty (NLCHP). 2019. *Housing Not Handcuffs 2019: Ending the Criminalization of Homelessness in U.S. Cities*. Washington, DC: National Law Center on Homelessness and Poverty. https://homelesslaw.org /wp-content/uploads/2019/12/HOUSING-NOT-HANDCUFFS-2019-FINAL.pdf.

National Low Income Housing Coalition (NLIHC). 2017. *Out of Reach 2017: The High Cost of Housing*. Washington, DC: NLIHC. https://nlihc.org/sites/default/files /oor/OOR_2017.pdf.

Nedelsky, Jennifer. 1990. *Private Property and the Limits of American Constitutionalism: The Madisonian Framework and Its Legacy*. Chicago: University of Chicago Press.

Needleman, Herbert L., and Philip J. Landrigan. 1981. "The Health Effects of Low-Level Lead Exposure." *Annual Review of Public Health* 2: 277–98.

Nellis, Ashley. 2017. *Still Life: America's Increasing Use of Life and Long-Term Sentences.* Washington, DC: Sentencing Project, May 3. https://www.sentencingproject.org/publications/still-life-americas-increasing-use-life-long-term-sentences/.

Nelson, Christina. 2022. "The Joint Distribution of Age and Race in Racially Integrated Neighbourhoods." *Population, Space and Place* 28, no. 2: 1–19.

Nelson, Geoffrey, Ana Stefancic, Jennifer Rae, Greg Townley, Sam Tsemberis, Eric Macnaughton, Tim Aubry, Jino Distasio, Roch Hurtubise, and Michelle Patterson. 2014. "Early Implementation Evaluation of a Multi-Site Housing First Intervention for Homeless People with Mental Illness: A Mixed Methods Approach." *Evaluation and Program Planning* 43: 16–26.

Nelson, Joan M. 1979. *Access to Power: Politics and the Urban Poor in Developing Nations.* Princeton, NJ: Princeton University Press.

Nelson, Kyle. 2021. "The Microfoundations of Bureaucratic Outcomes: Causes and Consequences of Interpretive Disjuncture in Eviction Cases." *Social Problems* 68, no. 1: 152–67.

Nelson, Kyle. 2022. "Litigating the Housing Crisis: Legal Assistance and the Institutional Life of Eviction in Los Angeles." PhD diss., University of California, Los Angeles. https://www.proquest.com/openview/bfbf06182ddd9c54967777693 85212c4/1?pq-origsite=gscholar&cbl=18750&diss=y.

Nelson, Kyle, Philip Garboden, Brian J. McCabe, and Eva Rosen. 2021a. "Evictions: The Comparative Analysis Problem." *Housing Policy Debate* 31, no. 3–5: 696–716.

Nelson, Kyle, Ashley Gromis, Yiwen Kuai, and Michael C. Lens. 2021b. "Spatial Concentration and Spillover: Eviction Dynamics in Neighborhoods of Los Angeles, 2005–2015." *Housing Policy Debate* 31, no. 3–5: 670–95.

Nelson, Margaret K. 2013. "Fictive Kin, Families We Choose, and Voluntary Kin: What Does the Discourse Tell Us?" *Journal of Family Theory and Review* 5, no. 4: 259–81.

Nelson, Robert K., LaDale Winling, Richard Marciano, and N. D. B Connolly. 2022. "Mapping Inequality." In *American Panorama*, edited by Robert K. Nelson and Edward L. Ayers. https://dsl.richmond.edu/panorama/redlining/.

Neuwirth, Robert. 2007. "Squatters and the Cities of Tomorrow." *City* 11, no. 1: 71–80.

Nevárez-Martínez, Deyanira, María G. Rendón, and Diego Arroyo. 2019. "Los Olvidados/The Forgotten: Reconceptualizing Colonias as Viable Communities." *Progress in Planning* 147: 100450.

New York State Department of Health. 2019. "What Your Child's Blood Lead Test Means." NYSDH, September. https://www.health.ny.gov/publications/2526/index.htm.

Newman, Katherine S. 2012. *The Accordion Family: Boomerang Kids, Anxious Parents, and the Private Toll of Global Competition.* Boston, MA: Beacon Press.

Ngai, Mae M. 2014. *Impossible Subjects: Illegal Aliens and the Making of Modern America.* Rev. ed., vol. 105. Princeton, NJ: Princeton University Press.

Noe-Bustamante, Luis. 2020. "Education Levels of Recent Latino Immigrants in the U.S. Reach New Highs as of 2018." Pew Research Center, April 7. https://www.pewresearch.org/fact-tank/2020/04/07/education-levels-of-recent-latino-immigrants-in-the-u-s-reached-new-highs-as-of-2018/.

Norgaard, Kari Marie. 2019. *Salmon and Acorns Feed Our People: Colonialism, Nature, and Social Action.* New Brunswick, NJ: Rutgers University Press.

Norman, Jon. 2011. "Housing for Families but Not for People: Federal Policy and Normative Family Ideals in Midcentury California." *Sociological Focus* 44: 210–30.

"Nuisance Property." n.d. City of Peoria, Illinois, Police Department. Retrieved October 17, 2022. https://www.peoriagov.org/704/Nuisance-Property.

Oakley, Deirdre. 2008. "Locational Patterns of Low Income Tax Credit Housing Developments: A Sociospatial Analysis of Four Metropolitan Areas." *Urban Affairs Review* 43, no. 5: 599–628.

Ocen, Priscilla. A. 2012. "The New Racially Restrictive Covenant: Race, Welfare and the Policing of Black Women in Subsidized Housing." *UCLA Law Review* 59: 1540–82.

O'Flaherty, Brendan. 1990. "The Option Value of Tax Delinquency: Theory." *Journal of Urban Economics* 28, no. 3: 287–317.

Oh, Sookhee, and Angie Chung. 2014. "A Study on the Sociospatial Context of Ethnic Politics and Entrepreneurial Growth in Koreatown and Monterey Park." *GeoJournal* 79, no. 1: 59–71.

Oh, Sun Jung, and John Yinger. 2015. "What Have We Learned from Paired Testing in Housing Markets?" *Cityscape* 17, no. 3: 15–60.

Oliver, Katherine. 1908. "The Cholo Question." *San Bernardino County Sun*, February 5: 4.

Oliver, Melvin L., and Thomas M. Shapiro. 1997. *Black Wealth, White Wealth: A New Perspective on Racial Inequality*. New York: Taylor and Francis.

Oliver, Melvin L., and Thomas M. Shapiro. 2019. "Disrupting the Racial Wealth Gap." *Contexts* 18, no. 1: 16–21.

Olsen, Skylar. 2014. "Doubled up for Dollars." Zillow, October 9. http://www.zillow.com/research/doubling-up-households-7947/.

Omi, Michael, and Howard Winant. 2014. *Racial Formation in the United States*. New York: Routledge.

Ondrich, Jan, Alex Stricker, and John Yinger. 1999. "Do Landlords Discriminate? The Incidence and Causes of Racial Discrimination in Rental Housing Markets." *Journal of Housing Economics* 8: 185–204.

O'Neil, Cathy. 2016. *Weapons of Math Destruction: How Big Data Increases Inequality and Threatens Democracy*. New York: Crown.

Ortega, Arnisson Andre. 2016. *Neoliberalizing Spaces in the Philippines: Suburbanization, Transnational Migration, and Dispossession*. Lanham, MD: Lexington Books.

Ortiz, Javier, Matthew Dick, and Sara Rankin. 2015. "The Wrong Side of History: A Comparison of Modern and Historical Criminalization Laws." Working paper 2602533, May 4, Social Science Research Network. https://ssrn.com/abstract=2602533.

Osborne, Melissa. 2019. "Who Gets 'Housing First'? Determining Eligibility in an Era of Housing First Homelessness." *Journal of Contemporary Ethnography* 48, no. 3: 402–28.

O'Sullivan, Arthur, Terri A. Sexton, and Steven M. Sheffrin. 1995. *Property Taxes and Tax Revolts*. New York: Cambridge University Press.

Owens, Ann. 2015. "Housing Policy and Urban Inequality: Did the Transformation of Assisted Housing Reduce Poverty Concentration?" *Social Forces* 94, no. 1: 325–48.

Owens, Ann. 2018. "Income Segregation between School Districts and Inequality in Students' Achievement." *Sociology of Education* 91, no. 1: 1–27.

Pacewicz, Josh. 2013. "Tax Increment Financing, Economic Development Professionals, and the Financialization of Urban Politics." *Socio-Economic Review* 11: 413–40.

Pager, Devah. 2003. "The Mark of a Criminal Record." *American Journal of Sociology* 108, no. 5: 937–75.

Pager, Devah. 2007. *Marked: Race, Crime, and Finding Work in an Era of Mass Incarceration.* Chicago: University of Chicago Press.

Pager, Devah, and Lincoln Quillian. 2005. "Walking the Talk? What Employers Say Versus What They Do." *American Sociological Review* 70, no. 3: 355–80.

Pager, Devah, and Hana Shepherd. 2008. "The Sociology of Discrimination: Racial Discrimination in Employment, Housing, Credit, and Consumer Markets." *Annual Review of Sociology* 34: 181–209.

Painter, Matthew A., II, and Zhenchao Qian. 2016a. "Wealth Inequality among Immigrants: Consistent Racial/Ethnic Inequality in the United States." *Population Research and Policy Review* 35, no. 2: 147–75.

Painter, Matthew A., II, and Zhenchao Qian. 2016b. "Wealth Inequality among New Immigrants." *Sociological Perspectives* 59, no. 2: 368–94.

Pais, Jeremy, and D. Matthew Ray. 2015. "Class Inequality and Adult Attainment Projects among Middle-Aged Men in the United States, 1980–2010." *Sociological Science* 2: 211–34.

Pais, Jeremy, Scott J. South, and Kyle Crowder. 2012. "Metropolitan Heterogeneity and Minority Neighborhood Attainment: Spatial Assimilation or Place Stratification?" *Social Problems* 59: 258–81.

Pallagst, Karina, Thorsten Wiechmann, and Cristina Martinez-Fernandez. 2013. *Shrinking Cities: International Perspectives and Policy Implications.* New York: Routledge.

Parisi, Domenico, Daniel T. Lichter and Michael C. Taquino. 2015. "The Buffering Hypothesis: Growing Diversity and Declining Black-White Segregation in America's Cities, Suburbs, and Small Towns?" *Sociological Science* 2: 125–57.

Park, Robert, and Ernest Burgess. 1925. *The City.* Chicago: University of Chicago Press.

Patterson, Ashleigh, and Richard Harris. 2017. "Landlords, Tenants, and the Legal Status of Secondary Suites in Hamilton, Ontario." *Canadian Geographer* 61, no. 4: 540–49.

Pattillo, Mary. 1999. *Black Picket Fences: Privilege and Peril among the Black Middle Class.* Chicago: University of Chicago Press.

Pattillo, Mary. 2008. *Black on the Block: The Politics of Race and Class in the City.* Chicago: University of Chicago Press.

Pattillo, Mary. 2013. "Housing: Commodity vs. Right." *Annual Review of Sociology* 39: 509–31.

Pattillo, Mary. 2019. "The Problem of Integration." In *The Dream Revisited,* edited by Ingrid Gould Ellen and Justin Peter Steil, 29–32. New York: Columbia University Press.

Pattillo, Mary, Erica Banks, Brian Sargent, and Daniel J. Boches. 2022. "Monetary Sanctions and Housing Instability." *RSF: The Russell Sage Foundation Journal of the Social Sciences* 8, no. 2: 57–75.

Paulauskaite, Dominyka, Raymond Powell, J. Andres Coca-Stefaniak, and Alastair M. Morrison. 2017. "Living like a Local: Authentic Tourism Experiences and the Sharing Economy." *International Journal of Tourism Research* 19, no. 6: 619–28.

Peck, Jamie, and Adam Tickell. "Neoliberalizing Space." In *Spaces of Neoliberalism: Urban Restructuring in North American and Western Europe,* edited by Neil Brenner and Nik Theodore, 33–57. New York: Blackwell Publishing.

Pedulla, David S. 2016. "Penalized or Protected? Gender and the Consequences of Nonstandard and Mismatched Employment Histories." *American Sociological Review* 81, no. 2: 262–89.

Pedulla, David S. 2018. "Emerging Frontiers in Audit Study Research: Mechanisms, Variation, and Representativeness." In *Audit Studies: Behind the Scenes with Theory, Method, and Nuance,* edited by S. Michael Gaddis, 179–85. Cham, Germany: Springer International Publishing.

Pell, M. B., Joshua Schneyer, and Andy Sullivan. 2017. "Hundreds More Lead Hotspots Are Identified as Trump Prepares to Gut Programs." *Huffington Post,* April 21. https://www.huffpost.com/entry/hundreds-more-lead-hotpsots-are-identified-as -trump-prepares-to-gut-programs_n_58fa207be4b00fa7de13b103.

Peng, Ilena, and Michael Tobin. 2022. "Airbnb Beats the Pandemic With 'Best Year' Yet; Shares Rise." *Bloomberg,* February 15. https://www.bloomberg.com/news/articles /2022-02-15/airbnb-beats-estimates-showing-resilience-despite-omicron-surge.

Pennington, Kate. 2021. "Does Building New Housing Cause Displacement? The Supply and Demand Effects of Construction in San Francisco." Working paper 3867764, Social Science Research Network, August 9. https://www.dropbox.com/s/oplls 6utgf7z6ih/Pennington_JMP.pdf?dl=0.

Peoria Police Department. n.d. *Armadillos: Starting a Trend.* Retrieved February 15, 2021. Peoria, IL: Peoria Police Department. https://popcenter.asu.edu/sites/default /files/library/awards/goldstein/2011/11-07.pdf.

Perkins, Kristin L. 2017a. "Household Complexity and Change among Children in the United States, 1984–2010." *Sociological Science* 4: 701–24.

Perkins, Kristin L. 2017b. "Reconsidering Residential Mobility: Differential Effects on Child Wellbeing by Race and Ethnicity." *Social Science Research* 63 (March): 124–37.

Perkins, Kristin L. 2017c. "Household Instability during Childhood and Young Adult Outcomes." PhD diss., Harvard University. https://dash.harvard.edu/handle/1 /41142076.

Perkins, Kristin L. 2019. "Changes in Household Composition and Children's Educational Attainment." *Demography* 56, no. 2: 525–48.

Perkins, Kristin L., and Robert J. Sampson. 2015. "Compounded Deprivation in the Transition to Adulthood: The Intersection of Racial and Economic Inequality among Chicagoans, 1995–2013." *RSF: The Russell Sage Foundation Journal of the Social Sciences* 1, no. 1: 35–54.

Perlman, Janice. 1976. *Myth of Marginality: Urban Poverty and Politics in Rio de Janeiro.* Berkeley: University of California Press.

Perlman, Janice. 2010. *Favela: Four Decades of Living on the Edge in Rio de Janeiro.* Oxford: Oxford University Press.

Perry, Andre, and David Harshbarger. 2019. *America's Formerly Redlined Neighborhoods Have Changed, and So Must Solutions to Rectify Them.* Washington, DC: Brookings Institute.

Perry, Andre, Jonathan Rothwell, and David Harshbarger. 2018. *The Devaluation of Assets in Black Neighborhoods: The Case of Residential Property.* Washington, DC: Metropolitan Policy Program, Brookings Institute.

Petersilia, Joan. 2003. *When Prisoners Come Home: Parole and Prisoner Reentry.* Oxford: Oxford University Press.

Pettit, Becky, and Bruce Western. 2004. "Mass Imprisonment and the Life Course: Race and Class Inequality in U.S. Incarceration." *American Sociological Review* 69, no. 2: 151–69.

Pettit, Kathryn L. S., G. Thomas Kingsley, Jennifer Biess, Kassie Bertumen, Nancy Pindus, Chris Narducci, and Amos Budde. 2014. *Continuity and Change: Demographic, Socioeconomic, and Housing Conditions of Native American Indians and Alaska Natives.*

Washington, DC: US Department of Housing and Urban Development, Office of Policy Development and Research.

Pew Charitable Trusts. 2022. *Millions of Americans Have Used Risky Financing Arrangements to Buy Homes*. Washington, DC: Pew Charitable Trusts, April. https://www.pewtrusts.org/-/media/assets/2022/05/millionsofamericans haveusedriskyfinancing_brief.pdf.

Pew Research Center. 2020. "What Census Calls Us: A Historical Timeline" Pew Research Center, February 6. https://www.pewresearch.org/interactives/what -census-calls-us/.

Philippine Statistics Authority (PSA). 1991–2000. *Philippine Statistical Yearbook*. Quezon City: Philippine Statistics Authority.

Phillips, David C. 2017. "Landlords Avoid Tenants Who Pay with Vouchers." *Economics Letters* 151 (February): 48–52.

Phillips, Shane. 2020. "We Need Rental Registries Now More Than Ever." *Shelterforce*, December 18. https://shelterforce.org/2020/12/18/we-need-a-rental-registry-now -more-than-ever/.

Phillips, Shane, Michael Manville, and Michael Lens. 2021. *Research Roundup: The Effect of Market-Rate Development on Neighborhood Rents*. Los Angeles, California: UCLA Lewis Center for Regional Policy Studies. https://escholarship.org/uc /item/5d00z61m?.

Pierce, Gregory, C. J. Gabbe, and Silvia R. Gonzalez. 2018. "Improperly-Zoned, Spatially-Marginalized, and Poorly-Served? An Analysis of Mobile Home Parks in Los Angeles County." *Land Use Policy* 76: 178–85.

Pierce, Gregory, and Silvia Jimenez. 2015. "Unreliable Water Access in U.S. Mobile Homes: Evidence from the American Housing Survey." *Housing Policy Debate* 25, no. 4: 739–53.

Piketty, Thomas. 2014. *Capital in the Twenty-First Century*. Cambridge, MA: Harvard University Press.

Pilkauskas, Natasha V. 2012. "Three-Generation Family Households: Differences by Family Structure at Birth." *Journal of Marriage and Family* 74, no. 5: 931–43.

Pilkauskas, Natasha V. 2014. "Living with a Grandparent and Parent in Early Childhood: Associations with School Readiness and Differences by Demographic Characteristics." *Developmental Psychology* 50, no. 12: 2587–99.

Pilkauskas, Natasha V., and Christina Cross. 2018. "Beyond the Nuclear Family: Trends in Children Living in Shared Households." *Demography* 55, no. 6: 2283–97.

Pilkauskas, Natasha V., Irwin Garfinkel, and Sara S. McLanahan. 2014. "The Prevalence and Economic Value of Doubling Up." *Demography* 51, no. 5: 1667–76.

Pinkster, Fenne M., and Willem R. Boterman. 2017. "When the Spell Is Broken: Gentrification, Urban Tourism and Privileged Discontent in the Amsterdam Canal District." *Cultural Geographies* 24, no. 3: 457–72.

Polanyi, Karl. 2001 (1944). *The Great Transformation: The Political and Economic Origins of Our Time*. Boston, MA: Beacon Press.

Popkin, Susan J., Mary Cunningham, and William Woodley. 2003. *Residents at Risk: A Profile of Ida B. Wells and Madden Park*. Washington, DC: Urban Institute.

Popkin, Susan J., Victoria E. Gwiasda, Lynn M. Olson, Dennis P. Rosenbaum, and Larry Buron. 2000. *The Hidden War: Crime and the Tragedy of Public Housing in Chicago*. New Brunswick, NJ: Rutgers University Press.

Portes, Alejandro. 1989. "Latin American Urbanization during the Years of Crisis." *Latin American Research Review* 24, no. 3: 7–44.

Portes, Alejandro, Carlos Dore-Cabral, and Patricia Landolt, eds. 1997. *The Urban Caribbean: Transition to the New Global Economy*. Baltimore, MD: Johns Hopkins University Press.

Portes, Alejandro, and Bryan R. Roberts. 2005. "The Free-Market City: Latin American Urbanization in the Years of the Neoliberal Experiment." *Studies in Comparative International Development* 40, no. 1: 43–82.

Portes, Alejandro, and John Walton. 1976. *Urban Latin America: The Political Conditions from Above and Below*. Austin: University of Texas Press.

Porton, Adam, Ashley Gromis, and Matthew Desmond. 2021. "Inaccuracies in Eviction Records: Implications for Renters and Researchers." *Housing Policy Debate* 31, no. 3–5: 377–94.

Potts, Deborah. 2020. *Broken Cities: Inside the Global Housing Crisis*. London: Zed Books.

Powell, Kathleen H. 2016. "A New Neighborhood Every Fall: Aging in Place in a College Town." *Journal of Gerontological Social Work* 59, no. 7–8: 537–53.

Powell, Walter W., and Paul J. DiMaggio, eds. 1991. *The New Institutionalism in Organizational Analysis*. Chicago: University of Chicago Press.

Powers, Jeanne M. 2008. "Forgotten History: Mexican American School Segregation in Arizona from 1900–1951." *Equity and Excellence in Education* 41, no. 4: 467–81.

Prasad, Shivangi, and Justin Stoler. 2016. "Mobile Home Residents and Hurricane Vulnerability in South Florida: Research Gaps and Challenges." *International Journal of Disaster Risk Science* 7, no. 4: 436–39.

Private Equity Stakeholder Project (PESP). 2019. *Private Equity Giants Converge on Manufactured Homes*. Chicago: PE Stakeholder, February 14. https://pestakeholder .org/wp-content/uploads/2019/02/Private-Equity-GIants-Converge-on-Manufac tured-Homes-PESP-MHAction-AFR-021419.pdf.

Proudfoot, Jesse, and Eugene J. McCann. 2008. "At Street Level: Bureaucratic Practice in the Management of Urban Neighborhood Change." *Urban Geography* 29: 348–70.

Pruijt, Hans. 2003. "Is the Institutionalization of Urban Movements Inevitable? A Comparison of the Opportunities for Sustained Squatting in New York City and Amsterdam." *International Journal of Urban and Regional Research* 27, no. 1: 133–57.

Pruitt, Anna S., and John P. Barile. 2020. *Unsheltered in Honolulu: Examining Unsheltered Homelessness in Honolulu from 2017–2020*. Honolulu, HI: Mayor's Office of Housing, City and County of Honolulu, and Partners in Care. https://www.honolulu.gov /rep/site/ohou/UnshelteredHNL-2020-compressed.pdf.

Puchalski, Vance Alan. 2016. "Credit at the Corner Store: An Analysis of Resource Exchange among Detroit-Area Urban Poor." *Sociological Forum* 31, no. 4: 1040–62.

Purser, Gretchen. 2016. "The Circle of Dispossession: Evicting the Urban Poor in Baltimore." *Critical Sociology* 42, no. 3: 393–415.

Quadlin, Natasha. 2018. "The Mark of a Woman's Record: Gender and Academic Performance in Hiring." *American Sociological Review* 83, no. 2: 331–60. https://doi .org/10.1177/0003122418762291.

Quealy, Kevin. 2020. "The Richest Neighborhoods Emptied Out Most as Coronavirus Hit New York City." *New York Times*, May 15. https://www.nytimes.com/interactive /2020/05/15/upshot/who-left-new-york-coronavirus.html.

Quillian, Lincoln, John J. Lee, and Brandon Honoré. 2020. "Racial Discrimination in the US Housing and Mortgage Lending Markets: A Quantitative Review of Trends, 1976–2016." *Race and Social Problems* 12, no. 1: 13–28.

Quillian, Lincoln, Devah Pager, Ole Hexel, and Arnfinn H. Midtbøen. 2017. "Meta-Analysis of Field Experiments Shows No Change in Racial Discrimination in Hiring over Time." *Proceedings of the National Academy of Sciences* 114, no. 41: 10870–75.

Quinn, Sarah. 2017. " 'The Miracles of Bookkeeping': How Budget Politics Link Fiscal Policies and Financial Markets." *American Journal of Sociology* 123, no. 1: 48–85.

Rabinowitz, Kate. 2019. "The Knowns and Unknowns of Airbnb in D.C." DC Policy Center, March 1. https://www.dcpolicycenter.org/publications/the-knowns-and-unknowns-of-airbnb-in-d-c/.

Rainwater, Lee. 1970. *Behind Ghetto Walls: Black Families in a Federal Slum.* New York: Aldine Publishing Company.

Raley, R. Kelly, Inbar Weiss, Robert Reynolds, and Shannon E. Cavanagh. 2019. "Estimating Children's Household Instability between Birth and Age 18 Using Longitudinal Household Roster Data." *Demography* 56, no. 5: 1957–73.

Ramsey, Kathryn V. 2018. "One-Strike 2.0: How Local Governments Are Distorting a Flawed Federal Eviction Law." *UCLA Law Review* 65: 1146–99.

Ramsey-Musolf, Darrel. 2018. "Accessory Dwelling Units as Low-Income Housing: California's Faustian Bargain." *Urban Science* 2, no. 3: 89.

Rankin, Sara. 2020. "Hiding Homelessness: The Transcarceration of Homelessness." *California Law Review* 109, no. 2: 1–55.

Raphael, Steven. 2010. "Housing Market Regulation and Homelessness." In *How to House the Homeless*, edited by Ingrid Gould Ellen and Brendan O'Flaherty, 110–40. New York: Russell Sage Foundation.

Rastogi, Ankit, and Katherine Curtis. 2020. "Beyond the City: Exploring the Suburban and Rural Landscapes of Racial Residential Integration Across the United States." *Population Research and Policy Review* 39, no. 5: 861–88.

Ray, Victor. 2019. "A Theory of Racialized Organizations." *American Sociological Review* 84, no. 1: 26–53.

Raymond, Elora Lee, Richard Duckworth, Benjamin Miller, Michael Lucas, and Shiraj Pokharel. 2018. "From Foreclosure to Eviction: Housing Insecurity in Corporate-Owned Single-Family Rentals." *Cityscape* 20, no. 3: 159–88.

Realtor.com. 2022. "Housing Inventory: Median Days on Market in the United States." FRED, Federal Reserve Bank of St. Louis, October 9. https://fred.stlouisfed.org/series/MEDDAYONMARUS.

Reardon, Sean F., Demetra Kalogrides, and Kenneth Shores. 2019. "The Geography of Racial/Ethnic Test Score Gaps." *American Journal of Sociology* 124, no. 4: 1164–221.

Reardon, Sean F., and Ann Owens. 2014. "60 Years After Brown: Trends and Consequences of School Segregation." *Annual Review of Sociology* 40: 199–281.

Reed, Chadwick, and Doug Ryan. 2021. *Manufactured Homes: A Key Element in Growing Latinx Homeownership.* Washington, DC: Prosperity Now, October. https://prosperitynow.org/sites/default/files/resources/Manufactured-Homes-Latinx-Commmunities_v2.pdf.

Reid, Carolina K. 2019. "Rethinking 'Opportunity' in the Siting of Affordable Housing in California: Resident Perspectives on the Low-Income Housing Tax Credit." *Housing Policy Debate* 29, no. 4: 645–69.

Ren, Xuefei. 2011. *Building Globalization: Transnational Architecture Production in Urban China*. Chicago: University of Chicago Press.

Rendall, Michael S., Margaret M. Weden, and Joey Brown. 2021. "Family and Household Sources of Poverty for Black, Hispanic, and White Newborns." *Journal of Marriage and Family* 84, no. 1: 330–46.

Reosti, Anna. 2020. "'We Go Totally Subjective': Discretion, Discrimination, and Tenant Screening in a Landlord's Market." *Law and Social Inquiry* 45, no. 3: 618–57.

Reskin, Barbara. 2012. "The Race Discrimination System." *Annual Review of Sociology* 38, no. 1: 17–35.

Reyes, Adriana M. 2018. "The Economic Organization of Extended Family Households by Race or Ethnicity and Socioeconomic Status." *Journal of Marriage and Family* 80, no. 1: 119–33.

Revitalizing and Rebuilding the City of Baltimore. Report commissioned by Mayor Martin O'Malley and Housing Commissioner Paul T. Graziano. Baltimore, MD: City of Baltimore, 2003. http://archives.ubalt.edu/aclu/pdfs/R0002_ACLU_S03A_B14_F002_P1.pdf.

Reyes, Adriana M. 2020. "Mitigating Poverty through the Formation of Extended Family Households: Race and Ethnic Differences." *Social Problems* 67, no. 4: 782–99.

Reyes, Marqueza C. L. 1998. "Spatial Structure of Metro Manila: Genesis, Growth, and Development." *Philippine Planning Journal* 29, no. 2 and 30, no. 1: 1–34.

Ribas, Vanessa. 2015. *On the Line: Slaughterhouse Lives and the Making of the New South*. Oakland: University of California Press.

Rice, Lisa, and Deidre Swesnik. 2013. "Discriminatory Effects of Credit Scoring on Communities of Color." *Suffolk University Law Review* 46, no. 3: 935–64. https://nationalfairhousing.org/wp-content/uploads/2017/04/NFHA-credit-scoring-paper-for-Suffolk-NCLC-symposium-submitted-to-Suffolk-Law.pdf.

Rice, Stuart A. 1918. "The Homeless." *Annals of the American Academy of Political and Social Science* 77, no. 1: 140–53.

Rich, Peter M., and Jennifer L. Jennings. 2015. "Choice, Information, and Constrained Options: School Transfers in a Stratified Educational System." *American Sociological Review* 80, no. 5: 1069–98.

Rieder, Jonathan. 1985. *Canarsie: The Jews and Italians of Brooklyn against Liberalism*. Cambridge, MA: Harvard University Press.

Riis, Jacob. 1890. *How the Other Half Lives: Studies among the Tenements of New York*. New York: Charles Scribner's Sons.

Riley, Lorinda. 2016. "When a Tribal Entity Becomes a Nation: The Role of Politics in the Shifting Federal Recognition Regulations." *American Indian Law Review* 39: 451–506.

Rimmer, Peter J., and Howard Dick. 2009. *The City in Southeast Asia: Patterns, Process, and Policy*. Honolulu: University of Hawai'i Press.

Rita, Nathalie, Philip Garboden, and Jennifer Darrah-Okike. 2021. "'You Have to Prove That You're Homeless': Vulnerability and Gatekeeping in Public Housing Prioritization Policies." Unpublished manuscript.

Roberto, Elizabeth. 2018. "The Spatial Proximity and Connectivity Method for Measuring and Analyzing Residential Segregation." *Sociological Methodology* 48, no. 1: 182–224.

Roberts, Bryan. 1973. *Organizing Strangers: Poor Families in Guatemala City*. Austin: University of Texas Press.

Roberts, Bryan. 1978. *Cities of Peasants: The Political Economy of Urbanization in the Third World*. New York: Sage Publications.

Roberts, Bryan. 1995. *The Making of Citizens: Cities of Peasants Revisited*. New York: Routledge.

Roberts, Bryan, and Alejandro Portes. 2006. "Coping with the Free Market City: Collective Action in Six Latin American Cities at the End of the Twentieth Century." *Latin American Research Review* 41, no. 2: 57–83.

Roberts, Sam. 2010. "In Harlem, Blacks Are No Longer a Majority." *New York Times*, January 6, section A: 16.

Robinson, Tony. 2019. "No Right to Rest: Police Enforcement Patterns and Quality of Life Consequences of the Criminalization of Homelessness." *Urban Affairs Review* 55, no. 1: 41–73.

Robinson, John N., III. 2019. "Fair Housing After 'Big Government': How Tax Credits Are Reshaping the Legal Fight Against Racial Segregation." *Housing Policy Debate* 29, no. 5: 752–68.

Robinson, John N., III. 2020a. "Capitalizing on Community: Affordable Housing Markets in the Age of Participation." *Politics and Society* 48, no. 2: 171–98.

Robinson, John N., III. 2020b. "Making Markets on the Margins: Housing Finance Agencies and the Racial Politics of Credit Expansion." *American Journal of Sociology* 125, no. 4: 974–1029.

Rodriguez-Lonebear, Desi. 2021. "The Blood Line: Racialized Boundary Making and Citizenship among Native Nations." *Sociology of Race and Ethnicity* 7, no. 4: 527–42. https://doi.org/10.1177/2332649220981589.

Roediger, David R. 2006. *Working toward Whiteness: How America's Immigrants Became White: The Strange Journey from Ellis Island to the Suburbs*. Cambridge, MA: Basic Books.

Roelofsen, Maartje. 2018. "Exploring the Socio-Spatial Inequalities of Airbnb in Sofia, Bulgaria." *Erdkunde* 72, no. 4: 313–28.

Roemer, J. E. 1982. "New Directions in the Marxian Theory of Exploitation and Class." *Politics and Society* 11, no. 3: 253–87.

Rolnik, Raquel. 2019. *Urban Warfare: Housing under the Empire of Finance*. Verso.

Romo, Ricardo. 1983. *East Los Angeles: History of a Barrio*. Vol. 12. Austin: University of Texas Press.

Roscigno, Vincent J., Diana L. Karafin, and Griff Tester. 2009. "The Complexities and Processes of Racial Housing Discrimination." *Social Problems* 56, no. 1: 49–69.

Rosen, Eva. 2014. "Rigging the Rules of the Game: How Landlords Geographically Sort Low-Income Renters." *City and Community* 13, no. 4: 310–40

Rosen, Eva. 2017. "Horizontal Immobility: How Narratives of Neighborhood Violence Shape Housing Decisions." *American Sociological Review* 82, no. 2: 270–96.

Rosen, Eva. 2020. *The Voucher Promise: "Section-8" and the Fate of an American Neighborhood*. Princeton, NJ: Princeton University Press.

Rosen, Eva. 2021. "If 'Housing Is a Right,' How Do We Make It Happen?" *New York Times*, February 17. https://www.nytimes.com/2021/02/17/opinion/eviction-housing-biden.html.

Rosen, Eva, and Philip M. E. Garboden. 2022. "Landlord Paternalism: Housing the Poor with a Velvet Glove." *Social Problems* 69, no. 2: 470–91.

Rosen, Eva, Philip M. E. Garboden, and Jennifer Cossyleon. 2021. "Racial Discrimination in Housing: How Landlords Use Algorithms and Home Visits to Screen Tenants." *American Sociological Review* 86, no. 5: 787–822.

Rosenbaum, Emily. 2012. "Home Ownership's Wild Ride, 2001–2011." US 2010 research brief, March. http://www.s4.brown.edu/us2010/Data/Report/report03212012.pdf.

Rosenberg, Erika, Kent Gardner, and Amelia Rickard. 2018. "Renewing Our Pledge: A Path to Ending Lead Poisoning for Buffalo's Most Vulnerable Citizens." Erie, NY: CGR, February. http://reports.cgr.org/details/1856.

Rosenberg, Mike. 2018. "Seattle Dethroned as Nation's Hottest Housing Market after Nearly Two Years." *Seattle Times*, August 28. https://www.seattletimes.com/business/real-estate/seattle-dethroned-as-nations-hottest-housing-market-for-first-time-in-nearly-two-years/.

Rosenblatt, Peter. 2012. "The Renaissance Comes to the Projects: Public Housing, Urban Redevelopment, and Racial Inequality in Baltimore." PhD diss., Johns Hopkins University. https://www.proquest.com/openview/c86276ba806d36a6fcaa3dfa2db12a63/1.pdf.

Rosenblatt, Peter, and Jennifer E. Cossyleon. 2018. "Pushing the Boundaries: Searching for Housing in the Most Segregated Metropolis in America." *City and Community* 17, no. 1: 87–108.

Rosenblatt, Peter, and Steven J. Sacco. 2018. "Investors and the Geography of the Subprime Housing Crisis." *Housing Policy Debate* 28, no. 1: 94–116.

Ross, Stephen, and John Yinger. 1999. "Does Discrimination in Mortgage Lending Exist? The Boston Fed Study and Its Critics." In *Mortgage Lending Discrimination: A Review of Existing Evidence*, edited by Margery Austin Turner and Felicity Skidmore, 43–83. Washington, DC: Urban Institute, June. https://www.urban.org/sites/default/files/publication/66151/309090-Mortgage-Lending-Discrimination.PDF.

Ross, Stephen, and John Yinger. 2002. *The Color of Credit*. Cambridge, MA: MIT Press.

Ross, Stephen L., and Margery A. Turner. 2005. "Housing Discrimination in Metropolitan America: Explaining Changes between 1989 and 2000." *Social Problems* 52, no. 2: 152–80.

Roth, Alvin. 2007. "Repugnance as a Constraint on Markets." *Journal of Economic Perspectives* 21, no. 3: 37–58.

Rothstein, Richard. 2017. *The Color of Law: A Forgotten History of How Our Government Segregated America*. New York: Liveright Publishing.

Rothwell, Jonathan, and Douglas S. Massey. 2009. "The Effect of Density Zoning on Racial Segregation in U.S. Urban Areas." *Urban Affairs Review* 44, no. 6: 779–806.

Rothwell, Jonathan, and Douglas S. Massey. 2010. "Density Zoning and Class Segregation in U.S. Metropolitan Areas." *Social Science Quarterly* 91, no. 5: 1123–43.

Roy, Ananya. 2002. *City Requiem, Calcutta: Gender and the Politics of Poverty*. Minneapolis: University of Minnesota Press.

Roy, Ananya. 2005. "Urban Informality: Toward an Epistemology of Planning." *Journal of the American Planning Association* 71, no. 2: 147–58.

Roy, Ananya, Terra Graziani, and Pamela Stephens. 2020. *Unhousing the Poor: Interlocking Regimes of Racialized Policing*. New York: Square One Justice Project, hosted by the Justice Lab at Columbia University. https://squareonejustice.org/wp-content/uploads/2020/08/Ananya-Roy-et-al-Unhousing-the-Poor-1.pdf.

Rucks-Ahidiana, Zawadi. 2017. "Cultural Implications of Historical Exclusion for the Racial Wealth Gap: How Ideal Financial Behavior Varies by Race." *American Journal of Cultural Sociology* 5, no. 1–2: 68–89.

Rucks-Ahidiana, Zawadi. 2020. "Racial Composition and Trajectories of Gentrification in the United States." *Urban Studies* 58, no. 13: 2721–41. https://doi.org/10.1177
/0042098020963853.

Ruggles, Steven, J. Trent Alexander, Katie Genadek, Ronald Goeken, Matthew B.
Schroeder, and Matthew Sobek. 2010. *Integrated Public Use Microdata Series:
Version 5.0.* Minneapolis: University of Minnesota.

Rugh, Jacob S. 2015. "Double Jeopardy: Why Latinos Were Hit Hardest by the US
Foreclosure Crisis." *Social Forces* 93, no. 3: 1139–84.

Rugh, Jacob S. 2020. "Why Black and Latino Home Ownership Matter to the Color
Line and Multiracial Democracy." *Race and Social Problems* 12, no. 1: 57–76.

Rugh, Jacob S., Len Albright, and Douglas S. Massey. 2015. "Race, Space, and
Cumulative Disadvantage: A Case Study of the Subprime Lending Collapse." *Social
Problems* 62, no. 2: 186–218.

Rugh, Jacob S., and Douglas S. Massey. 2010. "Racial Segregation and the American
Foreclosure Crisis." *American Sociological Review* 75, no. 5: 629–51.

Ruiz, Vicki L. 2001. "South by Southwest: Mexican Americans and Segregated
Schooling, 1900–1950." *OAH Magazine of History* 15, no. 2: 23–27.

Rumbach, Andrew, Esther Sullivan, and Carrie Makarewicz. 2020. "Mobile Home Parks
and Disasters: Understanding Risk to the Third Housing Type in the United States."
Natural Hazards Review 21, no. 2: 5020001.

Ryan, Brent D. 2012. *Design After Decline: How America Rebuilds Shrinking Cities.*
Philadelphia: University of Pennsylvania Press.

Saez, Emmanuel, and Gabriel Zucman. 2016. "Wealth Inequality in the United States
since 1913: Evidence from Capitalized Income Tax Data." *Quarterly Journal of
Economics* 131, no. 2: 519–78.

Saha, Lipon, Ron Nicholls, Alpana Sivam, and Sadasivam Karuppannan. 2019.
"Relationality: An Indigenous Approach to Housing Design." Paper presented at
the State of Australian Cities Conference, Perth, Western Australia, November 30–
December 5.

Sahn, Alexander. 2022. "Racial Diversity and Exclusionary Zoning: Evidence from
the Great Migration." Working paper, January 26. https://drive.google.com
/file/d/10_-WcJe4v6GfxVDfJ2h-R3pvjK4yjig0/view.

Saidel-Goley, Isaac, and Joseph William Singer. 2017. "Things Invisible to See: State
Action and Private Property." *Texas A and M Law Review* 5: 439–504.

Salamon, Sonya, and Katherine MacTavish. 2017. *Singlewide: Chasing the American
Dream in a Rural Trailer Park.* Ithaca, NY: Cornell University Press.

Salviati, Chris. 2019. "2019 Cost Burden Report: Half of Renter Households Struggle
with Affordability." *Apartment List*, October 9. https://www.apartmentlist.com
/research/cost-burden-2019.

Sampson, Robert J. 1988. "Local Friendship Ties and Community Attachment in Mass
Society: A Multilevel Systemic Model." *American Sociological Review* 53 no. 5: 766–79.

Sampson, Robert J. 2008. "Moving to Inequality: Neighborhood Effects and
Experiments Meet Structure." *American Journal of Sociology* 114, no. 11: 189–231.

Sampson, Robert J. 2012. *Great American City: Chicago and the Enduring Neighborhood
Effect.* Chicago: University of Chicago Press.

Sampson, Robert J., Jeffrey D. Morenoff, and Thomas Gannon-Rowley. 2002. "Assessing
'Neighborhood Effects': Social Processes and New Directions in Research." *Annual
Review of Sociology* 28, no. 1: 443–78.

Sampson, Robert J., and Patrick Sharkey. 2008. "Neighborhood Selection and the Social Reproduction of Concentrated Racial Inequality." *Demography* 45, no. 1:1–29.

Sampson, Robert J., Patrick Sharkey, and Stephen W. Raudenbush. 2008. "Durable Effects of Concentrated Disadvantage on Verbal Ability among African American Children." *Proceedings of the National Academy of Sciences of the United States of America* 105, no. 3: 845–52.

Sampson, Robert J., and Alix S. Winter. 2016. "The Racial Ecology of Lead Poisoning: Toxic Inequality in Chicago Neighborhoods, 1995–2013." *Du Bois Review: Social Science Research on Race* 13, no. 2: 261–83.

Samuels, Paul N., and Debbie A. Mukamal. 2004. *After Prison: Roadblocks to Reentry.* New York: Legal Action Center, January 2. https://law.stanford.edu/publications /after-prison-roadblocks-to-reentry-a-report-on-state-legal-barriers-facing-people -with-criminal-records/.

Sánchez, George. 1993. *Becoming Mexican American: Ethnicity, Culture, and Identity in Chicano Los Angeles 1900–1945.* New York: Oxford University Press.

Sánchez, George J. 2021. *Boyle Heights: How a Los Angeles Neighborhood Became the Future of American Democracy.* Berkeley: University of California Press.

Sandefur, Rebecca L. 2007. "The Importance of Doing Nothing: Everyday Problems and Responses of Inaction." In *Transforming Lives: Law and Social Process*, edited by Pascoe Pleasence, Alexy Buck, and Nigel J. Balmer, 112–32. Belfast, UK: Legal Services Commission.

Sandefur, Rebecca L. 2008. "Access to Civil Justice and Race, Class, and Gender Inequality." *Annual Review of Sociology* 34: 339–58.

Sandefur, Rebecca L. 2015. "Elements of Professional Expertise: Understanding Relational and Substantive Expertise through Lawyers' Impact." *American Sociological Review* 80, no. 5: 909–33.

Sanders, Welford. 1986. *Regulating Manufactured Housing.* Vol. 398. Chicago: American Planning Association.

San Francisco Budget and Legislative Analyst Office. 2016. *Performance Audit of Homeless Services in San Francisco.* Prepared for the Board of Supervisors of the City and County of San Francisco, June 13. https://sfbos.org/sites/default/files /FileCenter/Documents/56163-061316%20Homeless%20Services%20in%20SF _Bud%26LegAnalyst.pdf.

Sarat, Austin, ed. 2004. *The Blackwell Companion to Law and Society.* Malden, MA: Blackwell.

Sassen, Saskia. 2001. *The Global City: New York, London, Tokyo.* Princeton, NJ: Princeton University Press.

Sassler, Sharon, Desiree Ciambrone, and Gaelan Benway. 2008. "Are They Really Mama's Boys/Daddy's Girls? The Negotiation of Adulthood upon Returning to the Parental Home." *Sociological Forum* 23, no. 4: 670–98.

Satter, Beryl. 2009. *Family Properties: Race, Real Estate, and the Exploitation of Black Urban America.* New York: Metropolitan Books.

Scanlon, Kathleen, Christine Whitehead, and Melissa Fernández Arrigoitia. 2014. *Social Housing in Europe.* Chichester, UK: John Wiley and Sons.

Scarborough, William, Faith R. Kares, Iván Arenas, and Amanda E. Lewis. 2019. *Adversity and Resiliency for Chicago's First: The State of Racial Justice for American Indian Chicagoans.* Chicago: Institute for Research on Race and Public Policy, University of Illinois at Chicago.

Schäfer, Philipp, and Nicole Braun. 2016. "Misuse through Short-Term Rentals on the Berlin Housing Market." *International Journal of Housing Markets and Analysis; Bingley* 9, no. 2: 287–311.

Schmidt, Ryan W. 2011. "American Indian Identity and Blood Quantum in the 21st Century: A Critical Review." *Journal of Anthropology*. https://doi.org/10.1155/2011/549521.

Schor, Juliet B., and Steven P. Vallas. 2021. "The Sharing Economy: Rhetoric and Reality." *Annual Review of Sociology* 47, no. 1: 369–89.

Schwartz, Alex, Kirk McClure, and Lydia B. Taghavi. 2016. "Vouchers and Neighborhood Distress: The Unrealized Potential for Families with Housing Choice Vouchers to Reside in Neighborhoods with Low Levels of Distress." *Cityscape* 18, no. 3: 207–28.

Schwartz, Heather L. 2010. *Housing Policy Is School Policy: Economically Integrative Housing Promotes Academic Success in Montgomery County, MD.* New York: Century Foundation, January 1. https://www.rand.org/pubs/external_publications/EP2010 00161.html.

Schwegman, David. 2018. "Rental Market Discrimination Against Same-Sex Couples: Evidence from a Pairwise-Matched Email Correspondence Test." *Housing Policy Debate* 29: 250–72.

Scommegna, Paola. 2004. "Study Finds U.S. Manufactured-Home Owners Face 'Quasi-Homelessness.'" Population Reference Bureau, October 18. https://www.prb.org /resources/study-finds-u-s-manufactured-home-owners-face-quasi-homelessness/.

Seefeldt, Kristin S., and Heather Sandstrom. 2015. "When There Is No Welfare: The Income Packaging Strategies of Mothers without Earnings or Cash Assistance Following an Economic Downturn." *RSF* 1, no. 1: 139–58.

Selbst, Andrew. 2019. "A New HUD Rule Would Effectively Encourage Discrimination by Algorithm." *Slate*, August 19. https://slate.com/technology/2019/08/hud -disparate-impact-discrimination-algorithm.html.

Self, Robert O. 2003. *American Babylon: Race and the Struggle for Postwar Oakland.* Princeton, NJ: Princeton University Press.

Seron, Carroll, Gregg van Ryzin, Martin Frankel, and Jean Kovath. 2001. "The Impact of Legal Counsel on Outcomes for Poor Tenants in New York City's Housing Court: Results of a Randomized Experiment." *Law and Society Review* 35, no. 2: 419–34.

"Settlement Reached in Airbnb Discrimination Case." 2019. Stoll Berne, August 13. https://stollberne.com/news/settlement-reached-in-airbnb-discrimination-case/.

Sewell, Abigail A. 2010. "A Different Menu: Racial Residential Segregation and the Persistence of Racial Inequality." In *Race and Ethnic Relations in the 21st Century: History, Theory, Institutions, and Policy*, edited by R. Ray, 287–96. San Diego, CA: University Readers.

Sewell, Abigail A. 2016. "The Racism-Race Reification Process." *Sociology of Race and Ethnicity* 2, no. 4: 402–32.

Seymour, Eric, and Joshua Akers. 2021. "Building the Eviction Economy: Speculation, Precarity, and Eviction in Detroit." *Urban Affairs Review* 57, no. 1: 35–69.

Shabrina, Zahratu, Elsa Arcaute, and Michael Batty. 2021. "Airbnb and Its Potential Impact on the London Housing Market." *Urban Studies* 59, no. 1 (January): 197–221. https://doi.org/10.1177/0042098020970865.

Shannon, Sarah K. S., Christopher Uggen, Jason Schnittker, Melissa Thompson, Sara Wakefield, and Michael Massoglia. 2017. "The Growth, Scope, and Spatial

Distribution of People with Felony Records in the United States, 1948–2010." *Demography* 54, no. 5: 1795–818.

Shapiro, Thomas M. 2004. *The Hidden Cost of Being African American: How Wealth Perpetuates Inequality*. Oxford, UK: Oxford University Press.

Shapiro, Thomas M. 2017. *Toxic Inequality: How America's Wealth Gap Destroys Mobility, Deepens the Racial Divide, and Threatens Our Future*. New York: Basic Books.

Sharkey, Patrick. 2010. "The Acute Effect of Local Homicides on Children's Cognitive Performance." *Proceedings of the National Academy of Sciences of the United States of America* 107, no. 26: 11733–38.

Sharkey, Patrick. 2013. *Stuck in Place: Urban Neighborhoods and the End of Progress toward Racial Equality*. Chicago: University of Chicago Press.

Sharkey, Patrick, and Jacob William Faber. 2014. "Where, When, Why, and for Whom Do Residential Contexts Matter? Moving Away from the Dichotomous Understanding of Neighborhood Effects." *Annual Review of Sociology* 40, no. 1: 559–79.

Shatkin, Gavin. 2008. "The City and the Bottom Line: Urban Megaprojects and the Privatization of Planning in Southeast Asia." *Environment and Planning A* 40, no. 2: 383–401.

Shaw, Mary. 2004. "Housing and Public Health." *Annual Review of Public Health* 25: 397–418.

Shefner, Jon. 2001. "Coalitions and Clientelism in Mexico." *Theory and Society* 30, no. 5: 593–628.

Shen, G. 2005. "Location of Manufactured Housing and its Accessibility to Community Services: A GIS-Assisted Spatial Analysis." *Socio-Economic Planning Sciences* 39, no. 1: 25–41.

Shertzer, Allison, Tate Twinam, and Randall P. Walsh. 2021. "Zoning and Segregation in Urban Economic History." Working paper 28351, January, National Bureau of Economic Research. http://www.nber.org/papers/w28351.

Shiffer-Sebba, Doron. 2020. "Understanding the Divergent Logics of Landlords: Circumstantial Versus Divergent Pathways." *City and Community* 19, no. 4: 1011–37. https://doi.org/10.1111/cico.12490.

Shinn, Marybeth, and Jill Khadduri. 2020. *In the Midst of Plenty: Homelessness and What to Do About It*. Hoboken, NJ: Wiley Blackwell.

Shlay, Anne B. 2006. "Low-Income Homeownership: American Dream or Delusion?" *Urban Studies* 43: 511–31.

Shlay, Anne B., and Peter H. Rossi. 1992. "Social Science Research and Contemporary Studies of Homelessness." *Annual Review of Sociology* 18: 129–60.

Sigle-Rushton, Wendy, and Sara McLanahan. 2002. "The Living Arrangements of New Unmarried Mothers." *Demography* 39, no. 3: 415–33.

Simes, Jessica T. 2018a. "Place and Punishment: The Spatial Context of Mass Incarceration." *Journal of Quantitative Criminology* 34, no. 2: 513–33.

Simes, Jessica T. 2018b. "Place after Prison: Neighborhood Attainment and Attachment during Reentry." *Journal of Urban Affairs* (August 2): 1–21. https://doi.org/10.1080/07352166.2018.1495041.

Simes, Jessica T. 2021. *Punishing Places: The Geography of Mass Imprisonment*. Oakland: University of California Press.

Simone, Abdoumaliq. 2014. *Jakarta: Drawing the City Near*. Minneapolis: University of Minnesota Press.

Sisson, Patrick. 2018. "Why Do All New Apartment Buildings Look the Same?" *Curbed,*
December 4. https://archive.curbed.com/2018/12/4/18125536/real-estate
-modern-apartment-architecture.

Skidmore, Mark, Charles L. Ballard, and Timothy R. Hodge. 2010. "Property Value
Assessment Growth Limits and Redistribution of Property Tax Payments: Evidence
from Michigan." *National Tax Journal* 63, no. 3: 509–38.

Skobba, Kimberly, Marilyn J. Bruin, and Becky L. Yust. 2013. "Beyond Renting and
Owning: The Housing Accommodations of Low-Income Families." *Journal of
Poverty* 17, no. 2: 234–52.

Skobba, Kimberly, and Edward G. Goetz. 2013. "Mobility Decisions of Very Low-
Income Households." *Cityscape* 15, no. 2: 155–71.

Slater, Gene. 2021. *Freedom to Discriminate: How Realtors Conspired to Segregate Housing
and Divide America.* Berkeley, CA: Heyday Books.

Small, Mario Luis. 2004. *Villa Victoria: The Transformation of Social Capital in a Boston
Barrio.* Chicago: University of Chicago Press.

Small, Mario Luis. 2008. "Four Reasons to Abandon the Idea of 'the Ghetto.'" *City and
Community* 7, no. 4: 389–98.

Small, Mario Luis, Robert A. Manduca, and William R. Johnston. 2018. "Ethnography,
Neighborhood Effects, and the Rising Heterogeneity of Poor Neighborhoods across
Cities." *City and Community* 17, no. 3: 565–89.

Small, Mario Luis, and Monica McDermott. 2006. "The Presence of Organizational
Resources in Poor Urban Neighborhoods: An Analysis of Average and Contextual
Effects." *Social Forces* 84, no. 3: 1697–724.

Smith, Darren P. 2004. "'Studentification': The Gentrification Factory?" In
Gentrification in a Global Context, edited by Rowland Atkinson and Gary Bridge,
73–90. London: Routledge.

Smith, Janet L. 2006. "Public Housing Transformation: Evolving National Policy" In
Where Are Poor People to Live? Transforming Public Housing Communities, edited by
Larry Bennett, Janet L. Smith, and Patricia A. Wright, 19–40. New York: Routledge.

Smith, Jeffrey A., Miller McPherson, and Lynn Smith-Lovin. 2014. "Social Distance
in the United States: Sex, Race, Religion, Age, and Education Homophily among
Confidants, 1985 to 2004." *American Sociological Review* 79, no. 3: 432–56.

Smith, Linda Tuhiwai. 2012. *Decolonizing Methodologies: Research and Indigenous
Peoples.* London: Zed Books.

Smith, Neil. 1996. *The New Urban Frontier: Gentrification and the Revanchist City.*
London: Routledge.

Snell, Tracy L. 1995. *Correctional Populations in the United States, 1993.* NCJ 156241.
Washington, DC: Bureau of Justice Statistics, Office of Justice Programs, US
Department of Justice. http://www.bjs.gov/index.cfm?ty=pbdetail&iid=746.

Snelling, Charlotte, Catherine Colebrook, and Luke Murphy. 2016. *Homesharing and
London's Housing Market.* London: Institute for Public Policy Research, December.
https://www.ippr.org/files/publications/pdf/homesharing-and-london-housing
-market-dec16.pdf.

Snow, David A., and Leon Anderson. 1993. *Down on Their Luck: A Study of Homeless
Street People.* Los Angeles: University of California Press.

So, Wonyoung, Pranay Lohia, Rakesh Pimplikar, A. E. Hosoi, and Catherine D. Ignazio.
2022. "Beyond Fairness: Reparative Algorithms to Address Historical Injustices of
Housing Discrimination in the US." Presented at the 2022 ACM Conference on

Fairness, Accountability, and Transparency Conference on Fairness, Accountability, and Transparency, Seoul, Republic of Korea.

Somashekhar, Mahesh. 2020. "Racial Inequality between Gentrifiers: How the Race of Gentrifiers Affects Retail Development in Gentrifying Neighborhoods." *City and Community* 19, no. 4 (December): 811–44. https://doi.org/10.1111/cico.12421.

Somers, Margaret R., and Fred Block. 2005. "From Poverty to Perversity: Ideas, Markets, and Institutions over 200 Years of Welfare Debate." *American Sociological Review* 70, no. 2: 260–87.

Sørensen, A. B. 2005. "Foundations of a Rent-Based Class Analysis." In *Approaches to Class Analysis*, edited by E. O. Wright, 119–51. Cambridge: Cambridge University Press.

Soss, Joe, and Vesla Weaver. 2017. "Police Are Our Government: Politics, Political Science, and the Policing of Race-Class Subjugated Communities." *Annual Review of Political Science* 20, no. 1: 565–91.

South, Scott J., and Kyle D. Crowder. 1997. "Escaping Distressed Neighborhoods: Individual, Community, and Metropolitan Influences." *American Journal of Sociology* 102, no. 4: 1040–84.

South, Scott J., and Kyle D. Crowder. 1998. "Housing Discrimination and Residential Mobility: Impacts for Blacks and Whites." *Population Research and Policy Review* 17, no. 4: 369–87.

South, Scott J., Kyle Crowder, and Erick Chavez. 2005. "Exiting and Entering High-Poverty Neighborhoods: Latinos, Blacks and Anglos Compared." *Social Forces* 84, no. 2: 873–900.

South, Scott J., Kyle D. Crowder, and Katherine Trent. 1998. "Children's Residential Mobility and Neighborhood Environment Following Parental Divorce and Remarriage." *Social Forces* 77, no. 2: 667–93.

South, Scott J., and Glenn D. Deane. 1993. "Race and Residential Mobility: Individual Determinants and Structural Constraints." *Social Forces* 72, no. 1: 147–67.

South, Scott J., Ying Huang, Amy Spring, and Kyle Crowder. 2016. "Neighborhood Attainment over the Adult Life Course." *American Sociological Review* 81, no. 6: 1276–304.

South, Scott J., and Lei. 2015. "Failures-to-Launch and Boomerang Kids: Contemporary Determinants of Leaving and Returning to the Parental Home." *Social Forces* 94, no. 2: 863–90.

Sowell, John. 2019. "Want to Add a Cottage or Addition to Your Boise House to Rent out? Change Is Afoot." *Idaho Statesman*, May 6. https://www.idahostatesman.com/news/local/community/boise/article230106659.html.

Spalding, Sophie. 1992. "The Myth of the Classic Slum: Contradictory Perceptions of Boyle Heights Flats, 1900–1991." *Journal of Architectural Education* 45, no. 2: 107–19.

Spangler, Ian. 2020. "Hidden Value in the Platform's Platform: Airbnb, Displacement, and the Un-Homing Spatialities of Emotional Labour." *Transactions of the Institute of British Geographers* 45, no. 3: 575–88.

Sparks, Tony. 2017. "Citizens without Property: Informality and Political Agency in a Seattle, Washington Homeless Encampment." *Environment and Planning A* 49, no. 1: 86–103.

Spring, Amy, Elizabeth Ackert, Kyle Crowder, and Scott J. South. 2017. "Influence of Proximity to Kin on Residential Mobility and Destination Choice: Examining Local Movers in Metropolitan Areas." *Demography* 54, no. 4: 1277–304.

Squires, Gregory D. 1994. *Capital and Communities in Black and White: The Intersections of Race, Class, and Uneven Development*. Albany: State University of New York Press.

Squires, Gregory. 2011. *From Redlining to Reinvestment: Community Responses to Urban Disinvestment*. Philadelphia, PA: Temple University Press.

Squires, Gregory D. 2017. *The Fight for Fair Housing: Causes, Consequences, and Future Implications of the 1968 Federal Fair Housing Act*. New York: Routledge.

Squires, Gregory D., and William Velez. 1987. "Insurance Redlining and the Transformation of an Urban Metropolis." *Urban Affairs Quarterly* 23, no. 1: 63–83.

Stack, Carol B. 2008. *All Our Kin: Strategies for Survival in a Black Community*. New York: Basic Books.

Starecheski, Amy. 2016. *Ours to Lose: When Squatters Became Homeowners in New York City*. Chicago: University of Chicago Press.

Stark, Louisa R. 1994. "The Shelter as 'Total Institution' an Organizational Barrier to Remedying Homelessness." *American Behavioral Scientist* 37, no. 4: 553–62.

Stauffer, Robert H. 2004. "Kahana: How the Land Was Lost." Honolulu: University of Hawai'i Press.

Stefancic, Ana, and Sam Tsemberis. 2007. "Housing First for Long-Term Shelter Dwellers with Psychiatric Disabilities in a Suburban County: A Four-Year Study of Housing Access and Retention." *Journal of Primary Prevention* 28, no. 3–4: 265–79.

Stegman, Michael A. 1972. *Housing Investment in the Inner City: The Dynamics of Decline; a Study of Baltimore, Maryland, 1968–1970*. Cambridge, MA: MIT Press.

Steil, Justin P., Len Albright, Jacob S. Rugh, and Douglas S. Massey. 2018. "The Social Structure of Mortgage Discrimination." *Housing Studies* 33, no. 5: 759–76.

Steil, Justin P., J. de la Roca, and I. G. Ellen. 2015. "Desvinculado y Desigual: Is Segregation Harmful to Latinos?" *Annals of the American Academy of Political and Social Science* 660, no. 1: 57–76.

Steil, Justin P., and Laura Humm Delgado. 2018. "Contested Values: How Jim Crow Segregation Ordinances Redefined Property Rights." In *Global Perspectives on Urban Law*, edited by N. Davidson and G. Tewari, 7–26. London: Routledge.

Steinberg, Jessica K. 2015. "Demand Side Reform in the Poor People's Courts." *Connecticut Law Review* 47, no. 3: 741–807.

Steiner, Benjamin, Matthew D. Makarios, and Lawrence F. Travis. 2015. "Examining the Effects of Residential Situations and Residential Mobility on Offender Recidivism." *Crime and Delinquency* 61, no. 3: 375–401.

Steinman, Erich W. 2016. "Decolonization not Inclusion: Indigenous Resistance to American Settler Colonialism." *Sociology of Race and Ethnicity* 2, no. 2: 219–36.

Stergiou, Dimitrios P., and Anna Farmaki. 2020. "Resident Perceptions of the Impacts of P2P Accommodation: Implications for Neighbourhoods." *International Journal of Hospitality Management* 91(October): 102411.

Sternlieb, George, Robert W. Burchell, James W. Hughes, and Franklin J. James. 1974. "Housing Abandonment in the Urban Core." *Journal of the American Institute of Planners* 40, no. 5: 321–32.

Stewart, Robert, and Christopher Uggen. 2020. "Criminal Records and College Admissions: A Modified Experimental Audit." *Criminology* 58, no. 1: 156–88.

Stoker, Robert P., Clarence N. Stone, and Donn Worgs. 2015. "Neighborhood Policy in Baltimore: The Postindustrial Turn." In *Urban Neighborhoods in a New Era: Revitalization Politics in the Postindustrial City*, edited by Clarence N. Stone and Robert P. Stoker, 50–80. Chicago: University of Chicago Press.

Stokes, Susan C. 1995. *Cultures in Conflict: Social Movements and the State in Peru.* Berkeley: University of California Press.

Stout, Noelle. 2019. *Dispossessed: How Predatory Bureaucracy Foreclosed on the American Middle Class.* Berkeley: University of California Press.

Stovel, Katherine, and Lynette Shaw. 2012. "Brokerage." *Annual Review of Sociology* 38, no. 1: 139–58.

Stuart, Forrest. 2014. "From 'Rabble Management' to 'Recovery Management': Policing Homelessness in Marginal Urban Space." *Urban Studies* 51, no. 9: 1909–25.

Stuart, Forrest. 2015. "On the Streets, under Arrest: Policing Homelessness in the 21st Century." *Sociology Compass* 9, no. 11: 940–50.

Stuart, Forrest. 2016. *Down, Out, and under Arrest: Policing and Everyday Life in Skid Row.* Chicago: University of Chicago Press.

Stuber, Jenny. 2021. *Aspen and the American Dream: How One Town Manages Inequality in the Era of Supergentrification.* Berkeley: University of California Press.

Sugie, Naomi F. 2018. "Work as Foraging: A Smartphone Study of Job Search and Employment after Prison." *American Journal of Sociology* 123, no. 5: 1453–91.

Sugie, Naomi F., and Kristin Turney. 2017. "Beyond Incarceration: Criminal Justice Contact and Mental Health." *American Sociological Review* 82, no. 4: 719–43.

Sugrue, Thomas J. 1996. *The Origins of the Urban Crisis: Race and Inequality in Postwar Detroit.* Princeton, NJ: Princeton University Press.

Sugrue, Thomas J. 2014. *The Origins of the Urban Crisis: Race and Inequality in Postwar Detroit.* Rev. ed. Princeton, NJ: Princeton University Press.

Sullivan, Esther. 2017. "Displaced in Place: Manufactured Housing, Mass Eviction, and the Paradox of State Intervention." *American Sociological Review* 82, no. 2: 243–69.

Sullivan, Esther. 2018. *Manufactured Insecurity: Mobile Home Parks and Americans' Tenuous Right to Place.* Oakland: University of California Press.

Summers, Nicole. 2022. "Civil Probation." *Stanford Law Review* (forthcoming). https://dx.doi.org/10.2139/ssrn.3897493.

Sutherland, Edwin Hardin, and Harvey James Locke. 1936. *Twenty Thousand Homeless Men: A Study of Unemployed Men in the Chicago Shelters.* New York: Arno Press.

Sutton, Stacey. 2015. "The Geopolitics of Black Business Closure in Central Brooklyn." In *Race and Retail: Consumption across the Color Line*, edited by Mia Bay and Ann Fabian, 200–24. New Brunswick, NJ: Rutgers University Press.

Swartz, Mark, and Rachel Blake. 2010. *LCBH 2009 Report: Chicago Apartment Building Foreclosures: Impact on Tenants.* Chicago: Lawyers' Committee for Better Housing.

Tach, Laura, and Allison Dwyer Emory. 2017. "Public Housing Redevelopment, Neighborhood Change, and the Restructuring of Urban Inequality." *American Journal of Sociology* 123, no. 3: 686.

Taggart, Harriett Tee, and Kevin W. Smith. 1981. "Redlining: An Assessment of the Evidence of Disinvestment in Metropolitan Boston." *Urban Affairs Quarterly* 17, no. 1: 91–107.

Talerico, Kate. 2019. "How Airbnb Hurts Boise's Affordable Housing: 'It Has Driven up the Rental Prices.'" *Idaho Statesman*, April 12. https://www.idahostatesman.com/news/business/article227107254.html.

Taylor, Keeanga-Yamahtta. 2013. "Back Story to the Neoliberal Moment: Race Taxes and the Political Economy of Black Urban Housing in the 1960s." *Souls* 14, no. 3–4: 185–206.

Taylor, Keeanga-Yamahtta. 2019. *Race for Profit: How Banks and the Real Estate Industry Undermined Black Homeownership.* Chapel Hill: University of North Carolina Press.

Taylor, Keeanga-Yamahtta. 2020. "The Banality of Segregation: Why Hirsch Still Helps Us Understand Our Racial Geography." *Journal of Urban History* 46, no. 3: 490–93.

Taylor, Monique M. 2002. *Harlem: Between Heaven and Hell*. Minneapolis: University of Minnesota Press.

Te Awa Tupua (Whanganui River Claims Settlement) Act 2017 (Public Act 2017 no. 7) (New Zealand). https://www.legislation.govt.nz/act/public/2017/0007/latest /whole.html.

Telles, Edward E., and Vilma Ortiz. 2008. *Generations of Exclusion: Mexican-Americans, Assimilation, and Race*. New York: Russell Sage Foundation.

Tesfai, Rebecca. 2016. "The Interaction between Race and Nativity on the Housing Market: Homeownership and House Value of Black Immigrants in the United States." *International Migration Review* 50, no. 4: 1005–45. https://doi.org/10.1111 /imre.12190.

Thomas, June Manning. 2013. *Redevelopment and Race: Planning a Finer City in Postwar Detroit*. Detroit, MI: Wayne State University Press.

Thomas, June Manning, and Henco Bekkering. 2015. *Mapping Detroit: Land, Community, and Shaping a City*. Detroit, MI: Wayne State University Press.

Thomas, Melvin E., Richard Moye, Loren Henderson, and Hayward Derrick Horton. 2018. "Separate and Unequal: The Impact of Socioeconomic Status, Segregation, and the Great Recession on Racial Disparities in Housing Values." *Sociology of Race and Ethnicity* 4, no. 2: 229–44.

Thompson, Jeffrey P., and Gustavo A. Suarez. 2015. "Updating the Racial Wealth Gap." Finance and Economics Discussion Series working paper 2015-76, September, Board of Governors of the Federal Reserve System. http://dx.doi.org/10.17016 /FEDS.2015.076r1.

Thompson, M. Dion, and Gerard Shields. 2000. "O'Malley Pledges to Seek New Plan for Housing Poor." *Baltimore Sun*, October 4.

Thornhill, Ted. 2019. "We Want Black Students, Just Not You: How White Admissions Counselors Screen Black Prospective Students." *Sociology of Race and Ethnicity* 5, no. 4: 456–70. https://doi.org/10.1177/2332649218792579.

Tighe, J. Rosie, Megan E. Hatch, and Joseph Mead. 2017. "Source of Income Discrimination and Fair Housing Policy." *Journal of Planning Literature* 32, no. 1: 3–15.

Tighe, J. Rosie, and Stephanie Ryberg-Webster. 2019. *Legacy Cities: Continuity and Change amid Decline and Revival*. Pittsburgh, PA: University of Pittsburgh Press.

Timberlake, Jeffrey M. 2002. "Separate, but How Unequal? Ethnic Residential Stratification, 1980 to 1990." *City and Community* 1, no. 3: 251–66.

Torrats-Espinosa, Gerard. 2021. "Using Machine Learning to Estimate the Effect of Racial Segregation on COVID-19 Mortality in the United States." *Proceedings of the National Academy of Sciences* 118, no. 7. https://www.pnas.org/doi/full/10.1073 /pnas.2015577118.

Tran-Leung, Marie Claire. 2015. *When Discretion Means Denial: A National Perspective on Criminal Records Barriers to Federally Subsidized Housing*. Chicago: Sargent Shriver National Center on Poverty Law, February. https://www.povertylaw.org/files /docs/WDMD-final.pdf.

Transparent. 2020. "Airbnb at IPO Part I: Who Are Today's Airbnb Hosts and How Loyal Are They?" *Stay Informed with Data*, November 4. https://seetransparent

.com/blog/2020/11/04/airbnb-at-ipo-part-i-who-are-todays-airbnb-hosts-and-how-loyal-are-they/.

Trask, Haunani-Kay. 1999. *From a Native Daughter: Colonialism and Sovereignty in Hawaii*. Honolulu: University of Hawai'i Press.

Travis, Adam. 2019. "The Organization of Neglect: Limited Liability Companies and Housing Disinvestment." *American Sociological Review* 84, no. 1: 142–70.

Troesken, Werner, and Randall Walsh. 2019. "Collective Action, White Flight, and the Origins of Racial Zoning Laws." *Journal of Law, Economics, and Organization* 32, no. 2: 289–318.

"Trouble for Mexicans Brewing: West-End Residents Will Not Tolerate New Cholo Town—One Man Threatens to Get Gun Busy." 1909. *San Bernardino County Sun* XXX, no. 59 (June 6): 1.

Trounstine, Jessica. 2018. *Segregation by Design: Local Politics and Inequality in American Cities*. Cambridge: Cambridge University Press.

Trounstine, Jessica. 2020. "The Geography of Inequality: How Land Use Regulation Produces Segregation." *American Political Science Review* 114, no. 2: 443–55.

Tsemberis, Sam, Leyla Gulcur, and Maria Nakae. 2004. "Housing First, Consumer Choice, and Harm Reduction for Homeless Individuals with a Dual Diagnosis." *American Journal of Public Health* 94, no. 4: 651–56.

Turner, John C. 1967. "Barriers and Channels for Housing Development in Modernizing Countries." *Journal of the American Institute of Planners* 33, no. 3: 167–81.

Turner, Margery Austin, Carla Herbig, Deborah Kaye, Julie Fenderson, and Diane K. Levy. 2005. *Discrimination Against Persons with Disabilities: Barriers at Every Step*. Washington, DC: Urban Institute.

Turner, Margery Austin, and Stephen L. Ross. 2003. *Discrimination in Metropolitan Housing Markets, Phase II: Asians and Pacific Islanders*. Washington, DC: US Department of Housing and Urban Development, Office of Policy Development and Research.

Turner, Margery Austin, Stephen L. Ross, Julie Adams, Beata Bednarz, Carla Herbig, Seon Joo Lee, and Kimberlee Ross. 2003. *Discrimination in Metropolitan Housing Markets: Phase 3: Native Americans* Washington, DC: US Department of Housing and Urban Development, Office of Policy Development and Research, September. https://www.huduser.gov/Publications/pdf/hds_phase3.pdf.

Turner, Margery Austin, Robert Santos, Diane K. Levy, Doug Wissoker, Claudia L. Aranda, and Rob Pitingolo. 2013. *Housing Discrimination Against Racial and Ethnic Minorities 2012*. Washington, DC: US Department of Housing and Urban Development, Office of Policy Development and Research, June. https://www.huduser.gov/portal/Publications/pdf/HUD-514_HDS2012.pdf.

Turner, Margery Austin, Raymond J. Struyk, and John Yinger. 1991. *Housing Discrimination Study: Summary of Findings*. Washington, DC: Urban Institute.

Turney, Kristin. 2015. "Liminal Men: Incarceration and Relationship Dissolution." *Social Problems* 62, no. 4: 499–528.

Turney, Kristin, and Daniel Schneider. 2016. "Incarceration and Household Asset Ownership." *Demography* 53, no. 6 (December): 2075–103.

Turney, Kristin, Christopher Wildeman, and Jason Schnittker. 2012. "As Fathers and Felons: Explaining the Effects of Current and Recent Incarceration on Major Depression." *Journal of Health and Social Behavior* 53, no. 4: 465–81.

Tuttle, Steven. Forthcoming. "Towards a Theory of the Racialization of Space." *American Behavioral Scientist.*

Uggen, Christopher, and Jeff Manza. 2002. "Democratic Contraction? Political Consequences of Felon Disenfranchisement in the United States." *American Sociological Review* 67, no. 6: 777–803.

Uggen, Christopher, Mike Vuolo, Sarah Lageson, Ebony Ruhland, and Hilary K. Whitham. 2014. "The Edge of Stigma: An Experimental Audit of the Effects of Low-Level Criminal Records on Employment." *Criminology* 52, no. 4: 627–54.

Unger, Donald G., and Abraham Wandersman. 1985. "The Importance of Neighbors: The Social, Cognitive, and Affective Components of Neighboring." *American Journal of Community Psychology* 13, no. 2: 139–69.

United Nations. 2007. "United Nations Declaration on the Rights of Indigenous Peoples." https://www.un.org/development/desa/indigenouspeoples/declaration -on-the-rights-of-indigenous-peoples.html.

United Nations Center for Human Settlements (UN Habitat). 2003. *The Challenge of Slums: Global Report on Human Settlements 2003.* London: Earthscan.

United Nations Center for Human Settlements (UN Habitat). 2016. *Urbanization and Development: Emerging Futures.* Nairobi: UN Habitat.

United States Census Bureau. 1999. "Section 31: 20th Century Statistics." In *Statistical Abstract of the United States: 1999.* Washington, DC: US Census Bureau, December 9. https://www2.census.gov/library/publications/1999/compendia/statab/119ed /tables/sec31.pdf.

United States Census Bureau. 2017. *American Community Survey 5-Year Estimates: Household Type by Relationships.* Washington, DC: United States Census Bureau. https://www.census.gov/data/developers/data-sets/acs-5year.html.

United States Census Bureau. 2019a. "American Community Survey: 5-Year Estimates." United States Census Bureau. https://data.census.gov/cedsci/table? q=ACSDT 1Y2019.B25024&tid=ACSDT5Y2019.B25024&hidePreview=true.

United States Census Bureau. 2019b. "County Population Totals: 2010–2019." United States Census Bureau, last revised October 8, 2021. https://www.census.gov/data /datasets/time-series/demo/popest/2010s-counties-total.html.

United States Census Bureau. 2019c. "QuickFacts: Seattle City, WA." United States Census Bureau. https://www.census.gov/quickfacts/seattlecitywashington.

United States Census Bureau. n.d. "Boise City, Idaho, Profile 2020 ACS 5-Year Estimates." United States Census Bureau. Retrieved March 21, 2022. https://data .census.gov/cedsci/profile?g=1600000US1608830.

United States Commerce Department. 2010. *Cost and Size Comparison for Manufactured and Site Built Homes: 1995–2010.* Washington, DC: US Commerce Department.

United States Department of Housing and Urban Development (HUD). n.d. "HUD's Public Housing Program." HUD, accessed February 1, 2021. https://www.hud.gov /topics/rental_assistance/phprog.

United States Department of Housing and Urban Development (HUD). 1997. *Meeting the Challenge: Public Housing Authorities Respond to the "One Strike and You're Out" Initiative.* Washington, DC: HUD, September. https://www.ojp.gov/pdffiles1 /Photocopy/183952NCJRS.pdf.

United States Department of Housing and Urban Development (HUD). 2019. *Annual Homelessness Assessment Report.* Washington, DC: HUD. https://www.huduser .gov/portal/sites/default/files/pdf/2019-AHAR-Part-1.pdf.

United States Department of Housing and Urban Development (HUD). 2021. *FY21 Choice Neighborhoods Planning Grants NOFO*. Washington, DC: HUD.

United States Department of Housing and Urban Development (HUD). n.d. "About Place-Based Initiatives." HUD. Retrieved October 1, 2021. https://www.hud.gov /program_offices/economic_development/place_based/about.

United States Department of Housing and Urban Development (HUD) Office of General Counsel. 2016. *Office of General Counsel Guidance on Application of Fair Housing Act Standards to the Use of Criminal Records by Providers of Housing and Real Estate-Related Transactions*. Washington, DC: HUD, April 4. https://www.hud.gov /sites/documents/HUD_OGCGUIDAPPFHASTANDCR.PDF.

United States Environmental Protection Agency (EPA). 2012. "Settlement Reached with Mobile Home Park Owners over Drinking Water and Waste Water Violations." United States Environmental Protection Agency, October 1. https://www.epa.gov /enforcement/reference-news-release-settlement-reached-mobile-home-park -owners-over-drinking-water.

United States Federal Housing Finance Agency (US FHFA). 2022. "All-Transactions House Price Index for the United States [USSTHPI]." FRED, Federal Reserve Bank of St. Louis, October 8. https://fred.stlouisfed.org/series/USSTHPI.

United States General Accounting Office. 1998. *HOPE VI: Progress and Problems in Revitalizing Distressed Public Housing*. General Accounting Office publication 98–187. Washington, DC: US General Accounting Office.

United States Government Accountability Office (GAO). 2005. *Drug Offenders: Various Factors May Limit the Impacts of Federal Laws That Provide for Denial of Selected Benefits*. Washington, DC: United States Government Accountability Office, September 26. http://www.gao.gov/products/GAO-05-238.

United States National Commission on Severely Distressed Public Housing. 1992. *The Final Report of the National Commission on Severely Distressed Public Housing*. Washington, DC: Hon. Bill Green and Vincent Lane, co-commissioners.

United States Water Alliance / Dig Deep. 2019. *Closing the Water Access Gap in the United States: A National Action Plan*. Washington, DC: US Water Alliance. https:// www.digdeep.org/close-the-water-gap.

Urry, John. 2005. "The 'Consuming' of Place." In *Discourse, Communication and Tourism*, edited by Adam Joworski and Annette Pritchard, 19–27. Clevedon, UK: Channel View Publications.

Vale, Lawrence J. 2013. *Purging the Poorest: Public Housing and the Design Politics of Twice-Cleared Communities*. Chicago: University of Chicago Press.

Vale, Lawrence J. 2019. *After the Projects: Public Housing Redevelopment and the Governance of the Poorest Americans*. New York: Oxford University Press.

Vale, Lawrence J., and Shomon Shamsuddin. 2017. "All Mixed Up: Making Sense of Mixed-Income Housing Developments." *Journal of the American Planning Association* 83, no. 1: 56–67.

Valentin, Maxence. 2021. "Regulating Short-Term Rental Housing: Evidence from New Orleans." *Real Estate Economics* 49, no. 1: 152–86.

Vallas, Steven, and Juliet B. Schor. 2020. "What Do Platforms Do? Understanding the Gig Economy." *Annual Review of Sociology* 46: 273–94.

Valle, Melissa M. 2018. "Burlesquing Blackness: Racial Significations in Carnivals and the Carnivalesque on Colombia's Caribbean Coast." *Public Culture* 31, no. 1: 5–20.

Valverde, Mariana. 2012. *Everyday Law on the Street: City Governance in an Age of Diversity*. Chicago: University of Chicago Press.

Van Dyke, Jon M. 2008. *Who Owns the Crown Lands of Hawai'i?* Honolulu: University of Hawai'i Press.

Van Gunten, Tod, and Sebastian Kohl. 2020. "The Inversion of the 'Really Big Trade-Off': Homeownership and Pensions in Long-Run Perspective." *West European Politics* 43, no. 2: 435–63.

Van Zandt, Shannon, and Pratik C. Mhatre. 2009. "Growing Pains: Perpetuating Inequality Through the Production of Low-Income Housing in the Dallas/Fort Worth Metroplex." *Urban Geography* 30, no. 5: 490–513.

Vaughan, Mehana Blaich. 2018. "Kaiāulu: Gathering Tides." Corvallis: Oregon State University Press.

Venkatesh, Sudhir A. 2002. *American Project: The Rise and Fall of a Modern Ghetto*. Cambridge, MA: Harvard University Press.

Venkatesh, Sudhir. 2006. *Off the Books: The Underground Economy of the Urban Poor*. Cambridge, MA: Harvard University Press.

Ventry, Dennis. 2010. "The Accidental Deduction. A History and Critique of the Tax Subsidy for Mortgage Interest." *Law and Contemporary Problems* 73: 233–84.

Veracini, Lorenzo 2010. *Settler Colonialism: A Theoretical Overview*. Houndmills, UK: Palgrave Macmillan.

Vespa, Jonathan, Lauren Medina, and David Armstrong. 2020. *Demographic Turning Points for the United States: Population Projections for 2020 to 2060*. Current Population Reports P25–1144. Washington, DC: United States Census Bureau, March: 1–15. https://www.census.gov/content/dam/Census/library/publications/2020/demo/p25-1144.pdf.

Vigdor, Jacob. 2014. "Immigration and New York City: The Contributions of Foreign-Born Americans to New York's Renaissance, 1975–2013." Americas Society/ Council of Americas, April 10. https://www.as-coa.org/articles/immigration-and-new-york-city-contributions-foreign-born-americans-new-yorks-renaissance.

Villarreal, Ana. 2021. "Reconceptualizing Urban Violence from the Global South." *City and Community* 20, no. 1: 48–58.

Vogel, Matt, Lauren C. Porter, and Timothy McCuddy. 2017. "Hypermobility, Destination Effects, and Delinquency: Specifying the Link between Residential Mobility and Offending." *Social Forces* 95, no. 3: 1261–84.

Vrousalis, Nicholas. 2018. "Exploitation: A Primer." *Philosophy Compass* 13, no. 2: e12486.

Wachsmuth, David, and Alexander Weisler. 2018. "Airbnb and the Rent Gap: Gentrification through the Sharing Economy." *Environment and Planning A: Economy and Space* 50, no. 6: 1147–70.

Wacquant, Loïc. 2008. "Relocating Gentrification: The Working Class, Science and the State in Recent Urban Research." *International Journal of Urban and Regional Research* 32, no. 1: 198–205.

Wacquant, Loïc. 2016. "Revisiting Territories of Relegation: Class, Ethnicity and State in the Making of Advanced Marginality." *Urban Studies* 53, no. 6: 1077–88.

Wade, Lisa. 2013. "When Jews Dominated Professional Basketball." *Sociological Images* (blog), November 25. https://thesocietypages.org/socimages/2013/11/25/when-jews-dominated-professional-basketball/.

Waegemakers Schiff, Jeannette, and Rebecca A. L. Schiff. 2014. "Housing First: Paradigm or Program?" *Journal of Social Distress and the Homeless* 23, no. 2: 80–104.

Wagner, David. 2018. *No Longer Homeless: How the Ex-Homeless Get and Stay Off the Streets*. Rowman and Littlefield.

Wakin, M. 2005. "Not Sheltered, Not Homeless: RVs as Makeshifts." *American Behavioral Scientist* 48, no. 8: 1013–32.

Wallace, Deborah, and Rodrick Wallace. 1998. *A Plague on Your Houses: How New York Was Burned Down and National Public Health Crumbled*. New York: Verso.

Wallis, Allan. 1991. *Wheel Estate: The Rise and Decline of Mobile Homes*. Oxford: Oxford University Press.

Walsh, Camille. 2017. "White Backlash, the 'Taxpaying' Public, and Educational Citizenship." *Critical Sociology* 43, no. 2: 237–47.

Walter, Rebecca J., Yanmei Li, and Serge Atherwood. 2015. "Moving to Opportunity? An Examination of Housing Choice Vouchers on Urban Poverty Deconcentration in South Florida." *Housing Studies* 30, no. 7: 1064–91.

Wang, Ruoniu, and Rebecca J. Walter. 2018. "Tracking Mobility in the Housing Choice Voucher Program: A Household Level Examination in Florida, USA." *Housing Studies* 33, no. 3: 455–75.

Wang, Qi, Nolan Edward Phillips, Mario L. Small, and Robert J. Sampson. 2018. "Urban Mobility and Neighborhood Isolation in America's 50 Largest Cities." *Proceedings of the National Academy of Sciences* 115, no. 30: 7735–40.

Ward, Peter. 1999. *Colonias and Public Policy in Texas and Mexico: Urbanization by Stealth*. Austin: University of Texas Press.

Warner, Cody. 2015. "On the Move: Incarceration, Race, and Residential Mobility." *Social Science Research* 52 (July): 451–64.

Warner, Cody. 2016. "The Effect of Incarceration on Residential Mobility between Poor and Nonpoor Neighborhoods." *City and Community* 15, no. 4: 423–43.

Warner, Cody, and Brianna Remster. 2021. "Criminal Justice Contact, Residential Independence, and Returns to the Parental Home." *Journal of Marriage and Family* 83, no. 2: 322–39.

Way, Heather. 2010. "Informal Homeownership in the United States and the Law." *Saint Louis University Public Law Review* 29, no. 1: 113–92.

Wegmann, Jake. 2015. "Research Notes: The Hidden Cityscapes of Informal Housing in Suburban Los Angeles and the Paradox of Horizontal Density." *Building and Landscapes* 22, no. 2: 89–110.

Weinstein, Liza. 2014. *The Durable Slum: Dharavi and the Right to Stay Put in Globalizing Mumbai*. Minneapolis: University of Minnesota Press.

Weinstein, Liza. 2021. "Eviction: Reconceptualizing Housing Insecurity from the Global South." *City and Community* 20, no. 1: 13–23.

Weinstein, Liza, and Xuefei Ren. 2009. "The Changing Right to the City: Urban Renewal and Housing Rights in Globalizing Shanghai and Mumbai." *City and Community* 8, no. 4: 407–32.

Welsh, Megan, Joshua Chanin, and Stuart Henry. 2020. "Complex Colorblindness in Police Processes and Practices." *Social Problems* 68, no. 2: 374–92.

Welsh, Whitney, and Linda M. Burton. 2016. "Home, Heart, and Being Latina: Housing and Intimate Relationship Power among Low-Income Mexican Mothers." *Sociology of Race and Ethnicity* 2, no. 3: 307–22.

Wertheimer, A. 1999. *Exploitation*. Princeton, NJ: Princeton University Press.

Western, Bruce. 2002. "The Impact of Incarceration on Wage Mobility and Inequality." *American Sociological Review* 67, no. 4: 526–46.

Western, Bruce. 2018. *Homeward: Life in the Year After Prison*. New York: Russell Sage Foundation.

Western, Bruce, Anthony A. Braga, Jaclyn Davis, and Catherine Sirois. 2015. "Stress and Hardship after Prison." *American Journal of Sociology* 120, no. 5: 1512–47.

Westrich, Tim, John Taylor, David Berenbaum, Joshua Silver, and Anna Gullickson. 2007. *Are Banks on the Map? An Analysis of Bank Branch Location in Working Class and Minority Neighborhoods*. Washington, DC: National Community Reinvestment Coalition, March. https://community-wealth.org/content/are-banks-map-analysis -bank-branch-location-working-class-and-minority-neighborhoods.

Whitehead, Ellen. 2018a. "Paying for Their Stay: Race, Coresiding Arrangements, and Rent Payments among Fragile Families." *Journal of Family Issues* 39, no. 17: 4041–65.

Whitehead, Ellen M. 2018b. "'Be My Guest': The Link between Concentrated Poverty, Race, and Family-Level Support." *Journal of Family Issues* 39, no. 12: 3225–47.

Wienk, Ronald E., Clifford E. Reid, John C. Simonson, and Frederick J. Eggers. 1979. *Measuring Racial Discrimination in American Housing Markets: The Housing Market Practices Survey*. Washington, DC: Division of Evaluation, US Department of Housing and Urban Development, Office of Policy Development and Research.

Wild, Mark. 2005. *Street Meeting: Multiethnic Neighborhoods in Early Twentieth-Century Los Angeles*. Los Angeles: University of California Press.

Wildeman, Christopher. 2014. "Parental Incarceration, Child Homelessness, and the Invisible Consequences of Mass Imprisonment." *Annals of the American Academy of Political and Social Science* 651, no. 1: 74–96.

Wilkerson, Isabel. 2010. *The Warmth of Other Suns: The Epic Story of America's Great Migration*. New York: Vintage Books.

Wilkes, Rima, and John Iceland. 2004. "Hypersegregation in the Twenty-First Century." *Demography* 41, no. 1: 23–36.

Williams, Betsy A., Catherine F. Brooks, and Yotam Shmargad. 2018. "How Algorithms Discriminate Based on Data They Lack: Challenges, Solutions, and Policy Implications." *Journal of Information Policy* 8: 78–115.

Williams, David R., and Chiquite Collins. 2001. "Racial Residential Segregation: A Fundamental Cause of Racial Disparities in Health." *Public Health Reports* 116: 404–16.

Williams, Deidre. 2020. "Buffalo Looks to Change Locals Laws to Get the Lead Out." *Buffalo News*, November 17. http://www.buffalonews.com/news/local/buffalo -looks-to-change-local-laws-to-get-the-lead-out/article_ed8bee94-25e6-11eb-aada -6f81be8e46f9.html.

Williams, Monica. 2018. *The Sex Offender Housing Dilemma: Community Activism, Safety, and Social Justice*. New York: NYU Press.

Williams, Richard, Reynold Nesiba, and Eileen Diaz McConnell. 2005. "The Changing Face of Inequality in Home Mortgage Lending." *Social Problems* 52, no. 2: 181–208.

Williams, Robert A. 1991a. *The American Indian in Western Legal Thought: The Discourses of Conquest*. New York: Oxford University Press.

Williams, Terry. 1991b. "Letter from a Crackhouse." *City Journal* (Summer). https:// www.city-journal.org/html/letter-crackhouse-12755.html.

Wilson, William Julius. 1987. *The Truly Disadvantaged: The Inner City, the Underclass, and Public Policy*. Chicago: University of Chicago Press.

Wilson-Hokowhitu, Nālani. 2019. *The Past before Us: Moʻokūʻauhau as Methodology*. Honolulu: University of Hawaiʻi Press.

Wimmer, Andreas, and Kevin Lewis. 2010. "Beyond and below Racial Homophily: ERG Models of a Friendship Network Documented on Facebook." *American Journal of Sociology* 116, no. 2: 583–642.

Wirth, Louis. 1947. "Housing as a Field of Sociological Research." *American Sociological Review* 12, no. 2:137–43.

Wodtke, Geoffrey T., David J. Harding, and Felix Elwert. 2011. "Neighborhood Effects in Temporal Perspective." *American Sociological Review* 76, no. 5: 713–36.

Wolfe, Patrick. 2006. "Settler Colonialism and the Elimination of the Native." *Journal of Genocide Research* 8, no. 4: 387–409.

Wolff, Edward N. 2017a. *A Century of Wealth in America*. Cambridge, MA: Harvard University Press.

Wolff, Edward N. 2017b. "Household Wealth Trends in the United States, 1962 to 2016: Has Middle Class Wealth Recovered?" Washington, DC: National Bureau of Economic Research.

Won, Jongho. 2020. "Exploring Spatial Clustering over Time and Spillover Effects of the Low-Income Housing Tax Credit on Neighborhood-Level Segregation." *Urban Affairs Review* 58, no. 3: 799–831.

Wong, Weihuang. 2018. *Our Town: Support for Housing Growth When Localism Meets Liberalism*. New York: Mimeo.

Wood, A. 1995. "Exploitation." In *Philosophy and the Problems of Work: A Reader*, edited by Kory P. Schaff, 141–64. Lanham, MD: Rowman and Littlefield.

Woodhall-Melnik, Julia R., and James R. Dunn. 2016. "A Systematic Review of Outcomes Associated with Participation in Housing First Programs." *Housing Studies* 31, no. 3: 287–304.

Woodward, Susan E. 2008. *A Study of Closing Costs for FHA Mortgages*. Washington, DC: US Department of Housing and Urban Development, Office of Policy Development and Research, report 36, May. https://ssrn.com/abstract=1341045.

Woodward, Susan E., and Robert E. Hall. 2012. "Diagnosing Consumer Confusion and Suboptimal Shopping Effort: Theory and Mortgage-Market Evidence." *American Economic Review* 102, no. 7: 3249–76.

Wray, Matt, and Analee Newitz, eds. 1997. *White Trash: Race and Class in America*. New York: Routledge.

Wright, Bradley R. Entner, Avshalom Caspi, Terrie E. Moffitt, and Phil A. Silva. 1998. "Factors Associated with Doubled-Up Housing—a Common Precursor to Homelessness." *Social Service Review (Chicago)* 72, no. 1: 92–111.

Wyly, Elvin K., Mona Atia, and Daniel J. Hammel. 2004. "Has Mortgage Capital Found an Inner-City Spatial Fix?" *Housing Policy Debate* 15, no. 3: 623–85.

Wyly, Elvin K., and Daniel J. Hammel. 2000. "Capital's Metropolis: Chicago and the Transformation of American Housing Policy." *Geografiska Annaler B* 82, no. 4: 181–206

Wyly, Elvin, and C. S. Ponder. 2011. "Gender, Age, and Race in Subprime America." *Housing Policy Debate* 21: 529–64.

Yang, Yang, and Zhenxing (Eddie) Mao. 2019. "Welcome to My Home! An Empirical Analysis of Airbnb Supply in US Cities." *Journal of Travel Research* 58, no. 8: 1274–87.

Yelimeli, Supriya. 2021. "Berkeley Denounces Racist History of Single-Family Zoning, Begins 2-Year Process to Change General Plan." *Berkeleyside*, February 24. https://www.berkeleyside.com/2021/02/24/berkeley-denounces-racist-history-of-single-family-zoning-begins-2-year-process-to-change-general-plan.

Yeter, Deniz, Ellen C. Banks, and Michael Aschner. 2020. "Disparity in Risk Factor Severity for Early Childhood Blood Lead among Predominately African-American Black Children: The 1999 to 2010 U.S. NHANES." *International Journal of Environmental Research and Public Health* 17, no. 5: 1552–78.

Yinger, John. 1986. "Measuring Racial Discrimination with Fair Housing Audits: Caught in the Act." *American Economic Review* 76, no. 5: 881–93.

Yinger, John. 1995. *Closed Doors, Opportunities Lost: The Continuing Costs of Housing Discrimination.* New York: Russell Sage Foundation.

Yinger, John. 1998. "Housing Discrimination Is Still Worth Worrying About." *Housing Policy Debate* 9, no. 4: 893–927.

Zavisca, Jane R., and Theodore P. Gerber. 2016. "The Socioeconomic, Demographic, and Political Effects of Housing in Comparative Perspective." *Annual Review of Sociology* 42: 347–67.

Zhang, Li. 2001. *Strangers in the City: Reconfigurations of Space, Power, and Social Networks within China's Floating Population.* Stanford, CA: Stanford University Press.

Zhang, Li. 2010. *In Search of Paradise: Middle-Class Living in a Chinese Metropolis.* Ithaca, NY: Cornell University Press.

Ziol-Guest, Kathleen M., and Claire C. McKenna. 2014. "Early Childhood Housing Instability and School Readiness." *Child Development* 85, no. 1: 103–13.

Zubrinsky, Camille L., and Lawrence Bobo. 1996. "Prismatic Metropolis: Race and Residential Segregation in the City of the Angels." *Social Science Research* 25, no. 4: 335–74.

Zuk, Miriam, Ariel H. Bierbaum, Karen Chapple, Karolina Gorska, and Anastasia Loukaitou-Sideris. 2018. "Gentrification, Displacement, and the Role of Public Investment." *Journal of Planning Literature* 33, no. 1: 31–44.

Zuk, Miriam, and Karen Chapple. 2016. *Housing Production, Filtering, and Displacement: Untangling the Relationships.* Berkeley, CA: UC Berkeley Institute of Governmental Studies Research Brief, Urban Displacement Project.

Zukin, Sharon. 1989. *Loft Living: Culture and Capital in Urban Change.* New Brunswick, NJ: Rutgers University Press.

Zúñiga, Víctor, and Rubén Hernández-León. 2005. *New Destinations: Mexican Immigration in the United States.* New York: Russell Sage Foundation

Index

Page numbers in italics indicate figures or tables.

Asians (*cont.*)
47–49; in manufactured housing,
125; mortgage loans available to, 35;
racialization/racism experienced by,
40–42, 50
Atuahene, Bernadette, 210
audit studies, of housing discrimination,
93–106
Australian Aboriginals, 77
Auyero, Javier, 321

Bairoch, Paul, 320
Baldwin, James, 260
Baltimore (Maryland): neighborhood
decline in, 9, 206–7, 211; public housing
in, 53–65; segregation in, 6, 53–65, 294
Balto, Simon, 295
Balzarini, John, 88
Banking Act (1935), 18
Banks, Ellen C., 81
Barajas, Julia, 296
Bartram, Robin, 197, 200
Becher, Debbie, 196–97
Beck, Brenden, 301
Beck, Kevin R., 247
Beckett, Katherine, 166
Bedford (Ohio), 297
Belair-Edison Improvement Association,
57
Bell, Jeannine, 295
Bell, Monica C., 301
Benfer, Emily A., 88
Berner, Erhard, 327–28
Berry, Christopher, 210
Besbris, Max, 195, 200, 262
Bezdek, Barbara, 111
big data, 35, 128, 259–61
Black Lives Matter, 259
Blacks. *See* African Americans
Blackstone, 131
blight, 54–55, 57, 63
blockbusting, 187
blood quantum policies, 43, 74–75
Bogardus, Emory, 44
Boise (Idaho), 9, 214–15, 217–18, 221–22
Boterman, Willem R., 220
Bourdieu, Pierre, 132, 240, 320, 325
Boyd, Melody L., 88

Bracero Program, 45, 49
Brenner, Neil, 64
Bryan, Brielle, 309
Buchanan v. Warley (1917), 294
Buffalo (New York), 84–86
"buffer hypothesis," 33
Buffet, Warren, 131

Caldeira, Teresa, 322, 328–29
California, property rights in, 292, 296–
99. *See also* Los Angeles (California);
Southern California
California Real Estate Association
(CREA), 292
Candipan, Jennifer, 257
capitalism and capital accumulation:
housing insecurity linked to, 71–72,
131–32, 133; Indigenous alternatives to,
68, 70, 72, 76; manufactured housing
and, 131–32, 133; Marxist accounts
of exploitation in, 229–31; urban
redevelopment and, 53, 63, 65
Carlyle group, 131
Castells, Manuel, 153, 320, 321
Castles, Francis G., 242, 244
central business districts. *See* urban
redevelopment
Chanin, Joshua, 301
Chen, Cheng, 33
Chicago (Illinois), 294–95
Chicago Housing Authority, 55
Chicago School, 44, 163, 321, 329
children: housing-related outcomes
for, 37, 139–40, 143–44; landlords'
discrimination based on, 96; and lead
exposure, 79–91; poverty's effect on,
58, 63; and residential moves, 139–40;
in shared housing, 138–40, 142–44.
See also educational opportunity/
outcomes
Choice Neighborhoods, 64–65
Civil Rights Act (1968), 94
class: discrimination based on, 101–2;
in Global South, 322, 326–28; and
homeownership, 23–24, 24; and home
values, 25, 25; and inheritance, 22–23,
23. *See also* middle class
Clean Water Act (1972), 127

Housing Choice Voucher (HCV)
Program, 62, 82, 87–88, 96–99, 265–77,
292, 296, 298. *See also* vouchers
housing discrimination. *See* residential
segregation and discrimination
housing finance, 9
Housing First, 165, 170–72
housing inequality, 5–6; African
Americans and, 15–27; criminal justice
contact as result of, 310–11; housing
intermediaries and, 8; housing
supply related to, 182; impact of, 1;
intermediaries' role in, 192, 194–201;
Latinos and, 39–51; and lead exposure,
6, 79–91; manufactured housing and,
126–30, 133; Native Americans and,
72–74; Native Hawaiians and, 72–74;
neighborhood decline and, 209; race
linked to, 5–6; sociological study of,
51; tax policies and, 245, 247; wealth
inequality linked to, 15–27
housing informality. *See* informal housing
housing instability and insecurity, 6–8;
after criminal justice contact, 310–11;
capital production/accumulation linked
to, 71–72, 131–32, 133; evictions as factor
in, 109–20; manufactured housing and,
128–30; shared housing and, 135–47
housing market, 8–9; COVID-related,
35–37, 179, 258–59; fiscal relationships
as context for, 240–50; government
involvement in, 17–19; intermediaries
in, 8, 191–201; nonmarket relationships
as context for, 239–40; STRs'
impact on, 213–19, 222–23; urban
redevelopment and, 58–60; as Western
construct, 67, 68
Housing Opportunities for People
Everywhere (HOPE VI), 53, 58–65;
Fair Housing Center, 297
Housing Opportunity Extension Act
(1996), 295
housing search, 10, 279–90, 309. *See also*
residential mobility/displacement
housing segregation. *See* residential
segregation and discrimination
housing supply, 8, 179–89; affordability
of housing linked to, 180–81; data on,

185; declining/insufficient, 179–82;
gentrification in relation to, 181–82;
inequalities linked to, 182, 189; land
use in relation to, 182–89; regulations
and institutions governing, 184–
88; residents' perspective on, 186;
sociological study of, 180–82, 188–
89; as sociopolitical issue, 179–80,
184–89
Hoyt, Homer, 19
HUD. *See* US Department of Housing
and Urban Development (HUD)
Hurricane Andrew, 128

Indigenous peoples: concepts of land, 70,
72; defined, 68–69; racial identities of,
69; racialization of, 68; sociological
study of, 67–68. *See also* Native
Americans; Native Hawaiians
inequality. *See* housing inequality
informal housing: defined, 152–53; in
Global North, 149–50; in Global
South, 4, 7, 11, 151, 160, 319–20, 323–29;
neighborhood decline and, 211–12;
prevalence of, in United States, 150;
public policy and, 161; sociological
study of, 150–55, 161; squatting as, 7,
149; state role in, 153–54; types of,
153–54. *See also* squatting
informal subdivisions (ISes), 125–28
inheritance, 21–23
insecurity. *See* housing instability and
insecurity
instability. *See* housing instability and
insecurity
institutional investors, 113
intermediaries, in housing market,
8, 191–201; overview of, 191, 193;
practical and professional issues for,
200; private-sector, 197–98; public-
sector, 196–97; sociological study of,
192–93; stratification and inequalities
reproduced/contested by, 192, 194–201
International Crime Free Association,
296
international perspective, 4–5, 11
investors, real estate, 211
ISes. *See* informal subdivisions (ISes)

Printed and bound by CPI Group (UK) Ltd, Croydon, CR0 4YY

19/03/2024

14472759-0003